W9-AWB-402

Surviving Chemistry

Workbook

High School Chemistry

Surviving Chemistry Books

Student and Teacher-friendly High School Books to:

✓ *Excite* students to study

✓ *Engage* students in learning

✓ *Enhance* students understanding

Surviving Chemistry

Workbook

ISBN-13: 978-1508817192

ISBN-10: 1508817197

Printed in The United States of America

E3 Scholastic Publishing

Survivingchem.com
(877) 224 – 0484
info@e3chemistry.com

Now on
NYC DOE
Famis
E-catalog

New York City Teachers

Our books are now listed on Famis E-catalog through Ingram

Vendor #: ING032000
Contract #: 7108108

Worksheets

Table of Contents

Table of Contents

Multiple Choice Questions   Pg 117 - 359

Constructed Response Questions   Pg 360 - 415

Worksheets

Concept by Concept

Survivingchem.com

Set A: Terms and Definitions

Define or describe each of the following.

1. Pure substance

2. Mixture

3. Element

4. Compound

5. Law of Definite Composition

6. Homogeneous mixture

7. Heterogeneous mixture

8. Aqueous solution

9. Decantation

10. Filtration

11. Distillation

Set B: Comparing Types of Matter

Answer the following questions.

12. What are the two types of pure substances?

13. What are the two classifications of mixtures?

14. What methods are used to break down compounds?

15. What methods are used to separate the components of a mixture?

16. How are elements and compounds similar?

17. How are elements and compounds different?

18. How are compounds and mixtures similar

19. How are compounds and mixtures different?

Set C: Classification of Matter

Classify the following substances as:

    Pure substance – element   Mixture – homogenous

    Pure substance – compound   Mixture – heterogeneous

20. $HCl(aq)$ _____

21. $KBr(s)$ _____

22. $Cl_2(g)$ _____

23. $CH_2(OH)_2(aq)$ _____

24. $Hg(\ell)$ _____

25. $NH_3(\ell)$ _____

26. Sugar _____

27. Soil _____

28. Water _____

29. Sodium _____

30. Iron oxide _____

31. Salt water _____

Classify each diagram as: pure substance – element, pure substance – compound, or Mixture

| Atom Y: O |
| Atom Z: ● |
| **Key** |

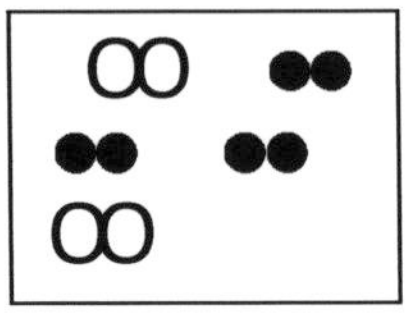

32. _____

_____

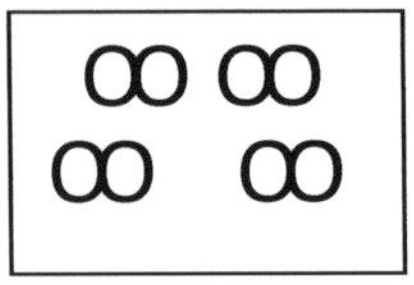

33. _____

_____

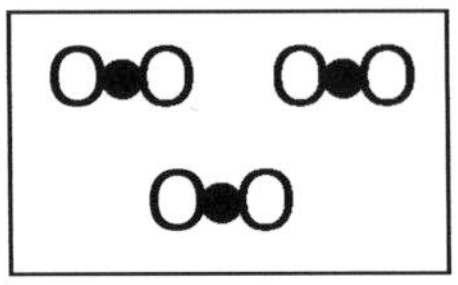

34. _____

_____

Set D: Diagrams of Matter

Two atoms are given below.

    Atom X: O   Atom Y: ●

Draw particle diagrams to represent each type of matter given in numbers 35 through 37.

35. Diatomic element X

Draw at least three units

36. Compound X_2Y_2

Draw at least three units

37. A mixture of diatomic element Y and compound X_2Y

Draw at least three units

 Survivingchem.com

Set A: Terms and Definitions

Define or describe each of the following.

1. Solid

2. Liquid

3. Gas

4. Melting

5. Freezing

6. Condensation

7. Evaporation

8. Sublimation

9. Deposition

10. Exothermic

11. Endothermic

12. Temperature

13. Kinetic energy

14. Potential energy

15. Ice / liquid equilibrium

16. Water / steam equilibrium

17. Phase change diagram

18. Absolute Zero

Set B: Phases of Matter and Temperature

Answer the following questions.

19. Which phase of matter have particles that are arranged in regular geometric?

20. In which phase of water can water molecules flow over each other?

21. Compare the force of attraction between particles of a substance in the liquid phase to those in the gas phases?

22. Which three phase changes are endothermic?

23. Which three phase changes are exothermic?

24. How many reference temperature points are needed to create a thermometer scale?

25. What temperatures are commonly used as reference points to make a Celsius or Kelvin thermometer?

26. How is the average kinetic energy of particles relates to the temperature of a substance?

Set C: Relating Phase Change to Energy

Above each arrow, write the phase change (*fusion, condensation. Etc.*) that is taking place.
Under each arrow, write "exothermic" or "endothermic" to indicate if the change releases or absorbs heat.

27. Au(ℓ) ⎯⎯⎯⎯⎯⎯→ Au(*s*)

28. $C_{10}H_8$(*s*) ⎯⎯⎯⎯⎯→ $C_{10}H_8$(*g*)

29. NaCl(*s*) ⎯⎯⎯⎯⎯⎯→ NaCl(ℓ)

30. $C_2H_3O_2$(*g*) ⎯⎯⎯⎯⎯→ $C_2H_3O_2$(ℓ)

Set D: Temperature

*Write "**Highest KE**" under the container or object that has particles with the highest kinetic energy.*
*Write "**Lowest KE**" under the container or object that has particles with the lowest kinetic energy.*

31.   32.

Convert the following temperatures to Kelvin.

33. -15°C

34.   30°C

35. 120°C

Convert the following temperatures to Celsius.

36.   27 K

37.   125 K

38.   325 K

Set E: Phase Change Diagrams

The diagram below shows the heating of a substance starting with the substance below its melting point.

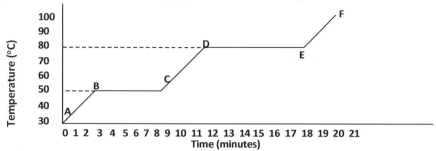

39. What is the boiling point of the substance?

40. At what temperature are solid and liquid exist at equilibrium?

41. At which segment or segments is the substance average kinetic energy increasing?

42. At which segment or segments is the substance exists in two phases?

43. Potential energy of the substance remains constant during which segment or segments?

44. What is the total length of the time that the substance exists only as a liquid?

45. What is the total length of time that the substance undergoes melting?

48. Is the diagram a heating curve for water or for a different substance? Explain your answer.

The diagram below shows the cooling of a substance starting with the substance at a temperature above its boiling point. The substance is losing heat at a rate of 155 Joules per minute.

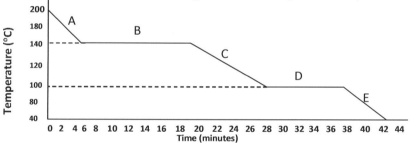

49. What is boiling point of the substance?

50. What is the freezing point of the substance?

51. What is the melting point of the substance?

52. Which segment or segments represents a time when the substance is going through a phase change?

53. Which segment or segments represents a time when the substance is in one phase?

54. What is the phase or phases of the substance during segment C?

55. What is the total length of time it took for the substance to change from liquid to solid?

56. Describe the change in kinetic energy of the substance during segment A.

57. How much heat is lost by the substance to completely change from gas to liquid?

58. How much heat is lost by the substance to completely change from liquid to solid?

Set A: Terms and Definitions

Define or describe each of the following terms.

1. Heat

2. Joules

3. Specific heat capacity

4. Heat of fusion

5. Heat of vaporization

6. Calorimeter

Set B: Direction of Heat Flow

For each question below, draw an arrow (---heat ------- >) or (< ------heat----) between the two objects to show the direction of heat will flow between them.

7.
| 67°C | 74°C |

8.
-50°C   -65°C

9.
-14°C   250 K

10.
390 K   125°C

Set C. Heat Calculations

For each question below: *Write down the heat equation to use, show your numerical setup, and solve the problem. Show all work in the space below each question.*

11. How much heat is absorbed when a 10-g sample of water changes its temperature from 23°C to 32°C?	12. How much heat is released by a 15 gram sample of water to cool from 50°C to 46°C?

Set C continues

13. How much heat is released by a 38-gram sample of water to freeze at it freezing point?	14. Calculate the number of joules of heat needed to change a 25 g sample of water to steam at its boiling point.
15. How much heat is absorbed by a 170-gram sample of ice to melt at 0°C?	16. The specific heat capacity of a substance is 15 J/g•°C. How much heat would be released by a 25 g sample of this substance to cool from 100°C to 90°C?
17. Substance Y has a heat of fusion of 3.5 kJ/g. How much heat is needed to melt a 30.-gram sample of substance Y at its melting point?	18. The heat of vaporization of propane is 356 Joules per gram. How much heat is needed to completely evaporate a 40.0-gram sample of propane at its boiling temperature of 230.K?
19. If 5000 Joules of energy is required to evaporate 36 grams of an unknown liquid at its boiling point, what is the heat of vaporization of the liquid?	20. A student determines that a sample of water absorbed 2200 joules of heat to change from 47°C to 59°C. What is the mass of the water sample?
21. A 5.7-g sample of copper absorbs 1023 Joules of heat to melt at its melting point. What is the heat of fusion of copper?	22. What is the specific heat capacity of an unknown substance if 550 Joules of heat is required to change the temperature of a 10-gram sample of the substance from 26°C to 33°C?

Set A: Kinetic Molecular Theory

The Kinetic Molecular Theory of Gases

Fill in the blanks to complete each statement.

1. Behavior of gases is influenced by these three factors: _____, _____ and _____

2. The kinetic molecular theory of an ideal gas is used to explain _____ of gases.

3. A gas is composed of _____ particles.

4. Distances between gas particles are _____ . _____.

5. Gas particles are in _____, _____, _____ line motion

6. When two particles of a gas collide, energy is _____ from one particle to another.

7. Particles of gases have no _____ to each other.

8. The volume of individual gas particles is _____ .

Deviation from the Ideal Gas Model.

Answer the following questions

9. Name four real gases that you know.
Oxygen, hydrogen, helium, neon, carbon dioxide. etc..(answers may vary)

10. Give two reasons why real gases do not behave exactly like an ideal gas.

11. Under what two conditions do real gases behave most like an ideal gas?

12. Under what two conditions do real gases behave least like an ideal gas?

13. Which two real gases behave most like (deviate least from) an ideal gas?

Set B: Avogadro's Law

14. According to the Avogadro's Law, under the same conditions of temperature and pressure;

Equal volume of gases contains _____ _____ _____ _____.

15. Gas A in the container below has the following properties:

volume	300 ml
pressure	150 kPa
temperature	280 K

Gas A

Circle all gases from the list below that contain the same number of molecules as Gas A in the container.

	volume	pressure	temperature
Gas B :	300 ml	280 kPa	150 K
Gas C :	300 ml	150 kPa	280 K
Gas D :	600 ml	300 kPa	560 K

Set C: Gas Law Calculations

Solve the following gas law problems.

For each question below, write down factors that are given in the problem, then use the Combined Gas Law equation to set up and solve the problem.

16. At constant pressure, a 3.5 L sample of oxygen gas is at 280 K. If the temperature is increased to 560 K, calculate the new volume of the gas.

    Determine factors from question.   *Show a numerical setup and the calculated result*

    P_1 = P_2 =

    V_1 = V_2 =

    T_1 = T_2 =

17. A 100 mL sample of a gas is at STP. What will be its new pressure if the volume is decreased to 50 ml and the temperature is increased to 480 K?

    Determine factors from question.   *Show a numerical setup and the calculated result*

    P_1 = P_2 =

    V_1 = V_2 =

    T_1 = T_2 =

18. A gas at constant temperature has a volume of 2 L at 101.3 kPa. What will be the new volume if the pressure is increased to 303.9 kPa?

    Determine factors from question.   *Show a numerical setup and the calculated result*

    P_1 = P_2 =

    V_1 = V_2 =

    T_1 = T_2 =

19. A gas at 300 K had its pressure changed from of 0.8 atm to 0.5 atm. If the volume is held constant, what will be the new temperature of the gas?

    Determine factors from question.   *Show a numerical setup and the calculated result*

    P_1 = P_2 =

    V_1 = V_2 =

    T_1 = T_2 =

20. A 0.8 L sample of a gas at STP had its temperature changed to 50°C and its pressure changed to 80 kPa. What is the new volume of the gas?

    Determine factors from question.   *Show a numerical setup and the calculated result*

    P_1 = P_2 =

    V_1 = V_2 =

    T_1 = T_2 =

Set A: Terms and Definitions

Define or describe each of the following terms.

1. Periodic Law

2. Group

3. Period

4. Metal

5. Nonmetal

6. Metalloid

7. Alkali metal

8. Alkaline earth metal

9. Transition element

10. Halogen

11. Noble gas

12. Malleable

13. Luster

14. Brittleness

15. Ionization energy

16. Electronegativity

17. Atomic radius

Set B: Properties of the Elements

Write in the space **"metals," "metalloids," or "nonmetals"** *to indicate the type of elements that is described by the statement.*

18. Located to the right of the Periodic Table.   18._____

19. Located to the left of the Periodic Table.   19._____

20. Located along the zigzag line of the Periodic Table.   20._____

21. The majority of the elements.   21._____

22. Gain electrons to form negative ions.   22._____

23. Solids tend to be brittle.   23._____

24. Solids tend to malleable   24._____

25. Tend to have low ionization energy.   25._____

26. Tend to lose electrons and form positive ions.   26._____

27. Have elements that are in the solid, liquid and gas phases at STP .   27._____

28. Elements only exist as solids at STP.   28._____

29. Have elements in the solid and liquid phases at STP.   29._____

30. Tend to have high ionization energy.   30._____

31. Ionic size (radius) is generally smaller than the atomic size.   31._____

32. Are good electrical and heat conductors.   32._____

33. May have properties of metals and of nonmetals?   33._____

34. Are poor electrical and poor heat conductors.   34._____

35. Atomic radius (size) is generally smaller than the ionic radius.   35._____

36. Solids may have luster.   36._____

37. Tend to have high electronegativity values.   37._____

38. Solids may have luster.   38._____

39. Tend to have low electronegativity values.   39._____

Set C: Properties of Groups

Write in the space provided: "**alkali metals**," "**alkaline earth metals**," "**transition metals**," "**Group 13**" "**halogens**," or "**noble gases**" to indicate the type of elements that is described by the statement.

40. Elements form oxide compounds with the general formula XO.

40._____

41. Elements tend to form compounds that can produce colored solution.

41._____

42. Elements have a full valence shell.

42._____

43. Elements are the most reactive of all metals.

43._____

44. Elements include the most reactive nonmetal.

44._____

45. Elements tend to have multiple positive oxidation numbers.

45._____

46. Elements form oxide compounds with the general formula of X_2O.

46._____

47. Elements form oxide compounds with the general formula of X_2O_3

47._____

48. Elements exist as monatomic gases.

48._____

49. Elements generally form +3 ions in a bond with other elements.

49._____

50. Elements have two electrons in their valence shell.

50._____

51. Elements always form a -1 ion.

51._____

52. Elements have seven valence electrons.

52._____

53. Elements form compounds with Group 1 elements (Y) with the general formula of XY.

53._____

54. Elements are obtained from electrolytic reduction of fused salts.

54._____

55. Elements neither gain nor lose electrons.

55._____

56. Elements exist mostly as diatomic molecules.

56._____

57. Elements combine with Group 17 elements in a ratio of 1 : 2.

57._____

58. Elements always form a +2 ion when bonding with other elements.

58._____

59. Elements combine with oxygen in a ratio of 1 : 1.

59._____

60. Elements are stable and rarely form compounds.

60._____

Set A: Classification of Elements

Symbols of elements are given below. Check one or more columns to classify each element.

	metal	nonmetal	metalloid	alkali	alkaline earth	transition element	halogen	noble gas	monatomic	diatomic
1. Sb										
2. Sr										
3. Rn										
4. P										
5. Pt										
6. Cs										
7. S										
8. Fe										
9. Br										
10. Ar										

Set B: Properties of the Elements

Symbols of elements are given below. Check one or more columns of properties to describe each element.

	Physical Properties				Conductivity		Ionization Energy		Electronegativity		Lose or Gain e-	
	luster	malleable	ductile	brittle	good	poor	low	high	low	high	lose	gain
11. C												
12. Ag												
13. Mg												
14. I												
15. S												
16. Au												
17. Pt												

Set A: Data and Graph for Group 2 (The Alkaline Earth Metals):

Using Reference Table S, complete the tables below for Group 2 Alkali Earth metals.
Once done, scale, plot and graph the data on the graphing grids to observe the trends of the four properties.

Group 2: Alkaline Earth Metals.   List the elements in the order of increasing atomic numbers.

Atomic Number	Elements Symbol	Electronegativity	Ionization Energy	Atomic Radius (pm)	Melting Point (K)

Trend in Electronegativity

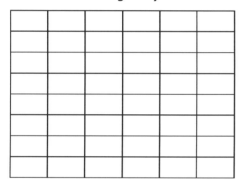

Electronegativity Value

Atomic Numbers

Trend in Ionization Energy

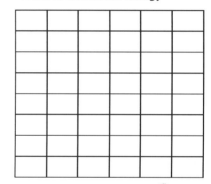

Ionization energy (kJ/mol)

Atomic Numbers

Trend in Atomic Radius (size)

Atomic Radius (pm)

Atomic Numbers

Trend in Melting Point

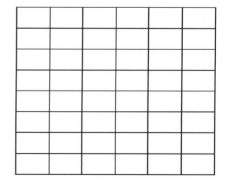

Melting Point (K)

Atomic Numbers

Set B: Data and Graph for Period 2 Elements

Using Reference Table S, complete the table below for the Period 2 elements.
Once done, scale, plot and graph the data on the graphing grids to observe trends of the four properties.

Period 2 Elements   List the elements in the order of increasing atomic numbers.

Atomic Number	Element Symbol	Electronegativity	Ionization Energy	Atomic Radius (pm)	Melting Point (K)

Trend in Electronegativity

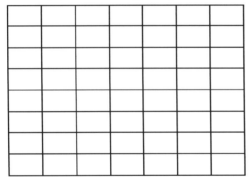

Trend in Ionization Energy

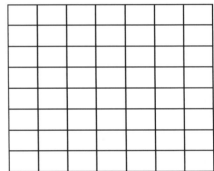

Trend in Atomic Radius (size)

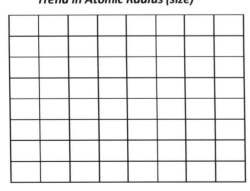

Trend in Melting Point

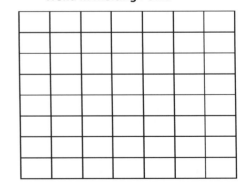

Set A: Models of the Atom

Draw and briefly describe each model of the atom.

1. Hard Sphere model

2. Plum-pudding model

3. Empty Space model

4. Bohr's model

5. Wave-mechanical model

6. State two conclusions from the Gold Foil experiment.

7. State two conclusions from the Cathode Ray experiment.

Set A: Terms and Definitions

Define or describe each of the following terms.

1. Nucleus

2. Neutron

3. Proton

4. Electron

5. Nucleons

6. Atomic number

7. Mass number

8. Atomic mass

9. Isotopes

10. Atomic mass unit

Set B: The Subatomic Particles

Complete the table below.

	Subatomic Particle	Symbol	Mass	Charge	Location
11.	Proton				
12.	Electron				
13.	Neutron				

Set C: Determining Number of Atomic Particles

14. Complete the table below based on the information provided for each _neutral_ atom.

	Protons	Electrons	Neutrons	Mass Number	Atomic Number	Nuclear Charge	Nucleons	Element Symbol
Atom A	44			102				
Atom B		84	125					
Atom C				56				Mn
Atom D					89		229	
Atom E		30				+28		
Atom F		92					233	
Atom G			82					Ba

Set D: Relating Number of Particles

15. Complete the table below based on the information provided for each _neutral_ atom.

	Isotope Symbol	Protons	Electrons	Neutrons	Mass Number	Atomic Number	Nuclear Charge	Nucleons	Atomic Nucleus
Atom H	$^{142}_{59}Pr$								
Atom I				31			+27		
Atom J	$^{243}_{95}Am$								
Atom K		77						194	
Atom L	^{80}Se								
Atom M									22 p 26 n

Set A: Atomic Mass Calculations

Calculate the atomic mass foe the elements given below. Show the numerical setup and calculated result for each.

1) 19.78% of ^{10}B

   80.22% of ^{11}B

2) 93.12% of ^{39}K

   6.88% of ^{41}K

3) 78.70% of ^{24}Mg

   10.13% of ^{25}Mg

   11.17% of ^{26}Mg

4) 80.0% of ^{70}X

   12.25% of ^{69}X

   7.75% of ^{68}X

5) A sample of chlorine contains 75% of chlorine-35 and 25% of chlorine-37. What is the atomic mass of chlorine? Show work.

6) Element X has two naturally occurring isotopes. If 72% of the atoms have a mass of 85 amu and 28% of the atoms have a mass of 87 amu, what is the atomic mass of element X? Show work.

7) The atomic mass of an element depends on what two factors?

                   Survivingchem.com

Set A: Drawing Bohr's Atomic Model

Based on the information from the Periodic Table, answer questions in each box about the given element. Then draw Bohr's atomic model for the element.

1. Magnesium-25

Electron configuration:

Number of electron shells: _____

Valence shell: _____

Number of valence electrons: _____

***Draw Bohr's atomic model for* Magnesium-25.**
Indicate the appropriate numbers of protons and neutrons in the nucleus, and use ⊖ to show The electrons in the electron shells.

2. Neon-21

Electron configuration:

Number of electron shells: _____

Valence shell: _____

Number of valence electrons: _____

Draw Bohr's atomic model for Neon-21.
Indicate the appropriate numbers of protons and neutrons in the nucleus, and use ⊖ to show The electrons in the electron shells.

3. Rubidium-86

Electron configuration:

Number of electron shells: _____

Valence shell: :   _____

Number of valence electrons: _____

***Draw Bohr's atomic model for* Rubidium-86.**
Indicate the appropriate numbers of protons and neutrons in the nucleus, and use ⊖ to show The electrons in the electron shells.

4. Selenium-78

Electron configuration:

Number of electron shells: _____

Valence shell: _____

Number of valence electrons: _____

Draw Bohr's atomic model for selenium-78.
Indicate the appropriate numbers of protons and neutrons in the nucleus, and use ⊖ to show The electrons in the electron shells.

Set B: Interpreting Electron Configurations

Electron configurations for six atoms are given. Complete the table below.

		Electron Configuration	Total Number of electrons	Number of electron shells	The Shell with highest energy electrons	Excited or ground state	Element Symbol
5.	**Atom A**	2 − 8 − 4					
6.	**Atom B**	2 − 3 − 1					
7.	**Atom C**	2 − 8 − 7 − 1					
8.	**Atom D**	2 − 8 − 18 − 6					
9.	**Atom E**	2 − 8 − 18 − 17 − 5					
10.	**Atom F**	1- 7					

Set C: Electron Transition Between Shells

An electron is moving from one electron shell.

Answer questions 11 to 16 based on the electron transition in these atoms.

Atom G: 3rd shell → 2nd shell   Atom I: 4th shell → 6th shell

Atom H: 1st shell → 4th shell   Atom J: 5th shell → 3rd shell

11. In which atom or atoms are energy absorbed during the electron transition?

12. In which atom or atoms are energy released during the electron transition?

13. In which atom or atoms can spectral lines be produces?

14. In which atom is the greatest amount of energy absorbed?

15. In which atom is the greatest amount of energy released?

16. In atom G, compare the energy of the electron in the 3rd shell to that of the electron in the 2nd shell.

Set D: Spectra Chart

Bright-line spectral chart for five elements and four unknown samples are given below.
Answer questions 17 - 21 based on the information given in the chart.

17. List all elements present in the unknown sample W .

18. List all elements present in the unknown sample X .

19. List all elements present in the unknown sample Y.

20. List all elements present in the unknown sample Z.

21. Explain, in terms of electron transition, how bright-line spectra are produced in atoms.

Set A: Terms and Definitions

Define or describe each of the following terms.

1. Neutral atom

2. Ion

3. Positive ion

4. Negative ion

5. Valence electron

Set B: Comparing Ions to Atoms

Answer the following questions.

6. Compare the number of electrons to the number of protons in a neutral atom.

7. Compare the number of electrons of a positive ion to that of the neutral atom.
    Include both positive ion and neutral atom in your answer.

8. Compare the number of electrons of a negative ion to that of the neutral atom.
    Include both negative ion and neutral atom in your answer.

9. Compare the number of protons to the number of electrons in a positive ion.
    Include both protons and electrons in your answer.

10. Compare the number of protons to the number of electrons in a negative ion.
    Include both protons and electrons in your answer.

11. Compare the size of a positive ion to that of the neutral atom.
    Include both positive ion and neutral atom in your answer.

12. Compare the size of a negative ion to that of the neutral atom.
    Include both negative ion and neutral atom in your answer.

Set C: Particles in Atoms and Ions

Symbols of atoms and ions given below. Complete the table below.

	Atom and Ion symbols	Atomic number	Number of protons	Number of electrons	Electron configuration
13.	C				
14.	C^{4-}				
15.	Sr				
16.	Sr^{2+}				
17.	Al				
18.	Al^{3+}				
19.	P				
20.	P^{-3}				

Set D: Determining Charge of Atoms

Determine the overall charge of each of the following atoms based on the information given.

21. **Atom A:** 46 protons, 61 neutrons, 42 electrons.   Charge =

22. **Atom B:** mass number of 209, nuclear charge of 83, and 81 electrons   Charge =

23. **Atoms C:** nuclear charge of 32, 36 electrons, 39 neutrons   Charge =

24. **Atoms D:** 54 electrons, 122 nucleons, atomic number of 51   Charge =

25. **Atom E:** 28 neutrons, nuclear charge of 22, 20 electrons   Charge =

Set A: Chemical Bonding Facts

Define each of the following terms, and answer the questions below.

1. Chemical bond

2. Octet rule

3. Potential energy

4. Exothermic

5. Endothermic

6. Why do atoms bond?

7. List three ways that an atom can get a full valence shell of electrons.

8. Atoms in a bond have electron configurations similar to elements in which Group of the Periodic Table?

10. In terms of energy, bond formation is _____ (endothermic or exothermic)

11. During bond formation, energy is always _____ (absorbed or released)

12. During bond formation, energy of the atoms _____ (increases or decreases)

13. During bond formation, the stability of the atoms _____ (increases or decreases)

14. During bond formation, the stability of the chemical system _____ (increases or decreases)

15. In terms of energy, bond breaking is _____ (endothermic or exothermic)

16. During bond breaking, energy is always _____ (absorbed or released)

17. During bond breaking, energy of the atoms _____ (increases or decreases)

18. During bond breaking, the stability of the atoms _____ (increases or decreases)

19. During bond breaking , the stability of the chemical system _____ (increases or decreases)

20. The amount of potential energy of a substance depends on _____ and _____ of the substance.

Set B: Noble Gas Configurations of Bonded Atoms

Ionic compounds are given below. Each element in the formulas has an electron configuration similar to the nearest noble gas atom. Indicate the correct noble gas in the space proved.

21   K_2O The electron configuration of K is similar to that of the element _____ .

The electron configuration of O is similar to that of the element _____ .

22.   CaS   The electron configuration of Ca is similar to that of the element _____ .

The electron configuration of S is similar to that of the element _____ .

23. AlI_3 The electron configuration of Al is similar to that of the element _____ .

The electron configuration of I is similar to that of the element _____ .

24. Cs_3N The electron configuration of Cs is similar to that of the element _____ .

The electron configuration of N is similar to that of the element _____ .

25. BeH_2 The electron configuration of Be is similar to that of the element _____ .

The electron configuration of H is similar to that of the element _____ .

26    $SrBr_2$ The electron configuration of Sr is similar to that of the element _____ .

The electron configuration of Br is similar to that of the element _____ .

27. Ba_3P_2 The electron configuration of Ba is similar to that of the element _____ .

The electron configuration of P is similar to that of the element _____ .

28. Al_2Se_3 The electron configuration of Al is similar to that of the element _____ .

The electron configuration of Se is similar to that of the element _____ .

29. Rb_3P The electron configuration of Rb is similar to that of the element _____ .

The electron configuration of P is similar to that of the element _____ .

30. B_2O_3 The electron configuration of B is similar to that of the element _____ .

The electron configuration of O is similar to that of the element _____ .

Set A: Terms and Definitions

Define or describe each of the following terms.

1. Intramolecular forces *- the forces that hold bonds together within a molecule*

2. Ionic bond *- a bond between a metal and a nonmetal - transfer of electrons*

3. Covalent bond *- a bond between 2 nonmetals - sharing of electrons*

4. Polar covalent bond

5. Nonpolar covalent bond

6. Network solid covalent bond

7. Coordinate covalent bond

8. Metallic bond

Set B: Bond Type Description

Indicate the type of chemical bond described by each statement below. Choose from the list below.
Ionic, covalent, polar covalent, nonpolar covalent, coordinate covalent, network solid covalent, metallic.

9. A bond in which two atoms share electrons unequally.   *polar covalent*

10. A bond in which two atoms have an electronegativity difference of zero.   *nonpolar covalent*

11. Bonding in which positive nuclei are immersed in the sea of mobile electrons.   *metallic*

12. A bond in which two atoms share electrons equally.   *nonpolar covalent*

13. A bond between a metal atom and a nonmetal atom.   *ionic*

14. A bond in which one atom transfers electron to another atom.   *ionic*

Set B cont.

15. One atom in this bond provides both shared electrons.   *covalent*

16. A bond in which electronegativity difference between two atoms is 2.0   *Ionic*

17. A bond holding atoms in diatomic molecules together.   *Covalent*

18. Bonding between different nonmetal atoms.   *covalent*

19. Bonding between atoms in a molecule.   ~~~~ *SKIP*

20. A bond in which the electronegativity difference between the two atoms is 0.8   *polar covalent*

21. Bonding resulting from one atom losing and another gaining electrons.   *ionic*

22. Bonding resulting from electrostatic attractions between opposite charges.   *SKIP*

23. Bonding found in polyatomic ions.   *covalent*

24. Atoms in diamonds are held together by this bond?   *metallic*

Set C: Determining Bond Types Between Atoms

Indicate the type of chemical bond that will form between the two atoms given in 25 – 32, or the type of bond that is found in the substances given in the 33 – 41. Use the list of bond types given below.

Ionic, polar covalent, nonpolar covalent, coordinate covalent, network solid covalent, metallic

25. Lithium and oxygen   *Ionic*

26. Aluminum and chlorine   *Ionic*

27. Nitrogen and nitrogen   *NP. Covalent*

28. Carbon and bromine   *P. Covalent*

29. Phosphorous and oxygen   *P. Covalent*

30. Calcium and fluorine   *Ionic*

31. Hydrogen and hydrogen   *NP. Covalent*

32. Sulfur and oxygen   *P. Covalent*

33. HCl   ~~P.~~ *P. Covalent*

34. Na_2SO_4 ~~~~ *Ionic*

35. Cl_2 *NP. Covalent*

36. Ag   *metallic*

37. CCl_4 *NP. Covalent*

38. SiC   *Ionic*

39. MgF_2 *Ionic*

40. $LiNO_3$ *Ionic*

41. H_3O^+ *P. Covalent*

Worksheet 15: Types of Substances and Properties   Topic 4

Set A: Determining Substance Type from Properties

Indicate type of substances that is described by each statement. Use the list of substances below.
Molecular substances, ionic substances, metallic substances, network solids

1. Substance that have high melting point, and is soluble in water.   *Ionic*

2. Substances that can conduct electricity in the solid and liquid phases.   *metallic*

3. Soft and brittle substances with covalent bonds between the atoms   *molecular/covalent*

4. Substances with low melting points and poor electrical conductivity   *molecular*

5. Substances that conduct electricity in aqueous solutions.   *Ionic*

6. Hard substances that are insoluble in water.   _____

7. Substances that can be a solid, liquid, or gas at STP.   *Metallic*

8. Substance that can be polar or nonpolar.   *molecular*

9. Substances that dissolve well in water.   *Ionic*

10. Hard and insoluble substances that are also a poor conductor of electricity_____

Set B: Determining Substance Type from Chemical Symbols

Identify each of the following substances as:

Polar molecular	metallic	binary ionic compound
nonpolar molecular	network solid	ionic compound with both ionic and covalent bonds

11. NH_3 *nonpolar molecular*

12. KNO_3 *Ionic*

13. O_2 *NP. molecular*

14. $AlCl_3$ *Ionic*

15. C   _____

16. Hg   *Metallic*

17. $C_6H_{12}O_6$ _____   _____

18. $CaSO_4$ *Ionic*

19. Cu   *Ionic*

20. CO_2 *NP. molecular*

21. $FeBr_2$ *Ionic*

22. HF   *P. molecular*

Set C: Determining Properties of Substances

Properties of substances are listed below. For each substance given in number 23 – 30, choose and write all properties of the substance from the list given below. Indicate the substance type to help you choose the correct set of properties for each.

Properties			**Use the following for Conductivity**
Soft solid	Soluble in water	High melting point	Conducts electricity as solid
Hard solid	Insoluble in water	Low melting point	Conducts electricity as liquid
	Slightly soluble		Conducts electricity as aqueous (electrolytes)
			Poor electrical conductor in all phases

            Type of Substance   *Properties*

23. $NaNO_3(s)$ _____   _____   _____

_____   _____   _____

_____   _____

24. $Ag(s)$ _____   _____   _____

_____   _____   _____

_____   _____

25. $I_2(s)$ _____   _____   _____

_____   _____   _____

_____   _____

26. $CO_2(s)$ _____   _____   _____

_____   _____   _____

_____   _____

27. $CuBr_2(s)$ _____   _____   _____

_____   _____   _____

_____   _____

28. $C_{12}H_{22}O_{11}(s)$ _____   _____   _____

_____   _____   _____

_____   _____

29. $P(s)$ _____   _____   _____

_____   _____   _____

_____   _____

30. $Au(s)$ _____   _____   _____

_____   _____   _____

_____   _____

Set A: Polarity and Shapes from Molecular Structures

Structures of molecular substances are given below. For each structure, indicate the correct information.

For bond polarity, write *"polar covalent"* or *"nonpolar covalent"*.
For molecular polarity, write *"polar molecule"* or *"nonpolar molecule"*
For symmetry, write *"symmetrical"* or *"asymmetrical"*
For molecular shape, indicate *"linear"* or *"pyramidal"* or *"tetrahedral"* or *"bent"*.

1. H – I

Bond polarity: ___polar Covalent___   Symmetry: asymmetrical

Molecular polarity: ___polar___   Molecular shape: linear

2.
$$
\begin{array}{c}
F \\
| \\
F-C-F \\
| \\
F
\end{array}
$$

Bond polarity: ___nonpolar___   Symmetry: Symmetrical

Molecular polarity: ___polar___   Molecular shape: tetrahedral

3. Br – Br

Bond polarity: ___NP___   Symmetry: Symmetrical

Molecular polarity: ___NP___   Molecular shape: linear

4.
$$
\begin{array}{c}
Cl \\
| \\
H-C-Cl \\
| \\
H
\end{array}
$$

Bond polarity: ___polar___   Symmetry: asymmetrial

Molecular polarity: ___polar___   Molecular shape: tetrahedral

5. O = O

Bond polarity: ___NP___   Symmetry: Symmetrical

Molecular polarity: ___NP___   Molecular shape: linear

6. O = C = O

Bond polarity: ___NP___   Symmetry: symmetrical

Molecular polarity: ___P___   Molecular shape: linear

7.
$$
\begin{array}{c}
H \quad Br \\
| \quad\ | \\
H-C-C-Br \\
| \quad\ | \\
H \quad H
\end{array}
$$

Bond polarity: ___P___   Symmetry: asymmetrical

Molecular polarity: ___P___   Molecular shape: tetrahedral

8.
$$
\begin{array}{c}
S \\
/ \ \backslash \\
H \quad H
\end{array}
$$

Bond polarity: ___P___   Symmetry: asymmetrical

Molecular polarity: ___NP___   Molecular shape: bent

9.
$$
\begin{array}{c}
H \\
| \\
H-C-H \\
| \\
H
\end{array}
$$

Bond polarity: ___NP___   Symmetry: Symmetrial

Molecular polarity: ___NP___   Molecular shape: tetrahedral

Set B: Degree of Bond Polarity

For each set of formulas: Determine the electronegativity value for each element. Calculate the electronegativity difference for each formula. Answer questions below each set.

Set I.	Formulas	HBr	HF	HI	HCl
	Electronegativity value	Br	F	I	Cl
	Electronegativity value	H	H	H	H
	Electronegativity difference	0.8	1.8	0.5	1.0

10. Which formula has the most covalent characteristics? HI
11. Which formula has the least ionic characteristics? HI
12. Which formula is the most polar? HF

Set II.	Formulas	CaO	K₂O	Al₃O₂	BaO
	Electronegativity value	O	O	O	O
	Electronegativity value	Ca	K	Al	Ba
	Electronegativity difference	2.4	2.6	1.8	2.5

Set II handwritten work:
CaO: 2.14 / 8.4 / -0.8 / 2.6
Al₃O₂: 2.14 / 3.4 / -1.6 / 1.8
BaO: 3.4 / -0.9 / 2.5

13. Which formula has the least covalent characteristics? K₂O
14. Which formula has the most ionic characteristics? K₂O
15. Which formula is the least polar? Al₃O₂

Set III.	Formulas	NH₃	CCl₄	H₂O	HCl
	Electronegativity value	N	Cl	O	Cl
	Electronegativity value	H	C	H	H
	Electronegativity difference	0.8	0.6	1.7	1.0

16. Which formula has the most covalent characteristics? CCl₄
17. Which formula has the least ionic characteristics? CCl₄
18. Which formula is the most polar? H₂O

Set IV.	Formulas	PCl₃	NaCl	MgCl₂	SCl₂
	Electronegativity value	Cl	Cl	Cl	Cl
	Electronegativity value	P	Na	Mg	S
	Electronegativity difference	1.0	2.3	1.9	0.6

19. Which formula has the least covalent characteristics? NaCl
20. Which formula has the most ionic characteristics? NaCl
21. Which formula is the least polar? NaCl

Set A: Drawing Electron-dot Diagrams

Draw the electron-dot diagram for the given atoms, ions and compounds.

For the formulas with two or more atoms (#9 – 20) use • for the electrons of one atom, and x for the electrons of the other atom.

1. Francium   2. Boron   3. Selenium   4. Fluorine   5. Argon

6. Beryllium ion   7. Nitrogen ion   8. Iodine ion

9. Lithium bromide   10. Barium Chloride   11. Potassium sulfide

12. Iodine (I_2)   13. Oxygen (O_2)   14. Nitrogen (N_2)

15. Hydrogen chloride (HCl)   16. Hydrogen fluoride (HF)   17. Ammonia (NH_3)

18. Methane (CH_4)   19. Carbon tetrafluoride (CF_4)   20. Carbon dioxide (CO_2)

Survivingchem.com

Set A: Terms and Definitions

Define or describe each of the following terms.

1. Chemical formula

2. Qualitative

3. Quantitative

4. Subscript

5. Molecular formula

6. Empirical formula

7. Binary compound

8. Polyatomic ion

Set B: Atoms in Chemical Compounds

Indicate the number of each atom and the total number of atoms in each of the given substances.

	Number of each atom	Total number of atoms in each formula
9. $HClO_3$	_____ H atoms	
	_____ Cl atoms	
	_____ O atoms	_____
10. $NH_4C_2H_3O_2$	_____ N atoms	
	_____ H atoms	
	_____ C atom	_____
	_____ O atoms	
11. $Mg(NO_3)_2$	_____ Mg atoms	
	_____ N atoms	
	_____ O atoms	_____

Set B cont.

12. $C_3H_5(OH)_3$ _____ C atoms   ***Total Number of Atoms in the Formula***
                          _____ H atoms
                          _____ O atoms   _____

13.   LiCl •$4H_2O$ _____ Li atoms
                          _____ Cl atoms
                          _____ H atoms   _____
                          _____ O atoms

14. $CuSO_4$•$3H_2O$ _____ Cu atoms
                          _____ S atoms
                          _____ O atoms   _____
                          _____ H atoms

15. NH_4Cl•$5H_2O$ _____ N atoms
                          _____ H atoms
                          _____ Cl atoms   _____
                          _____ O atoms

Set C: Ratio of Ions in ionic Substances

For each of the following ionic substance:
Write the symbols and names of both ions in the formula. Indicate the ratio of the ions in the formula.

Follow the example given below.

Ex. $MgCO_3$ *Ions in formula:* Mg^{2+} (magnesium ion) CO_3^{2-} (carbonate ion)

                     Ratio of ions :   1   :   1

16. KCl   *Ions in formula:*
                     Ratio of ions :

17. $SrBr_2$ *Ions in formula:*
                     Ratio of ions :

18 . Na_2CO_3 *Ions in formula:*
                     Ratio of ions :

19. $CaSO_4$ *Ions in formula:*
                     Ratio of ions :

20. $(NH_4)_3PO_4$ *Ions in formula:*
                     Ratio of ions :

21. $Mg(ClO_3)_2$ *Ions in formula:*
                     Ratio of ions :

Set A: Molecular and Empirical Formulas

Circle all empirical formulas.

22. a) CH_4 b) C_3H_6 c) N_2O_4 d) Na_2SO_4

     e) C_5H_{10} f) Al_2O_3 g) NH_4NO_3 h) $HC_2H_3O_2$

For each molecular formula given below: Determine and write down the greatest common factor (GCF), then write the correct empirical formula.

Molecular Formula	GCF	Empirical Formula
23. S_2O_4		
24. C_4H_{10}		
25. C_6H_{10}		
26. N_2F_2		
27. $C_6H_{12}O_6$		
28. $C_2H_4O_2$		
29. C_3H_6		
30. $K_2S_2O_4$		
31. N_2O_2		
32. $C_6H_{12}Cl_2O_2$		

Set A: Writing Chemical Formulas

Write the correct chemical formula for each of the given substances.

1. Write the correct formulas for the following <u>Binary Ionic Compounds</u>.

a)　Potassium fluoride

b)　Lithium oxide

c)　Barium iodide

d)　Magnesium sulfide

2. Write the correct formulas for the following <u>polyatomic ion</u> compounds.

e)　Sodium sulfate

f)　Barium Phosphate

g)　Magnesium hydrogen carbonate

h)　Aluminum chromate

3. Write the correct formulas for these compounds, which contain an element with <u>multiple positive charges.</u>

i)　Lead(II) Iodide

j)　Copper(I) nitrate

k)　Nitrogen(V) oxide

l)　Iron(III) Sulfate

m)　Chromium(V) Chloride

n)　Phosphorous(IV) oxide

4. Write the correct formulas for these compounds.

o)　Palladium(II) sulfide

p)　Strontium nitrite

q)　Calcium iodide

r)　Lithium permanganate

s)　Platinum(IV) oxide

t)　Barium chlorate

u)　Iron(III) Sulfate

v)　Chromium(VI) phosphide

w)　Manganese(III) oxide

　　　Copyright © 2015 E3 Scholastic Publishing. All Rights Reserved.　　Survivingchem.com

Set B: IUPAC Names from Chemical Formulas

Write the correct IUPAC names for each of the following compounds.

5. Name the following *binary ionic compounds.*

    a)   LiBr   b) Ag_2O

    c) Al_2O_3 d) Ba_3N_2

6. Name the following *polyatomic ion* compounds.

    e) $BeSO_4$ f) $Ca(NO_3)_2$

    g) $Al_2(Cr_2O_7)_3$ h) $(NH_4)_2S$

7. Name the following compounds containing an element with *multiple positive charges.*

    i) $CuCl_2$ j) Ti_2O_3 k) $Fe(NO_3)_2$

    l) $Ni_2(SO_4)_3$ m) Au_2O n) SnO

    o) NO_2 p) PCl_5 q) N_2O_5

8. Name the following substances.

    r) Na_3P s) Fe_2S_3 t) $Al_2(SO_3)_3$

    u) MnO v) $Ca(ClO_3)_2$ w) $PbSO_4$

    x) NO y) PBr_5 z) $Ba(HCO_3)_2$

Set C: Writing and Naming Compounds with Prefixes

9. Write the correct formulas for the following compounds containing prefixes.

a) Dibismuth trichloride   b) Silicon tetrafluoride   c) Ditatanium trioxide

d) Tetraphosphorous hexoxide   e) Carbon disulfide   f) Boron triiodide

10. Write the correct name for each of the following compounds using prefixes.

a) H_2S b) SiF_4 c) Hg_2Cl_2

d) XeF_6 e) V_2H f) PF_5

Set D: Formulas and Name of Hydrates

11. Write the correct name for each of the following hydrates.

a) $NH_4NO_3 \bullet 3H_2O$ b) $Na_2CO_3 \bullet 10H_2O$

c) $FeSO_4 \bullet 7H_2O$ d) $SnCl_2 \bullet 2H_2O$

12. Write the correct chemical formula for each of the following hydrates.

a) Barium hydroxide octahydrate   b) Cobalt(II) chloride hexahydrate

c) Iron(III) phosphate tetrahydrate   d) Lithium sulfite pentahydrate

Set A: Types of Chemical Reactions

Indicate the type of chemical reaction represented by each equation. Choose from the list below.
Synthesis, decomposition, single replacement, or double replacement.

1. Cl_2 + $2NaI$ → $2NaCl$ + I_2 _____

2. HNO_3 + $LiOH$ → H_2O + $LiNO_3$ _____

3. $2NaN_3$ → $2Na$ + $3N_2$ _____

4. $Ba(NO_3)_2$ + K_2SO_4 → $2KNO_3$ + $BaSO_4$ _____

5. P_4 + $6Cl_2$ → $4PCl_3$ _____

6. $4Al$ + $3Fe_3O_2$ → $2Al_2O_3$ + $9Fe$ _____

7. $2NaClO_3$ → $3O_2$ + $2NaCl$ _____

8. BaO + SO_3 → $BaSO_4$ _____

Set B: Interpreting Equations

In each balanced equation, determine the reactants, products, mole ratio, and sums of all coefficients.

9. $3Fe$ + $2O_2$ → Fe_3O_4

Reactants
Products
Mole ratio of Fe to Fe_3O_4
Sums of all coefficients:

10. N_2O_5 + H_2O → $2HNO_3$

Reactants
Products
Mole ratio of N_2O_5 to H_2O
Sum of all coefficients:

11. $2Al$ + $3CuSO_4$ → $Al_2(SO_4)_3$ + $3Cu$

Reactants
Products
Mole ratio of copper sulfate to copper
Sum of all coefficients

12. MnO_2 + $4HCl$ → $MnCl_2$ + Cl_2 + $2H_2O$

Reactants
Products
Mole ratio of hydrochloric acid to water :
Sum of all coefficients

Set C: Conservation of Atoms in Equations

Write *"balanced"* next to those equations that are correctly balanced (demonstrate conservation of mass). Write **"not balanced"** next to those equations that do no demonstrate conservation of mass.

12. $2Cu + O_2 \rightarrow 2CuO$ _____

13. $Cu + AgNO_3 \rightarrow Cu(NO_3)_2 + 2Ag$ _____

14. $P_4 + Cl_2 \rightarrow 4PCl_3$ _____

15. $2Ag + H_2S \rightarrow Ag_2S + H_2$ _____

16. $8Al + 3Fe_3O_4 \rightarrow 4Al_2O_3 + 9Fe$ _____

17. $4Fe + 3O_2 \rightarrow Fe_2O_3$ _____

18. $C_3H_8 + 3O_2 \rightarrow 3CO_2 + 4H_2O$ _____

D: Balancing Equations

Balance each equation below using the smallest whole number coefficients. Indicate the sum of all coefficients in the box after you had balanced each equation.

19. $Cu_2S \rightarrow Cu + S$

20. $Hg + O_2 \rightarrow HgO$

21. $FeCl_2 + Na_2CO_3 \rightarrow FeCO_3 + NaCl$

22. $AgNO_3 + MgCl_2 \rightarrow Mg(NO_3)_2 + AgCl$

23. $C_3H_6 + O_2 \rightarrow CO_2 + H_2O$

24. $C_8H_{16} + O_2 \rightarrow CO_2 + H_2O$

25. $C_2H_4O_2 + PCl_3 \rightarrow C_2H_3OCl + H_3PO_3$

Set A: Terms and Definitions

Define or describe each of the following terms.

1. Mole

2. Avogadro's number

3. Molar mass

4. Gram-atomic mass

5. Gram-formula mass

6. Gram-molecular

7. Percent composition

8. Hydrate

9. Anhydrous

Set B: Moles of Atoms in Formulas

Determine the number of moles of each atom and the total number of moles of atoms in the formula.

		Moles of Each Atom	**Total Moles of Atoms**
10.	1 mole of H_2SO_4		
11.	2 moles of $Mg(OH)_2$		
12.	0.5 moles of $C_7H_5(NO_2)_3$		

Set B cont.

	Moles of Each Atom	Total Moles of Atoms
13. 1 mole of $CuSO_4 \cdot 7H_2O$		
14. $2(NH_4)_3PO_4$		
15. $3Fe_2O_3$		

Set C: Molar or Formula Mass Calculations

Calculate the formula mass of the following compounds. Show work by listing each element in the formula, *their atomic mass, how many of the element, and the total mass of the element in the formula.*

	Element	Atomic Mass	How many	Total Mass	Formula Mass
18. Iron(III) sulfate $Fe_2(SO_4)_3$					
19. Ammonium chloride trihydrate $NH_4Cl \cdot 3H_2O$					
20. Octane C_8H_{18}					
21. Sucrose $C_{12}H_{22}O_{11}$					
22. $C_6H_{12}Cl_2O_2$					

Set D: Mole – Mass Calculations

Calculate the mass for the given number of moles of each substance.

*Use the mole equation on **Reference Table T** to set up and solve each problem..*

Write answers in the boxes below.

23. What is the mass of 0.5 moles of ammonia, NH_3?

24. What is the mass of 2.00 moles of $Ca(OH)_2$?

25. What is the mass of 4.2 moles of H_3PO_4?

26. What is the mass of 0.75 moles of butane, C_4H_8

27. What is the mass of 2.0 moles of gypsum, $CaCl_2 \bullet H_2O$?

Calculate the number of moles of each substance present in the given mass of the substance

Use the mole equation on Reference Table T to set up and solve each problem.

28. How many moles of HCl are there in 108 grams of the substance?

29. What is the number of moles of Na_2SO_4 in 300 grams of the substance?

30. What is the total number of moles in 576 g of $(NH_4)_2CO_3$?

31. How moles of $MgSO_4 \bullet 7H_2O$ are in 124 grams of the substance?

Set A: Percent Composition by Mass

For each formula below, calculate the percent composition for each element.

Use the Reference Table T equation below to set up and calculate the percent by mass of each element.

% of atom X = $\dfrac{\text{Total mass of atom X}}{\text{Formula Mass}} \times 100$	Table T equation

1. NH_3 % N =

         % H =

2. $NaNO_3$ % Na =

         % N =

         % O =

3 . $Ca(OH)_2$ % Ca =

         % O =

         % H =

4. $(NH_4)_3PO_4$ % N =

         % H =

         % P =

         % O =

Set B: Percent Composition of Hydrates

Calculate the percent by mass of water in each of the following hydrates.
Use the equation below to set up and calculate the percent of water.

$$\% \ H_2O \ = \ \frac{\text{Total mass of } H_2O}{\text{Formula mass of the hydrate}} \ \times \ 100$$

5. $CaCl_2 \cdot 2H_2O$ $\% \ H_2O \ =$

6. $Na_2CO_3 \cdot 10H_2O$ $\% \ H_2O \ =$

7. $Al(ClO_3)_3 \cdot 6H_2O$ $\% \ H_2O \ =$

For each problem below, calculate the percent of water in the hydrate.
For each: Determine the mass of water, setup the problem with an equation, and solve.

8. A student heated 10.5 grams of a hydrate until all water of hydration is driven off. The student determined the mass of the anhydrous to be 7.2 grams. What is the percent of water in the hydrate?

    Mass of water =   % water =

9. In a laboratory procedure, a student heated a 6.3-g sample of a hydrated salt to a constant mass of 3.8 grams. What is the percent of water in the hydrate?

    Mass of water =   % of water =

10. The data below was collected from a laboratory procedure to determine percent of water in a hydrate.
    Mass of evaporated dish + cover ……………………………………   26.0 g
    Mass of hydrate + evaporated dish + cover ……………………   31.0 g
    Mass of anhydrous + evaporate dish + cover …………………   28.9 g

    What is the percent by mass of water in the hydrate?
    Mass of water   =   % water =

Set A : Mole to Mole Problems

Solve the following problems. Show a numerical setup and the calculated result for each problem.

1. Given the balanced chemical equation: $Ca + 2H_2O \rightarrow Ca(OH)_2 + H_2$
   What is the total number of moles of Ca
   that will react with 6 moles of water?

2. Given the balanced chemical equation : $2N_2O_5(g) \rightarrow 4NO_2(g) + O_2(g)$
   What is the total number of moles of NO_2
   that will be produced from 5 moles of N_2O_5?

3. Given the balanced chemical equation: $CH_4(g) + 2O_2(g) \rightarrow CO_2(g) + 2H_2O(\ell)$
   How many moles of CO_2 will be produced
   from reacting 7.4 moles of O_2 ?

4. Given the balanced combustion reaction: $2C_2H_2 + 5O_2 \rightarrow 4CO_2 + 2H_2O$
   How many moles of C_2H_2 is needed to
   completely react with 11.5 moles of O_2?

5. Given the balanced chemical equation: $3Cu + 8HNO_3 \rightarrow 3Cu(NO_3)_2 + 2NO + 4H_2O$
   What is the total number of moles of Cu
   needed to produce 9.0 moles of NO?

6. Given the balanced chemical equation: $3H_2(g) + N_2(g) \rightarrow 2NH_3(g)$
   How many moles of ammonia can be
   produced by reacting 2.8 moles of nitrogen?

7. Given the balanced chemical equation: $2Li(s) + H_2SO_4(aq) \rightarrow Li_2SO_4(aq) + H_2(g)$
   How many moles of lithium must react to
   produce 3.3 moles of lithium sulfate, Li_2SO_4?

Set B : Volume to Volume Problems

Solve the following problems. Show a numerical setup and the calculated result for each problem.

1. Given the balanced chemical equation: $2Cl_2(g) + 2H_2O(\ell) \rightarrow 4HCl(aq) + O_2(g)$
   What is the total number of liters of $O_2(g)$
   produced when 8 liters of $Cl_2(g)$ is reacted with water?

2. Given the balanced chemical equation: $2SO_2(g) + O_2(g) \rightarrow 2SO_3(g)$
   At STP, how many liters of SO_2 will react with O_2
   to produce 9.0 liters of SO_3?

3. Given the balanced chemical equation: $CH_4(g) + 2O_2(g) \rightarrow CO_2(g) + 2H_2O(\ell)$
   What is the total volume of CO_2 produced
   when 5.7 liters of CH_4 reacted?

Set C: Mass to Mass Problems

Solve the following problems. Show a numerical setup and the calculated result for each problem.

1. Given the balanced combustion reaction: $2C_2H_6 + 7O_2 \rightarrow 4CO_2 + 6H_2O$
   What is the total mass of C_2H_6 that will react
   to produce 72 grams of H_2O?

1. Given the balanced chemical equation: $Mg + H_2SO_4 \rightarrow MgSO_4 + H_2$
   What is the total number of grams of $MgSO_4$
   produced when 100 grams of Mg is reacted?

3. Given the balanced chemical equation: $2KClO_3 \rightarrow 2KCl + 3O_2$
   What is the total number of grams of $KClO_3$
   that will react to produce 32 grams of O_2 at STP?

4. Given the balanced chemical equation: $2Li(s) + H_2SO_4(aq) \rightarrow Li_2SO_4(aq) + H_2(g)$
   How many grams of lithium sulfate is produced
   from reacting 27 grams of lithium?

Survivingchem.com

Set A: Terms and Definitions

Define or describe each of the following terms.

1. Aqueous solution

2. Homogeneous mixture

3. Solute

4. Solvent

5. Solubility

6. Soluble

7. Insoluble

8. Miscibility

9. Miscible

10. Immiscible

Set B: Solute and Solvent of Solutions

For each solution of the name or symbol, write the name and the formula of solute and solvent.

Solution symbol or name	Solute formula and name	Solvent formula
11. $MgBr_2(aq)$		
12. $K_2SO_4(aq)$		
13. $(NH_4)_2CO_3(aq)$		
14. Iron(III) chloride solution		
15. Copper(II) sulfate solution		
16. Barium nitrate solution		

Set C: Facts of Solubility Factors

Answer the following questions on factors that affect solubility.

17. List three factors that can affect the solubility of a substance.

18. How does temperature affect solubility of a solid?

19. How does temperature affect solubility of a gas?

20. How does pressure affect solubility of a solid?

21. How does pressure affect solubility of a gas?

22. What type of a substance is water?

23. What types of solutes dissolve well in water? Explain your answer.

Set D: Solubility

Below, solutes that will dissolve in water are given to the left. Four different temperature and pressure values are given. Answer the questions below based on the type of solute that is given.

24. NH_3 **32ºC**   **36ºC**   **40ºC**   **44ºC**   **1 atm**   **1.3 atm**   **1.6 atm**   **1.8 atm**
Does a change in temperature affect the solubility of NH_3?
   If Yes, at which temperature would NH_3 be most soluble?
Does pressure change has effect on the solubility of NH_3?
   If yes, at which pressure would NH_3 be most soluble?

25. $LiNO_3$ **40ºC**   **50ºC**   **60ºC**   **64ºC**   **.2 atm**   **.4 atm**   **.6 atm**   **.8 atm**
Does temperature change has effect on the solubility of $LiNO_3$?
   If Yes, at which temperature would $LiNO_3$ be least soluble?
Does pressure change has effect on the solubility of $LiNO_3$?
   If yes, at which pressure would $LiNO_3$ be least soluble?

26. $CaBr_2$ **60ºC**   **65ºC**   **70ºC**   **75ºC**   **100 kPa**   **150 kPa**   **200 kPa**   **250 kPa**
Does temperature change has effect on the solubility of $CaBr_2$?
   If Yes, at which temperature would $CaBr_2$ be most soluble?
Does pressure change has effect on the solubility of $CaBr_2$?
   If yes, at which pressure would $CaBr_2$ be most soluble?

27. CO   **273 K**   **283 K**   **293 K**   **303 K**   **2 atm**   **2.2 atm**   **2.4 atm**   **2.6 atm**
Does temperature change has effect the solubility of CO?
   If Yes, at which temperature would CO be least soluble?
Does pressure change has effect on the solubility of CO?
   If yes, at which pressure would CO be least soluble?

Set E: Determining Soluble and Insoluble Substances – Reading Reference Table F

Write "soluble" next to each substance that is soluble in water.
Write "insoluble" next each substance that is insoluble in water.

28. NaCl   _____   34. Calcium hydroxide   _____

29. $PbBr_2$ _____   35. Lithium hydroxide   _____

30. $CaSO_4$ _____   35. Lead sulfate   _____

31. NH_4NO_3 _____   36. Ammonium sulfide   _____

32. $MgCO_3$ _____   37. Lead nitrate   _____

33. K_3PO_4 _____   38. Potassium chromate   _____

Set F: Hydration of Ions

In each of the given solution, draw a diagram to show the interaction between the ions of the solute and molecules of water. Remember: Opposites attract!

39.   40.   41.

    LiBr*(aq)*   **MgSO₄*(aq)***   **NH₄NO₃*(aq)***

Set A : Terms and Definitions

Define or describe each of the following terms.

1. Saturation

2. Supersaturated

3. Unsaturation

4. Concentrated

5. Dilute

Set B: Reading the Solubility Curves - Reference Table G

Use the Solubility Curves on Reference Table G to answer the following questions.
Write your answers in the space to the right of each question.

6. Name three solutes from the table with an increase　　6.
   in solubility as water temperature increases.

7. Name two solutes from the table with a decrease　　7.
   In solubility as water temperature increases.

8. Which two solutes show the greatest change in solubility　　8.
   as the water temperature is changed from 10°C to 50°C?

9. Which two solutes show the least change in solubility　　9.
   as the water temperature is changed from 0°C to 100°C?

10. Which solid solute is most soluble at 60°C?　　10.

11. Which gaseous solute is least soluble at 40°C?　　11.

12. At 90°C, which salt is less soluble than $KClO_3$?　　12.

13. At 20°C, which gaseous solute is more soluble than NH_3?　　13.

Set C: Saturated Amount of Solutes in Solutions

Use Reference Table G to determine the amount of the solute needed to form a saturated solution.

14. In 100 g of H_2O at 70°C, what amount of KNO_3 will make a saturated solution?   *134g*

15. In 100 g of H_2O at 50°C, what amount of NH_4Cl will form a saturated solution?   *52 g*

16. In 100 g of H_2O at 30°C, what amount of HCl will make a saturated solution?   *48g*

17. In 50 g of H_2O at 20°C, what amount of $NaNO_3$ will form a saturated solution?   *44g*

18. In 200 g of H_2O at 60°C, what amount of $KClO_3$ will make a saturated solution?   *76g*

19. In 50 g of H_2O at 10°C, what amount of KI will make a saturated solution?   *68g*

20. In 300 g of H_2O at 90°C, what amount of NH_3 will form a saturated solution?   *30g*

21. In 25 g of H_2O at 80°C, what amount of NaCl will make a saturated solution?   *12.25g*

(margin work: 38 ×2 = 76)

(margin work: 68, 2⟌136, −12↓, 6)

Set D: Types of Solutions Using the Solubility Curves

Base on the given information, determine the type of solution that is formed.
Write "***Saturated***", "***Supersaturated***", or "***Unsaturated***" in the line provided.

22.   80 g of $NaNO_3$ is dissolved in 100 g of H_2O at 10°C.   *Saturated*

23.   75 g of $NaNO_3$ is dissolved in 100 g of H_2O at 10°C.   *Unsaturated*

24.   90 g of $NaNO_3$ is dissolved in 100 g of H_2O at 10°C.   *Supersaturated*

25.   90 g of KNO_3 is dissolved in 100 g of H_2O at 50°C.   *Supersaturated*

26.   5 g of $KClO_3$ is dissolved in 100 g of H_2O at 5°C   *Saturated*

27.   40 g of KCl is dissolved in 50 g of H_2O at 60°C.   *Unsaturated*

28.   40 g of $NaNO_3$ is dissolved in 50 g of H_2O at 10°C.   *Saturated*

29.   120 g of NH_3 is dissolved in 200 g of H_2O at 10°C.   *Unsaturated*

30.   90 g of NaCl is dissolved in 200 g of H_2O at 80°C.   *Supersaturated*

Set A: Terms and Definitions

Define or describe each of the following terms.

1. Molarity : *measures the number of moles of a solute in a 1 L solution*

2. Parts per million : *a ratio between the mass of a solute and the total mass of the solution*

Set B: Calculation of Molarity

Solve the molarity concentration problems below.
Show a numerical setup and the calculated result for each problem.

3. What is the molarity of 1.0 L NaCl solution containing 1.0 mole of the solute?

$$\frac{1}{1} = 1 \quad \boxed{1 M}$$

4. What is the concentration of 1.8 L KNO$_3$ solution containing 0.5 mol of the solute?

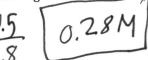

$$\frac{0.5}{1.8} \quad \boxed{0.28 M}$$

5. What is the concentration of a solution containing 3.3 moles of solute in every 6.0 L of the solution?

$$\frac{3.3}{6} \quad \boxed{0.55 M}$$

6. What is the concentration of NH$_4$Cl solution containing 2 moles of the solute in 500 ml of the solution?

$$\frac{2}{0.5} = \boxed{4M}$$

7. What is the molarity of a 1500-ml solution containing 3.0 moles of the solute?

$$\frac{3}{1.5} \quad \boxed{2M}$$

8. What is the molarity of a solution in which 28 g of NaCl is dissolved 2.0 liters of the solution?

$$\frac{28}{58} \quad \frac{0.48}{2} = \boxed{0.24 M}$$

9. What is the molar concentration of a solution in which 522 grams of K$_2$SO$_4$ is dissolved in 1.5 liters of the solution?

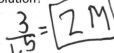

$$\frac{522}{174} \quad \frac{3}{1.5} = \boxed{2 M}$$

10. What is the molarity of a solution containing 12 g of HCl in 500 ml of the solution?

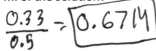

$$\frac{12}{36} = 0.33 \quad \frac{0.33}{0.5} = \boxed{0.67 M}$$

Set C: Calculation of Moles, Volume, and Mass in Solutions

Solve the concentration problems below.
Show a numerical setup and the calculated result for each problem.

11. How many moles of solute are there in a 2 L of 1 M solution? 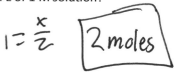 $1 = \frac{x}{2}$ 2 moles	12. What is the number of moles of LiBr in a 1.5 L of a 2 M LiBr solution? 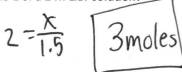 $2 = \frac{x}{1.5}$ 3 moles
13. How many moles of $NaNO_3$ must be dissolved in water to make 2 L of a 1.5 M solution? 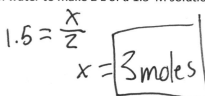 $1.5 = \frac{x}{2}$ $x = 3$ moles	14. What is the number of moles of NH_4Cl in 200 ml of a 0.4 M solution? 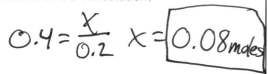 $0.4 = \frac{x}{0.2}$ $x = 0.08$ moles
15. What is the volume of a 1.5 M solution containing 2 moles of solutes? 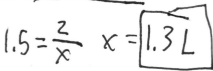 $1.5 = \frac{2}{x}$ $x = 1.3$ L	16. How much volume of a 0.4 M potassium iodide solution contains 0.12 moles of the solute? 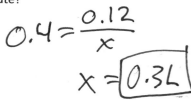 $0.4 = \frac{0.12}{x}$ $x = 0.3$ L
17. What volume of a 3 M H_2SO_4 solution will contain 0.75 moles of the solute? 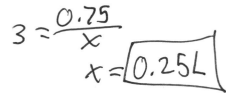 $3 = \frac{0.75}{x}$ $x = 0.25$ L	18. How many milliliters of a 2.5 M KNO_3 solution will contain 1.25 moles of the solute? 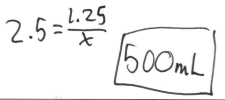 $2.5 = \frac{1.25}{x}$ 500 mL
19. How many grams of $CaCl_2$ are in a 1.0 L sample of a 0.5 M solution? 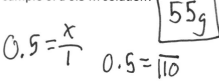 55 g $0.5 = \frac{x}{1}$ $0.5 = \overline{110}$	20. How many grams of NH_4NO_4 are in a 2.3 L sample of a 1.5 molar solution? 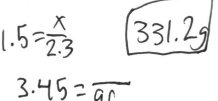 331.2 g $1.5 = \frac{x}{2.3}$ $3.45 = \overline{96}$

<u>SurvivingChem.com</u>   **59**

Set D: Parts Per Million Calculations

Solve the concentration problems below.
Show a numerical setup and the calculated result for each problem.

21. What the concentration of a solution, in parts per million, when 10 grams of the solute is dissolved in 2000 grams of water? $\dfrac{10}{2010}$ 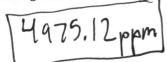	22. A 500 gram solution contains 0.02 gram of solute. What is the concentration of the solution in parts per million? $\dfrac{0.02}{500}$
23. A 1000-gram sample of CO_2 solution contains 0.5 gram of CO_2. What is the concentration, in parts per million, of the solution? $\dfrac{0.5}{1000}$ 	24. What is the concentration of KNO_3, in parts per million, in a solution that contains 100 grams of $KNO_3(s)$ dissolved in 2500 grams of water? $\dfrac{100}{2600}$ 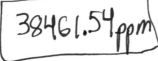
25. A 3800-gram of fish tank water contains 2.7×10^{-2} gram of dissolved oxygen. What is the concentration, in parts per million, of dissolved oxygen in the fish tank water? $\dfrac{0.027}{3800}$ 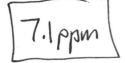	26. How many grams of HCl is in 1000 grams of a 2 ppm HCl solution? 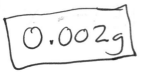
27. A 2200-gram $NH_3(aq)$ solution has a concentration of 0.5 ppm. What is the total mass of the solute in the solution? 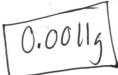	28. How many grams of $NH_4Cl(s)$ are needed to be dissolved in water to make 1500 grams of a 1.5 ppm solution? 

Set A: Terms and Definitions

Define or describe each of the following terms.

1. Vapor

2. Vapor pressure

3. Boiling

4. Boiling points

Answer the following questions.

5. Vapor pressure of a liquid depends on what factor?

6. Which of the four liquids on Table H has the weakest intermolecular forces between its molecules?

7. Which of the four liquids on Table H has the strongest intermolecular forces between its molecules?

8. Explain why water boils at 100°C at normal atmospheric pressure.

Set B: Vapor Pressure and Temperature

Use Reference Table H

Determine the vapor pressure of each of the following substances at the given temperature.

9. Propanone at 30°C _____   11. Ethanoic acid at 115°C   _____

10. Water at 75°C   _____   12. Ethanol at 58°C   _____

Determine the boiling point of each substance at the given atmospheric pressure.

13. Propanone at 50 kPa _____   15. Ethanoic acid at 80 kPa   _____

14. Water at 120 kPa _____   16.   Ethanol at 60 kPa   _____

Determine the normal boiling point of each substance given below.

17. Propanone _____   19.   Water   _____

18. Ethanol   _____   20.   Ethanoic acid _____

Set A: Comparing Freezing and Boiling Points of Solutions

The concentration of each solution in a set are given below.

For each set of solutions:

Write **"highest FP / Lowest BP"** underneath the beaker with solution that will freeze at the highest temperature and boils at the lowest temperature.

Write **"Lowest FP / Highest BP"** underneath the beaker with solution that will freeze at the lowest temperature and boils at the highest temperature.

Set 1.

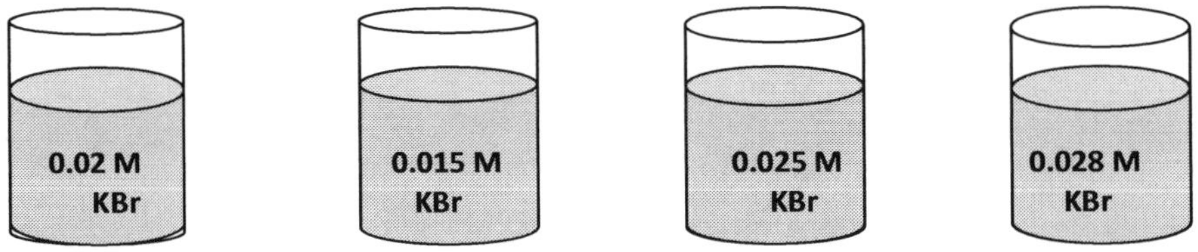

| 0.02 M KBr | 0.015 M KBr | 0.025 M KBr | 0.028 M KBr |

Set 2.

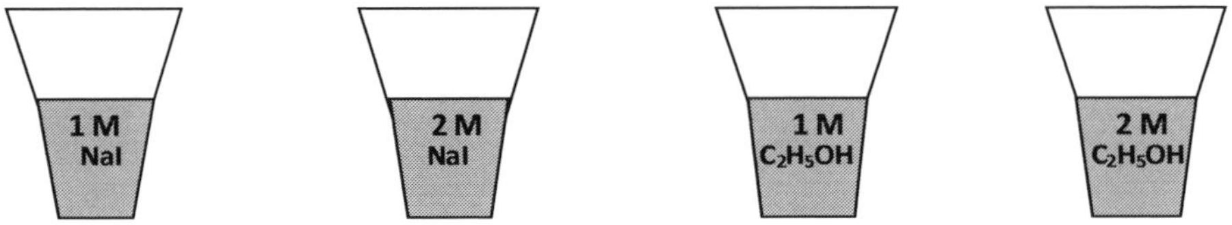

| 1 M NaI | 2 M NaI | 1 M C₂H₅OH | 2 M C₂H₅OH |

Set 3.

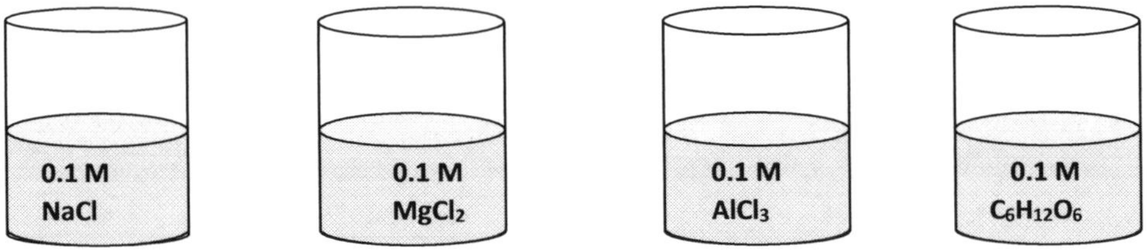

| 0.1 M NaCl | 0.1 M MgCl₂ | 0.1 M AlCl₃ | 0.1 M C₆H₁₂O₆ |

Set 4.

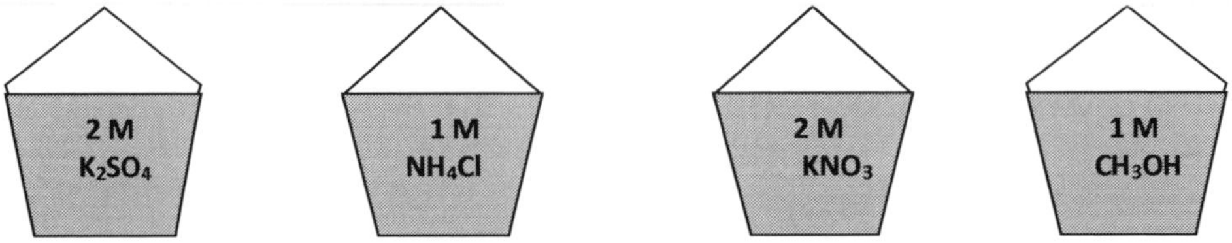

| 2 M K₂SO₄ | 1 M NH₄Cl | 2 M KNO₃ | 1 M CH₃OH |

Set 5.

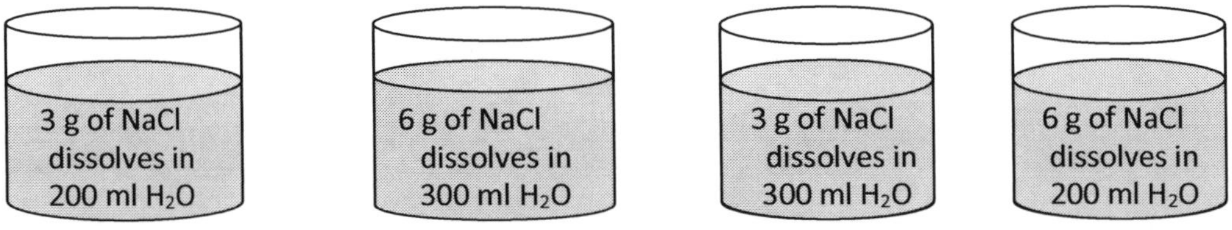

| 3 g of NaCl dissolves in 200 ml H₂O | 6 g of NaCl dissolves in 300 ml H₂O | 3 g of NaCl dissolves in 300 ml H₂O | 6 g of NaCl dissolves in 200 ml H₂O |

Set A: Terms and Definitions

Define or describe each of the following terms.

1. Arrhenius acid

2. Arrhenius base

3. Alternate acid theory

4. Alternate base theory

5. Hydrogen ion

6. Hydronium ion

7. Hydroxide ion

8. Acidity

9. Alkalinity

10. Electrolyte

11. Indicator

12. Neutralization

13. Salt

14. Titration

15. Hydrolysis

Set A: Properties of Acids and Bases

*Write **"acidic"** or **"basic"** or **" both acidic and basic"** or **"neutral"** to indicate if the property describes a solution that is an acid , a base , both, or neutral.*

1. A solution has a pH greater than 7.   _____

2. A solution turns the color of litmus to blue.   _____

3. A solution that has a higher concentration of H_3O^+ ions than OH- ions.   _____

4. A solution has a pH equal to 7.   _____

5. A solution in which phenolphthalein stays colorless.   _____

6. A solution that can change the color of an indicator.   _____

7. A solution is added to water, and the H^+ concentration of the water increases. _____

8. A solution changes phenolphthalein from colorless to pink.   _____

9. A solution has a higher concentration of hydroxide ion than hydrogen ion.   _____

10. A solution with equal number of H^+ ions to OH$^-$ ions.   _____

11. A solution contains electrolytes.   _____

12. A solution increases the OH$^-$ ion concentration of another solution.   _____

13. A solution decreases the alkalinity of another solution.   _____

14. A solution contains hydrogen ion as the only positive ion.   _____

15. A solution in which bromthymol will be yellow.   _____

16. A solution undergoes neutralization reaction.   _____

17. A solution reacts with a metal to produce hydrogen gas.   _____

18. A solution contains mobile ions that conduct electrical current .   _____

19. A solution that can turn litmus paper to red.   _____

20. A substance donates a proton in a reaction.   _____

21. A substance accepts a hydrogen ion in a reaction.   _____

Set B: Types of Solutions

*Test results for eight solutions are given below. In the space underneath each beaker, write **"Table K"** or **"Table L"** to indicate if the solution in the beaker is listed on Reference Table K or L.*

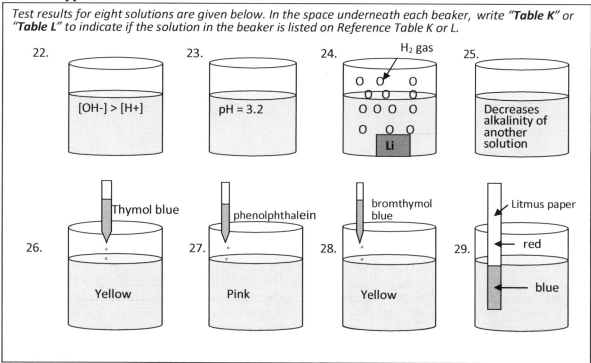

Set C: Determining Property Based on formula

Below, a solution is given in the left column. Three properties are listed in the right column. Put checks (✓) in [ ] next to those properties that best describe the solution given.

30. $Ca(OH)_2(aq)$ [ ]This solution will have a pH of 10.
                             [ ] This solution will turn litmus red
                             [ ]This solution will turn litmus blue.

31. $H_3PO_4(aq)$ [ ] Phenolphthalein will be pink in this solution
                             [ ] Phenolphthalein will be colorless in this solution
                             [ ]Concentration of H+ is less than that OH- in this solution.

32. $HF(aq)$ [ ]Concentration of H_3O+ is more than that of OH- in this solution
                             [ ] Bromthymol indicator is yellow in this solution
                             [ ]This solution will increase the pH of water.

33. $NH_3(aq)$ [ ] This solution will decrease the alkalinity of another solution.
                             [ ] Litmus will be red.
                             [ ] This solution will contain more hydroxide ion than hydrogen ion.

34. $CH_3COOH(aq)$ [ ] This solution will conducts electrical current
                             [ ] Thymol blue will change from yellow to blue in this solution
                             [ ] This solution will react with Tin to produce hydrogen gas.

Set A: Reactions of a Metal with an Acid

Below, equation showing reaction of a metal with an acid is given.

If the reaction will occur, write the products (salt and hydrogen gas) formulas to the right of the arrow. Be sure to balance these equations .

If the reaction will not occur, write "no reaction" to the right of the arrow.

| USE TABLE J |

	Metal	+	Acid		Salt	+	hydrogen gas
1.	Ca	+	HCl	→
2.	Ag	+	HNO_3	→
3.	Li	+	H_3PO_4	→
4.	Mg	+	$HC_2H_3O_2$	→
5.	Zn	+	HCl	→
6.	Au	+	H_2SO_4	→
7.	Al	+	HNO_3	→

Set B: Neutralization Reaction

Below, incomplete neutralization equation are given.

Write the products of each reaction to the right of the arrow. Be sure to balance the equations .

	Acid	+	Base		Salt	+	Water
8.	HCl	+	KOH	→
9.	HNO_3	+	NaOH	→
10.	H_2SO_4	+	KOH	→
11.	H_2CO_3	+	$Ca(OH)_2$	→
12.	H_3PO_4	+	LiOH	→
13.	$HC_2H_3O_2$	+	$Ba(OH)_2$	→

Titration Problems: *Show a numerical setup and the calculated result for each problem.*

Set A: Calculations of Moles	**Set B: Calculations of Molarity and Volume**
1. How many moles of KOH are needed to completely neutralize 0.5 L of 1.0 M HCl solution?	6. How many milliliters of 2.5 M HCl are required to exactly neutralize 100 mL of 0.1 M NaOH solution?
2. How many moles of HCl is needed to completely neutralize 1.5 L of a 0.3 M NaOH solution?	7. How many milliliters of 3 M KOH solution is required to neutralize 100 mL of 1.5 M HNO_3 solution?
3. How many moles of sodium hydroxide is needed to neutralize 0.3 L of 0.1 M nitric acid solution?	8. What is the molarity of a 60 ml HNO_3 solution if 180 ml of 0.2 M KOH is used to neutralize it?
4. How many moles of NaOH is needed to completely neutralize 0.1 L of 2 M H_2SO_4 solution.	9. What is the molarity of a 20 mL NaOH solution that is neutralized by 5 ml of 0.1 M HCl solution?
5. What is the number of moles of H_2SO_4 that will react of neutralize 0.5 L of a 6 M KOH solution?	10. What is the molarity of 80 mL H_2SO_4 solution that is neutralized by 40 mL of 2 M NaOH solution?

Set A: Relating H⁺ Concentration to pH

Determine the pH of the solutions given the [H⁺] or [H₃O⁺] concentrations.

1. $[H_3O^+]$ = 1.0 x 10^{-1} M   pH =

2. $[H^+]$ = 1.0 x 10^{-4} M   pH =

3. $[H^+]$ = 1.0 x 10^{-11} M   pH =

5. $[OH^-]$ = 1.0 x 10^{-7} M   pH =

6. $[OH^-]$ = 1.0 x 10^{-2} M   pH =

Determine the ion concentration of the solution

7. $[H^+]$ = 1.0 x 10^{-4} $[OH^-]$ =

8. $[H_3O^+]$ = 1.0 x 10^{-11} $[OH^-]$ =

9. $[OH^-]$ = 1.0 x 10^{-1} $[H^+]$ =

10. $[OH^-]$ = 1.0 x 10^{-7} $[H_3O^+]$ =

Below, the pH of two solutions are given. *You are asked to compare the H⁺ (hydrogen or hydronium ion) concentration of one solution to another. Follow the example comparison given below.*

	Solution A	Solution B	Examples comparison
Ex.	pH 6	pH 7	• Solution A has 10 times more H⁺ than solution B • Solution B has 1/10th the H⁺ ions of Solution A • As solution A changes to Solution B, there is a 10 fold decrease in the H⁺ concentration
11.	pH 8	pH 10	
12.	pH 13	pH 12	
13.	pH 5	pH 2	
14 .	pH 7	pH 11	

Set A: Names and Formulas of Binary Acids

Write names for these binary acids.	Write formulas for these binary acids.
1. HBr _____	4. Hydroiodic acid _____
2. H_2S _____	5. Hydrotelluric acid _____
3. HF _____	6. Hydrochloric acid _____

Set B: Names and Formulas of Ternary Acids

Write names for these ternary acids.	Write formulas for these ternary acids.
7. $HClO_2$ _____	12. Sulfurous acid _____
8. $H_2S_2O_3$ _____	13. Acetic acid _____
9. H_3PO_4 _____	14. Nitric acid _____
10. HNO_2 _____	15. Chloric acid _____
11. $HClO_4$ _____	16. Hypochlorous acid _____

Set A: Terms and Definitions

Define each term given below.

1. Kinetics

2. Rate

3. Collision theory

4. Effective collision

5. Catalyst

6. Activation energy

Set B: Facts related to effective collision, activation energy, and catalyst.

7. For a chemical reaction to occur, there must be _____ _____ .

8. For a collision to be effective, reacting particles must collide with sufficient _____ _____
   and at _____ _____

9. _____ of _____ _____ determines the rate of a reaction.

10. Activation energy is the energy needed to _____ a chemical reaction.

11. Both _____ and _____ reactions require activation energy.

12. Chemical reactions that require _____ amount of _____ _____ are
    faster than those that require _____ amount of _____ _____ .

13. Any substance that can _____ the activation energy for a reaction will _____
    the rate for that reaction.

14. A catalyst in a reaction provides _____ (_____ _____ _____)
    pathway so a reaction can start _____ .

Set C: Factors that Affect Reaction Rate

Each question below asked you to explain how a certain factor increases or decreases a reaction rate. Explain clearly.

15. Explain, in term of collision, how increasing the concentration of reactants will increase reaction rate.

16. Explain, in terms of kinetic energy and collision, how decreasing temperature of a reaction will decrease the rate of that reaction.

17. Explain, in terms of concentration and collision, how increasing pressure of gaseous reactants will increase the rate of the reaction.

18. Explain, in term of collision, how decreasing concentration of reactants will decrease the reaction rate.

19. Explain, in terms of kinetic energy and collision, how increasing the temperature of a reaction will increase the rate of that reaction.

20. Explain, in terms of collision, how increasing surface area of reacting solids causes an increase in reaction rate.

21. Explain, in terms of activation energy, how a catalyst speeds up a reaction.

22. Explain why reactions of ionic solutions occur very fast.

23. Explain why reactions of molecular substances are generally very slow.

Set D: Reaction Rate

24. For each set of reaction, write *"fastest rate"* under one container and write *"slowest rate"* under another container to indicate which reactions will occur at the fastest and at the slowest speed.

Equal mass of zinc is reacted in beakers of containing acidic solution of different molarity.

Set 1:

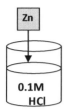 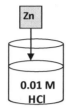 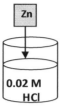 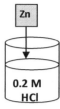

Set 2: Solution X and Solution Y from each water bath will be mixed in a beaker and allowed to react.

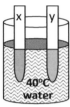 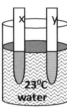 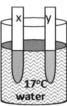 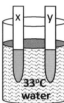

Set 3:

Gas particles o and • are reacting in a closed container under different pressures.

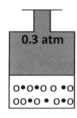 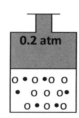 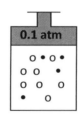 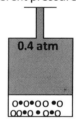

Different forms of metal M of equal mass are placed in an acid solution of equal concentration.

Set 4:

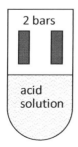 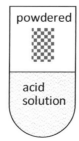 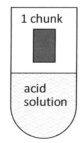 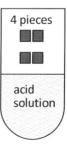

Set A: Terms and Definitions

> *Define each term given below.*
>
> 1. Potential energy — the energy ~~stored~~ held by an object
>
> 2. Heat (energy) of reactants
>
> 3. Heat (energy) of products
>
> 4. Heat of reaction (ΔH) — Difference between the potential energy of reactants and potential energy of products
>
> 5. Exothermic reaction — Reaction where energy is released
>
> 6. Endothermic reaction — Reaction where energy is absorbed
>
> 7. Activated complex — Where the reactants come together
>
> 8. Potential energy diagram — illustrates the potential energy change that occurs during a reaction

Set B: Energy of Reactions

> *Fill in the correct word or information.*
>
> 9. Potential energy of a substance depends on _____ and _____ of the substance.
>
> 10. ΔH (heat of reaction) is the __difference__ between energy of __reactants__ and that of __products__
>
> 11. ΔH = __products__ - __reactants__
>
> 12. - ΔH means that products of a reaction have ~~~~ __less__ __energy__ than the reactants.
>
> 13. - ΔH means that a reaction is __exothermic__ (__releases__ heat) .
>
> 14. +ΔH means that the products of a reaction have __more__ __energy__ than the reactants.
>
> 15. +ΔH means that a reaction is __endothermic__ (__absorbs__ heat).
>
> 16. In exothermic reactions, products always have __less__ __energy__ than the reactants
>
> 17. In exothermic reactions, energy is always _____, and temperature of surrounding _____.
>
> 18. In endothermic reactions, products always have __more__ __energy__ than the reactants
>
> 19. In endothermic reactions, energy is always _____, and temperature of surrounding _____

Set C: Exothermic and Endothermic Reactions

*Below, information or equation about a reaction is given. In the space write "**exothermic**" or
"**endothermic** " to indicate the type of reaction.*

19. A student measured the temperature of solution in a beaker
    before and after a reaction. The temperature after the
    reaction was 28°C higher than before the reaction.   *endothermic*

20. The heat of reaction of an unknown chemical reaction is +113 kJ   *endothermic*

21. Δ H of a reaction was calculated to be -45 kJ   *exothermic*

22. In a laboratory procedure, a student dropped a piece of metal
     into a solution and observed a reaction taking place in the test
     tube. When he had touched the test tube, the test tube felt colder   *exothermic*
     than it was before the reaction.

23. An unknown solid was place in a test containing water that was
     at 32°C. After the solid had completely dissolved, the temperature   *exothermic*
     of the liquid in the test tube was 5°C.

24. AB   +   Energy → A   +   B   *exothermic*

25. 2CO   + O_2 → $2CO_2$ + 566 kJ   *endothermic*

Set A: Potential Energy Measurements on a Diagram

For each diagram below, indicate the measurements represented by each arrow.

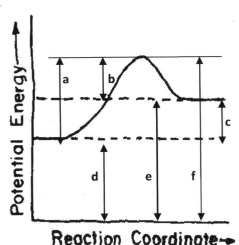

1.

a: activation energy

b: activation energy of reverse reaction

c: ΔH

d: P.E. of reactants

e: P.E. of products

f: P.E. of activated complex

Which measurements will change with addition of a catalyst?
activated complex, activation energy

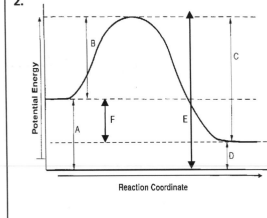

2.

A: P.E. of reactants

B: activation energy

C: activation energy of reverse reaction

D: P.E. of products

E: P.E. of activated complex

F: ΔH

Which measurements will change if a catalyst is added to the reaction?

Set B: Effect of Catalysts on Potential Energy Diagrams

For each diagram, draw a dotted curve to show the diagrams when a catalyst is added to the reaction.

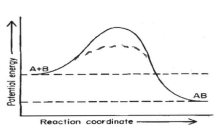

3.

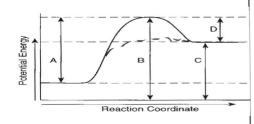

4.

Set C: Determining on Energy Values from Potential Diagrams

For each potential energy diagram, determine the value of the potential energy for the listed items.

Diagram 1

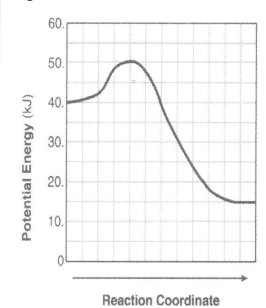

Determine the following potential energy measurements from diagram 1.

5. Potential energy of the Reactants: __40__

6. Potential Energy of the Products: : __15__

7. Potential Energy of the activated Complex: __90__

8. Heat of Reaction (ΔH) for forward reaction: __-25__

9. Heat of Reaction (ΔH) for reverse reaction: __25__

10. Activation energy for forward reaction: __10__

11. Activation energy for Reverse reaction: __35__

Diagram 2

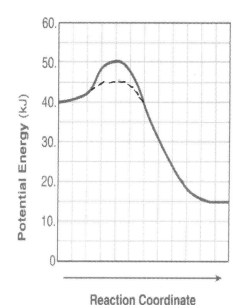

Using dash lines (---) or a different color pen, draw a curve on diagram 2 to show the energy diagram with a catalyst added to the reaction.

Determine the following potential energy measurements based on the curve you drew for the catalyzed reaction.

12. Potential energy of the Reactants: __40__

13. Potential Energy of the Products: : __15__

14. Potential Energy of the activated Complex: __45__

15. Heat of Reaction (ΔH) for forward reaction: __-30__

16. Heat of Reaction (ΔH) for reverse reaction: __30__

17. Activation energy for forward reaction: __5__

18. Activation energy for Reverse reaction: __30__

SurvivingChem.com

Set D: Drawing Potential Energy Diagrams

Drawing from Equation

On the axis given, sketch a potential energy diagram to represent the reaction given by the equation.

26. $2C(s)$ + $2H_2(g)$ + Energy $\rightarrow$ $C_2H_4(g)$

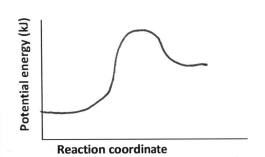

27. $2C(s)$ + $3H_2(g)$ $\rightarrow$ C_2H_6 + Heat

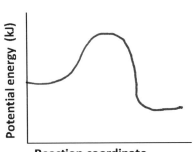

Drawing from information provided on Reference Table I

28. On the set of axis below, sketch a potential energy diagram to represent the formation of $NH_3(g)$ from its elements.

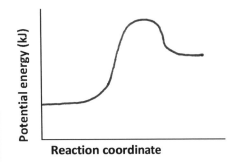

29. On the set of axis below, sketch a potential energy diagram to represent the formation of $HI(g)$ from its elements.

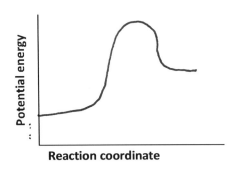

Drawing based on equation and activation energy.

Label the axis with appropriate potential energy values, and then draw a curve to represent the reaction.

30. CD + $50\,kJ$ $\rightarrow$ C + D .
The activation energy for this reaction is 80 kJ.

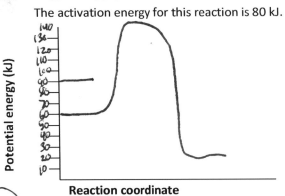

31. X + W $\rightarrow$ Z + $30\,kJ$.
The activation energy for this reaction is 20 kJ.

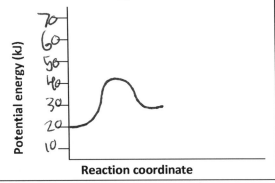

Set A: Terms and Definitions   .

Define each term given below.

1. Equilibrium

2. Physical equilibrium

3. Phase equilibrium

4. Solution equilibrium

5. Ice/water equilibrium

6. Water/steam equilibrium

7. La Chatelier's principle

8. Stress

Set B: Equilibrium Facts

Fill in the blanks or answer the question.

9. Describe the rate of two opposing reactions at equilibrium?

10. Describe the concentration (or the amount) of substances in a reaction at equilibrium?

11. What type of a reaction can reach equilibrium?

12. Equilibrium reactions can only occur in a _____ system.

13. Ice/liquid equilibrium occurs at which Celsius and Kelvin temperatures?

14. At ice/water equilibrium, the rates of _____ and _____ are _____.

15. At ice/water equilibrium, the amounts of ice and water remains _____.

16. Water/Steam equilibrium occurs at which Celsius and Kelvin temperature?

17. At water/steam equilibrium, the rates of _____ and _____ are _____.

18. At water/steam equilibrium, the amounts of water and steam remains _____.

19. What type of a solution can reach equilibrium?

Set C: Le Chatelier's Principle: Effects of Stress on a Reaction

Below, equilibrium reaction equation and different stresses to each reaction are given.

*Determine changes in concentration, rate and shift to the reaction based on the equation and each stress that are given. In the spaces, write "**increases**" or "**decreases**" For shift, write "**left**" or "**right**".*

Equation 1 : $2Cl_2$ + $2H_2O$ $\leftrightarrow$ $4HCl$ + O_2

20.   **Stress: *Increasing the concentration of O_2*:**
Concentration of HCl _____   Rate of forward reaction _____
Amount of H_2O _____   Rate of Reverse reaction _____
Concentration of Cl_2 _____   Reaction will shift _____

21.   **Stress: *Increasing the concentration of Cl_2***
Concentration of HCl _____   Rate of forward reaction _____
Amount of H_2O _____   Rate of Reverse reaction _____
Concentration of O_2 _____   Reaction will shift _____

22.   **Stress: *Decreasing the concentration of HCl***
Concentration of O_2 _____   Rate of forward reaction _____
Amount of H_2O _____   Rate of Reverse reaction _____
Concentration of Cl_2 _____   Reaction will shift _____

Equation 2: $2SO_3(g)$ +   heat $\leftrightarrow$ $2SO_2(g)$ + $O_2(g)$

23.   **Stress: *Increasing temperature (adding heat)***
Concentration of SO_3 _____   Rate of forward reaction _____
Concentration of SO_2 _____   Rate of reverse reaction _____
Concentration of O_2 _____   Reaction will shift _____

24.   **Stress: *Decreasing temperature (removing heat)***
Concentration of SO_3 _____   Rate of forward reaction _____
Concentration of SO_2 _____   Rate of reverse reaction _____
Concentration of O_2 _____   Reaction will shift _____

25.   **Stress: *Increasing pressure (decreasing volume)***
Concentration of SO_3 _____   Rate of forward reaction _____

Concentration of SO_2 _____   Rate of reverse reaction _____

Concentration of O_2 _____   Reaction will shift _____

Temperature (heat) _____

Set C cont.

> **Equation 3:**   BaSO$_4$(s)   ↔   Ba^{2+}(aq)   +   SO$_4^{2-}$(aq)

26. **Stress:** *Adding Na$_2$SO$_4$(s)*
      Concentration of SO$_4^{2-}$ ion _____   Rate of forward reaction _____
      Concentration of Ba^{2+} ion _____   Rate of Reverse reaction _____
      Concentration of BaSO$_4$ _____   Reaction will shift _____

27. **Stress:** *Adding Ba(NO$_3$)$_2$(s)*
      Concentration of Ba^{2+} ion _____   Rate of forward reaction _____
      Concentration of SO$_4^{2-}$ ion _____   Rate of Reverse reaction _____
      Concentration of BaSO$_4$ _____   Reaction will shift _____

28. **Stress:** *Removing SO$_4^{2-}$ ion (decreasing concentration of SO$_4^{2-}$)*
      Concentration of Ba^{2+} ions _____   Rate of forward reaction _____
      Concentration of BaSO$_4$ _____   Rate of Reverse reaction _____
                                                                                  Reaction will shift _____

> **Equation 4:**   3H$_2$ +   N$_2$ ↔   2NH$_3$ +   Heat

29. **Stress:** *Increasing temperature (Adding heat)*
      Concentration of H$_2$ _____   Rate of forward reaction _____
      Concentration of N$_2$ _____   Rate of reverse reaction _____
      Concentration of NH$_3$ _____   Reaction will shift _____

30. **Stress:** *Decreasing NH$_3$*
      Concentration of H$_2$ _____   Rate of forward reaction _____
      Concentration of N$_2$ _____   Rate of reverse reaction _____
      Heat (temperature) _____   Reaction will shift _____

31. **Stress:** *Increasing pressure (decreasing volume)*
      Concentration of H$_2$ _____   Rate of forward reaction _____
      Concentration of N$_2$ _____   Rate of reverse reaction _____
      Concentration of NH$_3$ _____   Reaction will shift _____
      Heat (temperature) _____

32. **Stress:** *Adding a catalyst*
      Concentration of H$_2$ _____   Rate of forward reaction _____
      Concentration of N$_2$ _____   Rate of reverse reaction _____
      Concentration of NH$_3$ _____   Reaction will shift _____
      Heat (temperature) _____

Set D: Le Chatelier's Principle: Determining stress.

Below, equilibrium reaction equation and different changes to the reaction are given.
You are to determine which stress or stresses to the reaction can cause the given change.

Base your choice of stresses to question 33 - 34 on the equilibrium equation 5 below.

Equation 5: $3H_2(g)$ + $N_2(g)$ $\leftrightarrow$ $2NH_3(g)$ + heat

33. **Change to reaction (result of stress) :**   *A decrease in concentration of N_2.*
    (Put a ✓ in [ ] next to each stress that will cause the concentration of N_2 to decrease)
    [ ]Increasing concentration of H_2 [ ]Adding heat (increasing temperature)
    [ ]Decreasing concentration of H_2 [ ]Removing heat (decreasing temperature)
    [ ]Increasing concentration of NH_3 [ ]Increasing pressure (decreasing volume)
    [ ]Decreasing concentration of NH_3 [ ]Decreasing pressure (increasing volume)
                                                                       [ ] Adding catalyst

34. **Change to reaction (result of stress) :**   *An increase in concentration of NH_3*
    (Put a ✓ in [ ] next to each stress that will cause the concentration of NH_3 to increase)
    [ ]Increasing concentration of H_2 [ ] Adding heat (increasing temperature)
    [ ]Decreasing concentration of H_2 [ ] Removing heat (decreasing temperature)
    [ ]Increasing concentration of N_2 [ ]Increasing pressure (decreasing volume)
    [ ]Decreasing concentration of N_2 [ ]Decreasing pressure (increasing volume)
                                                                       [ ] Adding catalyst

Base your choice of stresses to question 35 - 36 on the equilibrium equation 6 below.

Equation 6: $SO_2(g)$ + $NO_2(g)$ $\leftrightarrow$ $SO_3(g)$ + $NO(g)$ + heat

35. **Change to reaction (result of stress) :**   *A decrease in the reverse reaction*
    (Put a ✓ in [ ] next to each stress that will cause a decrease in the reverse reaction
    [ ]Increasing concentration of SO_2 [ ]Increasing concentration of NO
    [ ]Decreasing concentration of SO_2 [ ]Decreasing concentration of NO
    [ ]Increasing concentration of NO_2 [ ]Adding heat (increasing temperature)
    [ ]Decreasing concentration of NO_2 [ ]Removing heat (decreasing temperature)
    [ ]Increasing concentration of SO_3 [ ]Increasing pressure (decreasing volume)
    [ ]Decreasing concentration of SO_3 [ ]Decreasing pressure (increasing volume)
                                                                       [ ] Adding catalyst

36. **Change to reaction (result of stress) :**   *Reaction shift to the right*
    (Put a ✓ in [ ] next to each stress that will cause the reaction to shift to the right
    [ ]Increasing concentration of SO_2 [ ]Increasing concentration of NO
    [ ]Decreasing concentration of SO_2 [ ]Decreasing concentration of NO
    [ ]Increasing concentration of NO_2 [ ]Adding heat (increasing temperature)
    [ ]Decreasing concentration of NO_2 [ ]Removing heat (decreasing temperature)
    [ ]Increasing concentration of SO_3 [ ]Increasing pressure (decreasing volume)
    [ ]Decreasing concentration of SO_3 [ ]Decreasing pressure (increasing volume)
                                                                       [ ] Adding catalyst

Set A: Properties of Carbon and Organic Compounds:

Read and study Page 223 Set 1 of the Study book. As you study, answer the following questions.

1. A carbon atom has how many valence electrons?

2. What type of bond, and how many of it must a carbon atom form?

3. Which element is found in all organic compounds?

4. What are the three types of a covalent bond a carbon atom can form with another carbon atom?

5. Organic compounds are what type of substances?

6. What is general structural shape of simple organic molecules?

7. What is the molecular polarity of most organic compounds?

8. What type of forces hold molecules of organic compounds together?

9. Why do most organic compounds have low boiling and low melting points?

10. How would you compare the rate of reaction of organic compounds to those of inorganic compounds?

11. Most organic compounds are electrolytes (true or false)?

12. What type of organic compound is a weak electrolyte?

13. Why are most organic compounds insoluble (do not dissolve well) in water?

14. Why are most organic compounds decomposes easily under heat?

15. Draw the Lewis electron-dot diagram for a carbon atom?

Set A: Terms and Definitions

Define each term given below.

1. Homologous series

2. Hydrocarbon

3. Saturated hydrocarbon

4. Unsaturated hydrocarbon

5. Alkane

6. Alkene

7. Alkyne

8. Alkyl

9. Single covalent bond

10. Double covalent bond

11. Triple covalent bond

Set B: Facts of Organic Compounds

Answer the following questions about hydrocarbons.

12. What type of bonding is found in saturated hydrocarbons?

13. In a single covalent bond, how many electrons is /or are shared by each carbon atom? _____

14. How many pair of electrons is /or are shared between two atoms in a single bond? _____

15. How many total electrons does a single bond contain? _____

16. What type of bonding is found in unsaturated hydrocarbon? _____

17. In a double covalent bond, how many electrons is /or are shared by each carbon atom? _____

18. How many pair of electrons is /or are shared between two atoms in a double bond? _____

19. How many total electrons does a double bond contain? _____

20. In a triple covalent bond, how many electrons is /or are shared by each carbon atom? _____

21. How many pair of electrons is /or are shared between two atoms in a triple bond? _____

22. How many total electrons does a triple bond contain? _____

23. What is the general formula for alkanes? _____

24. What type of bonding is found in all alkanes? _____

25. What is the IUPAC name ending for all alkanes? _____

26. What is the general formula for alkenes? _____

27. What type of bonding is found in all alkenes?_____

28. What is the IUPAC name ending for all alkenes? _____

29. What is the general formula for alkynes? _____

30. What type of bonding is found in all alkynes? _____

31. What is the IUPAC name ending for all alkynes? _____

Set A: Terms and Definitions

Define each term given below.

1. Halide

2. Alcohol

3. Monohydroxy alcohol

4. Dihydroxy alcohol

5. Trihydroxyl alcohol

6. Primary alcohol

7. Secondary alcohol

8. Tertiary alcohol

9. Ether

10. Aldehyde

11. Ketone

12. Organic acid

13. Ester

14. Amine

15. Amide

16. Amino acid

     Survivingchem.com

Set B: Functional Group Compounds

Answer the following questions relating to functional group compounds.

17. What is the name ending for ester compounds?

18. What is the name ending for organic acid compounds?

19. What is the name ending for aldehyde compounds?

20. What is the name ending for ketone compounds?

21. What is the name ending for alcohol compounds?

22. What is the name ending for amine compounds?

23. Draw the functional group for ketones?

24. Draw the functional group for aldehydes.

25. Draw the functional group for esters.

26. Draw the functional group for organic acids.

27. Elements from which Group of the Periodic Table can be found in compounds of halides?

28. Name another element, other than carbon and hydrogen, that is found in amine compounds.

29. What three elements are found in molecules of alcohols and esters?

Set A: Identifying Classes of Organic Compounds

Determine the class of organic compound from the information given in each question.

1. A molecule of an organic compound contains a nitrogen atom.
   Which two classes of organic compounds could this molecule belongs?   _____

2. A molecule of organic compound contains two oxygen atom?
    Which two classes of compound could the molecule belongs?   _____

3. A molecule of a compound contains 10 Carbon and 20 Hydrogen atoms.
    What class of compound does this molecule belongs?   _____

4. A molecule contains four single bonds and one triple bond.
    Which class of compound does this molecule belongs?   _____

5. A solution of an organic compound conducts electrical current.
    What class of organic compound does this substance belongs?   _____

6. An organic compound has a distinctive smell of a fruit.
    To what class of organic compound does the substance belongs?   _____

7. A molecule contains 12 carbon and 26 hydrogen atoms.
    What class of compound is the molecule belongs?   _____

8. The functional group   – COOH is found in molecules of which
     class of organic compounds?   _____

9. An organic compound turns litmus red.
    This compound likely belongs to which class of organic compound?   _____

10. A compound that is classified as a saturated hydrocarbon likely belongs
     to which class of organic compound?   _____

11. An organic compound has a name that ends with –one. This compound
     likely belongs to which class of organic compound?   _____

12. A compound with the general formula R-COO-R' most likely belongs to
     which class of organic compound.   _____

13. An alcohol molecule has an –OH that is attached to an end carbon.
     What type of alcohol does this molecule belongs to ?   _____

14. An organic molecule contains 9 carbon atoms and 16 hydrogen.
     To which hydrocarbon class does this molecule belongs to?   _____

15. A compound contains 2 carbon, 4 hydrogen and 2 fluorine atoms.
     To what class of organic compound does this molecule belongs to?   _____

Set A: Drawing Structures of Hydrocarbon Compounds from IUPAC Names

Draw the structure for following hydrocarbon compounds.

1) Butane

2) Hexane

3) Octane

4) Propene

5) 2- hexene

6) 3-heptene

7) Propyne

8) 2 – pentyne

9) 3-octyne

10) 2-methyl butane

11) 2,4-dimethyl pentane

12) 2,2,3-trimethyl hexane

13) 4-ethyl, 3,5-dimethyl octane

14) 3-methyl, 2-pentene

15) 2,2,4-trimethyl, 4-heptene

Set B: Drawing Structures of Functional Group Compounds from IUPAC Names

Draw the following functional group compounds.

16) 3- iodohexane

17) 1,2-dichlobutane

18) pentanol

19) 3-hexanol

20) methyl pentyl ether

21) dipropyl ether

22) methanal

23) hexanal

24) Propanone

25) 3-hexanone

26) Methanoic acid

27) Pentanoic acid

28) Methyl butanoate

29) Butyl butanoate

Set C: Drawing and Naming Organic Compounds from Chemical Formulas

Name the substance and draw the structure for each condensed formula

30) $CH_3CH_2CH_2CH_3$

31) $CH_3CH(CH_3)CH_2CH_3$

32) $CH_2CHCH_2CH_2CH_3$

33) CH_3CCH

34) CH_3Cl

35) $CH_3CH(Br)CH_2CH_2CH_3$

36) CH_3CH_2OH

37) $CH_3CH_2CH(OH)CH_3$

38) CH_3CH_2COOH

39) $CH_3COOCH_2CH_2CH_3$

40) CH_3NH_2COOH

41) C_5H_8

Survivingchem.com

Set A: Facts about Isomers

Answer the following questions or fill in the blanks.

1. What are isomers ?

2. Two compounds are isomers if they have the same _____

3. Two isomers must have different _____, different _____ ,and

   also different _____.

4. For an hydrocarbon compound to have isomers, it must have at least how many carbon atoms?

5. As the number of carbon atoms increases, the number of possible isomers _____

Set B: Drawing and Naming Isomers

6.   Hexane C_6H_{14} Draw and name two isomers of hexane

```
    H   H   H   H   H   H
    |   |   |   |   |   |
H — C — C — C — C — C — C — H
    |   |   |   |   |   |
    H   H   H   H   H   H
```


7.   Heptene C_7H_{14} Draw and name two isomers of heptene

```
    H   H   H   H   H   H   H
    |   |   |   |   |   |   |
H — C — C — C — C — C — C = C — H
    |   |   |   |   |
    H   H   H   H   H
```

8.   Chloropentane C_4H_9Cl Draw and name two isomers of chloropentane

9.   Pentanol C_3H_7OH Draw and name two isomers of pentanol

Set A: Terms and Definitions

Define or describe the organic reactions given below.

1. Substitution

2. Addition

3. Fermentation

4. Saponification

5. Combustion

6. Esterification

7. Polymerization

8. Addition polymerization

9. Condensation polymerization

Set B: Facts of Organic Reactions

Answer the following questions about organic reactions.

10. What types of organic compounds undergo substitution reactions?

11. What is the main organic product in substitution reactions?

12. What type of organic compounds can undergo addition reactions with halogen?

13. What type of organic substance is produced in hydrogen addition with an alkene?

14. What organic product is produced in halogen addition with an alkene?

Set B cont.

15. In fermentation reactions, sugar is converted to _____ and _____ .

16. What are the two main products of a saponification reaction?

17. What are the two main products of combustion reactions?

18. Esterification is a reaction that involves molecules from which two classes of organic compounds?

19. What inorganic compound is produced in esterification and condensation polymerization reactions?

20. Monomers that are joined together in condensation polymerization reaction must have what kind of attached group?

21. Name two organic compounds that can be produced from condensation polymerization reaction?

22. Name some natural polymers.

23. Name some synthetic polymers.

Set C: Types of Organic Reactions

In the space provided, write the name of organic reaction represented by each equation. Use the following list of reactions: Substitution, addition, esterification, saponification, combustion, fermentation addition polymerization, condensation polymerization

24. C_4H_8 + F_2 $\rightarrow$ $C_4H_8F_2$ _____

25. $CH_4(g)$ + $O_2(g)$ $\rightarrow$ $H_2O(\ell)$ + $CO_2(g)$ _____

26. C_5H_{12} + Cl_2 $\rightarrow$ $C_5H_{11}Cl$ + HCl   _____

27   CH_3OH + CH_3OH $\rightarrow$ CH_3-O-CH_3 + H_2O _____

28.   Methanoic acid + Propanol $\rightarrow$ Methyl propanoate + water   _____

29.   Sugar $\rightarrow$ Ethanol   +   Carbon dioxide   _____

30. $n(CH_2CH_2)$ $\rightarrow$ $(CH_3CH_3)_n$ _____

Set D: Products of Organic Reactions

In the space provided, choose and write the organic reaction that will form the product that is given.

Substitution, addition, esterification, saponification, addition polymerization, condensation polymerization. combustion, fermentation

31. Glycerol   _____

32. Ethyl ethanoate _____

33. Chlorohexane   _____

34. Ethanol   _____

35. Diethyl ethyl ether _____

36. Polyethylene   _____

37. CH_2Cl_2 _____

38. CH_3CH_2Br _____

39. 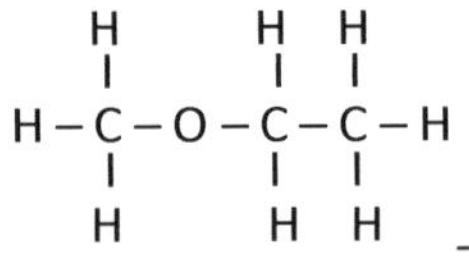
```
    H       H  H
    |       |  |
H – C – O – C – C – H
    |       |  |
    H       H  H
```
  _____

40. 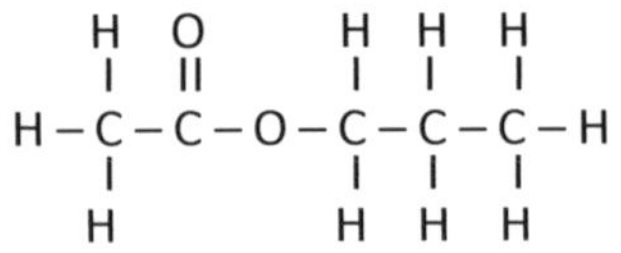
```
    H   O       H  H  H
    |   ||      |  |  |
H – C – C – O – C – C – C – H
    |           |  |  |
    H           H  H  H
```
  _____

Set E: Determining the Missing Reactant or Product of Organic Reactions

For each incomplete reaction, draw and name the formula of the missing substance in the equation.

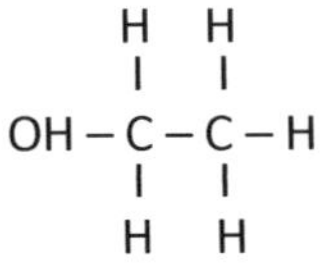

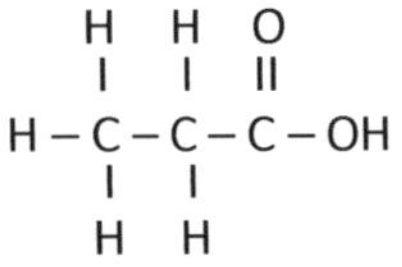

41. 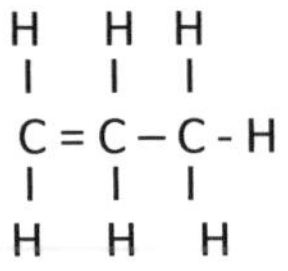
```
    H  H  H
    |  |  |
    C = C – C - H          +          F₂               →
    |  |  |
    H  H  H
```

42.
```
        H  H                H  H  O
        |  |                |  |  ||
OH – C – C – H     +    H – C – C – C – OH    →    + H₂O
        |  |                |  |
        H  H                H  H
```

43.   + Br_2 → $BrCH_2CH_3$ +   HBr

44. $CH_3 - CH_2 - CH_2 - OH$ +   → $CH_3 - CH_2 - CH_2 - O - CH_2 - CH_3$ + H_2O

           Survivingchem.com

Set A: Terms and Definitions

Define each term given below.

1. Redox

2. Oxidation

3. Reduction

4. Oxidized substance

5. Reduced substance

6. Oxidizing agent

7. Reducing agent

8. Oxidation number

9. Half-reaction

Set B: Oxidation Numbers

Fill in the blanks with the correct information related to oxidation numbers.

10. Oxidation number of a substance can be _____ , _____ , or _____ .

11. In neutral compounds, the sum of all oxidation numbers must equal _____ .

12. What is the oxidation number of a free element?

13. What is the oxidation number of a Group 1 element in compounds?

14. What is the oxidation number of a Group 2 element in compounds?

15. What is the oxidation number of a Group 13 element in compounds?

16. What is the oxidation number of hydrogen in most compounds?

17. What is the oxidation number of hydrogen in metal hydrides?

18. What is the oxidation number of oxygen in most compounds?

19. What is the oxidation number of oxygen in peroxides?

20. What is the oxidation number of oxygen in a compound with fluorine?

21. What is the oxidation number of a halogen element in most compounds?

Set C: Facts about Oxidation, Reduction, and Redox Reactions.

Fill in the blanks or answer the following questions about oxidation and reduction.

22. Redox reactions involve the _____ and _____ of _____ occurring _____.

23. Which three types of chemical reactions are considered redox?

24. Oxidation is the _____ of _____ during redox reactions.

25. Reduction is the _____ of _____ during redox reactions.

26. Oxidized substance is a substance that _____ _____.

27. Reduced substance is a substance that _____ _____.

28. Oxidized substance in a redox reaction acts as a _____ agent.

29. Reduced substance in a redox reaction acts as the _____ agent.

30. What happens to oxidation number of an oxidized substance in a redox reaction?

31. What happens to oxidation number of a reduced substance in a redox reaction?

Set D: Oxidation Numbers of Atoms in Substances

Write the correct oxidation number next to each element of the given chemical formula.

32.	F_2	F	33.	$MgCl_2$	Mg	34.	Al_2O_3	Al
					Cl			O
35.	CaH_2	Ca	36.	Na_2O_2	Na	37.	OF_2	O
		H			O			F
38.	$MnCl_2$	Mn	39.	N_2O_5	P	40.	PCl_3	P
		Cl			O			Cl
41.	$CaSO_4$	Ca	42.	Na_2CO_3	Na	43.	K_2PtCl_6	K
		S			C			Pt
		O			O			Cl
44.	SO_3^{2-}	S	45.	ClO_3^-	Cl	46.	H_3O^+	H
		O			O			O

     Survivingchem.com

Set A: Identifying Redox Reactions

*Next to the equations: Write "**redox**" next to those that represent redox reaction*
*Write "**not a redox**" next to those that DO NOT represent redox reactions.*

1. $Ni + Sn^{4+} \rightarrow Ni^{2+} + Sn^{2+}$ _____

2. $H_2O(g) \longrightarrow H_2O(s)$ _____

3. $KOH + HNO_3 \rightarrow KNO_3 + H_2O$ _____

4. $Mg + 2H_2O \rightarrow Mg(OH)_2 + H_2$ _____

5. $Sn + 2HCl \rightarrow SnCl_2 + H_2$ _____

6. $K^+ + Cl^- \rightarrow KCl$ _____

7. $2KClO_3 \rightarrow 2KCl + 3O_2$ _____

8. $2Mg + O_2 \rightarrow 2MgO$ _____

9. $2NaNO_3 + Li_2SO_4 \rightarrow Na_2SO_4 + 2LiNO_3$ _____

10. $NH_4Cl \rightarrow NH_4^+ + Cl^-$ _____

Set B: Changes in Oxidation Numbers

Oxidation number changes are given below.

*Indicate in the spaces if the change represents "**oxidation**" or "reduction."*

11. $0 \rightarrow +1$ _____

12. $+1 \rightarrow -2$ _____

13. $-3 \rightarrow -1$ _____

14. $-2 \rightarrow +2$ _____

15. $+3 \rightarrow +1$ _____

16. $+1 \rightarrow 0$ _____

Answer questions below based on the changes given in # 11 – 16.

Write only the question number in the blanks.

17. Which of the changes represents the greatest number of electrons lost? _____

18. Which of the changes represents the least number of electrons lost? _____

19. Which of the changes represents the greatest number of electrons gained? _____

20. Which of the changes represents the least number of electrons gained? _____

Set C: Half-reactions: Identifying Oxidation and Reduction

For half-reactions given below.

*Write "**Oxidation**" next to those that correctly represent oxidation half-reactions.*

*Write "**Reduction**" next to those that correctly represent reduction half-reactions.*

*Write "**Neither**" next to those that are neither oxidation nor reduction reaction.*

21. $Ca^{2+} + 2e^- \rightarrow Ca$ _____

22. $2N^{3-} \rightarrow N_2 + 6e^-$ _____

23. $Br_2 + e^- \rightarrow 2Br^-$ _____

24. $Cu^{2+} + e^- \rightarrow Cu^+$ _____

25. $P^{3-} \rightarrow P + 2e^-$ _____

26. $Li \rightarrow Li^+ + e^-$ _____

27. $Cl_2 + 2e^- \rightarrow 2Cl^-$ _____

28. $Mg \rightarrow Mg^{2+} + e^-$ _____

29. $S^{2-} \rightarrow S + 2e^-$ _____

30. $Mn^{7+} + 3e^- \rightarrow Mn^{4+}$ _____

Set D: Balancing Half-reactions with Electrons

Below, incomplete half-reaction equations are given. *Add correct number of electrons to either side of the arrow to equalize the charge (show conservation of charge).*

31. Fe^{2+}	$\rightarrow$	Fe^{3+}	36. Mn^{4+}	$\rightarrow$	Mn^{3+}
32 K^+	$\rightarrow$	K	37. Cr^{2+}	$\rightarrow$	Cr^{3+}
33. Sn^{4+}	$\rightarrow$	Sn^{2+}	38. Cl^{7+}	$\rightarrow$	Cl^+
34. Cr^{3+}	$\rightarrow$	Cr^{6+}	39. $3Cl_2$	$\rightarrow$	$6Cl^-$
35. O_2	$\rightarrow$	$2O^-$	40. $4H^-$	$\rightarrow$	$2H_2$

           Survivingchem.com

Set A: Interpreting Half-reaction Equations

Below, a balanced half-reaction equation is given. *Fill each blank with the appropriate* **"bold"** *term that best describe what is occurring in the half-reaction equation.*

Choose from the **list of terms** *below.*

Oxidation, reduction , oxidized, reduced, oxidizing agent, **reducing** agent, **lost** electrons, **gained** electrons

1. Br_2 + 2e- →   2Br-

This half-equation represents _____
Br_2 is _____
Br_2 is the _____ agent

Br_2 had _____ electrons

2. Zn^o → $2e^-$ + Zn^{2+}

This half-equation represents _____
Zn^0 is _____
Zn^0 is the _____ agent

Zn^0 had _____ electrons

3. Au^+ →   2e-   + Au^{3+}

This half-equation represents _____
Au^+ is _____
Au^+ is the _____ agent

Au^+ had _____ electrons

4. Mn^{4+} +   e-   → Mn^{3+}

This half-equation represents _____
$Mn^{4+}$is _____
Mn^{4+} is the _____ agent

Mn^{4+} _____ electrons

5. 2F $^-$ → F_2^o +   2e-

This half-equation represents _____
F $^-$ is _____
F $^-$ is the _____ agent

F $^-$ had _____ electrons

6. 2S   + $2e^-$ → S^{2-}

This half-equation represents _____
S is _____
S is the _____ agent

S had _____ electrons

Need Help? Study Book   Pg 267 S et 10

Set B: Interpreting Redox Reactions

Below, redox equations are given. Fill in the blank with the correct information from each equation.

7. Cr^{2+} + Mg $\rightarrow$ Cr + Mg^{2+}

The oxidized substance is _____
The reduced substance is _____
The oxidizing agent is _____
The reducing agent is _____
The species gaining electrons is _____
The species losing electrons is _____
The total number of electrons lost and gained is ____
Oxidation half equation:

Reduction half equation:

8. Br^2 + Hg $\rightarrow$ Hg^{2+} + $2Br^-$

The oxidized substance is _____
The reduced substance is _____
The oxidizing agent is _____
The reducing agent is _____
The species gaining electrons is _____
The species losing electrons is _____
Total number of electrons lost and gained is ____
Oxidation half equation:

Reduction half equation:

9. $3Sn$ + $2Fe^{3+}$ $\rightarrow$ $3Sn^{2+}$ + $2Fe$

The oxidized substance is _____
The reduced substance is _____
The oxidizing agent is _____
The reducing agent is _____
The species gaining electrons is _____
The species losing electrons is _____
Total number of electrons lost and gained is ____
Oxidation half equation:

Reduction half equation:

10. Mg^{2+} + $2F^-$ $\rightarrow$ Mg + F_2

The oxidized substance is _____
The reduced substance is _____
The oxidizing agent is _____
The reducing agent is _____
The species gaining electrons is _____
The species losing electrons is _____
Total number of electrons lost and gained is ____
Oxidation half equation:

Reduction half equation:

11. O_2 + $2H_2$ $\rightarrow$ $4H^+$ + $2O^{2-}$

The oxidized substance is _____
The reduced substance is _____
The oxidizing agent is _____
The reducing agent is _____
The species gaining electrons is _____
The species losing electrons is _____
Total number of electrons lost and gained is ____
Oxidation half equation:

Reduction half equation:

                   <u>Survivingchem.com</u>

Set B cont.

12. Ca   +   HCl   →   CaCl$_2$ +   H$_2$

The oxidized substance is _____
The reduced substance is _____
The oxidizing agent is _____
The reducing agent is _____
The species gaining electrons is _____
The species losing electrons is _____
Total number of electrons lost and gained is ___
Oxidation half equation:

Reduction half equation:

13. PbCl$_2$*(aq)* + Co*(s)* →   Pb*(s)* + CoCl$_2$*(aq)*

The oxidized substance is _____
The reduced substance is _____
The oxidizing agent is _____
The reducing agent is _____
The species gaining electrons is _____
The species losing electrons is _____
Total number of electrons lost and gained is ___
Oxidation half equation:

Reduction half equation:

14. CuNO$_3$ +   Fe   →   FeNO$_3$ +   Cu

The oxidized substance is _____
The reduced substance is _____
The oxidizing agent is _____
The reducing agent is _____
The species gaining electrons is _____
The species losing electrons is _____
Total number of electrons lost and gained is ___
Oxidation half equation:

Reduction half equation:

15. 2KBr   +   F$_2$ →   2KF   +   Br$_2$

The oxidized substance is _____
The reduced substance is _____
The oxidizing agent is _____
The reducing agent is _____
The species gaining electrons is _____
The species losing electrons is _____
Total number of electrons lost and gained is ___
Oxidation half equation:

Reduction half equation:

16. MgH$_2$ →   Mg   +   H$_2$

The oxidized substance is _____
The reduced substance is _____
The oxidizing agent is _____
The reducing agent is _____
The species gaining electrons is _____
The species losing electrons is _____
Total number of electrons lost and gained is ___
Oxidation half equation:

Reduction half equation:

Set A: Balancing ionic redox equations:

Balance the following ionic redox equations using the ***"smallest whole-number coefficients."***

REMEMBER: *A Balanced equation must show conservation of atoms and charges.*
That means, the sum of atoms and charges on both sides of the equation must be equal.

1. Cu + Ag^+ $\rightarrow$ Cu^{2+} + Ag

2. Hg^{2+} + I^- $\rightarrow$ Hg + I_2

3. Fe^{3+} + Ni $\rightarrow$ Fe + Ni^{2+}

4. Fe^{3+} + Sn^{2+} $\rightarrow$ Fe^{2+} + Sn^{4+}

5. Cr + Cu^{2+} $\rightarrow$ Cr^{3+} + Cu

6. Mn^{4+} + Ti $\rightarrow$ Mn^{2+} + Ti^+

7. Na^+ + O^{2-} $\rightarrow$ Na + O_2

8. Fe^{3+} + Al $\rightarrow$ Fe^{2+} + Al^{3+}

9. Mg + H^+ $\rightarrow$ Mg^{2+} + H_2

10. Al + Cu^{2+} $\rightarrow$ Al^{3+} + Cu

              Survivingchem.com

Set A: Terms and Definitions

Define each term given below.

1. Electrochemical cell

2. Electrode

3. Anode

4. Cathode

5. Voltaic cell

6. Electrolytic cell

7. Electroplating

8. Electrolytic reduction

9. Electrolysis

10. Salt Bridge

11. Battery

           SurvivingChem.com

Set B: Fact about of Electrochemical Cells

*Write "**voltaic cell**" next to each statement that describes a voltaic cell.*

*Write "**electrolytic cell**" next to each statement that describes an electrolytic cell.*

*Write "**both**" if the statement describes both voltaic and electrolytic cells.*

12. Redox reaction is nonspontaneous   _____

13. Battery is a type of this cell.   _____

14. Redox reaction occurs in two separate cells.   _____

15. Oxidation occurs at the anode   _____

16. Redox reaction is spontaneous   _____

17. Redox reaction occurs in one cell   _____

18. Uses external energy source   _____

19. Anode is positive   _____

20. Redox reaction is endothermic   _____

21. Reduction occurs at cathode.   _____

22. Anode is negative   _____

23. Chemical energy is converted to electrical energy   _____

24. Contains a salt bridge   _____

25. Negative electrode gains mass during redox reaction   _____

26. Cathode is negative   _____

27. Electrons travel from positive to negative electrode   _____

28. Electrical energy is converted to chemical energy   _____

29. Electrons travel from anode to cathode   _____

30. Cathode is positive   _____

31. Electrons travel from negative to positive electrode _____

32. Positive electrode gains mass during redox reaction   _____

33. Redox reaction is exothermic   _____

34. Anode loses mass during redox reactions   _____

35. Use in electroplating of jewelry and silverwares   _____

36. Cathode gains mass during redox reactions   _____

Set A: Components of Electrochemical Cells

Identify the components of the electrochemical cells shown below.

Diagram 1

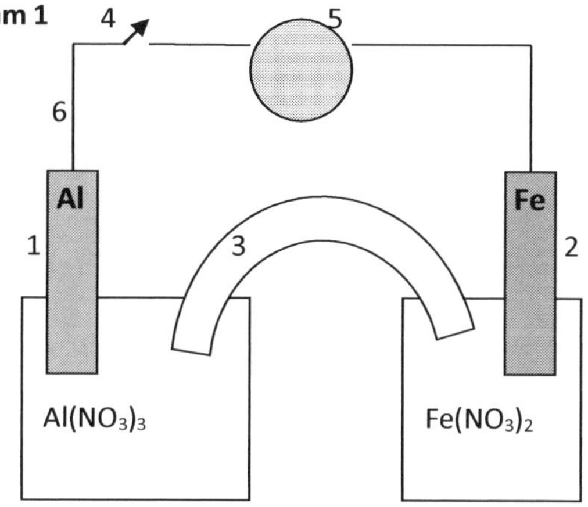

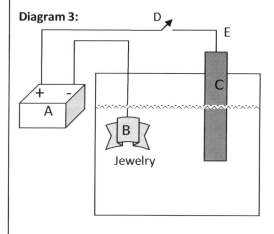

Al(NO₃)₃   Fe(NO₃)₂

1. _____
2. _____
3. _____
4. _____
5. _____
6. _____
7. Type of electrochemical cell: _____
8. Describe the reaction in this cell (circle two):

exothermic, endothermic,

nonspontaneous, spontaneous.

Diagram 2

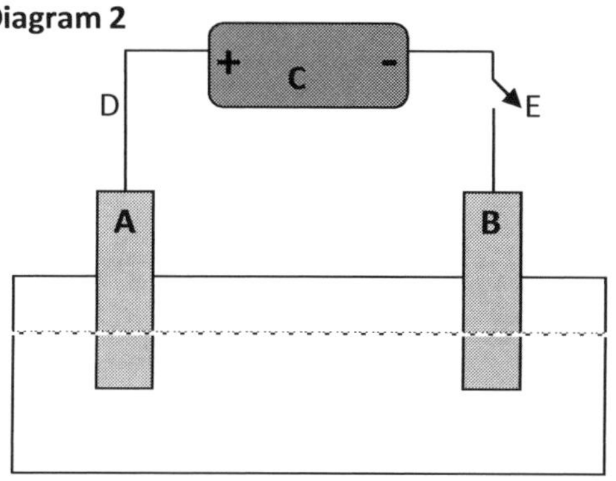

A. _____
B. _____
C. _____
D. _____
E. _____

F. Type of electrochemical cell: _____
G. Describe the reaction in this cell (circle two):

exothermic, endothermic,

nonspontaneous, spontaneous.

Diagram 3:

Jewelry

A. _____
B. _____
C. _____
D. _____
E. _____

E. Type of electrochemical cell: _____
F. Describe the reaction in this cell (circle two):

exothermic, endothermic,

nonspontaneous, spontaneous.

Set B: Voltaic Cell Diagrams

Diagram 4

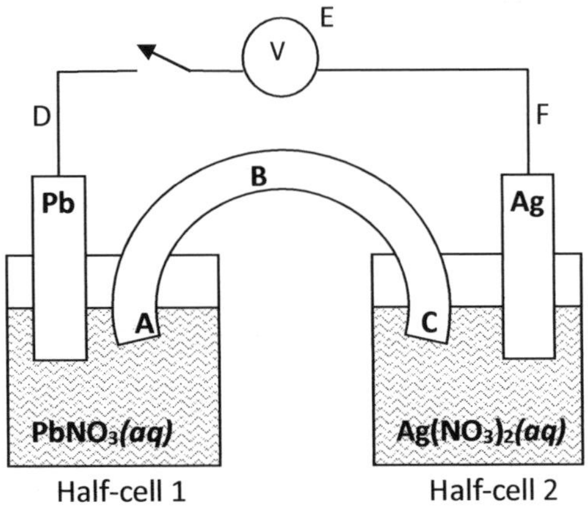

PbNO₃(aq)   Ag(NO₃)₂(aq)

Half-cell 1   Half-cell 2

$$Pb \quad + \quad 2Ag^+ \quad \rightarrow \quad 2Ag \quad + \quad Pb^{2+}$$

Answer these questions based on diagram 4.

1. Oxidized substance: _____
2. Reduced substance: _____
3. Oxidizing agent: _____
4. Reducing agent: _____
5. Species gaining electrons: _____
6. Species losing electrons: _____
7. Anode or negative electrode: _____
8. Cathode or positive electrode: _____
9. Indicate with letters:

    Direction of electron flow:

    Direction of ions flow:

10. Half-cell where oxidation is occurring: ___
11. Half-cell where reduction is occurring: ___
12. Write a balance oxidation half-reaction:

13. Write a balance reduction half-reaction:

Diagram 5

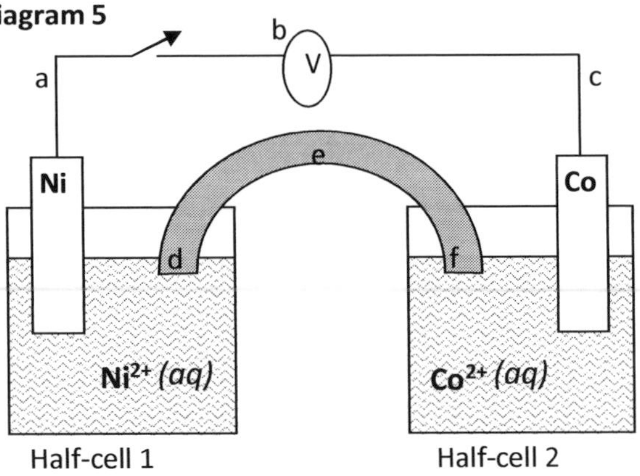

Ni²⁺ (aq)   Co²⁺ (aq)

Half-cell 1   Half-cell 2

Answer these questions based on diagram 5.

1. Oxidized substance: _____
2. Reduced substance: _____
3. Oxidizing agent: _____
4. Reducing agent: _____
5. Species gaining electrons: _____
6. Species losing electrons: _____
7. Anode or negative electrode: _____
8. Cathode or positive electrode: _____
9. Indicate with letters:

    Direction for the flow of electrons:

    Direction for the flow of ions:

10. Half-cell where oxidation is occurring: ___
11. Half-cell where reduction is occurring: ___

12. Write a balanced oxidation half-reaction:

13. Write a balance reduction half-reaction:

Set C: Electrolytic Cell Diagrams

Diagram 6

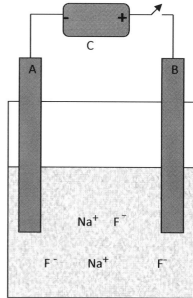

NaF + electricity $\longrightarrow$ Na + F$_2$

Answer these questions based on diagram 6.

1. Oxidized substance or object: _____
2. Reduced substance or object _____
3. Oxidizing agent: _____
4. Reducing agent: _____
5. Species gaining electrons: _____
6. Species losing electrons: _____
7. Cathode: _____
8. Anode: _____
9. Indicate with letters:

   Direction of the flow of electrons:

10. Write a balance oxidation half-reaction:

11. Write a balance reduction half-reaction:

Diagram 7

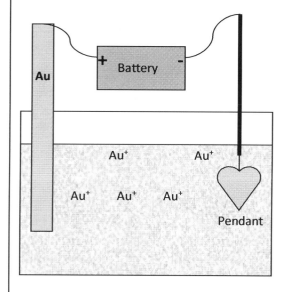

Answer these questions based on diagram 7.

1. Oxidized substance or object: _____
2. Reduced substance or object: _____
3. Substance or object gaining electrons: _____
4. Substance or object losing electrons: _____
5. Cathode: _____
6. Anode : _____
7. Substance or object gaining mass: _____
8. Substance or object losing mass: _____

9. Write a balanced oxidation half-reaction:

10. Write a balanced reduction half-reaction:

Set A: Terms and Definitions

Define each term given below.

1. Transmutation

2. Natural transmutation

3. Artificial transmutation

4. Alpha particle

5. Beta particle

6. Accelerator

7. Positron

8. Gamma ray

9. Alpha decay

10. Beta decay

11. Positron emission

12. Fission

13. Fusion

14. Half-life

15. Radioisotope

16. Tracer

Set B: Facts of Nuclear Decays

Answer the following questions relating to nuclear decay particles and transmutations.

17. Which nuclear particle has the greatest mass?

18. Which nuclear particle has the highest penetrating power?

19. List three particles that can be accelerated in an accelerator?

20. Which nuclear particle has the greatest positive charge?

21. List these nuclear radiations in order of increasing mass: Alpha, beta, neutron.

22. List these nuclear emissions in order of decreasing penetrating power? Beta, gamma, alpha.

23. As a nucleus emits an alpha particle, the number of protons in the nucleus _____.

24. As an atom emits an alpha particle, the mass number of the atom _____.

25. As an atom emits a beta particle, the number of protons.

26. As a unstable nucleus emits a beta particle, the number of neutrons in the nucleus _____.

27. As an atom emits a positron, the mass number of the atom _____.

28. As an unstable nucleus emits a positron, the number of neutrons in the atom _____.

29. Name two ways nuclear particles can be separated from a radioactive source?

30. Which elements has no stable isotope?

31. What is transmutation?

32. Explain the difference between natural transmutation and artificial transmutation?

Copyright © 2015 E3 Scholastic Publishing. All Rights Reserved.   <u>Survivingchem.com</u>

Set A: Types of Nuclear Reactions

Below, nuclear equations are given. Identify the type of nuclear process shown by each equation.
Choose from these lists of reactions: *Alpha decay, beta decay, positron emission,*

artificial transmutation, fission, or fusion

1. $^{99}_{44}Tc \longrightarrow \ ^{0}_{-1}e \ + \ ^{99}_{45}Ru$ _____

2. $^{54}_{26}Fe \ + \ ^{1}_{0}n \longrightarrow \ ^{1}_{1}H \ + \ ^{54}_{25}Mn$ _____

3. $^{243}_{94}Pm \longrightarrow \ ^{239}_{92}U \ + \ ^{4}_{2}He$ _____

4. $^{29}_{14}Si \longrightarrow \ ^{0}_{+1}e \ + \ ^{29}_{13}Al$ _____

5. $^{1}_{1}H \ + \ ^{3}_{1}H \longrightarrow \ ^{4}_{2}He$ _____

6. $^{235}_{92}U \ + \ ^{1}_{0}n \longrightarrow 4^{1}_{0}n \ + \ ^{72}_{30}Zn \ + \ ^{160}_{62}Sm$ _____

Set B: Balancing Nuclear Equations

For each incomplete nuclear equation, determine and write down the missing particle.
Be sure that the missing particle has the correct mass (top #), charge (bottom #) and symbol.

7. $^{235}_{92}U \ + \ ^{1}_{0}n \longrightarrow$ _____

8. _____ $+ \ ^{1}_{1}H \longrightarrow \ ^{4}_{2}He \ + \ ^{6}_{3}Li$

9. $^{70}_{33}As \longrightarrow$ _____ $+ \ ^{70}_{32}Ge$

10. _____ $+ \ ^{0}_{-1}e \longrightarrow \ ^{54}_{24}Cr$

11. $^{4}_{2}He \ + \ ^{14}_{7}N \longrightarrow$ _____ $+ \ ^{1}_{0}n$

12. _____ $+ \ ^{4}_{2}He \longrightarrow \ ^{245}_{97}Bk \ + \ 2^{1}_{0}n$

13. $^{238}_{92}U \ + \ ^{12}_{6}C \longrightarrow$ _____ $+ \ 4^{1}_{0}n$

Set C: Writing Nuclear Decay Equations

Use information provided in Reference Table N to write balanced nuclear equations for the decay of following radioisotopes.

14. Krypton – 85

15.   Uranium – 233

16. Neon - 19

17. Iodine – 131

18. Radon – 222

Write a balanced nuclear equation based on the information provided for each reaction

19. Alpha emission of $^{214}_{84}$Po

20. Electron absorption of $^{116}_{51}$Sb

21. Proton emission of $^{41}_{19}$K

22. Neutron emission of $^{107}_{47}$Ag

23. Positron absorption of $^{40}_{18}$Ar

24. Alpha absorption by $^{14}_{7}$N with neutron emission

25.   Neutron absorption by $^{209}_{83}$Bi with alpha emission

Set A: Half-life Problems

Solve the following half-life related problems. Use Reference Tables N to get the half-life of a radioisotope if necessary.

1. In how many years would radium – 226 undergoes 5 half-life periods?

2. How many half-life periods will it take for a sample of ^{198}Au to decay from original mass of 25 grams to a remaining mass of 1.56 grams?

3. In how many days will it take for a sample of P-32 to decay from an original mass of 250 mg to a remaining mass of 62.5 mg?

4. How many milligrams of a 72 mg of a radioisotope will remain unchanged after 4 half-life periods?

5. How much of a 100-gram sample of Gold – 198 is left after 8.10 days.

6. How much of a 750-gram sample of ^{42}K is left after 62 hours?

7. A 12 g sample of plutonium – 239 decays for 7.32 x 10^4 years. How many grams of the sample is left unchanged?

8. If there are 50 grams of a radioisotope remaining after 3 half-life period of decaying, how many grams were in the original sample?

Set A: cont.

9. There are 2.25 grams of iodine – 131 left after 40.35 days. How many grams were in the original sample?

10. An unknown radioisotope that decays from 500 grams to 62.5 grams in approximately 91 years.

    Calculate the half-life of this radioisotope?

    Identify the unknown radioisotope using Reference Table N.

11. A 50 g sample of a radioisotope decays to 12.5 grams in 14.4 seconds.

    Calculate the half-life of this radioisotope?

    Identify the radioisotope using Reference Table N.

12. In 7.38 days, a radioisotope undergoes 6 half-life periods.

    What is the half-life of this radioisotope?

    Identify the radioisotope using Reference Table N

13. What fraction of a radioisotope will remain after 5 half-life periods?

14. What fraction of a sample of Hydrogen – 3 radioisotope will remain unchanged after 49 years of decaying?

15. What fraction of ^{14}C will remain unchanged after 17190 years.

     Survivingchem.com

Multiple Choices

Concept by Concept

Survivingchem.com

Topic 1 – Matter and Energy

1. Types of Matter: Recalling Facts and Definitions

1. A substance that is composed only of atoms having the same atomic number is classified as
   1) A compound   2) An element   3) A solution   4) A mixture

2. Which type of matter can be separated only by physical methods?
   1) A mixture   2) A pure substance   3) An element   4) A compound

3. Which two types of matter are considered chemical pure substances?
   1) Elements and mixtures   3) Solutions and mixtures
   2) Elements and compounds   4) Solutions and compounds

4. Which type of matter is composed of two or more different elements chemically combined in a definite ratio?
   1) A compound   3) A homogeneous mixture
   2) An element   4) A heterogeneous mixture

5. Which of these terms refers to matter that could be heterogeneous?
   1) Element   3) Mixture
   2) Compound   4) Solution

6. Two substances, X and Y, are to be identified. Substance X cannot be broken down by a chemical change. Substance Y can be broken down by a chemical change. What can be concluded about these substances?
   1) X and Y are both elements   3) X is an element and Y is a compound
   2) X and Y are both compounds   4) X is a compound and Y is an element

7. Which must be a mixture of substances?
   1) An element   3) A liquid
   2) A solution   4) A gas

8. Which is true of all elements?
   1) They have fixed ratio of composition   3) They are composed of atoms
   2) They cannot be decomposed   4) All of the above

9. Which property correctly describes all compounds?
   1) They are always homogenous   3) They can be physically separated
   2) They are always heterogeneous   4) They cannot be decomposed

10. Which statement correctly describes a mixture?
    1) A mixture can consist of a single element   3) A mixture can be separated by physical means
    2) A mixture must have definite composition   4) A mixture must be homogeneous

11. One similarity between all mixtures and compounds is that both
    1) Are heterogeneous   3) Combine in definite ratio
    2) Are homogeneous   4) Consist of two or more substances

12. Bronze contains 90 to 95 percent copper and 5 to 10 percent tin. Because these percentages can vary, bronze is classified as
    1) A compound   3) A mixture
    2) An element   4) A substance

13. When a teaspoon of sugar is added to water in a beaker, the sugar dissolves. The resulting mixture is
    1) A compound   3) A heterogeneous solution
    2) An element   4) A homogeneous solution

2. Types of Matter: Recognizing and Interpreting Chemical Symbols of Matter

1. Which is a formula of an element?
   1) $Cl_2(g)$
   2) $MgCl_2(s)$
   3) $H_2O(\ell)$
   4) $HF(aq)$

2. Which substance represents a compound?
   1) $C(s)$
   2) $Co(s)$
   3) $CO(g)$
   4) $O_2(g)$

3. Which symbol represents a mixture?
   1) $NaCl(s)$
   2) $NaCl(aq)$
   3) $NaCl(\ell)$
   4) $H_2O(\ell)$

4. Which formula is composed of atoms with the same atomic number?
   1) CO_2
   2) CO
   3) Cu
   4) CuO

5. Which material is a mixture?
   1) Water
   2) Sugar
   3) Air
   4) Hydrogen

6. Which substance is an element?
   1) Calcium
   2) Ammonia
   3) Calcium chloride
   4) Ammonium chloride

7. Which substance can be decomposed by a chemical change?
   1) Ammonia
   2) Aluminum
   3) Potassium
   4) Helium

8. Which of these contains only one substance?
   1) Sugar water
   2) Saltwater
   3) Rain water
   4) Distilled water

9. The formula, $N_2(g)$, represents a(n)
   1) compound
   2) mixture
   3) element
   4) solution

10. The formula $AlBr_3(s)$ would be best described as
    1) compound
    2) mixture
    3) element
    4) solution

11. When $NaNO_3(s)$ is dissolved in water, the resulting solution is classifies as a
    1) heterogeneous compound
    2) homogeneous compound
    3) heterogeneous mixture
    4) homogeneous mixture

12. When sample X is passed through a filter a white residue, Y, remains on the filter paper and a clear liquid, Z, passes through. When liquid Z is vaporized, another white residue remains. Sample X is best classified as a(n)
    1) element
    2) compound
    3) heterogeneous mixture
    4) homogeneous mixture

13. Which is true of the symbol $KCl(aq)$?
    1) It is composed substances chemically combined
    2) It composed of substances physically combined
    3) It is a pure substance
    4) It is a compound

14. A mixture of crystals of salt and sugar is added to water and stirred until all solids have dissolved. Which statement best describes the resulting mixture.
    1) The mixture is homogeneous and can be separated by filtration
    2) The mixture is homogeneous and cannot be separated by filtration
    3) The mixture is heterogeneous and can be separated by filtration
    4) The mixture is heterogeneous and cannot be separated by filtration

3. Types of Matter: Recognizing and Interpreting Diagrams of Matter

Answer questions 1 – 4 based on the diagrams and information provided below.

KEY   I   II   III   IV

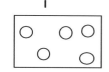 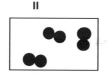

Atom A   Atom B

1. Which diagrams contain only pure substances?

    1) I and II only   2) II and III only   3) I, II, and III only   4) II, III, IV only

2. Which diagram represents an element?

    1) I only   2) II only   3) I and II only   4) II and IV only

3. Which diagram represents a compound?

    1) II only   2) III only   3) II and III only   4) II and IV only

4. Which diagram is showing a mixture of substances?

    1) I   2) II   3) III   4) IV

Given diagrams A, B and C below: Answer questions 5 - 7 based on the diagrams.

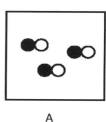 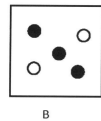 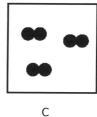

       A   B   C   ● = particle X
                                                 ○ = particle Y

5. Which diagram or diagrams represent a compound of X and Y?

    1) A and B   2) A and C   3) A only   4) B only

6. Which diagrams represent chemical pure substances?

    1) A and B   2) A and C   3) B and C   4) A, B and C

7. Which best describes diagram B?

    1) It is a mixture that is composed of substances physically combined

    2) It is a mixture that is composed of substances chemically combined

    3) It is a compound that is composed of substances physically combined

    4) It is a compound that is composed of substances chemically combined

4. Phases of Matter: Recalling Facts and Definitions

1. Which phase of matter has a definite volume but no definite shape?
   1) Aqueous   2) Solid   3) Liquid   4) Gas

2. Which phase of matter has a definite volume and a definite shape?
   1) Solid   2) Liquid   3) Gas   4) Aqueous

3. A substance in which phase has molecules that are arranged in a regular geometric pattern?
   1) Solid   2) Aqueous   3) Liquid   4) Gas

4. Molecules of a substance are most random in which phase?
   1) Aqueous   2) Gas   3) Solid   4) Liquid

5. Substance X is a gas and substance Y is a liquid. One similarity between substance X and substance Y is that
   1) Both have definite shape
   2) Both have definite volume
   3) Both are compressible
   4) Both take the shapes of their containers

6. Which correctly describe particles of substances in the gas phase?
   1) Particles are arranged in regular geometric pattern and are far apart
   2) Particles are in fixed rigid position and are close together
   3) Particles are moving freely in a straight path
   4) Particles are move freely and are close together.

5. Phases of Matter: Recognizing and Interpreting Formulas in Different Phases

1. Which form of water contains water molecules that are in a regular geometric pattern?
   1) $H_2O(g)$ 2) $H_2O(\ell)$ 3) $H_2O(aq)$ 4) $H_2O(s)$

2. Which form of carbon dioxide is most likely to take the shape and volume of its container?
   1) $CO_2(g)$ 2) $CO_2(s)$ 3) $CO_2(aq)$ 4) $CO_2(\ell)$

3. Which substance has no definitely shape nor volume?
   1) $NH_3(g)$ 2) $NH_3(\ell)$ 3) $H_2O(s)$ 4) $H_2O(g)$

4. Which formula correctly represents a substance that has a definite volume but no definite shape?
   1) $Hg(\ell)$ 2) $HCl(g)$ 3) $Na(s)$ 4) $H_2(g)$

5. Which statement is correct for $Fe(s)$?
   1) It has a definite shape, and is compressible
   2) It has a definite shape, and is incompressible
   3) It has no definite shape, and is compressible
   4) It has no definite shape, and is incompressible

6. Which characteristics best describe $O_2(g)$ at room temperature?
   1) no definite shape and incompressible
   2) definite shape and compressible
   3) no definite shape and no definite volume
   4) definite shape and definite volume

6. Phase Changes: Recalling Phase Changes

1. Which term refers to a change of a substance from solid to liquid?
   1) Freezing 2) Condensation 3) Evaporation 4) Fusion

2. Which term correctly describes the change of water from steam to liquid?
   1) Sublimation 2) Condensation 3) Evaporation 4) Fusion

3. When a substance evaporates, it is changing from
   1) liquid to gas 2) gas to liquid 3) solid to gas 4) gas to solid

4. Which equation is showing sublimation of iodine?
   1) $I_2(g) \rightarrow I_2(s)$ 3) $I_2(s) \rightarrow I_2(l)$
   2) $I_2(s) \rightarrow I_2(g)$ 4) $I_2(g) \rightarrow I_2(l)$

5. Which phase change correctly shows condensation of water?
   1) $H_2O(g) \rightarrow H_2O(l)$ 3) $H_2O(s) \rightarrow H_2O(l)$
   2) $H_2O(l) \rightarrow H_2O(s)$ 4) $H_2O(s) \rightarrow H_2O(g)$

6. Which equation represents fusion of water?
   1) $H_2O(g) \rightarrow H_2O(l)$ 3) $H_2O(s) \rightarrow H_2O(l)$
   2) $H_2O(l) \rightarrow H_2O(s)$ 4) $H_2O(s) \rightarrow H_2O(g)$

7. The change, $NH_3(g) \rightarrow NH_3(s)$, is best described as
   1) sublimation 3) condensation
   2) evaporation 4) deposition

7. Heat and Energy: Recalling Facts and Definitions

1. Which term describes a form of energy that can be absorbed or released?
    1) Temperature   2) Degree   3) Kelvin   4) Heat

2. Which unit is appropriate for measuring heat energy?
    1) Kilojoules   2) grams   3) Celsius   4) kilopascal

3. Energy that is stored in chemical substances is called
    1) potential energy   2) activation energy   3) kinetic energy   4) ionization energy

4. Energy due to movement of particles of a substance is called
    1) kinetic energy   2) entropy energy   3) potential energy   4) activation energy

5. When a substance absorbs heat energy, the process is described as
    1) transmutation   2) radioactivity   3) endothermic   4) exothermic

6. In endothermic processes, heat is
    1) released, only   3) both absorbed and released
    2) absorbed, only   4) neither absorbed nor released

7. As a substance undergoes exothermic phase change, heat energy is
    1) released, only   3) both absorbed and released
    2) absorbed, only   4) neither absorbed nor released

8. Phase Change and Energy: Relating Phase Changes to Heat Energy

1. Which phase change is exothermic?
    1) Freezing   2) Sublimation   3) Evaporation   4) Fusion

2. Which phase change is endothermic?
    1) Fusion   2) Condensation   3) Freezing   4) All of the above

3. Which change will result in heat energy being absorbed by the substance?
    1) Liquid to solid   2) Gas to liquid   3) Liquid to gas   4) Gas to solid

4. Which phase change is accompanied by the release of heat energy?
    1) Gas to liquid   2) Liquid to gas   3) Solid to gas   4) Solid to liquid

5. Which change in iodine is endothermic?
    1) $I_2(g) \rightarrow I_2(s)$ 3) $I_2(\ell) \rightarrow I_2(s)$
    2) $I_2(s) \rightarrow I_2(g)$ 4) $I_2(g) \rightarrow I_2(\ell)$

6. Which phase change correctly shows the release of heat to the surrounding?
    1) $NH_3(\ell) \rightarrow NH_3(g)$ 3) $NaCl(s)) \rightarrow NaCl(\ell)$
    2) $CO_2(s) \rightarrow CO_2(g)$ 4) $H_2O(g) \rightarrow H_2O(\ell)$

7. Which equation shows a phase change of water at 0^oC
    1) $H_2O(\ell) \rightarrow H_2O(g)$ 3) $H_2O(s) \rightarrow H_2O(aq)$
    2) $H_2O(\ell) \rightarrow H_2O(s)$ 4) $H_2O(s) \rightarrow H_2O(g)$

8. Which equation correctly shows liquid/steam equilibrium of water at its boiling point?
    1) $H_2O(\ell) \rightarrow H_2O(g)$ 3) $H_2O(s) \rightarrow H_2O(\ell)$
    2) $H_2O(\ell) \rightarrow H_2O(s)$ 4) $H_2O(s) \rightarrow H_2O(g)$

9. The change, $NH_3(g) \rightarrow NH_3(\ell)$, is best described as
    1) evaporation, which is exothermic   3) condensation, which is exotherm
    2) evaporation, which is endothermic   4) condensation, which is endothermic

10. A change of Iodine solid to iodine gas is best described as
    1) sublimation, in which heat is absorbed   3) evaporation, in which heat is absorbed
    2) sublimation, in which heat is released   4) evaporation, in which heat is released

 Survivingchem.com

9. Phase Change Diagrams: Recognizing Phase Change Diagrams

1. Which diagram is showing a uniform cooling of a substance starting with the substance in the gas phase?

 1) 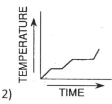 2)  3)  4)

2. Which diagram shows the uniform heating of a substance starting with the substance in the solid phase?

  1)  2)   3)   4)

3. Which diagram is showing a change in temperature of a substance as it is cooling?

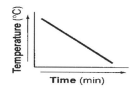 1) 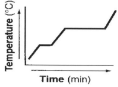 3)

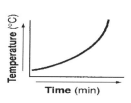 2)  4)

4. Which diagram is showing exothermic phase change taking place?

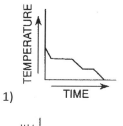 1) 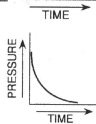 3)

  2) 4)

10. Phase Change Diagrams: Determining Boiling, Melting and Freezing Points

Answer questions 1 – 3 based on the graph below.

The graph below represents a uniform heating of a substance, starting with the substance as a solid below its melting point.

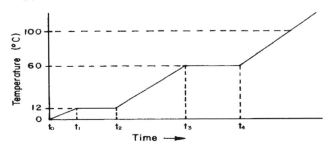

1. What is the melting point of this substance?
    1) 0°C   2) 12°C   3) 60°C   4) 100°C

2. What is the boiling point of the substance?
    1) 100°C   2) 60°C   3) 12°C   4) 0°C

3. The freezing point of the substance is
    1) 100°C   2) 0°C   3) 60°C   4) 12°C

Answer question 4 – 6 based on the graph below.

The graph below represents a uniform cooling of a substance starting with the substance as a gas above its boiling point.

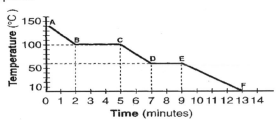

4. What is the freezing point of this substance?
    1) 60°C   2) 10°C   3) 150°C   4) 100°C

5. What is the boiling point of the substance?
    1) 150°C   2) 100°C   3) 60°C   4) 10°C

6. The melting point of the substance is
    1) 100°C   2) 10°C   3) 100°C   4) 60°C

 Survivingchem.com

11. Phase Change Diagrams: Determining Phases on a Curve

Answer questions 1 – 5 based on the graph below.

The graph below represents the relationship between temperature and time as heat is added at a constant rate to a substance, starting when the substance is a solid below its melting point

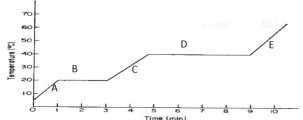

1. During which segment is the substance exists as a solid?
    1) B   2) D   3) C   4) A

2. During which segment is the substance exists as a gas?
    1) D   2) C   3) A   4) E

3. During which segment is the liquid phase at equilibrium with the gas phase?
    1) D   2) E   3) C   4) B

4. During which segment or segments does the substance exist in one phase?
    1) A only   2) A and C, only   3) A, C and E, only   4) B and D, only

5. Which segment or segments of the curve represent a fixed point on a thermometer?
    1) B and D   2) A, C, and E   3) A   4) E

Answer questions 6 – 10 based on the graph below

The graph below represents the relationship between temperature and time as heat is added at a constant rate to a substance, starting when the substance is a gas above its boiling point.

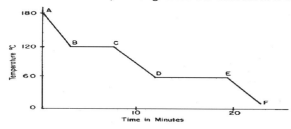

6. The liquid phase of the substance is represented by segment
    1) BC   2) DE   3) CD   4) EF

7. The substance exists as a gas during segment
    1) AB   2) CD   3) EF   4) B

8. Liquid/solid equilibrium of the substance is represented by which segment of the curve?
    1) BC   2) AB   3) EF   4) DE

9. During which segment or segments does the substance exist in one phase?
    1) AB only   2) BC only   3) AB and CD, only   4) AB, CD and EF, only

10. During which segment or segments of the graph is the substance exists in two phases?
    1) AB and EF only   2) BC and DE, only   3) EF only   4) AB, BC, CD

12. Phase Change Diagrams: Relating Heat to Phase Changes

Answer questions 1 – 5 based on the graph below.

The graph below represents the uniform heating of a substance, starting with the substance as a solid below its melting point.

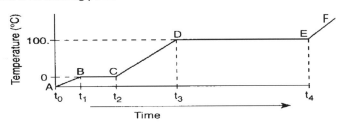

1. Which portions of the graph represent times when kinetic energy is increasing while potential energy remains constant?
   1) AB, CD, and EF   2) BC and DE   3) AB , BC, and CD   4) CD and EF

2. Which portions of the graph represent times when potential energy is increasing while kinetic energy remains constant?
   1) AB, CD, and EF   2) CD and EF   3) AB , BC, and CD   4) BC and DE

3. Between which time intervals could the heat of fusion be determined?
   1) t_0 and t_1 2) t_1 and t_2 3) t_3 and t_4 4) t_2 and t_4

4. Which time interval could the heat of vaporization be determined?
   1) t_0 and t_1 2) t_1 and t_2 3) t_3 and t_4 4) t_2 and t_4

5. The process shown in the diagram above can be described as
   1) endothermic, because heat is release   3) exothermic, because heat is released
   2) endothermic, because heat is absorbed   4) exothermic, because heat is absorbed

Answer question 6 – 10 based on your understanding of the diagram below:

The graph below represents the uniform cooling of an unknown substance, starting with the substance as a gas above its boiling point.

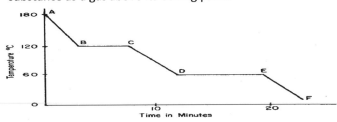

6. Which portions of the graph represent times when kinetic energy is decreasing while potential energy remains constant?
   1) AB , BC, and CD   2) BC and DE   3) AB , CD, and EF   4) CD and EF

7. Which portions of the graph represent times when potential energy is decreasing while kinetic energy remains constant?
   1) AB , CD, and EF   2) BC and DE   3) AB , BC, and CD   4) CD and EF

8. Between which two points could the heat of fusion be determined?
   1) A and B   2) B and C   3) C and D   4) D and E

9. Which interval could the heat of vaporization be determined?
   1) A and B   2) B and C   3) C and D   4) D and E

10. The process shown in the diagram above can be described as
   1) endothermic, because heat is release   3) exothermic, because heat is released
   2) endothermic, because heat is absorbed   4) exothermic, because heat is absorbed

13. Phase Change Data

Answer questions 1 – 4 based on the data below:

The data below was collected as a substance in the liquid state cools.

DATA TABLE

Time (minutes)	Temperature (°C)
0	65
1	58
2	52
3	53
4	53
5	53
6	53
7	53
8	51
9	47
10	42

1. Which temperature represents the freezing point of this substance?
   1) 65°C   2) 42°C   3) 47°C   4) 53°C

2. Between which time is the a solid?
   1) 0 – 2 minutes   2) 2 – 7 minutes   3) 3 – 10 minutes   4) 8 – 10 minutes

3. Between which time is the kinetic energy of molecules of the substance remains constant while the potential energy of the molecule is changing?
   1) 3 – 7 min   2) 0 – 2 min   3) 8 – 9 min   4) 0 – 10 min

4. Which is true of the kinetic energy and the potential energy of the substance from time 0 and 2 minute?
   1) The kinetic energy is increasing and the potential energy is remaining constant
   2) The kinetic energy is decreasing and the potential energy is remaining constant
   3) The kinetic energy is remaining constant and the potential energy is decreasing
   4) Both the kinetic energy and the potential energy are decreasing

Answer questions 5 – 9 based on the data below:

The data below represents the data collected during a laboratory experiment in which heat was added at a constant rate to a solid below its freezing point.

Time (minute)	0	2	4	6	8	10	12	14	16	18	20	22	24	26	28	30	32	34
Temperature (°C)	20	24	28	32	32	32	35	38	41	44	47	51	54	54	54	54	58	64

5. What is the melting point of the substance?
   1) 0°C   2) 32°C   3) 62°C   4) 54°C

6. The boiling point of the substance is
   1) 32°C   2) 41°C   3) 54°C   4) 100°C

7. Which temperature measurement is of the substance when it a liquid only?
   1) 20°C   2) 44°C   3) 38°C   4) 64°C

8. Which is true of kinetic energy and potential energy of the substance between the 24th - 30th minutes?
   1) The kinetic energy is increasing and the potential energy is remaining constant
   2) The kinetic energy is decreasing and the potential energy is increasing
   3) The kinetic energy is remaining constant and the potential energy is increasing
   4) Both the kinetic energy and the potential energy are remaining constant

9. The process taking place during this laboratory experiment is best describe as
   1) Exothermic chemical change   3) Endothermic chemical change
   2) Exothermic physical change   4) Endothermic physical change

14. Temperature and Kinetic Energy

1. Which temperature of water will contain molecules with the highest kinetic energy?
   1) 40°C   2) 30°C   3) 20°C   4) 10°C

2. Which temperature of a solid substance will have particles with the highest kinetic energy?
   1) 273 K   2) 373 K   3) 170°C   4) 70°C

3. The average kinetic energy of water molecules is greatest in which of these sample?
   1) 10 g of water at 35°C   3) 100 g of water at 25°C
   2) 10 g of water at 55°C   4) 100 g of water at 45°C

4. A substance at which temperature will have the lowest average kinetic energy?
   1) 19°C   2) 27°C   3) 38°C   4) 42°C

5. Molecules of which substance have the lowest average kinetic energy?
   1) $NO(g)$ at 5°C   2) $NO_2(g)$ at -10°C   3) $NO_2(g)$ at 25 K   4) $N_2O_3(g)$ at 100 K

6. Which flask below contains molecules with the highest kinetic energy?

     20.ml   40.ml   30.ml   10.ml

     10°C   20°c   30°C   40°C

   1)   2)   3)   4)

7. Given four beakers containing different volume of HCl solution.

   10 milliliters   50 milliliters   200 milliliters   400 milliliters
   0.1 M HCl at 20°C   0.1 M HCl at 10°C   0.1 M HCl at 30°C   0.1 M HCl at 15°C
     A   B   C   D

    Which is true of the average kinetic energy of the molecules in the beakers?
   1) All four beakers have the same average kinetic energy
   2) Beaker D has the highest kinetic energy and beaker A has the lowest kinetic energy
   3) Beaker C has the highest kinetic energy and beaker B has the lowest kinetic energy
   4) Beaker B has the highest kinetic energy and beaker A has the lowest kinetic energy

8. Which change in temperature of a 1-gram sample of water would cause the greatest increase in the average kinetic energy of the molecules?
   1) 1°C to 10°C   2) 10°C to 1°C   3) 50°C to 60°C   4) 60°C to 50°C

9. Which change in temperature of a sample of water would result in the smallest decrease in the average kinetic energy of its molecule?
   1) 25°C to 32°C   2) 15°C to 9°C   3) 25°C to 29°C   4) 12°C to 2°C

10. A sample of substance X can change from one temperature to another. Which change will result in the highest increase in the average kinetic energy of the molecules?
   1) 250 K to -10°C   2) 300 K to 57°C   3) 400K to 100°C   4) 100K to -60°C

15. Temperature Conversions

1. Which temperature is equivalent to 50°C?
   1) 50 K   2) 223 K   3) 373 K   4) 323 K

2. What is the equivalent of 23°C on a Kelvin scale?
   1) +50   2) +296   3) -250   4) -296

3. The temperature of -30°C is the same as
   1) 243 K   2) 303 K   3) 30 K   4) 70 K

4. What is the equivalent of 546K on a Celsius scale?
   1) 273°C   2) -273°C   3) 818°C   4) 546°C

5. The temperature of 30 K is equivalent to
   1) 243°C   2) -243°C   3) 303°C   4) -303°C

6. Which temperature is equivalent to 300 K?
   1) 23°C   2) 300°C   3) 573°C   4) 73°C

7. The temperature of a sample of water is changed from 10°C to 30°C. The difference between these temperatures in Kelvin will be
   1) 273 K   2) 100 K   3) 20 K   4) 303 K

8. At STP, the difference between the boiling point and the freezing point of water in Kelvin scale is
   1) 373   2) 273   3) 180   4) 100

9. A liquid's freezing point is -38°C and its boiling point is 357°C. What is the number of Kelvin degrees between the boiling and the freezing point of the liquid?
   1) 319   2) 592   3) 668   4) 395

10. Heat is being added to a given sample. Compared to the Celsius temperature of the sample, the Kelvin temperature will
    1) Always be 273° lower
    2) Always be 273° greater
    3) Have the same reading at 0°C
    4) Have the same reading at 273°C

16. Heat Flow and Temperature

1. Solid A and Solid B are adjacent to each other. Object B has a temperature of 30°C . Heat will flow from A to B when the temperature of A is
   1) 10°C   2) 20°C   3) 30°C   4) 40°C

2. A solid material X is place in liquid Y. Heat will flow from Y to X when the temperature of
   1) Y is 20°C and X is 30°C   3) Y is 15°C and X 10°C
   2) Y is 10°C and X is 20°C   4) Y is 30°C and X is 40°C

3. Object A is at 40°C and Object B is at 50°C. Which is true of the heat flow between these two objects?
   1) Object B will lose heat to A and A will increase in temperature
   2) Object B will lose heat to A and A will decrease in temperature
   3) Object A will lose heat to B and B will increase in temperature
   4) Object A will lose heat to B and B will decreases in temperature

4. Which diagram correctly shows direction of heat flow between the two objects?

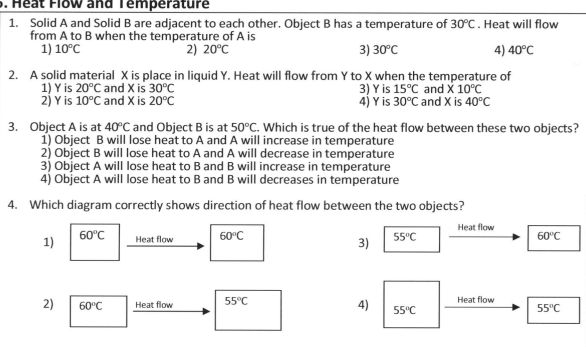

17. Heat Calculations: Recalling Concept Facts and Definitions

1. The specific heat capacity of a substance can be measured as the substance changes
   1) Phase 2) Temperature 3) Chemical composition 4) Nucleus composition

2. Heat of vaporization of a substance can be measured during
   1) melting 2) freezing 3) fusion 4) boiling

3. Heat of fusion of a substance can be measured during a
   1) Phase change 2) chemical change 3) nucleus change 4) nuclear change

4. The amount of heat needed to change the temperature of 1 gram of a substance 1°C is called
   1) Heat of fusion
   2) Entropy
   3) Heat of vaporization
   4) Specific heat

5. The amount of heat needed to change a one gram sample of a substance from solid to liquid is called
   1) Heat of vaporization
   2) Heat of reaction
   3) Specific heat capacity
   4) Heat of fusion

6. The amount of heat needed to change a unit mass of a liquid to a gas at a constant temperature is called
   1) Heat of combustion
   2) Entropy
   3) Heat of vaporization
   4) Specific heat capacity

7. The specific heat capacity of water is 4.18 J/°C•g . Adding 4.18 Joules of heat to a 1 gram sample of water will cause the water to
   1) Change from solid to liquid
   2) Change from liquid to solid
   3) Change its temperature 1 degree Celsius
   4) Change its temperature 4.18 degree Celsius

8. The heat of fusion of ice is 334 Joules per gram. Adding 334 Joules to one gram of heat to ice at STP will cause the ice to
   1) Increase in temperature
   2) Decrease in Temperature
   3) Change to water at a higher temperature
   4) Change to water at the same temperature

9. As water evaporates into steam, its temperature
   1) Increases as heat is absorbed
   2) Decreases as heat is absorbed
   3) Remains the same as heat is released
   4) Remains the same as heat is absorbed

10. The heat of vaporization of water is 2260 J/g. Adding 2260 Joules of heat to a one gram sample of water at STP will cause the water to
    1) Change to steam at a constant temperature
    2) Change to steam at higher temperature
    3) Change to ice at a constant temperature
    4) Change to ice at a higher temperature

  Survivingchem.com

18. Heat Calculations with Specific Heat Capacity

1. What is the total number of joules absorbed by a 10-gram sample of water as it changes its temperature from 60°C to 80°C?
    1) 42   2) 84   3) 420   4) 840

2. How much heat is released by 15 grams of water when it is cooled from 40°C to 30°C?
    1) 630 J   2) 42 J   3) 63 J   4) 130 J

3. How many kilojoules of heat are needed to raise the temperature of a 500 g of water from 15°C to 20°C?
    1) 4.20 kJ   2) 10.5 kJ   3) 32.0 kJ   4) 105 kJ

4. What is the total amount of heat energy needed to change the temperature of a 65-gram sample of water from 40.°C to 25°C?
    1) 6.3×10^{-2} kJ   2) 1.1×10^{-1} kJ   3) 4.1×10^{1} kJ   4) 6.8×10^{1} kJ

5. A water sample absorbed 168 joules of heat to change from 10°C to 30°C. What was the mass of the water sample?
    1) 1.00 g   2) 2.00 g   3) 20.0 g   4) 30.0 g

6. A sample of water is cooled from 15°C to 5°C by the removal of 1700 Joules of heat energy. What is the mass of the water?
    1) 200 g   2) 800 g   3) 41 g   4) 400 g

19. Heat Calculations with Heat of Fusion

1. How many joules of heat energy are needed to change a 5 gram sample of ice to water at the 0°C?
    1) 21.0 J   2) 66.8 J   3) 1670 J   4) 11300 J

2. How many Joules of heat must be removed from a 25 gram sample of water to change it to ice at its freezing point?
    1) 8350   2) 13.4   3) 56500   4) 334

3. How many kilojoules of heat must be removed from a 180 g sample of water to change it to ice at 0°C?
    1) 180 kJ   2) .75 kJ   3) 60 kJ   4) 40.6 kJ

4. The heat of fusion of an unknown substance is 220 J/g. How much heat is required to melt a 35 gram sample of this substance at its melting point?
    1) 255 J   2) 73480 J   3) 11690 J   4) 7700 J

5. 1200 Joules is added to a sample of ice to change it to water at its melting. What is the mass of the ice?
    1) 3.6 g   2) 0.27 g   3) 334 g   4) 1.9 g

20. Heat Calculations with Heat of Vaporization

1. How much heat is required to vaporize a 10 gram sample of water at its boiling point?
   1) 2260 J   2) 3340 J   3) 22600 J   4) 33.4 J

2. What is the total number of heat needed to vaporize a 25 g sample of water to steam at 100°C?
   1) 83.5 kJ   2) 2.5 kJ   3) 90.4 kJ   4) 56.5 kJ

3. The heat of vaporization of a liquid substance is 670 J/g. How much heat must be added to a 40 g sample of this liquid to change it to vapor at its boiling point?
   1) 16.75 J   2) 26800 J   3) 1640 J   4) 670 J

4. How much heat must be removed from a 5 gram sample of steam to condense it to water at a constant temperature of 100°C?
   1) 1657 J   2) 11300 J   3) 500 J   4) 2100 J

5. A 23 g sample of an unknown liquid substance absorbed 34 kJ of heat to change to gas at its boiling point. What is the heat of vaporization of the unknown liquid?
   1) 2.26 kJ/g   2) 782 kJ/g   3) 7.7 kJ/g   4) 1.5 kJ/g

21. Heat Calculations: Mixed Problems

1. What is the total number of kilojoules of heat needed to change 150 grams of ice to water at 0°C?
   1) 50.1   2) 2.22   3) 184   4) 484

2. How much heat is needed to change a 5.0 gram sample of water from 65°C to 75°C?
   1) 210 J   2) 14 J   3) 21 J   4) 43 J

3. When 200 grams of water is cooled from 50.°C to 25°C, the total amount of heat energy released by the water is
   1) 34 kJ   2) 21 kJ   3) 42 kJ   4) 17 kJ

4. What amount of heat energy is needed to change a 20 g sample of water at 100°C to steam at the same temperature?
   1) 905 kJ   2) 45.2 kJ   3) 1.13 kJ   4) .200 kJ

5. What is the total number of joules of heat energy released by a 2.5 gram sample of water to change to ice at 0°C?
   1) 133 J   2) 8.4 J   3) 10.5 J   4) 835 J

6. A 100 grams sample of water releases 1672 Joules of heat to cool to a lower temperature. What is the change in the temperature of the water sample?
   1) 16.72 °C   2) 1572 °C   3) 4°C   4) 24 °C

7. A 12 g sample of water at 40°C absorbed 252 Joules of heat to change to a different temperature. What would be the final temperature of the water?
   1) 5°C   2) 45°C   3) 35°C   4) 21°C

 Survivingchem.com

21. Continues

8. 900 Joules of heat energy was added to a sample of ice to melt it at its freezing. What is the mass of the water?
   1) 2.7 g   2) .37 g   3) 30060 g   4) 900 g

9. The heat of fusion of a solid is 15 kJ/g. If a sample of this substance released 45 kJ of heat to freeze at its freezing point, what is the mass of the substance?
   1) 3 g   2) .33 g   3) 675 g   4) 60 g

10. If a 25 grams sample of a solid requires 12000 Joules of heat to completely change to a liquid at its melting point, what is the heat of fusion of this substance?
    1) 12000 J/g   2) 334 J/g   3) 480 J/g   4) 36 J/g

11. What is the heat of vaporization of an unknown liquid if 5 grams of this liquid requires 22 kJ of heat to change to vapor at its boiling point?
    1) 4.4 J/g   2) 100 J/g   3) 4400 J/g   4) 11300 J/g

22. Heat Calculations from Lab Data

1. In an experiment using a calorimeter, the following data were obtained:

Mass of calorimeter + water	150 g
Mass of calorimeter	100 g
Initial temperature of water	35°C
Final temperature of water	65°C

   What is the total number of joules of heat energy absorbed by the water?
   1) 4500   2) 6270   3) 12600   4) 18900

2. A student collected the following data from a calorimeter laboratory experiment:

Mass of calorimeter + water	72.5g
Mass of calorimeter	40.5 g
Final temperature of water	22°C
Initial temperature of water	30°C

   Based on the data collected by the student, how much heat is released by the water in the calorimeter?
   1) 2436 J   2) 1361 J   3) 960 J   4) 1070 J

3. The following information was collected by a student from a calorimetric experiment.

Mass of calorimeter + water	48.0 g
Mass of calorimeter	37.0 g
Initial temperature of water	60.0 °C
Final temperature of water	?

   If the student determined that the water in the calorimeter had absorbed 299 Joules of heat, what would be the final temperature of the water?
   1) 6.5°C   2) 66.5°C   3) 53.5°C   4) 360°C

23. Kinetic Molecular Theory

1. An ideal gas is made up of gas particles that
   1) Have volume
   2) Attract each other
   3) Can be liquefied
   4) Are in random motion

2. Which is true of real gases but not of ideal gas?
   1) Real gases have volume
   2) Real gases do not have volume
   3) Real gases have mass
   4) Real gases do not have mass

3. Real gases differ from an ideal gas because the molecules of real gases have
   1) Some volume and no attraction for each other
   2) Some attraction and some attraction for each other
   3) No volume and no attraction for each other
   4) No volume and some attraction for each other

4. According to the kinetic molecular theory of gases, which assumption is correct?
   1) Gas particles strongly attract each other.
   2) Gas particles travel in curves path
   3) The volume of gas prevents random movement
   4) Energy may be transferred between particles when they collide

5. The kinetic molecular theory assumes that the particles of ideal gas
   1) Are in random, constant, straight line-motion
   2) Are arranged in regular geometric pattern
   3) Have strong attractive forces between them
   4) Have collision that result in the system losing energy

6. An assumption of the kinetic molecular theory of gases is that the particles of a gas have
   1) Little attraction for each other and a significant volume
   2) Little attraction for each other and an insignificant volume
   3) Strong attraction for each other and a significant volume
   4) Strong attraction for each other and an insignificant volume

7. Under which two conditions do real gases behave least like an ideal gas?
   1) High pressure and low temperature
   2) Low pressure and high temperature
   3) High pressure and high temperature
   4) Low pressure and low temperature

8. Under which two conditions do real gases behave most like (deviate least from) an ideal gas?
   1) High pressure and low temperature
   2) Low pressure and high temperature
   3) High pressure and high temperature
   4) Low pressure and low temperature

     Survivingchem.com

24. Deviation from an Ideal Gas: Effect of Molecular Mass

1. Which two gases behave most like an ideal gas under the same temperature and pressure?
    1) CO_2 and O_2 2) NH_3 and CH_4 3) H_2 and He   4) O_2 and N_2

2. Under the same temperature and pressure, which gas behaves least like an ideal gas?
    1) Xe   2) Kr   3) Ne   4) He

3. Under the same temperature and pressure, which gas is most likely to behave like an ideal gas?
    1) H   2) He   3) O_2 4) Ne

4. Which gas is least likely to obey the ideal gas model under same temperature and pressure?
    1) Xe   2) Kr   3) Ne   4) He

5. At STP, which will behave least like an ideal gas?
    1) Fluorine   2) Oxygen   3) Nitrogen   4) Hydrogen

25. Deviation from an Ideal Gas: Effect of Temperature and Pressure

1. Under which conditions of temperature and pressure would a real gas behaves least like an ideal gas?
    1) 0°C and 100 kPa   3) 0°C and 300 kPa
    2) 150°C and 100 kPa   4) 150°C and 300 kPa

2. A real gas behaves least like an ideal under which two conditions?
    1) 273 K and 1 atm   3) 546 K and 1 atm
    2) 273 K and 2 atm   4) 546 K and 2 atm

3. Under which conditions of temperature and pressure would a real gas behaves most like an ideal gas?
    1) 0°C and 100 kPa   3) 0°C and 300 kPa
    2) 150°C and 100 kPa   4) 150°C and 300 kPa

4. A real gas will behave most like an ideal gas under which conditions of temperature and pressure?
    1) 273 K and 1 atm   3) 546 K and 2 atm
    2) 273 K and 2 atm   4) 546 K and 1 atm

5. Under which two conditions would helium behaves most like an ideal gas?
    1) 50 K and 20 kPa   3) 50 K and 600 kPa
    2) 750 K and 20 kPa   4) 750 K and 600 kPa

26: Avogadro's Law

1. Under the same temperature and pressure, which is true of 1 L of Oxygen gas and 1 L of Nitrogen gas?
   1) They have equal number of molecules
   2) They have equal mass
   3) They have equal density
   4) They have the same structure

2. AT STP, 2 L of He and 2 L of H_2 have the same
   1) Mass   2) density   3) number of molecules   4) number of atoms

3. At STP, a 2 L sample of CO_2 contains the same number of molecules as
   1) 1 L of He   2) 2 L of He   3) 3 L of SO_2 4) 4 L of SO_2

4. At STP, which gas sample contains the same number of molecules as a 22.4 L sample of Hydrogen?
   1) 1 L of helium   2) 101.3 L of helium   3) 273 L of neon   4) 22.4 L of neon

5. Under which conditions would a 2 L sample of O_2 has the same number of molecules as a 2 L sample of N_2 that is at STP?
   1) 0 K and 1 atm   2) 0 K and 2 atm   3) 273 K and 1 atm   4) 273 K and 2 atm

6. The table below gives temperature and pressure of four different gas samples, each in a 1.5 L container:

Gas sample	Temperature (K)	Pressure (atm)
He	150	1.8
Ne	150	2.6
O_2	150	1.8
CO_2	100	2.6

Which two gas samples contain the same number of molecules?
   1) He and Ne   2) He and O_2 3) Ne and CO_2 4) Ne and O_2

27. Grahams Law of Diffusion

1. The particles of which gas will diffuse at the fastest rate under the same temperature and pressure?
   1) Xe   2) Kr   3) Ne   4) He

2. At STP, the molecules of which gas will travel the fastest?
   1) Fluorine   2) Oxygen   3) Nitrogen   4) Chlorine

3. Which gas molecule will diffuse at the slowest rate under the same conditions?
   1) H_2 2) N_2 3) O_2 4) F_2

4. Gas A, B, C and D have a mass of 20 g/mole, 30 g/mole, 40 g/mole, and 50 g/mole respectively. If all gases are at the same temperature and pressure, which gas will diffuse the slowest?
   1) A   2) B   3) C   4) D

28. Gas Law at Constant Temperature: Recalling Concept Facts

1. At constant temperature, the volume of a confined gas varies
   1) Directly with the pressure
   2) Indirectly with the pressure
   3) Directly with the mass of the gas
   4) Indirectly with the mass of the gas

2. At constant temperature, as pressure of a gas in a closed cylinder increases, volume of the gas
   1) Increases
   2) Decreases
   3) Remains the same

3. At constant temperature, as the pressure of a gas in a cylinder is decreased by half, the volume of the gas will
   1) Remain the same
   2) Decrease by half
   3) Increase 2 folds
   4) Increase by 4 folds

4. A gas is at STP. If the temperature of the gas is held constant while the volume of the gas is cut in half, the pressure of the gas will be
   1) Double
   2) Triple
   3) Halve
   4) Quadruple

5. Which graph best illustrates the relationship between pressure and volume of a gas when the temperature is held constant?

   1)   2)   3)   4)

29. Gas Law at Constant Temperature Calculations

1. At constant temperature, a gas at 2 atm of pressure has a volume of 6 L. What will be the new volume if the pressure is changed to 4 atm?
   1) 6.0 L
   2) 8.0 L
   3) 3 L
   4) 12.0 L

2. The pressure on 80 milliliters of a gas at constant temperature is changed from 16 atm to 8 atm. The new volume of the gas is
   1) 160 ml
   2) 40 ml
   3) 5 ml
   4) 10 ml

3. A gas sample occupies 10. ml at 1.0 atmospheric pressure. If the volume changes to 20. ml and the temperature remains the same, the new pressure will be
   1) 1.0 atm
   2) 2.0 atm
   3) 0.25 atm
   4) 0.50 atm

4. The volume of a $CO_2(g)$ changes from 50 ml to 100 ml when pressure on the gas is changed to 0.6 atm. If the temperature of the gas is constant, what was the initial pressure on the gas?
   1) 1.2 atm
   2) 0.3 atm
   3) 60 atm
   4) 2 atm

5. A 60 ml sample of hydrogen gas is at STP. If the temperature of the gas is held constant and the pressure is changed to 3 atm, what will the new volume of the hydrogen gas be?
   1) 20 ml
   2) 180 ml
   3) 1 ml
   4) 0.05 ml

6. A 2.0 L sample of $O_2(g)$ at STP had its volume changed to 1.5 L. If the temperature of the gas was held constant, what is the new pressure of the gas in kilopascal?
   1) 3.0 kPa
   2) 152 kPa
   3) 101.3 kPa
   4) 135 kPa

7. A 500 ml sample of a gas has its pressure change from 30 kPa to 15 kPa. If the temperature is held constant, the new volume of the gas can calculated from which set up?
   1) $15 \times \dfrac{30}{500}$
   2) $500 \times \dfrac{30}{15}$
   3) $500 \times \dfrac{15}{30}$
   4) $15 \times 30 \times 500$

30. Gas Law at Constant Pressure: Recalling Concept Facts

1. At constant pressure, the volume of a confined gas varies
   1) Directly with the Kelvin temperature
   2) Indirectly with the Kelvin temperature
   3) Directly with the mass of the gas
   4) Indirectly with the mass of the gas

2. At constant pressure, as temperature of a gas in a closed cylinder increases, the volume of the gas
   1) Decreases
   2) Increases
   3) Remains the same

3. At constant pressure, as the pressure of a gas in a cylinder is decreased by half, the volume of the gas will
   1) Increase by 2 times
   2) Increase by 4 times
   3) Decrease by half
   4) Remain the same

4. A gas is at STP. If the pressure on the gas is held constant while the volume of the gas is doubled, the new temperature of the gas will be
   1) Twice as much
   2) Four times as great
   3) Half as much
   4) One-fourth as much

5. Which graph best illustrates the relationship between the Kelvin temperature of a gas and its volume when the pressure on the gas is held constant?

   1) 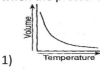　2) 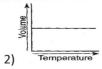　3) 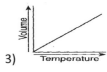　4)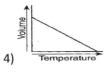

31. Gas Law at Constant Pressure Calculations

1. A sample of oxygen gas has a volume of 150. ml at 300 K. If the pressure is held constant and the temperature is raised to 600 K, the new volume of the gas will be
   1) 75.0 ml
   2) 150 ml
   3) 300 ml
   4) 600 ml

2. A 4.0 L of O_2 gas has a pressure of 100 K at constant pressure. What will the new volume be if the temperature of the gas is decreased to 25 K?
   1) 16 L
   2) 1 L
   3) 2 L
   4) 100 L

3. At constant pressure, a 200. milliliter sample of a gas is at a temperature of 600 K. What temperature of the gas will produce a new volume of 400. milliliters?
   1) 300 K
   2) 400 K
   3) 600 K
   4) 1200 K

4. A 1.5 L sample of carbon dioxide gas has its temperature changed to 200 K in order to produce a new volume of 6.0 L of carbon dioxide gas. Assuming the pressure of the gas is constant, what was the initial temperature of the gas?
   1) 500 K
   2) 750 K
   3) 100 K
   4) 50 K

5. At STP, the volume of a hydrogen gas is 40 ml. What will be the new volume of the hydrogen gas if the temperature is changed to 546 K and the pressure is held constant?
   1) 80 ml
   2) 20 ml
   3) 273 ml
   4) 546 ml

6. A gas originally at STP has a volume of 0.8 L. If the pressure of the gas is held constant, at what temperature will the volume of the gas decreased to 0. 6 L?
   1) 273 K
   2) 205 K
   3) 364 k
   4) 131 K

7. A 20 ml sample of a gas is at 30°C. If, at constant pressure, the temperature of the gas is changed to 60°C, what will the new volume of the gas be?
   1) 40 ml
   2) 10 ml
   3) 22 ml
   4) 18 ml

 　Survivingchem.com

32. Gas Law at Constant Volume: Recalling Concept Facts

1. At constant volume , the pressure of a confined gas varies
   1) Indirectly with the mass of the gas
   2) Directly with the Kelvin temperature
   3) Directly with the mass of the gas
   4) Indirectly with the Kelvin temperature

2. At constant volume , as temperature of a gas in a closed cylinder increases, the pressure of the gas
   1) Remains the same   2) Decreases   3) Increases

3. At constant volume, as the Kelvin temperature of a gas in a cylinder is decreased by half, the pressure on the gas will
   1) Increase by 2 times   2) Increase by 4 times   3) Decrease by half   4) Remain the same

4. A gas is at STP. If the volume of the gas is held constant while the pressure of the gas is doubled, the new temperature of the gas will be
   1) Four times as great   2) One-fourth as much   3) Half as much   4) Twice as much

5. Which graph best illustrates the relationship between the Kelvin temperature of a gas and the pressure on the gas when the volume of the gas is held constant?

1) 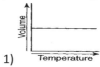   2) 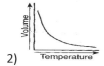   3) 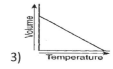   4)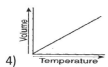

33. Gas Law at Constant Volume Calculations

1. A gas sample at 546 K has a pressure of 0.4 atm. If the volume of the gas sample is unchanged, what will

   be the new pressure of the gas if its temperature is changed 136.5 K ?
   1) 0.4 atm   2) 0.8 atm   3) 0.1 atm   4) 0.2 atm

2. Helium gas is at a pressure of 50 kPa and at a temperature of 300 K. What will be the temperature of gas if the pressure is changed to 120 kPa at constant volume?
   1) 720 K   2) 125 K   3) 20 K   4) 250 K

3. A sample of CO_2 is at STP. If the volume of the CO_2 gas remains constant and its temperature is changed to 45°C, what will be the new pressure of the gas?
   1) 90.1 kPa   2) 101.3 kPa   3) 591 kPa   4) 118 kPa

34. Combined Gas Laws: Recalling Concept Facts and Definitions

1. If the Kelvin temperature of a gas is doubled while the pressure is halved, the volume of the gas will
   1) Remain the same
   2) Increase 2 times
   3) Decrease by half
   4) Increase 4 times

2. As the Kelvin temperature of a gas is halved and the pressure is doubled, the volume of the gas will
   1) Increase 4 times as much
   2) Decrease by 4
   3) Decrease to half
   4) Remains the same

3. Under which conditions would a volume of a given sample of a gas decrease?
   1) Decrease pressure and increase temperature
   2) Decrease pressure and decrease temperature
   3) Increase pressure and decrease temperature
   4) Increase pressure and increase temperature

4. The volume of a 1.0 mole sample of an ideal gas will increase when the
   1) Pressure decreases and the temperature decreases
   2) Pressure decreases and the temperature increases
   3) Pressure increases and the temperature decreases
   4) Pressure increases and the temperature increases

35. Combined Gas Law Calculations

1. At a temperature of 273.0 K , a 400.0 milliliter gas sample has a pressure of 101.3 kPa. If the pressure is changed to 50.65 kPa, at what temperature will the gas have a volume of 551 milliliters?
   1) 100 K   2) 273 K   3) 188 K   4) 546 K

2. A gas sample has a volume of 1.4 L at a temperature of 20.K and a pressure of 1.0 atm. What will be the new volume when the temperature is changed to 40.K and the pressure is changed to 0.50 atm ?
   1) 0.35 L   2) 0.75 L   3) 1.4 L   4) 5.6 L

3. A sample of hydrogen gas occupies a volume of 15.0 liters at a pressure of 2.00 atmospheres and a temperature of 300 K. If the temperature is raised to 400 K, what pressure will allow the hydrogen to occupy a volume of 40.0 liters?
   1) 0.5 atm   2) 1.0 atm   3) 2.0 atm   4) 4.0 atm

4. At STP, a gas has a volume of 4.0 L. If the temperature of the gas is changed to 600 K and the pressure is increased to 160 kPa, what is the new volume of the gas sample?
   1) 2.8 L   2) 4.0 L   3) 5.6 L   4) 8.0 L

5. At 40°C and 2 atm, the volume of a sample of $O_2(g)$ is 380 ml. What will be the new volume of the $O_2(g)$ at STP?
   1) 57 .5 ml   2) 111 ml   3) 871 ml   4) 663 ml

6. A gas occupies a volume of 3 L at 1.5 atm and 80°C. Which setup is correct for calculating the new volume of the gas if the temperature is changed to 150°C and the pressure is dropped to 1.0 atm?

   1) $3 \times \dfrac{1.5 \times 150}{1 \times 80}$ 3) $3 \times \dfrac{1.5 \times 423}{1 \times 353}$

   2) $3 \times \dfrac{1.5 \times 80}{1 \times 150}$ 4) $3 \times \dfrac{1.5 \times 353}{1 \times 423}$

36. Mixed Gas Law Calculations

1. A gas in a closed container has a pressure of 300 kPa at 303 K. If the volume is held constant and the temperature is lowered to 101 K, what will be the new pressure?
   1) 900 kPa
   2) 200 kPa
   3) 800 kPa
   4) 100 kPa

2. A gas has a volume of 1000 mL at a temperature of 20 K and a pressure of 1 atm. If the temperature is changed to 40 K and the pressure is changed to 0.5 atm, what will the new volume of the gas?
   1) 250 ml
   2) 1000 ml
   3) 4000 ml
   4) 5600 ml

3. A gas has a volume of 5 L at 0.2 atm. If the temperature of the gas remains the same and the pressure is changed to 0.6 atm, what is the new volume of the gas ?
   1) 15 L
   2) 12 L
   3) 0.6 L
   4) 1.7 L

4. A gas sample has a volume of 12 liters at 0°C and 0.5 atm. What will be the new volume of the gas when the pressure is changed to 1 atm and the temperature is held constant?
   1) 24 L
   2) 18 L
   3) 12 L
   4) 6.0 L

5. At STP, a gas has a volume of 250 ml. If the pressure remained constant, at what Kelvin temperature would the gas has a volume of 500 ml?
   1) 137 K
   2) 500 K
   3) 546 K
   4) 273 K

6. A gas has a pressure of 120 kPa and a volume of 50.0 milliliters when its temperature is 127°C. What volume will the gas occupies at a pressure of 60 kPa and at a temperature of -73°C?
   1) 12.5 ml
   2) 50.0 ml
   3) 100 ml
   4) 200 ml

7. The graph below shows a change in the volume of a gas sample as its temperature rises at constant pressure.

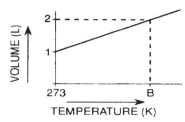

What temperature is represented by point B?
   1) 546 K
   2) 298 K
   3) 273 K
   4) 2 K

8. The graph below represents the relationship between pressure and volume of a gas at constant temperature.

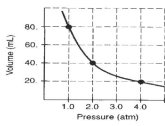

The product of pressure and volume is constant. According to the graph, what is the

product in atm·ml ?
   1) 20
   2) 40
   3) 60
   4) 80

37. Physical and Chemical Properties

1. Which is a physical property of Sodium?
   1) It is flammable
   2) It is shiny
   3) It reacts with water
   4) It reacts with chlorine

2. Which is a chemical property of water?
   1) It freezes
   2) It boils
   3) It evaporates
   4) It decomposes

3. Which best describes a chemical property of sodium?
   1) It is a shiny metal
   2) It is smooth
   3) It reacts vigorously with water
   4) It is a hard solid

4. An example of a physical change is
   1) Boiling of water
   2) Combining magnesium with oxygen
   3) Burning of magnesium
   4) Exploding fireworks

5. An example of a physical property of an element is the element's ability to
   1) Form a compound
   2) React with oxygen
   3) React with an acid
   4) Form an aqueous solution

6. Which is a physical change of iodine?
   1) Iodine can react with sugar
   2) Iodine can react with hydrogen
   3) It can decompose to two iodine molecule
   4) Iodine can dissolve in water

7. Which physical property makes it possible to separate the components of crude oil by means of distillation?
   1) Boiling Point
   2) Solubility
   3) Conductivity
   4) Melting point

8. During a chemical change, a substance changes its
   1) Density
   2) Composition
   3) Solubility
   4) Phase

9. Which list consists of physical properties of an element?
   1) Good solubility, High density, has luster
   2) React with water, it is a solid, it is malleable
   3) It explodes, low melting point, good conductivity
   4) Low density, poor conductivity, combines with oxygen

10. Given the particle diagram representing four molecules of a substance.

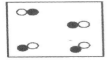

Which particle diagram best represents this same substance after a physical change has taken place?

1)

3)

2)

4)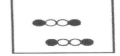

 Survivingchem.com

Survivingchem.com

Topic 2: The Periodic Table

1. Periodic Table: Recalling Concept Facts and Definitions

1. The observed regularities in the properties of the elements are periodic functions of their
   1) atomic numbers   2) atomic mass   3) oxidation state   4) reactivity

2. The vertical columns of the Periodic Table are called
   1) periods   2) energy levels   3) rows   4) groups

3. The horizontal arrangements of the elements on the Periodic Table are called
   1) periods   2) energy levels   3) rows   4) groups

4. Majority of the elements on the Periodic Table are
   1) metals   2) nonmetals   3) metalloids   4) noble gases

5. More than two third of the elements on the Periodic Table are
   1) halogens   2) metalloids   3) nonmetals   4) metals

6. The majority of the elements on the Periodic Table exist as
   1) solids   2) liquids   3) gases   4) aqueous

7. Which of the following information cannot be found in the box of elements on the Periodic Table?
   1) Oxidation state   2) Atomic number   3) Atomic mass   4) Phase

8. The Periodic Table of the elements contains elements that are
   1) solids only   3) liquids and gases only
   2) solid and liquids only   4) solid, liquids and gases

9. The modern Periodic Table of the elements is arranged by increasing
   1) mass number   3) atomic number
   2) atomic mass   4) oxidation numbers

2. Characteristics of Elements in Groups and Periods

1. Which is true of elements within the same group on the Periodic table ?
   1) The have same number of electrons   3) They have the same energy levels
   2) They have the same number of valence electrons   4) They have the same nuclear charge

2. In general, elements within each group of the Periodic Table share similar
   1) chemical properties   3) mass number
   2) electron configuration   4) number of occupied energy levels

3. Elements in the same period of the Periodic Table are similar in that they all have the same
   1) number of electron shells   3) oxidation state
   2) valence electrons   4) chemical properties

4. The similarities in chemical properties of elements within the same group is due to similarity in
   1) number of electron shells   3) number of protons
   2) number of neutrons electrons 4) number of valence electrons

5. The Period number of an element represents
   1) the number of electron shells in the atom of that element
   2) the number of neutrons and protons in the atom of that element
   3) the number of valence electrons in the atom of that element
   4) the atomic size of that element

3. Characteristics of Groups: Determining Elements with Similar Chemical Characteristics

1. Which element has chemical properties most similar to oxygen?
   1) N   2) F   3) S   4) H

2. Which list of elements contains element with similar chemical characteristics?
   1) Be, Li, and B   2) Be, Mg, and Ca   3) Na, Mg, and Al   4) K, Ca, and Mg

3. Which list contains elements with greatest variation in chemical properties?
   1) O, S and Se   2) N, P and As   3) Be, N, O   4) Ba, Sr and Ca

4. Which element will react in a similar manner as the element Chlorine?
   1) Fluorine   2) Sulfur   3) Argon   4) Calcium

5. Element Oxygen and Sulfur can both form a bond with sodium with similar chemical formula. The similarity in their formulas is due to
   1) Oxygen and Sulfur having the same number of kernel electrons
   2) Oxygen and sulfur having the same number of valence electrons
   3) Oxygen and sulfur having the same number of protons
   4) Oxygen and sulfur having the same molecular structure

4. Group Names

1. The elements in Group 1 of the Periodic Table are called
   1) Alkaline earth   2) Alkali   3) Transition elements   4) Halogens

2. Elements in Group 3 to Group 12 of the Periodic Table are collectively known as
   1) Transition metals   2) Noble gas   3) Halogens   4) Alkali metals

3. Group 18 elements on the periodic table are called
   1) Transition metals   2) Halogens   3) Alkaline earth   4) Noble gases

4. Elements of which group are known as alkaline earth metals?
   1) 1   2) 13   3) 17   4) 2

5. Which group of the periodic table contains elements that are call the halogens?
   1) 18   2) 17   3) 2   4) 1

     Survivingchem.com

5. Physical Properties of the Elements: Recalling Terms and Definitions

1. Elements that can be hammered into thin sheet are said to be
   1) Ductile   2) Luster   3) Malleable   4) Brittle

2. Property of an element that describes its ability to be drawn into thin sheet is called
   1) luster   2) Ductile   3) Malleable   4) Brittle

3. Shininess of an element means that the element
   1) Is brittle   2) is dull   3) has conductivity   4) has luster

4. Atomic radius indicates which information about the elements?
   1) Atomic size   2) Atomic hardness   3) Atomic density   4) Bonding size

5. Ionization energy values of an element measures the element's ability to
   1) Lose electrons   2) Attract electrons   3) Carry heat   4) Carry electricity

6. Electronegativity values of the elements measure the elements' ability to
   1) Lose electrons   2) Attract electrons   3) Carry heat   4) Carry electricity

7. Brittleness describes how easily
   1) A solid sublimes   3) A solid shatters when struck
   2) A solid melts   4) A solid can be drawn into a thin wire

8. Conductivity refers to atom's ability to
   1) Reacts with other elements   3) Lose electrons
   2) Carry electrical current   4) Break easily

9. Atoms ability to gain electrons from another atom during bonding is determined by the atom's
   1) Density value   3) Electronegativity value
   2) Ionization energy value 4) Conductivity value

10. The tendency for an atom to give away its electrons during chemical bonding is measured by its
    1) Atomic radius value   3) Electronegativity value
    2) Density value   4) Ionization energy value

6. Types of Elements and Properties: Recalling Concept Facts

1. Which is a property of most metallic solids?
   1) Ductile   2) Brittleness   3) Low conductivity   4) High ionization energy

2. Solid nonmetal elements tend to be
   1) Malleable   2) Brittle   3) Ductile   4) Luster

3. An element has luster as one of its physical properties. Which is most likely true of this element?
   1) It is a gas   2) It is a metal   3) It is a nonmetal   4) It is gas

4. Which properties are characteristics of metallic elements?
   1) Malleable and luster   3) Brittleness and dullness
   2) Low heat conductivity and luster 4) Brittleness and ductile

5. Which characteristics describe most metals?
   1) Good electrical conductivity and poor heat conductivity
   2) Poor electrical conductivity and poor heat conductivity
   3) Good heat conductivity and good heat conductivity
   4) Poor electrical conductivity and good heat conductivity

6. continues.

6. Low ionization energy and low electronegativity are characteristics that best describe
   1) Nonmetals   2) Metals   3) Metalloids   4) Liquids

7. An element has luster, yet it is brittle. This element is most likely a

   1) Metalloid   2) Metal   3) Nonmetal   4) Liquid

8. Metalloids tend to have properties resembling
   1) Nonmetals only   3) Metals only
   2) Both metals and nonmetals   4) Neither a metal nor a nonmetal

9. Compared to atoms of nonmetals, atoms of metallic elements tend to
   1) Gain electrons and form negative ions   3) Lose electrons and form negative ions
   2) Gain electrons and form positive ions   4) Lose electrons and form positive ions

10. A nonmetallic element is likely to
    1) Gain electrons and form negative ions   3) Lose electrons and form negative ions
    2) Gain electrons and form positive ions   4) Lose electrons and form positive ions

11. When an atom of a metallic element forms a bond, it
    1) Loses electrons, and its atomic radius decreases in size
    2) Loses electrons, and its atomic radius increases in size
    3) Gains electrons, and its atomic radius decreases in size
    4) Gains electrons, and its atomic radius increases in size

12. During bonding with a metal, an atom of a nonmetal is likely
    1) Loses electrons, and its atomic radius will decreases in size
    2) Loses electrons, and its atomic radius will increases in size
    3) Gains electrons, and its atomic radius will decreases in size
    4) Gains electrons, and its atomic radius will increases in size

13. At STP, metallic elements on the Periodic Table can be found in which phase or phases?
    1) Solid only   3) Solid and liquid only
    2) Solid, liquid and gas   4) Gas only

14. Nonmetal elements on the Periodic Table can exist in which phase or phases?
    1) Solid only   3) Liquid only
    2) Solid or liquid only   4) Solid, liquid and gas

15. Element X is a solid at STP. Element X
    1) Must be a metal
    2) Must be a nonmetal
    3) Must be a metalloid or metal
    4) Could be a metal, a nonmetal or a metalloid

7. Metals, Nonmetals, and Metalloids

1. Which element is a metal?
   1) Br   2) He   3) Br   4) Hg

2. Which of these Group 14 elements has characteristics of a metal?
   1) Pb   2) Ge   3) Si   4) C

3. Which of these Period 4 elements exists as a metallic solid at STP?
   1) Arsenic   2) Selenium   3) Calcium   4) Krypton

4. Which of these elements has nonmetallic properties?
   1) Bismuth   2) Antimony   3) Arsenic   4) Phosphorous

5. Which list of elements contains only nonmetals?
   1) Br and Kr   2) Al and Si   3) Li and Be   4) Ca and Cl

6. Which list of elements contains only metalloids?
   1) Pb and Bi   2) Si and Ge   3) B and C   4) H and He

7. Which element is a metalloid?
   1) B   2) Al   3) Sn   4) Au

8. The element in which group contains only metallic elements?
   1) Group 2   2) Group 13   3) Group 14   4) Group 17

9. Which group contains the most number of metallic elements?
   1) Group 13   2) Group 14   3) Group 15   4) Group 18

10. Which of these groups contains only of nonmetallic elements?
    1) Group 17   2) Group 14   3) Group 2   4) Group 2

11. Which of these groups contains the least amount of nonmetallic elements?
    1) Group 16   2) Group 14   3) Group 15   4) Group 17

12. The element Antimony is a
    1) Metal   2) Nonmetal   3) Metalloid   4) Halogen

13. The element Iodine is best described as a
    1) Metal   2) Nonmetal   3) Metalloid   4) Noble gas

14. The element lead is best described as
    1) A metal   2) A nonmetal   3) A metalloid   4) A noble gas

15. Which is true of Hydrogen?
    1) It is a nonmetal   2) It is a metalloid   3) It is a metal   4) It is a halogen

16. The element in Group 13 Period 2 is
    1) A metalloid   2) A nonmetal   3) A noble gas   4) A metal

17. The element in Period 3 Group 16 is
    1) A metal   2) A nonmetal   3) A metalloid   4) A transition metal

18. The element in Group 3 Period 3 has
    1) Nonmetallic properties   3) Both metallic and nonmetallic properties
    2) Metallic properties   4) Neither metallic nor nonmetallic properties

8. Types of Elements: Relating Elements to Properties

1. Which of these elements is ductile and malleable?
   1) C   2) Cu   3) S   4) Se

2. Which element is malleable and has luster?
   1) Ag   2) Br   3) He   4) P

3. Which element is brittle?
   1) Al   2) He   3) Mg   4) S

4. Element X has luster and is brittle. Which could be element X?
   1) Silicon   2) Neon   3) Iron   4) copper

5. Which of these elements in Period 2 is likely to form a negative ion?
   1) Oxygen   2) Boron   3) Ne   4) Li

6. Which of these elements is likely to lose an electron and form a positive ion?
   1) K   2) S   3) P   4) Kr

7. During chemical bonding, which of these elements will lose an electron?
   1) Carbon   2) Nitrogen   3) Chlorine   4) Magnesium

8. A solid element is tested in a laboratory and was found to be a nonconductor of electricity and heat. Which of these could be the element that was tested?
   1) S   2) Au   3) Ag   4) Ne

9. Which of these elements has high thermal and electrical conductivity?
   1) Iodine   2) Carbon   3) Phosphorous   4) Iron

10. Which of these Period 3 solids has the lowest heat and electrical conductivity?
    1) Sodium   2) Magnesium   3) Aluminum   4) Sulfur

11. Which properties best described the element Silver?
    1) Malleable and low electrical conductivity   3) Malleable and high electrical conductivity
    2) Brittle and low electrical conductivity   4) Brittle and high electrical conductivity

12. Which of these characteristics best describes the element phosphorous?
    1) It is brittle   2) It is malleable   3) It has luster   4) It is ductile

13. Which is true of carbon?
    1) It is malleable   3) It has low electrical conductivity
    2) It has Luster   4) It is a gas at STP

14. Which is true of element mercury at STP?
    1) It is a liquid, and has low conductivity   3) It is a liquid, and has high conductivity
    2) It is a solid, and has low conductivity   4) It is a solid, and has high conductivity

15. Which is true of element sodium during chemical bonding?
    1) It tends to gain electrons and form a positive ion
    2) It tends to lose electrons and form a positive ion
    3) It tends to gain electrons and form a negative ion
    4) It tends to lose electrons and form a negative ion

9. Group Properties: Recalling Concept Facts

1. Which is true of the alkali metal elements?

   1) They tend to gain electrons easily
   2) They tend to lose electrons easily
   3) They tend to form multiple oxidation number
   4) They tend to form colored compounds

2. Which are characteristics of elements in Group 1 of the Periodic Table?

   1) They all have one valence electron and share similar chemical properties
   2) They all have one valence electron and share different chemical properties
   3) They all have one energy level and share similar chemical characteristics
   4) They all have one energy level and share different chemical characteristics

3. What is the most likely formula for an oxide formed between a Group 1 atom X and oxygen?

   1) XO   2) X_2O 3) XO_2 4) XO_{16}

4. . Which is NOT true of the alkaline earth metals?

   1) They are obtain from their fused salts
   2) They all have two valence electrons
   3) They are more reactive than Group 1 atoms
   4) They tend to form a positive ion

5. Alkaline earth elements tend to

   1) Gain electrons easily
   2) Lose electrons easily
   3) Form multiple oxidation number
   4) Form colored compounds

6. Which set of characteristics of is true of elements in Group 2 of the Periodic Table?

   1) They all have two energy level and share different chemical characteristics
   2) They all have two energy level and share similar chemical characteristics
   3) They all have two valence electrons and share similar chemical properties
   4) They all have two valence electrons and share different chemical properties

7. What is the most likely formula for an oxide formed between a Group 2 element M and oxygen?

   1) MO   2) M_2O 3) MO_2 4) MO_{16}

8. Which property best describes transition elements?

   1) They tend to gain electrons
   2) They tend to gain protons
   3) They tend to form colorful compounds
   4) They form molecular compounds

9. Which statement best describes element in Group 3 to 12?

   1) They tend to form multiple positive oxidation numbers and produce colorful compounds
   2) They tend to form multiple negative oxidation numbers and produce colorful compounds
   3) They tend to be diatomic molecules and produce colorful solution
   4) They tend to be monatomic molecules and produce colorful solutions

10. Which physical characteristic of a solution indicates the presence of a transition element?

   1) Its density   2) Its color   3) Its effect on litmus   4) Its reactivity

9. cont.

11. In general, the elements in Group 17 of the Periodic Table tend to have
    1) Similar physical characteristics
    2) Similar chemical characteristics
    3) Similar number of electrons
    4) similar number of protons

12. Halogens in their elemental state exist as
    1) Monatomic molecule 2) Diatomic molecule 3) Polyatomic ions 4) Triatomic ions

13. Which is true of all Group 17 halogens?
    1) They all have seven valence electrons, and will lose 1 electron during bonding
    2) They all have seven valence electrons, and will lose 2 electrons during bonding
    3) They all have seven valence electrons, and will gain 1 electron during bonding
    4) They all have seven valence electrons, and will gain 2 electrons during bonding

14. The general formula of a halide salt formed between a halogen Y and an alkali element X would be
    1) XY   2) XY_2 3) X_2Y 4) XY_{17}

15. When a halide salt is formed between a halogen Y and a Group 2 element M, the general formula of the halide will be
    1) MY_{17} 2) MY   3) M_2Y 4) MY_2

16. The most active halogen is
    1) I   2) Br   3) Cl   4) F

17. Which halogens exist as gases?
    1) Cl and I   2) F and Br   3) F and Cl   4) Br and Cl

18. Which halogen is correctly paired with the phase it exists at STP?
    1) Br is a liquid   2) F is a solid   3) I is a gas   4) Cl is a liquid

19. All Group 18 elements, at STP, exist as
    1) Monatomic liquids
    2) Monatomic gases
    3) Diatomic liquids
    4) Diatomic gases

20. The noble gases are similar in that they
    1) Have full valence shell
    2) Have eight electrons shells
    3) Gain electrons easily
    4) Lose electrons easily

21. Which are true of all Group 18 noble gases?
    1) They are very stable, and tend to form many compounds
    2) They are very stable, and tend to form very few compounds
    3) They are not very stable, and tend to form many compounds
    4) They are not very stable, and tend to form very few compounds

22. Which two noble gases have been found to form stable compounds?
    1)He and Ne   2) Ne and He   3) Ar and Xe   4) Ra and Xe

10. Groups of the Elements

1. Which element is a member of the halogen family?
    1) H　　　　　　　　2) He　　　　　　　3) Br　　　　　　　4) B

2. Which element is an alkali metal?
    1) H　　　　　　　　2) Li　　　　　　　3) Al　　　　　　　4) Mg

3. Which of these elements is NOT an alkaline earth metal?
    1) Mg　　　　　　　2) Be　　　　　　　3) Ca　　　　　　　4) Na

4. Which element is a noble gas?
    1) Neon　　　　　　2) Fluorine　　　　3) Oxygen　　　　4) Nitrogen

5. Which is a transition metal?
    1) Sr　　　　　　　2) Ag　　　　　　　3) I　　　　　　　　4) Xe

6. Which of these is an alkaline earth element?
    1) Na　　　　　　　2) K　　　　　　　3) H　　　　　　　4) Ra

7. Which element is a transition metal?
    1) Strontium　　　　2) Selenium　　　　3) Mercury　　　　4) Iodine

8. Xenon is
    1) an alkali　　　　2) an alkaline earth　3) a halogen　　　4) a noble gas

9. Iron is best classified as a(n)
    1) alkaline earth metal　2) noble gas　　　3) transition metal　4) halogen

10. Helium is
    1) a noble gas　　　2) a halogen　　　　3) a transition metal　4) an alkali metal

11. Element beryllium is
    1) an alkali metal　2) an alkaline metal　3) a transition metal　4) a halogen

12. The element in Group 17 Period 4 is a(n)
    1) transition metal　2) alkali metal　　3) halogen　　　　4) noble gas

13. Potassium and cesium are classified as
    1) transition metals　2) alkali metals　3) halogens　　　4) noble gases

11. Group Properties

1. An element forms an oxide with the formula X_2O. Element X could be
    1) Mg   2) K   3) Cl   4) He

2. A Period 2 element Z forms a compound with oxygen with a formula of Z_2O?
    Element Z could be
    1) Neon   2) Boron   3) Be   4) Li

3. If element M forms an oxide with oxygen with a formula of MO. Which element could M be?
    1) H   2) He   3) Li   4) Be

4. Element Z is in Period 3 of the Periodic Table, and forms an oxide with the formula Z_2O_3?
    Element Z is
    1) Na   2) Mg   3) Al   4) Cl

5. A compound of halide has a formula YCl_2. Which element is Y?
    1) H   2) Sr   3) Na   4) Li

6. A Period 4 element L forms a halide with bromine with the formula LiBr. Which element could L be?
    1) Kr   2) Se   3) Ca   4) K

7. Which element is commonly found in nature only in compounds?
    1) Au   2) Cs   3) Ag   4) He

8. Which of these period 2 elements is found in nature only as a fused compound?
    1) Lithium   2) Carbon   3) Nitrogen   4) Neon

9. Which of these nonmetals occurs in nature only in compounds?
    1) Carbon   2) Phosphorous   3) Fluorine   4) Sulfur

10. Which set contains elements that are never found in nature in their atomic state?
    1) K and Na   2) K and S   3) Na and Ne   4) Na and C

11. Which of these element is obtained from its fused salt?
    1) Rubidium   2) Iron   3) Iodine   4) Neon

12. Which of these oxides will likely form a colored solution when dissolved in water?
    1) Na_2O 2) CaO   3) SO_2 4 FeO

13. Chlorine will bond with which metallic element to form a colorful compound?
    1) Aluminum   2) Sodium   3) Strontium   4)Manganese

14. Which salt contains an ion that forms a colored solution?
    1) $CaSO_4$ 2) $Ni_2(SO_4)_3$ 3) $Al_2(SO_4)_3$ 4) $MgSO_4$

15. A solution of a compound containing element Z is blue. Element Z could be
    1) Fluorine   2) Copper   3) Beryllium   4) Neon

12. Trends in Atomic Size (Radius) of the Elements: Recalling Concept Facts

1. As the elements in Group 1 are considered in order from top to bottom, the atomic radius of each successive element generally
    1) Increases   2) Decreases   3) Remains the same

2. As the elements in Group 17 of the Periodic Table are considered in order of increasing atomic number, the atomic size of each successive element generally
    1) Increases   2) Decreases   3)) Remains the same

3. When the elements in Group 13 are considered in order of decreasing atomic number, the size of each successive element
    1) Increases   2) Decreases   3) Remains the same

4. As the elements in Period 2 are considered in order from left to right, the atomic radius of each successive element generally
    1) Increases   2) Decreases   3) Remains the same

5. As the elements in Period 4 of the Periodic Table are considered in order of increasing atomic number, the atomic size of each successive element generally

    1) Increases   2) Decreases   3) Remains the same

6. When the elements within a period on the Periodic Table are considered in order of decreasing atomic number, the size of each successive element
    1) Decreases   2) Increases   3) Remains the same

7. When the elements are considered from right to left of Period 2 the atomic radius of the successive element generally will

    1) Increase   2) Decrease   3) Remain the same

8. As the elements in Group 1 of the Periodic Table are considered in order of increasing atomic number, the atomic radius of each successive element increases. This is primarily due to an increase in the number of
    1) Neutrons in the nucleus   3) Valence electrons
    2) Unpaired electrons   4) Electrons shells

9. As the elements in a given group are considered in order from bottom to top, the atomic size of each successive element decreases. This decrease is mostly due to a decrease in
    1) Atomic number   3) The number of occupied energy levels
    2) Mass number   4) The number of protons occupying the nucleus

10. As the elements in Period 3 of the Periodic Table are considered in order of increasing atomic number, the atomic radius of each successive element decreases. This is primarily due to an increase in the number of
    1) Nuclear charge   3) Valence electrons
    2) Electron shells   4) Kernel electrons

11. When the elements are considered in order of decreasing atomic number across any given Period of the Periodic Table, the size of each successive atom increases. This increase is primarily due to
    1) Increase in occupied electron shells   3) Increase in nuclear charge
    2) Decrease in occupied electron shells   4) Decrease in nuclear charge

13. Atomic Radii: Comparing Atomic Sizes of Elements

1. Which of the following elements has the largest atomic radius?
   1) Li   2) B   3) C   4) F

2. Which of these elements has the largest atomic radius?
   1) Kr   2) Br   3) Si   4) Ca

3. Which of these elements has the smallest atomic size?
   1) C   2) N   3) O   4) F

4. Which of these elements has the smallest radius?
   1) Mg   2) Cl   3) S   4) Al

5. Which of these elements in Group 2 of the Periodic Table has the largest atomic radius?
   1) Be   2) Mg   3) Ca   4) Sr

6. The atom of which of these elements has the biggest atomic radius?
   1) F   2) Cl   3) Br   4) I

7. Which of these Group 14 elements has the smallest atomic radius?
   1) Lead   2) Tin   3) Silicon   4) Carbon

8. Which atom has a bigger atomic radius than the atom of Sulfur?
   1) Oxygen   2) Phosphorous   3) Chlorine   4) Argon

9. The atom of which element is bigger than the atom of the element calcium?
   1) Sr   2) Sc   3) Mg   4) Be

10. According to the Periodic Table, which sequence correctly places the elements in order of increasing atomic size?
    1) Na $\rightarrow$ Li $\rightarrow$ H $\rightarrow$ K
    2) Ba $\rightarrow$ Sr $\rightarrow$ Sr $\rightarrow$ Ca
    3) Te $\rightarrow$ Sb $\rightarrow$ Sn $\rightarrow$ In
    4) H $\rightarrow$ He $\rightarrow$ Li $\rightarrow$ Be

14. Trends in Metallic and Nonmetallic Properties: Recalling Concept Facts

1. As the elements in Group 1 are considered in order from top to bottom, the metallic property of each successive element generally
   1) Increases   2) Decreases   3) Remains the same

2. When the elements in Group 2 are considered in order of decreasing atomic number, the reactivity of the elements generally
   1) Increases   2) Decreases   3) Remains the same

3. When the elements are considered from bottom to top of any group on the Periodic Table, the nonmetallic characteristics of successive element
   1) Increases   2) Decreases   3) Remains the same

4. As the halogens in Group 17 are considered in order from bottom to top , the number of valence electrons of successive element generally
   1) Increases   2) Decreases   3) Remains the same

5. As the elements in Period 4 of the Periodic Table are considered in order of increasing atomic number, the metallic properties of successive element
   1) Increases   2) Decreases   3)) Remains the same

6. When the elements within a Period on the Periodic Table are considered in order of increasing atomic number, the nonmetallic properties of successive element
   1) Increases   2) Decreases   3) Remains the same

 Survivingchem.com

15. Metallic and Nonmetallic Properties: Comparing Elements

1. Which element is the most reactive metal in Group 1 of the Period Table?
   1) Fr   2) Na   3) Li   4) Cs

2. Which of these alkaline earth metals is the most reactive?
   1) Be   2) Mg   3) Ca   4) Sr

3. Which of these Period 3 elements has the most metallic properties?
   1) Cl   2) S   3) P   4) Si

4. Which of these elements has the most metallic properties?
   1) Radium   2) Strontium   3) Magnesium   4) Beryllium

5. Which of these elements has the least metallic characteristics
   1) Fr   2) Na   3) Li   4) Cs

6. Which of these element is the most reactive metal?
   1) Li   2) Be   3) Na   4) Mg

7. Which of these elements in Period 2 has the least metallic characteristics?
   1) Beryllium   2) Carbon   3) Nitrogen   4) Oxygen

8. Which of these halogens is the most reactive on the Period Table?
   1) I   2) Br   3) Cl   4) F

9. Which of these elements has the most nonmetallic properties?
   1) H   2) Li   3) Na   4) K

10. Which of these elements has the most nonmetallic characteristics?
    1) Radium   2) Strontium   3) Magnesium   4) Beryllium

11. Which of these elements has the least nonmetallic properties?
    1) Rb   2) Na   3) Li   4) Cs

12. Which of these elements is the most reactive nonmetal in Period 2?
    1) Carbon   2) Oxygen   3) Nitrogen   4) Neon

13. Which of these elements is more reactive than Cs?
    1) Rb   2) Ba   3) Sr   4) Fr

14. Which of these element has more metallic properties than Chlorine?
    1) S   2) Ar   3) F   4) O

15. Which of these elements has stronger metallic characteristics than Aluminum?
    1) He   2) Mg   3) Ga   4) Si

16. Which part of the Periodic Table contains elements with the strongest metallic properties?
    1) Upper right   2) Upper left   3) Lower right   4) Lower left

17. As the elements in Group 15 are considered in order of increasing atomic number, which sequence in properties occurs?

    1) metalloid $\rightarrow$ metal $\rightarrow$ nonmetal   3) nonmetal $\rightarrow$ metalloid $\rightarrow$ metal

    2) metal $\rightarrow$ metalloid $\rightarrow$ nonmetal   4) metal $\rightarrow$ nonmetal $\rightarrow$ metalloid

16. Trends in Electronegativity and Ionization Energy: Recalling Concept Facts

1. As the elements in Group 1 are considered in order from top to bottom, the electronegativity value of each successive element generally
   1) Increases   2) Decreases   3) Remains the same

2. As the elements in Group 17 of the Periodic Table are considered in order of increasing atomic number, the tendency of each successive atom to attract electron generally
   1) Increases   2) Decreases   3)) Remains the same

3. When the elements within Group 16 are considered in order of decreasing atomic number, the electronegativity value of successive element
   1) Increases   2) Decreases   3) Remains the same

4. As the elements in Period 2 are considered in order from left to right, the electronegativity value of each successive element generally
   1) Increases   2) Decreases   3) Remains the same

5. As the elements in Period 4 of the Periodic Table are considered in order of decreasing atomic number, the tendency for each successive element to gain electron during chemical bonding generally
   1) increases   2) Decreases   3)) Remains the same

6. As the elements in Group 2 are considered in order from top to bottom, the first ionization energy of each successive element generally
   2)Increases   2) Decreases   3) Remains the same

7. As the elements in Group 16 are considered in order of increasing atomic number, the tendency of each successive to lose its most loosely bound electron generally
   1) Increases   2) Decreases   3)) Remains the same

8. When elements within Group 16 are considered in order of decreasing atomic number , the first ionization energy of successive element generally
   1) Increases   2) Decreases   3) Remains the same

9. As the elements in Period 2 are considered in order from left to right, the ionization energy of each successive element generally
   1) Increases   2) Decreases   3) Remains the same

10. As the elements in Period 4 of the Periodic Table are considered in order of increasing atomic number, the tendency for each successive element to lose its electron to another atom during chemical bonding generally
    1) increases   2) Decreases   3)) Remains the same

11. When elements within Period 3 are considered in order of decreasing atomic number, ionization energy of each successive element generally
    1) Increases due to increase in atomic size
    2) Increase due to decrease in atomic size
    3) Decrease due to increase in atomic size
    4) Decrease due to decrease in atomic size

12. As the elements in Group 17 are considered in order from bottom to top, electronegativity of the elements
    1) Decreases due to increase in atomic radius
    2) Decreases due to decrease in atomic radius
    3) Increases due to increase in atomic radius
    4) Increases due to decrease in atomic size

17. Electronegativity and Ionization Energy: Comparing Elements

1. Which of these Group 2 elements has the highest electronegativity value?
   1) Be   2) Mg   3) Ca   4) Sr

2. Which of these Period 2 element has the highest electronegativity value?
   1) Nitrogen   2) Carbon   3) Boron   4) Beryllium

3. Which element has the greatest tendency to attract electrons during bonding?
   1) Se   2) S   3) Te   4) O

4. Which element has the least tendency to gain electrons?
   1) Cl   2) S   3) P   4) Si

5. Which element has the highest ionization energy?
   1) Cs   2) Na   3) K   4) Rb

6. Which of these Period 2 elements has the greatest tendency to lose its most loosely bound valence electrons?
   1) Li   2) Be   3) B   4) C

7. Which element has the least tendency to lose its electron to another atom during bonding?
   1) Potassium   2) Selenium   3) Bromine   4) Calcium

8. Which elements has a greater tendency to attract electron than phosphorous?
   1) Silicon   2) Arsenic   3) Boron   4) Sulfur

9. Which sequence of elements is arranged in order of decrease tendency to attract electrons during chemical bonding?
   1) Al, Si, P   3) Cs, Na, Li
   2) I, Br, Cl   4) C, B, Be

10. Which sequence correctly places the elements in order of increasing ionization energy?
    1) H $\rightarrow$ Li $\rightarrow$ Na $\rightarrow$ K   3) I $\rightarrow$ Br $\rightarrow$ Cl $\rightarrow$ F
    2) O $\rightarrow$ S $\rightarrow$ Se $\rightarrow$ Te   4) H $\rightarrow$ Be $\rightarrow$ Al $\rightarrow$ Ga

Survivingchem.com

Topic 3 - The Atomic Structure

1. History of Atomic Models: Recalling Concept Facts and Definitions

1. In the wave-mechanical model of the atom, the orbital is a region of the most probable location of
   1) Protons   2) Neutrons   3) Positrons   4) Electrons

2. According to the wave-mechanical model of the atom, electrons in the atom
   1) Travel in defined circle
   2) Are most likely to be found in an excited state
   3) Have a positive charge
   4) Are located in orbital outside the nucleus

3. The modern model of an atom shows that electrons are
   1) Orbiting the nucleus in fixed path
   2) Found in regions called orbital
   3) Combined with neutrons in the nucleus
   4) Located in a solid sphere covering the nucleus

4. In the wave-mechanical model, the orbital is a region in space of an atom where there is
   1) High probability of finding an electron
   2) High probability of finding a neutron
   3) Circular path in which electrons are found
   4) Circular path in which neutrons are found

5. The modern model of the atom is based on the work of
   1) One Scientist over a short period of time
   2) One scientist over a long period of time
   3) Many Scientists over a short period of time
   4) Many scientists over a long period of time

6. Over the course of the historical development of the modern atomic model, there
   1) Has been one proposed model of atom by many Scientists
   2) Has been one proposed model of atom by one Scientist
   3) Have been many proposed models of atom by many Scientists
   4) Have been many proposed models of atom by one Scientist

7. Which conclusion is based on the "gold foil experiment" and the resulting model of the atom?
   1) An atom is mainly empty space, and the nucleus has a positive charge
   2) An atom is mainly empty space, and the nucleus has a negative charge
   3) An atom has hardly any empty space, and the nucleus is positive charge
   4) An atom has hardly any empty space, and the nucleus is negative charge

8. Which group of atomic models is listed in order from the earliest to the most recent?
   1) Hard-sphere model, wave-mechanical model, electron-shell model
   2) Hard-sphere model, electron-shell model, wave mechanical model
   3) Electron-shell model, wave-mechanical model, hard-sphere model
   4) Electron-shell model, hard-sphere model, wave-mechanical model

9. Which sequence represents a correct order of historical developments leading to the modern model of the atom?
   1) Atom is a hard sphere → atom is mostly empty space → electrons exist in orbital outside the nucleus
   2) Atom is a hard sphere → electrons exist in orbital outside the nucleus → atom is mostly empty space
   3) Atom is mostly empty space → the atom is a hard sphere → electrons exist in orbital outside the nucleus
   4) Atom is empty space → electrons exist in orbital outside the nucleus → the atom is a hard sphere

10. Which order of diagrams correctly shows the historical models of the atom from the earliest to the most modern?

1)   3)

2)   4)

2. Atomic Structure: Recalling Concept Facts and Definitions

1. According to the modern atomic theory, the major portion of an atom is mostly
   1) Hard sphere 2) Electron 3) Empty space 4) Protons

2. Subatomic particles can usually pass undeflected through an atom because the volume of an atom is composed mainly by
   1) Uncharged nucleus 2) Unoccupied space 3) Neutrons only 4) Protons only

3. Which particles are found in the nucleus of an atom?
   1) Electron, only
   2) Neutrons, only
   3) Protons and electrons
   4) Protons and neutrons

4. The nucleus of an tom is the part of an atom that
   1) Consist mostly of empty space
   2) Has a negative charge
   3) Occupies most of the atom's total volume
   4) Contains most of atom's total mass

5. Experiment evidence indicates that atoms
   1) Have uniform distribution of positive charges
   2) Have uniform distribution of negative charges
   3) Contains a positively charged , dense center
   4) Contains a negatively charged, dense center

6. Compare to the entire atom, the nucleus of an atom is
   1) Smaller and contains most of atom's mass
   2) Smaller and contains little of atom's mass
   3) Larger and contains most of atom's mass
   4) Larger and contains little of atom's mass

7. What are the three subatomic particles?
   1) Positron, protons and neutrons
   2) Positron, protons, and electrons
   3) Protons, electrons and alpha particle
   4) Protons, electrons and neutrons

8. The nucleons consist of
   1) Protons and electrons
   2) Protons and neutrons
   3) Electrons and positrons
   4) Electrons and neutrons

3. Subatomic Particles: Recalling Concept Facts and Definitions

1. Which particle has a mass approximately one atomic mass unit and a unit positive charge?
   1) A neutron 2) A Proton 3) A beta particle 4) An alpha particle

2. Which particle has approximately the same mass as a proton?
   1) Alpha 2) Beta 3) Electron 4) Neutrons

3. Which subatomic particle has no charge?
   1) Protons 2) Electrons 3) Neutrons 4) Beta

4. Which of the following particles has the least mass?
   1) Protons 2) Positrons 3) Neutrons 4) Electrons

5. Which particles have approximately one atomic mass unit?
   1) Protons and electrons
   2) Protons and neutrons
   3) Electrons and positrons
   4) Electrons and neutrons

6. What is the charge and mass of an electron?
   1) Charge of +1 and a mass of 1 amu
   2) Charge of -1 and a mass of 1 amu
   3) Charge of +1 and a mass of 1/1836 amu
   4) Charge of -1 and a mass of 1/1836 amu

3. Continues

7. What are the characteristics of a neutron?
   1) It has no charge and no mass
   2) It has no charge and a mass of 1 amu
   3) It has a charge of +1 and no mass
   4) It has a charge of +1 and a mass of 1 amu

8. An electron has a charge of
   1) -1 and the same mass as a proton
   2) +1 and the same mass a proton
   3) -1 and a smaller mass than a proton
   4) +1 and a smaller mass than a proton

9. Compared to an electron, a neutron has
   1) The same mass and the same charge
   2) The same mass but a different charge
   3) A different mass but the same charge
   4) A different mass and a different charge

10. Which are true of neutrons?
    1) They have a mass of zero and are found outside the nucleus
    2) They have a mass of zero and are found inside the nucleus
    3) They have a mass 0f 1 amu and are found outside the nucleus
    4) They have a mass of 1 amu and are found inside the nucleus

11. The mass of an atom is due primarily to the
    1) Mass of protons plus the mass of electron
    2) Mass of neutrons plus the mass of electron
    3) Mass of protons plus the mass of positron
    4) Mass of neutrons plus the mass of protons

12. Which is true of protons and neutrons?
    1) They have approximately the same mass and the same charge
    2) They have approximately the same mass but different charge
    3) The have different mass and different charge
    4) They have different mass but the same charge

13. Compared with an electron, a proton has
    1) More mass and the same charge
    2) More mass and an opposite charge
    3) Equal mass and the same charge
    4) Equal mass and an opposite charge

14. The mass of a proton is approximately
    1) 1/2000 times the mass of a neutron and a unit positive charge
    2) 1/2000 times the mass of a neutron and a unit negative charge
    3) 2000 times the mass of an electron and a unit positive charge
    4) 2000 times the mass of an electron and a unit negative charge

15. A student constructs a model for comparing the mass of subatomic particles. The student selected a small metal sphere with a mass of 1 gram to represent an electron. A sphere with which mass would be most appropriate to represent a proton?
    1) 1 g   2) ½ g   3) ½000 g   4) 2000 g

4. Subatomic Particles: Relating One Particle to Another

1. The atomic number of an element is always equal to the number of
   1) Protons   2) Positrons   3) Neutrons   4) Electrons

2. In a neutral atom, the number of electrons is always equal to the number of
   1) Protons plus neutrons   2) Protons minus neutrons   3) Protons only   4) Neutrons only

3. Nuclear charge of an atom is equal to the number of
   1) Neutrons   2) Protons plus electrons   3) Neutrons plus neutrons   4) Protons

4. The mass number of an element is always equal to the number of
   1) Protons plus electron   3) Neutrons plus protons
   2) Protons plus positrons   4) Neutrons plus positrons

5. The total number of nucleons in an atom is
   1) Equal to the number of protons plus the number of electrons
   2) Equal to the number of protons plus the number of neutrons
   3) Equal to the number of protons minus the number of electrons
   4) Equal to the number of protons minus the number of electrons

6. The number of neutrons in the nucleus of an atom can be determined by
   1) Adding the mass number to the atomic number of the atom
   2) Adding the mass number to the number of electrons of the atom
   3) Subtracting the atomic number from the mass number of the atom
   4) Subtracting the mass number from the atomic number of the atom

7. The number of protons in the nucleus of an unknown element can be determined by
   1) Adding the mass number to the number of electrons of the element
   2) Subtracting the mass number from the number of neutrons of the element
   3) Adding mass number to the number of neutrons of the element
   4) Subtracting the number of neutrons from the mass number of the element

5. Subatomic Particles: Determining the Number of Subatomic Particles

1. What is the atomic number of an atom with 13 protons, 14 electrons, and 15 neutrons?
   1) 42   2) 14   3) 13   4) 27

2. An atom contains 23 electrons, 21 protons, and 24 neutrons. What is the atomic number of this atom?
   1) 44   2) 23   3) 24   4) 21

3. A particle of an atom contains 26 protons, 23 electrons, and 56 neutrons. What will be the correct atomic number for this particle?
   1) 26   2) 23   3) 56   4) 33

4. What is the total number of neutron in the nucleus of a neutral atom that has 19 electrons and a mass number of 39?
   1) 19   2) 20   3) 39   4) 58

5. An atom has a mass number of 18 and 8 protons. What is the total number of nucleons in this atom?
   1) 18   2) 8   3) 10   4) 26

6. What is the number of nucleons in an atom with 18 protons, 18 electrons, and 22 neutrons?
   1) 40   2) 36   3) 18   4) 4

7. An atom contains 83 protons, 80 electrons, and 126 neutrons. What is the mass number of this atom?
   1) 163   2) 209   3) 206   4) 46

5. Cont.

8. What is the nuclear charge of an atom with 16 protons, 18 electrons, and 17 neutrons?
   1) +16   2) +33   3) +18   4) +17

9. Which is true of an atom with 76 electrons, 117 neutrons, and a mass number 198 ?
   1) It has 79 protons and 315 nucleons   3) It has 79 protons and 198 nucleons
   2) It has 41 protons and 315 nucleons   4) It has 41 protons and 198 nucleons

10. An atom with 21 neutrons and 40 nucleons has
    1) A nuclear charge of +19   3) A mass number of 61
    2) A nuclear charge of +40   4) A mass number of 19

11. A neutral atom with atomic number of 9 and a mass number of 17 will also have
    1) 9 protons, 9 electrons, and 9 neutrons   3) 9 protons, 9 electrons, and 8 neutrons
    2) 9 protons, 8 electrons, and 9 neutrons   4) 9 protons, 8 electrons, and 8 neutrons

12. Which is true of a neutral atom with 35 protons and a mass number of 80?
    1) It has 35 electrons and 35 neutrons   3) It has 45 electrons and 80 neutrons
    2) It has 35 electrons and 45 neutrons   4) It has 45 electrons and 115 neutrons

6. Subatomic Particles: Determining Identity of an Atom

1. Atom X has 16 protons, 18 electrons, and 17 neutrons. Which element is atom X?
   1) S   2) Ge   3) In   4) Cl

2. An atom of which element could have a mass number of 39 and 20 neutrons?
   1) Y   2) Ca   3) K   4) Pr

3. A neutral atom with 7 electrons and 8 neutrons could be of element
   1) Nitrogen   2) Oxygen   3) Sulfur   4) Hydrogen

4. A neutral atom with 179 nucleons and 101 neutrons could be of element
   1) Au   2) Md   3) Si   4) Se

5. Which neutral atom could have 15 electrons, 17 neutrons and a mass of 32?
   1) Germanium   2) Phosphorous   3) Chlorine   4) Cadmium

6. Which element could have a mass number of 86 atomic mass unit and 49 neutrons in its nucleus?
   1) In   2) Rb   3) Rn   4) Au

7. An atom of fluorine has a mass of 19 amu. The total number of protons and neutrons in its nucleus is
   1) 9   2) 10   3) 19   4) 28

8. A neutral magnesium atom with 26 nucleons and 12 electrons will also has
   1) 26 protons and 12 neutrons   3) 12 protons and 38 neutrons
   2) 26 protons and 14 neutrons   4) 12 protons and 14 neutrons

7. Isotopes: Recalling Concept Facts and Definitions

1. All atoms of the same element with the same number of protons but different number of neutrons are called
   1) Charge atoms   2) Charged nuclei   3) Isomers   4) Isotopes

2. Isotopes of an element have different
   1) Number of electrons   2) Number of protons   3) Atomic numbers   4) Mass numbers

3. Isotopes are atoms that have the same number of protons but a different
   1) Atomic number   2) Number of neutron   3) Nuclear number   4) Positron

4. All isotopes of a given atom have
   1) The same mass number and the same atomic number
   2) The same mass number but different atomic number
   3) Different mass number but the same atomic number
   4) Different mass number and different atomic number

8. Isotopes: Recognizing Isotope Notations

1. Which pair of atoms are isotopes?

   1) $^{14}_{6}C$ and $^{14}_{7}N$ 2) $^{40}_{19}K$ and $^{40}_{18}Ar$ 3) $^{222}_{88}Ra$ and $^{232}_{86}Rn$ 4) $^{40}_{19}K$ and $^{42}_{19}K$

2. Which two atoms are isotopes?

   1) $^{24}_{11}Mg$ and $^{24}_{12}Na$ 2) $^{21}_{11}Na$ and $^{23}_{11}Na$ 3) $^{3}_{1}H$ and $^{3}_{3}He$ 4) $^{7}_{3}Li$ and $^{9}_{4}Be$

3. Which pair of atoms are isotopes of the same element X?

   1) $^{226}_{91}X$ and $^{226}_{91}X$ 2) $^{226}_{91}X$ and $^{227}_{91}X$ 3) $^{227}_{91}X$ and $^{227}_{90}X$ 4) $^{226}_{90}X$ and $^{227}_{91}X$

4. Which pair must represent isotopes of the same element?

   1) $^{14}_{6}X$ and $^{14}_{7}X$ 2) $^{12}_{6}X$ and $^{6}_{12}X$ 3) $^{2}_{1}X$ and $^{4}_{2}X$ 4) $^{12}_{6}X$ and $^{13}_{6}X$

5. Which pair are isotopes?
   1) Ba-56 and Mn-56   3) Ba-137 and Ba-139
   2) Cs-137 and Ba-137   4) Cr- 52 and Mn-55

6. Which two symbols correctly show two isotopes of the same elements?
   1) Iodine-53 and Xenon-54   3) Iodine-53 and Bromine-35
   2) Iodine-127 and Iodine-128   4) Iodine-127 and Iodine-53

7. Which two nucleus symbols are from atoms of the same element?

   1) (10 p / 10 n) (11 p / 11 n)   3) (18 p / 20 n) (18 p / 22 n)

   2) (10 p / 11 n) (11 p / 10 n)   4) (18 p / 20 n) (20 p / 10 n)

8. Which atom is an isotope of oxygen?
   $^{14}_{7}N$ 2) $^{16}_{8}N$ 3) $^{14}_{7}O$ 4) $^{17}_{8}O$

9. Which symbol could be an isotope of calcium ?

   1) $^{20}_{20}X$ 2) $^{20}_{40}X$ 3) $^{40}_{20}X$ 4) $^{40}_{40}X$

10. Which name is correct for the isotope symbol represented as $^{19}_{9}X$?

    1) Potassium – 19   2) Potassium - 9   3) Fluorine – 19   4) Fluorine - 9

11. If one isotope of an element has the symbol $^{86}_{37}X$. Which symbol could represent a different isotope of element X?
    1) Rb - 88   2) Rb - 37   3) Rn – 86   4) In - 49

9. Isotope Symbols: Determining Number of Subatomic Particles

1. What is the mass number of $^{31}_{15}P$?

   1) 31   2) 15   3) 16   4) 46

2. What is the total number of protons in the nucleus of the symbol $^{40}_{18}Ar$?

   1) 40   2) 12   3) 58   4) 18

3. What will be the total number of protons and neutrons in the nucleus of $^{227}_{91}X$?

   1) 91   2) 136   3) 227   4) 318

4. What is the total number of nucleons in the nuclide $^{65}_{30}Zn$?

   1) 65   2) 30   3) 35   4) 95

5. The atom of $^{21}_{10}Ne$ has a nuclear charge of

   1) +21   2) +10   3) +11   4) +31

6. The number of electrons in the neutral atom of $^{15}_{8}O$ is

   1) 7   2) 15   3) 8   4) 23

7. How many neutrons can be found in the neutral atom of Mg-26?
   1) 12   2) 14   3) 26   4) 38

8. What is the mass number of sodium – 23 ?
   1) 23   2) 11   3) 12   4) 34

9. What is the total number of neutrons in an atom of Pb - 207?
   1) 82   2) 125   3) 207   4) 289

10. Which information is correct for the nuclide $^{34}_{16}X$?

    1) It has 16 protons, 15 electron, and 16 neutron
    2) It has 16 protons, 15 electrons and 16 neutrons
    3) It has 16 protons, 16 electrons, and 34 neutrons
    4) It has 16 protons, 16 electrons, and 18 neutrons

11. Which is true of the isotope symbol $^{9}_{4}Be$?

    1) It has 4 protons, 4 electrons, and 9 neutrons
    2) It has 9 protons , 9 electrons, and 4 neutrons
    3) It has 4 protons, 4 electrons, and 5 neutrons
    4) It has 9 protons, 4 electrons, and 5 neutrons

9. Continues

12. The atom of chlorine – 37 has
   1) 17 protons and a mass number of 37
   2) 17 protons and a mass number of 18

   3) 37 protons and a mass number of 17
   4) 37 protons and a mass number of 18

13. The nucleus of $^{127}_{53}$ I contains

   1) 53 neutrons and 127 protons
   2) 53 protons and 127 neutrons

   3) 53 protons and 74 electrons
   4) 53 protons and 74 neutrons

14. The nucleus of which atom contains 48 neutrons?

   1) $^{32}_{16}$ S
   2) $^{48}_{21}$ Ti
   3) $^{85}_{37}$ Rb
   4) $^{112}_{48}$ Cd

15. Which atom contains only 12 nucleons in its nucleus?

   1) $^{12}_{6}$ C
   2) $^{24}_{12}$ Mg
   3) $^{8}_{4}$ Be
   4) $^{23}_{11}$ Na

16. An isotope of element krypton has 46 neutrons and 36 protons. Which symbol correctly identifies this isotope?

   1) $^{46}_{36}$ Kr
   2) $^{36}_{46}$ Kr
   3) $^{82}_{36}$ Kr
   4) $^{82}_{46}$ Kr

17. Which nuclide contains exactly 15 protons?
   1) Sulfur – 32
   2) Phosphorous – 32
   3) Oxygen – 15
   4) Nitrogen – 14

18. Which nuclide contains 15 neutrons?
   1) Phosphorous – 15
   2) Nickel – 28
   3) Silicon – 29
   4) Oxygen – 15

10. Isotope symbols: Comparing Number of Particles in Nuclides

1. Compare to the atom of $^{40}_{20}$ Ca, the atom of $^{38}_{18}$ Ar has

   1) Greater nuclear charge
   2) Greater number of neutrons

   3) The same number of nuclear charge
   4) The same number of neutrons

2. Compare to an atom of ^{12} C, an atom of ^{14} C has
   1) More protons
   2) More neutrons

   3) Fewer protons
   4) Fewer neutrons

3. Compare to a neutral atom of Potassium - 42 , a neutral atom of Calcium – 40 contains fewer
   1) Protons
   2) Electrons

   3) Neutrons
   4) Nuclear charge

4. An atom of K- 37 and an atom of K – 42 differ in their total number of
   1) Electrons
   2) Protons

   3) Neutrons
   4) Positron

 Survivingchem.com

10. **Continues**

5. The nuclides ^{14}C and ^{14}N are similar in that they both have the same
    1) Mass number 2) Atomic Number 3) Number of neutrons 4)Nuclear charge

6. Which pair of atoms do the nuclei contain the same number of neutrons?

    1) $^{7}_{3}Li$ and $^{9}_{4}Be$ 2) $^{40}_{19}K$ and $^{41}_{19}K$ 3) $^{42}_{20}Ca$ and $^{40}_{18}Ar$ 4) $^{14}_{7}N$ and $^{16}_{8}O$

7. In which pair do the atoms have the same number of neutrons?

    1) ^{24}Mg and ^{24}Na 2) ^{15}N and ^{16}O 3) ^{32}Si and ^{31}P 4) ^{32}S and ^{33}S

8. Which two isotopes contain the same number of neutrons?
    1) H-1 and He-3   2) H-2 and He-4   3) H-3 and He-3   4) H-3 and He-4

9. In which pair of atoms do the nuclei contain the same number of neutrons?
    1) Calcium-40 and Calcium-42   3) Bromine – 83 and Krypton - 83
    2) Chlorine-35 and Sulfur- 34   4) Iodine – 127 and Bromine – 80

10. Which pair of atom does the nuclide contains the same number of nucleons?

    1)$^{121}_{50}Sn$ and $^{119}_{50}Sn$ 2) $^{19}_{8}O$ and $^{20}_{9}F$ 3) $^{222}_{88}Ra$ and $^{222}_{86}Rn$ 4) $^{226}_{88}Ra$ and $^{228}_{88}Ra$

11. Which isotope contains the greatest nuclear charge?
    1)^{37}Cl 2) ^{42}K 3) ^{40}Ar 4) ^{40}Ca

12. Which symbol has the smallest nuclear charge?
    1) Cu – 65   2) Zn – 64   3) Ga – 69   4) Ge - 72

13. Which nucleus contains the greatest number of neutrons?
    1)S – 32   2) S – 33   3) P – 31   4) P – 33

14. Which of the following nuclei has a nucleus with the fewest number of neutrons?

    1) $^{58}_{27}Co$ 2) $^{60}_{27}Co$ 3) $^{58}_{28}Ni$ 4) $^{60}_{28}Ni$

15. In which isotope does the nucleus contains the greatest number of nucleons?

    1) $^{226}_{88}Ra$ 2) $^{224}_{87}Fr$ 3) $^{223}_{86}Rn$ 4) $^{210}_{85}At$

16. Which symbol shows a proton to neutron ratio of 1 : 1 ?

    1) $^{1}_{1}H$ 2) $^{19}_{9}F$ 3) $^{32}_{16}S$ 4) $^{39}_{19}K$

17. In which nucleus is the ratio of protons to neutrons 1 : 1?
    1) N - 14   2) N - 16   3) O – 15   4) O – 17

18. For most atoms with an atomic number of less than 20, nuclear stability occurs when the ratio of
    neutrons to protons is 1 : 1 . Which of the following atoms is likely to have a stable nucleus?
    1)^{3}He 2) ^{13}C 3) ^{16}N 4) ^{24}Mg

11. Isotope symbols: Recognizing Notation of Nuclides

1. Chlorine − 37 can also be represented as

   1) $^{35}_{17}\text{Cl}$

   2) $^{37}_{17}\text{Cl}$

   3) $^{17}_{35}\text{Cl}$

   4) $^{17}_{37}\text{Cl}$

2. Magnesium -26 is the same as

   1) $^{26}_{26}\text{Mg}$

   2) $^{26}_{12}\text{Mg}$

   3) $^{12}_{26}\text{Mg}$

   4) $^{12}_{12}\text{Mg}$

3. The symbol $^{223}_{85}\text{Fr}$ can also be represented as

   1) Fr − 85

   2) Fr − 138

   3) Fr − 223

   4) Fr − 308

4. The isotope symbol $^{27}_{13}\text{Al}$ can also be represented as

   1) Aluminum−27

   2) Aluminum−13

   3) Aluminum−14

   4) Aluminum-40

5. Which diagram represents the nucleus of an atom $^{27}_{13}\text{Al}$?

   1) (14 n / 27 p)

   2) (14 n / 13 p)

   3) (27 n / 13 p)

   4) (40 n / 13 p)

6. Which diagram correctly represents the nucleus of the symbol $^{37}_{17}\text{X}$?

   1) (17 n / 37 p)

   2) (37 n / 17 p)

   3) (20 n / 17 p)

   4) (17 n / 20 p)

7. The nucleus diagram can also be written as

   1) $^{31}_{15}\text{P}$

   2) $^{16}_{15}\text{P}$

   3) $^{31}_{16}\text{S}$

   4) $^{15}_{16}\text{S}$

8. The nucleus diagram of an atom is . Which symbol correctly represents this atom?

   1) $^{35}_{45}\text{Rh}$

   2) $^{80}_{45}\text{Rh}$

   3) $^{80}_{35}\text{Br}$

   4) $^{45}_{35}\text{Br}$

12. Electron Shells: Determining Number of Electron Shells in an Atom

1. How many electron shells containing electrons are in a neutral atom of Oxygen?
   1) 1   2) 2   3) 6   4) 16

2. What is the total number of electron shells in an atom of Bromine?
   1) 1   2) 2   3) 4   4) 7

3. The electron configuration of an atom in the ground state is $2 - 4$. The total number of occupied electron shells in this atom is
   1) 2   2) 4   3) 6   4) 8

4. How many electron shells are in a ground state atom with atomic number of 18?
   1) 1   2) 2   3) 3   4) 4

5. Which is a ground state electron configuration of an atom in the fourth electron shell?
   1) $2 - 8 - 4$ 2) $2 - 8 - 18 - 4$ 3) $2 - 8 - 18 - 18 - 4$ 4) $2 - 4$

6. Which electron configuration is of an atom with three electron shells?
   1) 2   2) $2 - 3$ 3) $2 - 8 - 8$ 4) $2 - 8 - 18 - 3$

7. An atom has atomic number of 56. What is the minimum number of electrons shells that is need to contain all of its electrons in the ground state?
   1) 5   2) 18   3) 56   4) 6

8. A neutral atom with 48 electrons has a ground state electron configuration with
   1) one electron shell containing the electrons
   2) three electron shells containing the electrons
   3) four electron shells containing the electrons
   4) five electron shells containing the electrons

9. Which of these atoms in the ground state has the most number of electron shells containing electrons?
   1) Cs-132   2) Xe - 134   3) I - 127   4) Na - 23

10. Which of the following elements has an atom with the least number of electron shells containing electrons?
    1) Cl   2) F   3) Na   4) K

13. Electron Shells

1. Which electron shell of a sulfur atom contains electrons with the least amount of energy?
   1) 1   2) 2   3) 3   4) 6

2. In the configuration, $2 - 8 - 8 - 1$, which electron shell contains electrons with the most energy?
   1) 4th 2) 3rd 3) 8th 4) 1st

3. In the ground state configuration of calcium, in which electron shell would one find electrons with the most energy?
   1) 2nd shell   2) 3rd shell   3) 4th shell   4) 8th shell

4. In the ground state atom of silicon, which electron shell contains electron with the greatest amount of energy?
   1) First electron shell   3) Third electron shell
   2) Second electron shell   4) Fourth electron shell

5. In a bromine atom in the ground state, the electrons that has the least amount of energy are located in the
   1) first electron shell   3) third electron shell
   2) second electron shell   4) fourth electron shell

14. Electron Shells: Maximum Number of Electrons

1. What is the maximum number of electrons that can occupy the second energy level of an atom?
   1) 2   2) 8   3) 7   4) 17

2. What is the most number of electrons that can be found in the 4th energy level of an atom?
   1) 2   2) 8   3) 18   4) 32

3. Which electron shell of an atom can hold a maximum of 72 electrons?
   1) 7th shell   2) 6th shell   3) 5th shell   4) 4th shell

15. Electron Configurations: Determining Number of Electrons in a Shell

1. How many electrons are in the 3rd electron shell of a neutral strontium atom in the ground state?
   1) 2   2) 3   3) 8   4) 18

2. What is the number of electrons in the second electron shell of a ground state atom of calcium?
   1) 1   2) 2   3) 8   4) 20

3. How many electrons are found in the 5th electron shell of an element with atomic number of 52?
   1) 6   2) 5   3) 8   4) 18

4. The element with atomic number of 9 has how many electrons in the 2nd energy level?
   1) 2   2) 7   3) 9   4) 8

5. The total number of electrons found in the configuration of a neutral chromium atom is
   1) 24   2)6   3)13   4) 1

6. In the electron configuration $2 - 8 - 18 - 18 - 1$, how many electrons are in the electron shell with the least amount of energy?
   1) 1   2) 2   3) 8   4) 18

7. What is the total number of electron in the atom with a configuration of $2 - 8 - 18 - 4$?
   1) 2   2) 18   3) 32   4) 28

8. How many total electrons are in the configuration $2 - 2 - 1$?
   1) 1   2) 2   3) 4   4) 5

9. Which electron shell of a potassium atom in the ground state contains 1 electron?
   1) 1   2) 2   3) 3   4) 4

10. An atom in the ground state has a configuration of $2 - 8 - 18 - 3$. Which electron shell of this atom contains a total of three electrons?
   1) 1   2) 2   3) 3   4) 4

16. Electron Configurations: Determining Partially Filled Shells

1. Which of these ground state electron configurations is of an atom with two partially filled electron shells?
   1) 2 − 8 − 8 − 1   2) 2 − 8 − 18 − 2   3) 2 − 8 − 18 − 7   4) 2 − 8 - 2

2. An atom of which element in the ground state has a partially filled second electron shell ?
   1) Hydrogen   2) Lithium   3) Potassium   4) Sodium

3. The atom of which element has an incomplete third electron shell?
   1) Calcium   2) Bromine   3) Krypton   4) Silver

4. Which Period 2 atom in the ground state has a half- filled second electron shell?
   1) Be   2) B   3) C   4) N

5. Which of these elements has a completely filled third electron shell?
   1) Al   2) Cl   3) Kr   4) Ne

17. Electron Configurations: Relating Number of Protons to Configuration

1. What is the total number of protons in a neutral atom with a ground state electron configuration of 2 − 8 − 18 − 32 − 18 − 1?
   1) 69   2) 79   3) 118   4) 197

2. A neutral atom with a configuration of 2 − 8 − 8 − 3 will have how many total protons in its nucleus?
   1) 2   2) 3   3) 8   4) 21

3. An atom has a configuration of 2 − 8 − 18 − 4 − 1. How many protons are there in the nucleus of this atom?
   1) 1   2) 32   3) 33   4) 18

4. What is the nuclear charge of an atom with a configuration of 2 − 8 − 13 − 1 ?
   1) +6   2) -6   3) -24   4) +24

5. What is the nuclear charge of an atom with a configuration of 2–8–18–18–7 ?
   1) +53   2) +7   3) -1   4) +1

6. What is the ground state electron configuration of a neutral atom with 27 protons?
   1) 2 − 8 − 14 − 3   3) 2 − 8 − 15 − 2
   2) 2 − 8 − 8 − 8 − 1   4) 2 − 8 − 17

7. An atom has 17 protons in its nucleus. What is the ground state configuration of this atom?
   1) 2 − 8 − 7   3) 2 − 8 − 8 − 7
   2) 2 − 8 − 8 - 1   4) 2 − 8 − 6 − 1

8. An atom with a nuclear charge of +48 will have a ground state configuration of
   1) 2 − 8 − 8 − 8 − 8 − 8 − 8   3) 2 − 8 − 18 − 17 − 3
   2) 2 − 8 − 18 − 18 − 2   4) 2 − 18 − 18 − 2

9. An atom with 19 electrons will have a ground state configuration of
   1) 2 − 8 − 8 − 1   2) 2 − 8 − 7 − 2   3) 2 − 8 − 6- 3   4) 2 − 8 − 5 − 4

9. A neutral atom has 34 electrons? What is the ground state electron configuration for this atom?
   1) 2 − 8 − 8 −16   2) 2 − 8 − 18 − 6   3) 2 − 18 − 8 − 6   4) 2 − 18 − 14

18. Ground and Excited States: Recalling Concept Facts and Definitions

1. As an electron of an atom moves from the ground state to the excited state, its energy
       1) Decreases   2) Increases   3) Remains the same

2. As an electron of an atom moves from the excited to the ground state, the total energy of the atom
       1) Decreases   2) Increases   3) Remains the same

3. When compared with the energy of a carbon atom in the excited state, the energy of the carbon atom in the ground state is
       1) Greater   2) Lower   3) Same

4. What happens as an electron in an atom moves from a high electron shell to a lower electron shell?
    1) The energy of the electron increases
    2) The energy of the electron decreases
    3) The total number of electrons increases
    4) The total number of electrons decreases

5. Compared to a sodium atom in the ground state, the sodium atom in the excited state must have
    1) A greater number of electrons   3) An electron with greater energy
    2) A smaller number of electrons   4) An electron with smaller energy

6. As an electron in an atom moves from the ground state to the excited state, the electron
    1) Releases energy as it moves to a lower energy level
    2) Releases energy as it moves to a higher energy level
    3) Absorbs energy as it moves to a lower energy level
    4) Absorbs energy as it moves to a higher energy level

7. When an electron in an atom moves from the excited state to the ground state, the result is the
    1) Absorption of energy by the electron as it moves to a lower energy state
    2) Absorption of energy by the electron as it moves to a higher energy state
    3) Emission of energy by the electron as it moves to lower energy state
    4) Emission of energy by the electron as it moves to a higher energy state

8. As an electron moves from a higher energy level to a lower energy level, the electron will
       1) Lose energy   2) Lose a proton   3) Gain energy   4) Gain a proton

9. When an electron in excited atom returns to a lower energy state, the energy emitted can result in the production of
    1) Alpha particle   3) Isotopes
    2) Protons   4) Spectral lines

10. The characteristic bright-line spectrum of an element occurs when electrons
    1) Move from lower to higher energy levels   3) Are lost by a neutral atom
    2) Moves from higher to lower energy levels   4) Are gained by a neutral atom

11. During a flame test, ions of a specific metal are heated in the flame of a gas burner. A characteristic color of light is emitted by those ions in the flame when the electrons
    1) Gain energy as they return to lower energy levels
    2) Gain energy as they return to higher energy levels
    3) Emit energy as they return to lower energy levels
    4) Emit energy as they return to higher energy levels

12. Electron X can change to a higher or a lower electron shell. Which statement is true of electron X?
    1) Electron X absorbs energy and produces spectral lines when moving to lower shell
    2) Electron X absorbs energy and produces spectral lines when moving to higher shell
    3) Electron X emits energy and produces spectral lines when moving to lower shell
    4) Electron X emits energy and produces spectral lines when moving to higher shell

     Survivingchem.com

19. Electron Transition: Relating Electron Transition to Energy and Spectral Lines

1. Which electron transition represents a gain of energy by the electron?
   1) From 3rd to 2nd shell
   2) From 3rd to 1st shell
   3) From 4th to 1st shell
   4) From 1st to 2nd shell

2. An electron in the atom of lithium can move from one level to another. The transition between which two levels will result in the emission of energy by the electron ?
   1) 3rd to 2nd level
   2) 1st to 3rd level
   3) 2nd to 3rd level
   4) 1st to 2nd level

3. Which electron transition will result in the greatest amount of energy released by the electron?
   1) 1st to 2nd
   2) 3rd to 2nd
   3) 1st to 3rd
   4) 3rd to 1st

4. The highest amount of energy will be emitted by an electron when it moves from
   1) 4th to 1st electron shell
   2) 1st to 4th electron shell
   3) 1st to 5th electron shell
   4) 5th to 4th electron shell

5. Which energy level change by an electron of hydrogen atom will cause the greatest amount of energy to be absorbed?
   1) Second to fourth level
   2) Fourth to second level
   3) Second to fifth level
   4) Fifth to second level

6. An electron in an atom of neon will gain the most energy when moving from
   1) 2nd to 3rd electron shell
   2) 3rd to 2nd electron shell
   3) 2nd to 4th electron shell
   4) 4th to 2nd electron shell

7. Which electron transition will produce spectral lines?
   1) From 2nd to 1st shell
   2) From 3rd to 5th shell
   3) From 2nd to 3rd shell
   4) From 3rd to 4th shell

8. Electron transition between which shells in an atom of magnesium will cause the emission of bright line spectra by the atom?
   1) 4th to 3rd
   2) 1st to 3rd
   3) 3rd to 4th
   4) 2nd to 3rd

9. An atom of oxygen is in the excited state. When an electron in this atom moves from third to second shell, energy is
   1) Emitted by the nucleus
   2) Absorbed by the nucleus
   3) Emitted by the electron
   4) Absorbed by the electron

10. An electron in the fourth electron shell of an atom moves to the second electron shell. Which statement is true of the electron?
    1) The electron gains energy and produces spectral lines
    2) The electron gains energy and produces an alpha particle
    3) The electron emits energy and produces spectral lines
    4) The electron emits energy and produces an alpha particle

11. How do the energy and the most probable location of an electron in the third shell of an atom compares to the energy and the most probable location of an electron in the first shell of the same atom?
    1) In the third shell, an electron has more energy and is closer to the nucleus
    2) In the third shell, an electron has more energy and is farther from the nucleus
    3) In the third shell, an electron has less energy and is closer to the nucleus
    4) In the third shell, an electron has less energy and is farther from the nucleus

20. Ground and Excited State Configurations

1. What is the electron configuration of a sulfur atom in the ground state?
   1) $2 - 4$ 2) $2 - 6$ 3) $2 - 8 - 4$ 4) $2 - 8 - 6$

2. Which electron configuration represents an atom of lithium in an excited state?
   1) $1 - 1$ 2) $1 - 2$ 3) $2 - 1$ 4) $2 - 2$

3. Which electron configuration could represent a strontium atom in the excited state?
   1) $2 - 8 - 18 - 7 - 1$ 2) $2 - 8 - 18 - 7 - 3$ 3) $2 - 8 - 18 - 8 - 1$ 4) $2 - 8 - 18 - 8 - 2$

4. An atom has 16 protons and 16 electrons. Which is the electron configuration of this atom in the excited state?
   1) $2-18-8-4$ 2) $2-8-6$ 3) $2-18-8-8-3-1$ 4) $2-8-5-1$

5. Atom X has 8 protons and 8 electrons. Which configuration shows this atom in the excited state?
   1) $2 - 6$ 2) $1 - 7$ 3) $2 - 8 - 6$ 4) $2 - 8 - 8$

6. Which is a configuration of an atom in the excited state?
   1) $2 - 8 - 1$ 2) $2 - 8 - 3$ 3) $2 - 8$ 4) $2 - 1 - 2$

7. Which configuration shows an atom in the excited state?
   1) $2 - 8 - 7 - 8$ 2) $2 - 8 - 8$ 3) 2 4) $2 - 8 - 1$

8. The electron configuration $2 - 8 - 2$ is of a
   1) sodium atom in the ground state
   2) sodium atom in the excited state
   3) magnesium atom in the ground state
   4) magnesium atom in the excited state

9. The electron configuration $2 - 8 - 5 - 1$ is of a(n)
   1) oxygen atom in the ground state
   2) oxygen atom in the excited state
   3) sulfur atom in the ground state
   4) sulfur atom in the excited state

10. The electron configuration $2 - 8 - 18 - 2 - 1$ is of
    1) Ga atom in the excited state
    2) Ga atom in the ground state
    3) Al atom in the excited state
    4) Al atom in the ground state

21. Neutral Atoms and Ions: Recalling Concept Facts and Definitions

1. An atom with equal number of protons to electrons are called
   1) Positive ion 2) Negative ion 3) Neutral atom 4) Isotope

2. What type of particle contains more protons than electrons?
   1) A neutral atom 2) A Positive ion 3) A negative ion 4) An isomer

3. An atom that contains less electrons than protons is called
   1) A neutral atom 2) An alpha particle 3) A Positive ion 4) A negative ion

4. A neutral atom must have the same number of protons and
   1) Electrons 2) Neutrons 3) Positrons 4) Nuclear charge

5. The total number of electrons in a neutral atom must always be equal to the atom's
   1) Mass number 2) Atomic number 3) Atomic mass 4) Number of nucleons

6. An atom that has a negative charge must have
   1) Greater number of protons than electrons
   2) Equal number of protons to electrons
   3) Greater number of electrons to protons
   4) Equal number of electrons and neutrons

7. Which statement is true of all negative ions?
   1) They contain equal number of protons to electrons
   2) They contain equal number of protons to neutrons
   3) They contain more electrons than protons
   4) They contain less electrons than protons

Survivingchem.com

22. Neutral Atoms and Ions: Comparing Particles

1. A positive ion is formed when a neutral atom
    1) Loses electrons
    2) Loses protons
    3) Gains electrons
    4) Gains electrons

2. A neutral atom can become a positive charge ion by
    1) Losing neutrons
    2) Losing energy
    3) Losing protons
    4) Losing electrons

3. A neutral oxygen atom (O) differs from an ion of oxygen (O^{2-}) in that the atom has
    1) more protons
    2) more electrons
    3) fewer protons
    4) fewer electrons

4. Compared to Be^{2+} ion, a Be^0 atom has
    1) more protons
    2) more electrons
    3) fewer protons
    4) fewer electrons

5. Compared to a neutral nonmetal, a negative ion of the same nonmetal atom has
    1) more electrons
    2) less electron
    3) more protons
    4) less protons

6. When an atom becomes a positive ion, the radius of the atom
    1) Remains the same   2) Increases   3) Decreases

7. When an atom becomes a negative ion, the size of the atom
    1) Remains the same   2) Increases   3) Decreases

8. A nonmetal atom is likely to
    1) Lose electrons and become a positive ion
    2) Gain electrons and become a positive ion
    3) Lose electrons and become a negative ion
    4) Gain electrons and become a negative ion

9. Which change occurs as a metallic atom loses electrons and becomes a positive ion?
    1) The ion has less electron and a smaller size than the atom
    2) The ion has less electron and a bigger size than the atom
    3) The ion has more electrons and a smaller size than the atom
    4) The ion has more electrons and a bigger size than the atom

10. Which changes occur as an atom becomes a positively charge ion?
    1) The atom gains electrons, and the number of protons increases
    2) The atom gains electrons, and the number of protons remains the same
    3) The atom loses electrons, and the number of protons decreases
    4) The atom loses electrons, and the number of protons remains the same

11. Which statement is correct as a nonmetallic element gains electron and becomes a negative ion?
    1) The ion has less electron and smaller size than the atom
    2) The ion has less electron and a bigger size than the atom
    3) The ion has more electrons and a smaller size than the atom
    4) The ion has more electrons and a bigger size than the atom

12. Compared to a negative ion, a neutral atom of the same element
    1) Is smaller because it has less electrons
    2) Is smaller because it has more electrons
    3) Is bigger because it has less electrons
    4) Is bigger because it has more electrons

23. Ions: Determining Number of Particles

1. What is the total number of electrons in S^{2-} ion?
   1) 10   2) 14   3) 16   4) 18

2. The total number of electrons in F^- ion is
   1) 9   2) 8   3) 10   4) 17

3. What is the total number of electrons in a Cr^{3+} ion?
   1) 3   2) 21   3) 24   4) 27

4. The total number of electrons in a Mg^{2+} ion is
   1) 10   2) 2   3) 12   4) 24

5. How many electrons are in a potassium atom with a +1 charge?
   1) 18   2) 19   3) 21   4) 1

6. What is the ionic charge of an atom of strontium with 36 electrons?
   1) +2   2) -2   3) +38   4) − 36

7. An atom has 16 protons, 17 neutrons and 18 electrons. What is the charge of this atom?
   1) +2   2) -1   3) +2   4) -2

8. An atom has a nuclear charge of 50 and 46 electrons. The net ionic charge of this atom is
   1) +46   2) -46   3) -4   4) +4

9. An atom contains has a nuclear charge of +7, 10 electrons, and 8 neutrons. What is the ionic charge of this atom?
   1) +7   2) − 1   3) − 3   4) +3

10. The ion P^{3-} has
    1) 15 protons and 15 electrons   3) 18 protons and 15 electrons
    2) 15 protons and 18 electrons   4) 18 protons and 18 electrons

11. An atom with a nuclear charge of +14 and an ionic charge of -4 has
    1) 14 protons and 18 electrons   3) 14 protons and 4 electrons
    2) 14 protons and 14 electrons   4) 4 protons and 14 electrons

12. The ion Mn^{4+} has
    1) 25 protons and 25 electrons   3) 25 protons and 21 electrons
    2) 25 protons and 4 electrons   4) 21 protons and 25 electrons

13. Which is true of a sodium ion ($Na^{+)}$?
    1) It has a nuclear charge of +1 and 11 electrons
    2) It has a nuclear charge of +11 and 12 electrons
    3) It has a nuclear charge of +1 and 10 electrons
    4) It has a nuclear charge of +11 and 10 electrons

Survivingchem.com

24. Ionic Configurations: Determining and Interpreting Electron Configurations of Ions

1. Which is the correct electron configuration for a sodium ion (Na^+) ?
   1) $2 - 8 - 1$ 2) $2 - 8 - 8$ 3) $2 - 7 - 1$ 4) $2 - 8$

2. Which electron configuration is correct for B^{3+} ion?
   1) 2 2) $2 - 3$ 3) $2 - 8$ 4) $2 - 2 - 1$

3. The configuration for Sr^{2+} is
   1) $2 - 8 - 18 - 8 - 2$ 2) $2 - 8 - 18 - 10$ 3) $2 - 8 - 18$ 4) $2 - 8 - 18 - 8$

4. The ionic configuration for a calcium ion is
   1) $2 - 8 - 8 - 2$ 2) $2 - 8 - 2$ 3) $2 - 8 - 8$ 4) $2 - 8 - 8 - 8$

5. Which electron configuration is correct for P^{3-} ion?
   1) $2 - 8 - 8$ 2) $2 - 8$ 3) $2 - 8 - 8 - 8$ 4) $2 - 8 - 5 - 3$

6. Which configuration is correct for a Br^- ion?
   1) $2 - 8 - 18 - 7$ 2) $2 - 8 - 18$ 3) $2 - 8 - 18 - 8$ 4) $2 - 18 - 8 - 8$

7. The electron configuration for an ion of oxygen could be
   1) $2 - 4$ 2) $2 - 5$ 3) $2 - 7$ 4) $2 - 8$

8. The electron configuration $2 - 8 - 18 - 8$ could represent which particle?
   1) Ca^{2+} 2) Ge^{4-} 3) Cl^- 4) Br^{5+}

9. A ionic configuration of $2 - 8$ could be of element
   1) Nitrogen   2) Beryllium   3) Calcium   4) Sulfur

10. The configuration 2 could represent a configuration for
    1) An atom of B   2) An ion of B   3) An atom of F   4) An ion of F

Topic 4: Chemical bonding

1. Chemical Bonding: Recalling Concept Facts and Definitions

1. Chemical bonding is the simultaneous attraction of two nuclei to
   1) Protons   2) Neutrons   3) Electrons   4) Positron

2. When atoms bond, their stability
   1) Increase   2) Decrease   3) Remain the same

3. When atoms bond, the electron configuration of each atom in the bond resembles that of the nearest
   1) Noble gas   2) Halogen   3) Alkaline earth   4) Alkali

4. Atoms bond due to the interaction between
   1) Protons and neutrons   3) Neutrons and electrons
   2) Protons and electrons   4) Neutrons and positrons

5. One main reason atoms bond is to
   1) Get a stable electron configuration   3) To gain protons
   2) Get an unstable electron configuration   4) To lose x

2. Bonded Atoms and Noble Gas Configurations

1. When a hydrogen atom bonds with another atom, the electron configuration of the hydrogen atom will be similar to that of the element
   1) Lithium   2) Oxygen   3) Neon   4) Helium

2. When an atom of oxygen bonds with a metal, the electron configuration of the oxygen ion will be similar to the configuration of which atom?
   1) Neon   2) Fluorine   3) Helium   4) Sulfur

3. When the atom of calcium bonds with oxygen to produce calcium oxide, the electron configuration of the calcium ion in the compound is similar to that of the atom of
   1) O   2) Ar   3) Kr   4)) K

4. Which compound contains ions with electron configurations of both ions similar to that of Helium?
   1) LiH   2) LiF   3) NaH   4) NaCl

5. In which compound would the configuration of the atoms in the compound resembles that of Argon?
   1) Al_2O_3 2) K_2O 3) $CaCl_2$ 4) NaCl

6. A bond between which two atoms will produce ions with electron configurations that are similar to those of Kr and Ne, respectively ?
   1) Li and Cl   2) K and Cl   3) Al and Br   4) Sr and F

7. When sodium and fluorine atoms combine to produce the compound NaF, the ions formed have the same electron configuration as the atom of
   1) Argon, only   3) Both argon and neon
   2) Neon, only   4) Neither argon and neon

8. When the atoms of magnesium and chlorine bond to form the compound $MgCl_2$, the electron configurations of the ions in this compound is similar to those of the atoms of
   1) Calcium and Bromine   3) Neon and Helium
   2) Beryllium and Fluorine   4) Neon and Argon

9. Atom X and atom Y bond to form a compound. The electron configuration of X in the bond is $2 - 8 - 8$. The electron configuration of Y in the compound is $2 - 8$. Which two atoms could be X and Y?
   1) X could be magnesium and Y could be sulfur   3) X could be calcium and Y could be sulfur
   2) X could be magnesium and Y could be oxygen   4) X could be calcium and Y could be oxygen

10. Which statement is true of the electron configurations of the ions in the compound potassium bromide?
    1) Potassium ion will resemble that of Krypton, and bromine ion will resemble that of Argon
    2) Potassium ion will resemble that of Argon, and bromine ion will resemble that of Krypton
    3) Both potassium and bromine ions will resemble the configuration of argon
    4) Both potassium and bromine ions will resemble the configuration of krypton

3. Bonding and Energy: Recalling Concept Facts and Definitions

1. When a bond is formed between two atoms, the stability of the atoms
   1) Increases   2)Decreases   3) Remained the same

2. As a bond is formed between atoms, potential energy of the atoms generally
   1) Decreases   2) Increases   3) Remains the same

3. When a bond is broken in a chemical substance, the stability of the atoms
   1) Remained the same   2) Decreases   3) Increases

4. As a bond is broken in a compound, the potential energy of the atoms generally
   1) Remained the same   2) Decreased   3) Increased

5. Bond formation between two atoms is generally
   1) Exothermic , which absorbs energy   3)Endothermic , which absorbs energy
   2) Exothermic, which releases energy   4) Endothermic, which releases energy

6. The breaking of a bond of a chemical substance is
   1) Exothermic , which absorbs energy   3) Endothermic , which absorbs energy
   2) Exothermic, which releases energy   4) Endothermic, which releases energy

7. When a bond is form between atoms, energy is generally
   1) Released   3) Both released and absorbed
   2) Absorbed   4) Neither released not absorbed

8. When a bond is broken in compounds, energy is generally
   1) Released   3) Both released and absorbed
   2) Absorbed   4) Neither released not absorbed

9. When two atoms form a bond to produce a chemical substance, the stability of the chemical system
   1) Decreases as energy is absorbed   3) Increases as energy is absorbed
   2) Decreases as energy is released   4) Increases as energy is released

10. When a bond is broken in a chemical substance, the stability of the chemical system
    1) Decreases as energy is absorbed   3) Increases as energy is absorbed
    2) Decreases as energy is released   4) Increases as energy is releases

11. What type of energy is stored in the bonds of chemical substances?
    1) Kinetic energy   3) Activation energy
    2) Potential energy   4) Ionization energy

12. The amount of potential energy in chemical bonds of substances depends on
    1) The composition of the chemical substances only
    2) The structure of the chemical substances only
    3) Both the composition and the structure of chemical substances
    4) Neither the composition nor the structure of chemical substances

    Survivingchem.com

4. Bonding and Energy

1. Which statement is true concerning the reaction

$$N(g) \quad + \quad N(g) \quad \rightarrow \quad N_2(g)$$

   1) A bond is broken and energy is absorbed   3) A bond is formed and energy is absorbed
   2) A bond is broken and energy is released   4) A bond is formed and energy is released

2. Given the balanced equation:

$$I_2 \quad \rightarrow \quad I \quad + \quad I$$

   Which statement describes the process represented by this equation?

   1) A bond is formed, and energy will be absorb   3) A bond is broken, and energy will be absorb
   2) A bond is formed, and energy will be release   4) A bond is broken, and energy will be release

3. Given the equation

$$H \quad + \quad H \quad \rightarrow \quad H_2$$

   Which statement best describes this process?

   1) It is exothermic, and a bond is formed   3) It is endothermic, and a bond is formed
   2) It is exothermic, and a bond is broken   4) It is endothermic, and a bond is broken

4. Which statement is true concerning the process taking place in the reaction

$$AB \quad + \quad energy \quad \rightarrow \quad A \quad + \quad B$$

   1) A bond is broken and energy is absorbed   3) A bond is formed and energy is absorbed
   2) A bond is broken and energy is released   4) A bond is formed and energy is released

5. Given the balanced equation representing a reaction

$$Cl_2(g) \quad + \quad energy \quad \rightarrow \quad Cl(g) \quad + \quad Cl(g)$$

   What occurs during this change?

   1) Energy is released and a bond is formed   3) Energy is absorbed and a bond is formed
   2) Energy is released and a bond is broken   4) Energy is absorbed and a bond is broken

6. In the balanced equation

$$HCl \quad \rightarrow \quad H_2 \quad + \quad Cl_2$$

   Which is correct of the process taking place as bonds are broken and formed?

   1) The breaking of H–Cl bond is exothermic   3) The forming of H–H bond is exothermic
   2) The breaking of H–Cl bond is exothermic   4) The forming of Cl–Cl bond is endothermic

7. Given the reaction:

$$H_2 \quad + \quad Cl_2 \quad \rightarrow \quad 2\,HCl$$

   Which statement best describes the energy changes as bonds are formed and broken in this reaction?

   1) The breaking of Cl–Cl bond absorbs energy   3) The forming of H–Cl bond absorbs energy
   2) The breaking of H–H bond releases energy   4) The forming of H–Cl bond absorbs energy

4. Continues

8. What occurs as a molecule of bromine separates into two bromine atoms?
    1) Energy would be absorbed as a bond is broken   3) Energy would be released as a bond is broken
    2) Energy would be absorbed as a bond is formed 4) Energy would be released as a bond is formed

9. When two fluorine atoms combined to form a molecule of fluorine, energy is
    1) Always absorbed   3) Sometimes absorbed
    2) Always released   4) Sometimes released

10. When a molecule of water is formed from oxygen and hydrogen atoms,
    1) A bond will be formed, and energy will be absorbed
    2) A bond will be broken, and energy will be absorbed
    3) A bond will be formed, and energy will be released
    4) A bond will be broken, and energy will be released

5. Ionic Bond: Recalling Concept Facts and Definitions

1. Ionic bonding usually occurred between the atoms of
    1) A metal and another metal   3) A metal and a nonmetal
    2) A nonmetal and another nonmetal   4) Two of the same metalloid

2. When combining with nonmetallic atoms, metallic atoms generally
    1) Lose electrons and form negative ions   3) Gain electrons and form negative ions
    2) Lose electrons and form positive ions   4) Gain electrons and form positive ions

3. When combining with a metallic atom, a nonmetallic atom tends to
    1) Lose electrons and forms a negative ion   3) Gain electrons and forms a negative ion
    2) Lose electrons and forms a positive ion   4) Gain electrons and forms a positive ion

4. When two atoms form an ionic bond, the electronegativity difference between these two atoms is generally
    1) Greater than 1.7   3) Exactly zero
    2) Less than 1.7   4) Less than Zero

5. In ionic bonding, electrons are
    1) Always shared between a metal and a nonmetal atoms
    2) Always shared between two different nonmetals atoms
    3) Always transferred from a metal atom to a nonmetal atom
    4) Always transferred from a nonmetal atom to a metal atom

6. Ionic bonding is formed when
    1) A Nonmetal loses electrons to a metal, which gains the electrons
    2) A Nonmetal loses electrons another nonmetal, which gains the electron
    3) A Metal atom loses electrons to a another metal, which gains the electrons
    4) A Metal atom loses electrons to a nonmetal, which gains the electrons

7. Which is true of a metallic atom in ionic bond with a nonmetal atom?
    1) The metal is usually a positive charged ion, because it had loss electrons
    2) The metal is usually a positive charged ion, because it had gained electrons
    3) The metal is usually a negative charged ion, because it had loss electrons
    4) The metal is usually a negative charged ion, because it had gained electrons

8. When a nonmetal atom forms ionic bond with a metal, the nonmetal becomes a
    1) positive ion, because it had gained electrons
    2) positive ion, because it had gained protons
    3) negative ion, because it had gained electrons.
    4) negative ion, because it had gained protons.

     Survivingchem.com

6. Covalent Bond: Recalling Concept Facts and Definitions

1. A Covalent bond is formed between atoms of
    1) Two nonmetals
    2) Two metals
    3) A metal and a nonmetal
    4) A metal and a metalloid

2. Covalent bonding occurs when electrons are
    1) Transferred from a metallic atom to a nonmetallic atom
    2) Transferred from a nonmetallic atom to a metallic atom
    3) Shared between metallic atoms
    4) Shared between nonmetallic atoms

3. When two atoms form a covalent bond, the electronegativity difference between these two atoms is generally
    1) Greater than 1.7
    2) Less than 1.7
    3) Exactly zero
    4) Less than Zero

4. The sharing of electrons in covalent bonding
    1) Must always be equal
    2) Must always be unequal
    3) Is either equal nor unequal
    4) Can be equal or unequal

5. Which list includes only types of covalent bonding?
    1) Polar, Nonpolar, and metallic
    2) Polar, nonpolar, and network solid
    3) Network solid, polar, and metallic
    4) Network solids, metallic, and nonpolar

7. Polar and Nonpolar Covalent Bonds: Recalling Concept Facts and Definitions

1. The bonding in polar covalent bonding occurs when
    1) Two of the same metals share electrons
    2) Two of the same nonmetals share electrons
    3) Two different metals share electrons
    4) Two different nonmetals share electrons

2. Sharing of electrons in polar covalent bonding is usually
    1) Unequal between two different nonmetals
    2) Unequal between two of the same nonmetals
    3) Equal between two different nonmetals
    4) Equal between two of the same nonmetals

3. Nonpolar covalent bonding occurs when
    1) Two of the same metals share electrons
    2) Two of the same nonmetals share electrons
    3) Two different metals share electrons
    4) Two different nonmetals share electrons

4. Sharing in nonpolar covalent bonding is usually
    1) Unequal between two different nonmetals
    2) Unequal between two of the same nonmetals
    3) Equal between two of the same nonmetals
    4) Equal between two different nonmetals

5. When two atoms form a polar covalent bond, the electronegativity difference between these two atoms is generally
    1) Exactly zero
    2) Below Zero
    3) Less than 1.7 but greater than zero
    4) Greater 1.7

6. When two atoms formed a nonpolar covalent bond, the electronegativity difference between these two atoms is usually
    1) About zero
    2) Below Zero
    3) Exactly 1.7
    4) Greater 1.7

8. Network Solid and Coordinate Covalent Bonds: Recalling Concept Facts and Definitions

1. The bonding in network solids is
   1) Ionic   2) Covalent   3) Metallic   4) Hydrogen

2. Substances containing network solid bonding contain
   1) Particles that are molecule
   2) Particles that are ions
   3) Particles that are metallic
   4) No discrete particles

3. Network solid bonding forms substances that have
   1) Low melting points
   2) High melting points
   3) High electrical conductivity
   4) High solubility in water

4. A coordinate covalent bonding is formed when
   1) An atom transfers one of its electron to a hydrogen ion
   2) An atom shares one of its electron with a hydrogen ion
   3) An atom transfers two of its electrons to a hydrogen ion
   4) An atom shares two of its electron with a hydrogen ion

5. A coordinate covalent bond can be form between
   1) A hydrogen ion and a hydrogen atom of ammonia molecule
   2) A hydrogen ion and a nitrogen atom of ammonia molecule
   3) A sodium ion and a hydrogen atom of ammonia molecule
   4) A sodium ion and a nitrogen atom of ammonia molecule

6. A coordinate covalent bonding will form by interaction between
   1) A hydrogen ion and an oxygen atom of a water molecule
   2) A hydrogen ion and a hydrogen atom of a water molecule
   3) A chlorine ion and an oxygen atom of a water molecule
   4) A chlorine ion and a hydrogen atom of a water molecule

7. Which two substances can form a coordinate covalent bond with a proton?
   1) NH_3 and NH_4^+
   2) H_2O and H_3O^+
   3) NH_3 and H_2O
   4) NH_4^+ and H_3O^+

9. Metallic Bond: Recalling Concept Facts and Definitions

1. Metallic bonding is best described as
   1) Positive ions in the sea of positive electrons
   2) Positive ions in the sea of mobile electrons
   3) Negative ions in the sea of positive electrons
   4) Negative ions in the sea of mobile electrons

2. Metallic bonding occurs between metal atoms that have
   1) Filled energy levels and low ionization energy
   2) Filled energy levels and high ionization energy
   3) Unfilled energy levels and low ionization energy
   4) Unfilled energy levels and high ionization energy

3. The ability to conduct electricity in the solid state is a characteristic of metallic substances. This characteristics is best explained by the presence of
   1) High ionization energy
   2) High electronegativity
   3) Mobile protons
   4) Mobile electrons

        Survivingchem.com

10. Types of Bonding: Determining bond type from bond descriptions

1. Which type of bond is formed when electrons are shared between two atoms?
   1) Covalent   2) Ionic   3) Metallic   4) Hydrogen

2. Which kind of bond is formed between a proton (H^+) and a water molecule?
   1) Nonpolar covalent   2) Coordinate covalent   3) Polar   4) Network solid

3. Which type of bonding involves positive ions immersed in a sea of mobile electrons?
   1) Polar covalent   2) Nonpolar covalent   3) Ionic   4) Metallic

4. Atom X loses electrons to atom Y. The bond that is formed between X and Y is best described as
   1) Metallic   2) Ionic   3) Covalent   4) Coordinate

5. The transfer of electrons from a metal to a nonmetal will result in the formation of
   1) Hydrogen bond   3) Ionic bond
   2) Covalent bond   4) Metallic bond

6. Two atoms with an electronegativity difference of 0.4 form a bond that is
   1) Ionic, because electrons are shared   3) Covalent, because electrons are shared
   2) Ionic, because electrons are transferred   4) Covalent, because electrons are transferred

7. Two atoms share electrons equally, the bond formed is mostly
   1) Polar and covalent   3) Metallic and covalent
   2) Ionic and covalent   4) Nonpolar and covalent

8. Which type of bond exists in a molecule in which electrons are shared unequally between the two atoms of the molecule?
   1) A polar covalent bond with an electronegativity difference of zero
   2) A polar covalent bond with an electronegativity difference greater than zero
   3) A nonpolar covalent bond with an electronegativity difference of zero
   4) A nonpolar covalent bond with an electronegativity difference greater than zero

9. When one atom loses one or more electrons to another, the bond that is formed between the two atoms is
   1) Ionic with electronegativity difference of greater than 1.7
   2) Ionic with electronegativity difference of less than 1.7
   3) Covalent with electronegativity difference of greater than 1.7
   4) Covalent with electronegativity difference of less than 1.7

10. Atom X bonds with another atom X to form X_2 molecule. The bond in this molecule is
    1) Polar because electrons are shared equally
    2) Nonpolar because electrons are shared equally
    3) Polar because electrons are shared unequally
    4) Nonpolar because electrons are shared unequally

11. Ionic Bonding: Determining formulas and names containing ionic bonding

1. In which formula would the bonding between the atoms is described as ionic?
   1) HNO_3 2) NH_4 3) H_2O 4) KCl

2. Which bond is ionic?
   1) N − O 2) Na − O 3) C − O 4) H − F

3. Which pair of elements form a bond that is mostly ionic?
   1) $CaCl_2$ 2) CCl_4 3) HCl 4) PCl_5

4. Atoms in which compound are held together by ionic bonds?
   1) CH_4 2) $AlCl_3$ 3) H_2O 4) NH_3

5. Which element would most likely form an ionic bond with chlorine?
   1) O 2) N 3) S 4) Sr

6. Which electron configuration belongs to an elements that would form ionic bond with aluminum?
   1) 2 − 3 2) 2 − 8 − 14 − 2 3) 2 − 8 − 6 4) 2

7. Which compound contains elements that are held together by ionic bonds?
   1) Carbon dioxide 3) Lithium bromide
   2) Carbon monoxide 4) Hydrogen bromide

8. Which pair of atoms will form ionic bond?
   1) Hydrogen and sulfur 3) Magnesium and magnesium
   2) Hydrogen and oxygen 4) Magnesium and phosphorous

9. Elements in which two Groups of the Periodic Table would combine to form a bond that is ionic?
   1) Group 1 and Group 2 3) Group 2 and Group 16
   2) Group 2 and Group 13 4) Group 17 and Group 18

10. Element X combines with rubidium to form an ionic bond. In which Group of the Periodic Table could element X be found?
    1) Group 1 3) Group 2
    2) Group 13 4) Group 16

12. Covalent Bond: Determining formulas and names containing covalent bonding

1. Which chemical formula contains atoms that are held together by covalent bonds?
   1) KCl 2) $CaCl_2$ 3) $AlCl_3$ 4) HCl

2. Which pair of atoms are held together by a covalent bond?
   1) N-H 2) Li-H 3) Na-H 4) Ca − H

3. Which substance has atoms held together by a covalent bond?
   1) H_2 2) Na 3) NaCl 4) NaH

4. Which compound contains atoms held together by covalent bonds?
   1) Sodium chloride 3) Aluminum oxide
   2) Calcium hydride 4) Nitrogen (II) oxide

5. Which element would most likely form a covalent bond with a chlorine atom?
   1) Iron 3) Phosphorous
   2) Beryllium 4) Potassium

6. A covalent bond will form between elements from which two groups of the Periodic Table?
   1) Group 16 and Group 18 3) Group 1 and Group 2
   2) Group 16 and Group 17 4) Group 13 and Group 17

Survivingchem.com

13. Polar/nonpolar/coordinate/network solid: Determining formulas and names

1. Which formula contains nonpolar covalent bonds?
   1) NH_3 2) H_2O 3) O_2 4) NaCl

2. In which formula are the atoms held together by nonpolar covalent bonds?
   1) F_2 2) OF_2 3) HF   4) LiF

3. Which pair of atoms are held together by a nonpolar covalent bond?
   1) Co – Cl   2) K – O   3) N – H   4) N – N

4. The bonding in which formula is polar covalent?
   1) H_2O 2) H_2 3) O_2 4) Na_2O

5. Which compound contains atoms held together by polar bonds?
   1) $CaCl_2$ 2) CO_2 3) O_2 4) Li_2O

6. Which two atoms are held together by a polar covalent bond?
   1) Br-Cl   2) Al-Cl   3) Cl-Cl   4) Sr-Cl

7. In which substance is the bonding network covalent?
   1) O_2 2) SiO_2 3) NaCl   4) HCl

8. Which substance contains network solid covalent bonding?
   1) H_2O 2) SO_2 3) C   4) Br_2

9. Coordinate covalent bonding would be found in which species?
   1) Hydronium ion   2) Hydrogen ion   3) Oxygen   4) Sodium chloride

10. Which formula contains atoms held together by a coordinate covalent bond?
    1) SiC   2) $CaCl_2$ 3) NH_3 4) NH_4^+

14. Metallic bonding: Determining formula and names containing metallic bonding

1. In which substance would the atoms be held together by a metallic bonding?
   1) Calcium   2) Carbon   3) Oxygen   4) Helium

2. The atoms of which substance are held together by a metallic bond?
   1) H_2(g)   2) H_2O(ℓ)   3) SiC(s)   4) Fe(s)

3. Which substance contains metallic bonding?
   1) Sodium Chloride   3) Hydrogen chloride
   2) Carbon   4) Copper

4. Which electron configuration belongs to a substance whose atoms are held together by metallic bonds?
   1) 2 – 8 – 8   2) 1   3) 2 – 8 – 18 – 18   4) 2 – 8 – 18 – 5

15. Ionic and covalent bonding: Determining formula containing both ionic and covalent

1. Which formula contains both ionic and covalent bonds?
   1) MgS
   2) NaBr
   3) $C_6H_{12}O_6$
   4) $MgSO_4$

2. Which compound contains atoms that are held together by ionic and covalent bonds?
   1) H_2O
   2) SiC
   3) $NaNO_3$
   4) CH_4

3. Which formula contains both ionic and covalent bonds?
   1) $Ca(OH)_2$
   2) HCl
   3) CH_3OH
   4) P_2O_4

4. Which compound contains both ionic and covalent bonds?
   1) Ammonia
   2) Lithium sulfate
   3) Methane
   4) Potassium chloride

5. Which compound has atoms that are held together by both ionic and covalent bonds?
   1) Ammonium chloride
   2) Hydrogen chloride
   3) Sodium Chloride
   4) Copper(II) Chloride

16. Bond Types Determining formula based on bond description

1. Which substance contains bonds resulting from a transfer of electrons from one atom to another?
   1) CO_2
   2) NH_3
   3) KBr
   4) Cl_2

2. Which pair of atoms will share electrons when a bond is formed between them?
   1) Ba and I
   2) Br and F
   3) K and Cl
   4) Li and I

3. In which compound do the atoms form bonds by sharing electrons?
   1) CCl4
   2) Na_2O
   3) CaO
   4) MgO

4. In which substance is the bonding between the atoms a result of equal sharing of electrons?
   1) Br_2
   2) Na
   3) CO_2
   4) NH_3

5. In which substance is the bonding between the atoms a result of positive ions in the sea of mobile electrons?
   1) C
   2) N_2
   3) He
   4) Ni

6. The bonding in which compound a result of unequal sharing of electrons between the atoms?
   1) H_2S
   2) H_2
   3) Cl_2
   4) NaCl

7. Which pair of atoms will form a bond when electrons are transferred from one atom to the other?
   1) C and O
   2) Ca and O
   3) N and O
   4) O and O

8. Which pair of electrons configurations belong to atoms that will share electrons when they bond with each other?
   1) $2-8-2$ and $2-8-1$
   2) $2-8-18-8$ and $2-8-13-1$
   3) $2-8-6$ and $2-8-18-7$
   4) $2-8-5$ and $2-8-18-8-1$

 Survivingchem.com

Topic 4: Chemical bonding

17. Bond Types: Determining bond based on atoms in formula or name

1. The bonding in calcium phosphate, $Ca_3(PO_4)_2$, can be best described as
   1) Covalent, only
   2) Both covalent and ionic
   3) Ionic, only
   4) Neither covalent nor ionic

2. Which best describes the bonding in Cl_2?
   1) Polar and covalent
   2) Nonpolar and covalent
   3) Network sold and covalent
   4) Coordinate and covalent

3. Which type of bond is found between the C and H atoms in a molecule of methane, CH_4?
   1) Covalent bonds
   2) Ionic bonds
   3) Hydrogen bonds
   4) Metallic bonds

4. The bonding in a hydronium ion, H_3O^+, is best described as
   1) Polar and covalent
   2) Nonpolar and covalent
   3) Network solid and covalent
   4) Coordinate and covalent

5. The C – Cl bond in CCl_4 is best described as
   1) Ionic, because electrons are transferred
   2) Ionic, because electrons are shared
   3) Covalent, because electrons are transferred
   4) Covalent, because electrons are shared

6. Bonding between the two bromine atoms in a bromine molecule is best described as
   1) Ionic
   2) nonpolar covalent
   3) polar covalent
   4) Network Covalent

7. The transfer of electrons from a sodium atom to a chlorine atom results in the formation of
   1) Coordinate covalent bond
   2) Polar covalent bond
   3) Nonpolar covalent bond
   4) Ionic bond

8. The carbon atoms in diamond are held together by
   1) Metallic bonds
   2) Ionic bonds
   3) Hydrogen bonds
   4) Covalent bonds

9. A bond that holds atoms of nickel together is
   1) Metallic bond
   2) Network covalent bond
   3) Ionic bonds
   4) Coordinate covalent bond

10. As a bond between a hydrogen atom and a sulfur atom is formed, electrons are
    1) Shared to form an ionic bond
    2) Shared to form a covalent bond
    3) Lost and gained to form an ionic bond
    4) Lost and gained to form a covalent bond

11. As a bond is formed between atoms of lithium and Iodine, electrons are
    1) Shared to form an ionic bond
    2) Shared to form a covalent bond
    3) Lost and gained to form an ionic bond
    4) Lost and gained to form a covalent bond

17. Cont.

12. Bonding in ammonia is best described as
    1) Covalent
    2) Coordinate
    3) Ionic
    4) Metallic

13. Magnesium nitrate contains chemical bonds that are
    1) Covalent only
    2) Both covalent and ionic
    3) Ionic Only
    4) Neither covalent nor ionic

14. Bonding between the atoms in a water molecule is
    1) Nonpolar covalent
    2) Polar covalent
    3) coordinate covalent
    4) Network solid

15. When a reaction occurs between atoms with ground state electron configurations of 2 -1 and 2 – 7, the bond formed is mainly
    1) Polar covalent
    2) Metallic
    3) Nonpolar covalent
    4) Ionic

16. Element magnesium bonds with oxygen to form magnesium oxide, MgO. This bond is mostly
    1) Ionic, because electrons are shared between Mg and O
    2) Ionic, because electrons are transferred from Mg to O
    3) Covalent, because electrons are shared between Mg and O
    4) Covalent, because electrons are transferred from Mg to O

17. Which type of bond exists in a molecule of hydrogen iodide?
    1) A polar covalent bond, with an electronegativity difference of zero
    2) A polar covalent bond, with an electronegativity difference greater than zero
    3) A nonpolar covalent bond, with an electronegativity difference of zero
    4) A nonpolar covalent bond, with an electronegativity difference greater than zero

18. Two atoms with ground state electron configurations of 2 – 8 – 8 – 1 and 2- 8 – 6 would most likely form a bond that is
    1) Covalent, because there will be a sharing of electrons
    2) Covalent, because there will be a transferring of electrons
    3) Ionic, because there will be a sharing of electrons
    4) Ionic, because there will be a transferring of electrons

19. An atom with electronegativity of 0.9 bonds with an atom with electronegativity of 3.1. Which phrase best describes the bond between the elements of these atoms?
    1) Mostly covalent in character, and is formed between two nonmetals
    2) Mostly covalent in character, and is formed between a metal and a nonmetal
    3) Mostly ionic in character, and is formed between a metal and a nonmetal
    4) Mostly ionic in character, and is formed between two nonmetals

20. An element with electronegativity value of 3.5 bonds with an element with electronegativity value of 3.0.
    Which best describes the bond between these two elements?
    1) Mostly covalent in character, and is formed between two nonmetals
    2) Mostly covalent in character, and is formed between a metal and a nonmetal
    3) Mostly ionic in character ,and is formed between a metal and a nonmetal
    4) Mostly ionic in character, and is formed between two nonmetals

 Survivingchem.com

18. Molecular substances, shapes and polarity: Recalling Concept Facts and Definitions

1. Which term refers to the smallest unit of a covalent substance?
   1) Allotrope   2) Molecule   3) Isomer   4) Isotope

2. When two atoms form a chemical bond by sharing electrons, the resulting molecule will be
   1) Polar, only   3) Either polar or nonpolar
   2) Nonpolar, only   4) Neither polar nor nonpolar

3. Two nonmetal atoms of the same element share electrons equally. The resulting molecule is
   1) Polar, only   3) Either polar or nonpolar
   2) Nonpolar, only   4) Neither polar nor nonpolar

4. Symmetrical distribution of charge in a molecule resulted in the molecule being
   1) Ionic   3) Network solid
   2) Polar   4) Nonpolar

5. Asymmetrical distribution of charge in a molecule usually resulted in the molecule being
   1) Polar   3) Nonpolar
   2) Metallic   4) Ionic

6. Bonding in all diatomic molecules is
   1) Polar, and the molecule is always polar
   2) Nonpolar, and the molecule is always polar
   3) Polar, and the molecule is always nonpolar
   4) Nonpolar, and the molecule is always nonpolar

7. The bonding in nonpolar molecules usually resulted in the molecule having
   1) Asymmetrical shape with equal charge distribution
   2) Asymmetrical shape with unequal charge distribution
   3) Symmetrical shape with equal charge distribution
   4) Symmetrical shape with unequal charge distribution

8. Which best describes the shape and charge distribution in polar molecules?
   1) Asymmetrical shape with equal charge distribution
   2) Asymmetrical shape with unequal charge distribution
   3) Symmetrical shape with equal charge distribution
   4) Symmetrical shape with unequal charge distribution

19. Molecular polarity: Determining formula of polar and nonpolar molecules

1. Which formula represents a polar molecule?
   1) Br_2 2) CO_2 3) CH_4 4) NH_3

2. Which molecule is polar?
   1) H_2 2) N_2 3) CH_4 4) HF

3. Which formula represents a polar molecule?
   1) KCl   2) PCl_2 3) Cl_2 4) NaCl

4. The molecule of which substance is polar?
   1) H_2S 2) N_2 3) H_2 4) CH_4

5. Which formula represents a polar molecule containing polar covalent bonds.
   1) HBr   2) CCl_4 3) CH_4 4) CO_2

6. The molecules of which substance is nonpolar?
   1) NaCl   2) H_2O 3) CH_4 4) HI

7. Which formula represent a nonpolar molecule containing nonpolar bonds?
   1) KCl   2) O_2 3) NH_3 4) CH_4

8. The formula of which substance represents a nonpolar molecule containing nonpolar bonds?
   1) CH_4 2) CO_2 3) H_2O 4) N_2

9. Which formula represents a nonpolar molecule containing polar covalent bonds?
   1) CO_2 2) HBr   3) K_2O 4) H_2

10. The formula of which substance represents a nonpolar molecule with polar covalent bonds?
    1) NH_3 2) Na   3) CH_4 4) Cl_2

11. The shape and bonding in Hydrogen fluoride, HF, are best described as
    1) Symmetrical and polar
    2) Symmetrical and nonpolar
    3) Asymmetrical and polar
    4) Asymmetrical and nonpolar

12. The shape and bonding in diatomic bromine molecule are best described as
    1) Symmetrical and polar
    2) Symmetrical and nonpolar
    3) Asymmetrical and polar
    4) Asymmetrical and nonpolar

13. Which best explains why CCl_4 molecule is nonpolar?
    1) CCl_4 has a symmetrical charge distribution
    2) C and Cl have the same electronegativity
    3) CCl_4 is a gas at room temperature
    4) C and Cl are nonmetals

14. Two fluorine atoms are held together by a covalent bond to form F_2. Which statement correctly describes the bond and the molecular polarity of F_2?
    1) The bond is polar, and F_2 is a polar molecule
    2) The bond is polar, and F_2 is a nonpolar molecule
    3) The bond is nonpolar, and F_2 is a polar molecule
    4) The bond is nonpolar, and F_2 is a nonpolar molecule

15. Which best describes the bonding in a molecule of ammonia, NH_3?
    1) The bonding is polar, and NH_3 is a polar molecule
    2) The bonding is polar, and NH_3 is a nonpolar molecule
    3) The bonding is nonpolar, and NH_3 is a polar molecule
    4) The bonding is nonpolar, and NH_3 is a nonpolar molecule

 Survivingchem.com

20 . Molecular structures and shapes: Recognizing bond and molecular polarity by structures

1. Which diagram best represents a polar molecule?

 1)

Cl_2

 2)

HCl

3) ∞

H_2

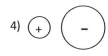 4) (+) (−)

Na Cl

2. Which molecule is polar?

1) H − S
     |
     H

2) H − C − H
   (with H above and H below C)

3) O = C = O

4) N ≡ N

3. Which molecule is polar?

1) Li − Cl

2) H − N − H
         |
         H

3) Cl − Cl

4) H-C-H
   (with H above and H below C)

4. Which structural formula represents a polar molecule?

1) H − H

2) Na − H

3) H − Br

4) O = O

5. Which structural formula represents a nonpolar symmetrical molecule?

1) Na − Cl

2) O = C = O

3) H − I

4) O with H and H

6. Which structural formula is linear and nonpolar?

1) H − Cl

2) H − C − H
   (with H above and H below C)

3) H − N − H
         |
         H

4) Cl − Cl

7. The structure of which molecule is nonpolar with polar covalent bonds?

1) Cl − C − Cl
   (with Cl above and Cl below C)

2) O with H and H

3) N − N

4) H − F

8. Which formula has a tetrahedral shape and is symmetrical?

1) H − N − H
         |
         H

2) S with H and H

3) F − C − F
   (with F above and F below C)

4) H − H

21. Degree of bond and molecular polarity: Determining formula with most and least polarity

1. The degree of bond and molecular polarity of a compound can be predicted by determining the difference in
    1) Melting points of the elements in the compound
    2) Densities of the elements in the compound
    3) Electronegativity values of the elements in the compound
    4) Atomic masses of the elements in the of the compound

2. Which of these formulas contain a bond with the most ionic characteristics?
    1) $NaCl$ 2) $MgCl_2$ 3) KCl 4) $CaCl_2$

3. Which bond is the least ionic?
    1) $Al - O$ 2) $Li - O$ 3) $N - O$ 4) $S - O$

4. The bonding in which compound has the least degree of ionic character?
    1) KBr 2) HF 3) MgO 4) PCl_3

5. Which bond has the greatest degree of covalent characteristics?
    1) $C - O$ 2) $H - O$ 3) $F - O$ 4) $N - O$

6. The bonding in which molecule has the greatest degree of covalent characteristics?
    1) CF_4 2) BeF_2 3) BF_3 4) LiF

7. A bond between which two atoms has the least covalent characteristics?
    1) CaO 2) NO_2 3) SO_2 4) H_2

8. Which pair of atoms forms a bond that is the least covalent?
    1) Ba and I   2) Br and Cl   3) K and Cl   4) Li and I

9. Which molecule is the most polar?
    1) $H - Br$ 2) $H - Cl$ 3) $H - F$ 4) $H - I$

10. Which molecule is the most polar?
    1) NH_3 2) CCl_4 3) CH_4 4) CO_2

11. Which molecule is the least polar?
    1) H_2O 2) HCl 3) HBr 4) H_2

12. In which substance are the molecule the most polar?
    1) H_2Te 2) H_2Se 3) H_2S 4) H_2O

     Survivingchem.com

Topic 4: Chemical bonding

22. Electrons in bonding: Determining Number of electrons lost, gained, or shared

1. As sodium reacts with fluorine to form the compound NaF, each sodium atom will
   1) Gain 1 electron
   2) Gain 2 electrons
   3) Lose 1 electron
   4) Lose 2 electrons

2. When magnesium reacts with oxygen to form MgO, magnesium atom will
   1) Transfer 1 electron to oxygen
   2) Transfer 2 electrons to oxygen
   3) Share 1 electron with oxygen
   4) Share 2 electrons with oxygen

3. What is the total number of pairs of electrons shared in a molecule of N_2?
   1) One pair
   2) Two pairs
   3) Three pairs
   4) Four Pairs

4. An oxygen molecule contains a double bond because the two atoms of oxygen share a total of
   1) 1 electron
   2) 2 electrons
   3) 3 electrons
   4) 4 electrons

5. The Cl – Cl bond in Cl_2 means that the chlorine atoms share
   1) 1 pair of electrons
   2) 2 pairs of electrons
   3) 3 pairs of electron
   4) 4 pairs of electrons

6. The total number of electrons shared between the atom of oxygen and the two atoms of hydrogen of a water molecule is
   1) 2
   2) 4
   3) 6
   4) 8

7. Which is true of a lithium atom and a chlorine atom when they react to form LiF?
   1) Lithium will lose 1 electron and chlorine will gain 1 electron
   2) Lithium will lose 2 electrons and chlorine will gain 2 electron
   3) Lithium will gain 1 electron and chlorine will lose 1 electron
   4) Lithium will gain 2 electrons and chlorine will lose 2 electrons

8. When potassium atom bonds with oxygen to form the compound K_2O,
   1) Each oxygen will gain 1 electron from each potassium atom
   2) Each oxygen atom will gain 2 electrons from each potassium atom
   3) Each oxygen will lose 1 electron to each potassium atom
   4) Each oxygen will lose 2electron to each potassium atom

23. Atoms in bonding: Determining number of atoms needed to form a stable configuration:

1. For an atom of oxygen to form a stable configuration during bonding with element beryllium, it must bond with
   1) One beryllium atom
   2) Two beryllium atoms
   3) Three beryllium atoms
   4) Four beryllium atom

2. A barium atom attains a stable electron configuration when it bonds with
   1) One chlorine atom
   2) Two chlorine atoms
   3) One sodium atom
   4) Two sodium atom

3. A potassium atom attains a stable electron configuration when it bonds with
   1) 1 chlorine atom
   2) 2 chlorine atoms
   3) 3 chlorine atoms
   4) 4 chlorine atoms

4. An atom of nitrogen is most stable when it bonds with
   1) One sodium atom
   2) One magnesium atom
   3) One aluminum atom
   4) One calcium atom

5. An atom of fluorine can attain a stable noble gas configuration if it bonds by sharing
   1) One electron with a hydrogen atom to form an ionic bond
   2) One electron with a hydrogen atom to form a covalent bond
   3) Two electrons with a hydrogen atom to form an ionic bond
   4) Two electrons with a hydrogen atom to form a covalent bond

24. Types of substances: Identifying ionic, molecular, and network solid substances:

1. Which formula represents an ionic compound?
   1) NaCl   2) N_2O 3) HCl   4) H_2O

2. Which formula represents an ionic compound?
   1) $FeCl_2$ 2) Fe   3) Cl_2 4) PCl_3

3. Which of the following compound is ionic compound?
   1) K I   2) CO_2 3) HCl   4) H_2O

4. The formula of which compound ionic?
   1) H_2 2) NH_4Cl 3) CH_4 4) CH_3OH

5. Which compound is ionic?
   1) H_2SO_4 2) CO   3) Na_2SO_4 4) H_2

6. Which formula represents a molecular substance?
   1) KCl   2) NaCl   3) LiCl   4) HCl

7. Which substance is a molecular compound?
   1) O_2 2) Cu   3) CuO   4) FeO

8. Which is a molecular compound?
   1) $NaC_2H_3O_2$ 2) NH_3 3) $C_6H_{12}O_6$ 4) NaCl

9. Which is a network solid substance?
   1) SiO_2 2) NaCl   3) NH_3 4) H_2O

10. Which substance can exist as a network solid?
    1) Carbon dioxide   2) Carbon   3) Zinc   4) Oxygen

11. Which is a metallic substance?
    1) He   2) O_2 3) Cl   4) Au

12. Which is a metallic substance?
    1) Diamond   2) Calcium Oxide   3) Nickel   4) Neon

13. Which two substances are covalent compounds?
    1) $C_6H_{12}O_6(s)$ and KI(s)   3) KI(s) and NaCl(s)
    2) $C_6H_{12}O_6(s)$ and HCl(g)   4) NaCl(s) and HCl(g)

14. Which compound is ionic?
    1) Water   3) Methane
    2) Ammonia   4) Lithium bromide

15. Which compound is ionic?
    1) Carbon dioxide   3) Nitrogen dioxide
    2) Sodium nitrate   4) Hydrogen chloride

16. Which name represents a covalent substance?
    1) Magnesium oxide   3) Mercury
    2) Aluminum oxide   4) Ammonia

17. Which is a molecular substance?
    1) Water   3) Sodium chloride
    2) Diamond   4) Copper

25. Identifying Properties of Substances: Recalling Concept Facts

1. A characteristic of ionic solids is that they have
   1) High melting points
   2) Low melting points
   3) High electrical conductivity
   4) Low solubility water

2. Which characteristic is a property of molecular substances?
   1) Good heat conductivity
   2) Good electrical conductivity
   3) Low melting point
   4) High melting point

3. Which two characteristics are properties of metallic substances?
   1) High solubility in water and high electrical conductivity
   2) High solubility in water and low electrical conductivity
   3) Low solubility in water and high electrical conductivity
   4) Low solubility in water and low electrical conductivity

4. Which is true of the conductivity of metallic substances?
   1) Metallic substances conduct electricity as solids and liquids
   2) Metallic substances conduct electricity only as liquids
   3) Metallic substances conduct electricity due to mobile ions
   4) Metallic substances conduct electricity due to mobile protons

5. Which is true of conductivity of ionic substances?
   1) Ionic substances can conduct electricity as solids
   2) Ionic substances can conduct electricity as liquids only
   3) Ionic substances conduct electricity as aqueous and as liquids
   4) Ionic substances do not conduct electricity at all

6. Which properties best accounts for the high conductivity of metallic substances?
   1) High electronegativity
   2) High ionization energy
   3) Highly mobile electrons
   4) Highly mobile protons

7. Conductivity of ionic substances when dissolved in water is primarily due to the presence of
   1) Mobile positive ions, only
   2) Mobile negative ions, only
   3) Mobile positive and negative ions
   4) Mobile electrons in valence shell

8. Which type of substance has low melting point, and is a poor conductor of heat and electricity?
   1) Network solids
   2) Molecular solids
   3) Metallic solids
   4) Ionic solids

9. A substance has a melting point of 1074 K and conducts electricity when dissolved in water, but does NOT conduct electricity in the solid phase. The substance is most likely
   1) Network solid
   2) Molecular solid
   3) Metallic solid
   4) Ionic solid

10. Which terms describe a substance that has a low melting point and poor electrical conductivity?
    1) Covalent and metallic
    2) Covalent and molecular
    3) Ionic and molecular
    4) ionic and metallic

11. The table below contains properties of compounds A, B, C, and D.

Compound	Melting point	Conductivity	Solubility in water
A	High	Excellent (liquid	soluble
B	High	Very poor (solid)	Insoluble
C	Low	Poor (solid)	Slightly soluble
D	High	Excellent (solid)	Insoluble

Which list identifies the type of solid each compound represents?

1) A – ionic, B – network ,   C – metallic, D-molecular
2) A – network,   B – ionic,   C – molecular, D – metallic
3) A – metallic, B – molecular, C – network, D – ionic
4) A – ionic, B – network,   C – molecular, D - metallic

26. Types of substances: Determining formula of compounds based on given properties

1. Which substance, when dissolved in water, forms a solution that conducts an electrical current?
    1) C_2H_5OH 2) $C_6H_{12}O_6$ 3) N_2 4) KCl

2. Which substance at STP conducts electricity because the substance contains mobile electrons?
    1) NaCl   2) S   3) Mg   4) H_2O

3. Based on bond type, which compound has the highest melting point?
    1) CH_3OH 2) C_6H_{14} 3) $CuCl_2$ 4) CCl_4

4. Which of the following substances is the best conductor of electricity?
    1) $H_2O(g)$ 2) $H_2O(s)$ 3) $NaCl(s)$ 4) $NaCl(\ell)$

5. Which substance is a conductor of electricity in the liquid phase but NOT in the solid phase?
    1) Br_2 2) HBr   3) Na   4) NaCl

6. Which of the following solids has the highest melting point?
    1) $H_2O(s)$ 2) $Na_2O(s)$ 3) $SO_2(s)$ 4) $CO_2(s)$

7. A solid substance was tested in the laboratory. The test results are listed below.
    - Dissolves in water   • Is an electrolyte   • Melts at a high temperature

    Based on these results, the solid substance could be
    1) Cu   2) $CuBr_2$ 3) C   4) $C_6H_{12}O_6$

8. A solid substance is found to have the following properties:
    - Non electrolytes   • Low solubility in water   • Low melting point

    Based on the above properties, the solid substance could be
    1) $I_2(s)$ 2) $Ag(s)$ 3) $NaCl(s)$ 4) $SiO_2(s)$

9. A solid substance has a high melting point and is a good conductor of electricity as a solid and as a liquid. This substance could be
    1) Calcium chloride   2) Carbon dioxide   3) Silver   4) Carbon

10. A certain substance is a poor conductor of electricity and has a high melting point. The substance is most likely
    1) $CO_2(s)$ 2) $SiO_2(s)$ 3) $H_2O(s)$ 4) $C_6H_{12}O_6(s)$

11. Which property is true of copper?
    1) It has a low melting point   3) It has a high melting point
    2) It is a nonconductor   4) It is soluble in water

12. Which is true of the compound $NaCl(s)$
    1) It is a good electrolyte with high melting point
    2) It is a poor electrolyte with high melting point
    3) It is a good electrolyte with low melting point
    4) It is a poor electrolyte with low melting point

13. Which set of properties best describes $NH_4Cl(s)$?
    1) Low solubility in water and poor conductor of electricity as aqueous
    2) Low solubility in water and good conductor of electricity as aqueous
    3) High solubility in water and poor conductor of electricity as aqueous
    4) High solubility in water and good conductor of electricity as aqueous

14. The compound $C_{12}H_{22}O_{11}$ is best described as
    1) A molecular solid with low melting point and low electrical conductivity as aqueous
    2) A molecular solid with high melting point and high electrical conductivity as aqueous
    3) An ionic solid with low melting point and low electrical conductivity as aqueous
    4) An ionic solid with high melting point and high electrical conductivity as aqueous

27. Intermolecular forces / Hydrogen bonding: Recalling Concept Facts and Definitions

1. Which type of forces exist between atoms of compounds and molecules?
   1) Intermolecular forces
   2) Intramolecular forces
   3) Catalytic forces
   4) Magnetic forces

2. The type of forces between molecules in molecular substances are called
   1) Intermolecular forces
   2) Intramolecular forces
   3) Catalytic forces
   4) Magnetic forces

3. Compare to intramolecular forces, the strength of intermolecular forces are generally
   1) Stronger
   2) Weaker
   3) The same

4. Which list includes only intramolecular forces?
   1) Ionic , covalent, and hydrogen bonds
   2) Ionic, covalent, and metallic bonds
   3) Covalent, hydrogen, metallic bonds
   4) Metallic, hydrogen, and ionic bonds

5. Which is an example of an intermolecular force?
   1) Polar covalent bond
   2) Network solid bond
   3) Coordinate covalent bond
   4) Hydrogen bond

6. The strength of intermolecular forces in molecular substance depends largely on the
   1) Polarity of the molecules
   2) Mass of the molecules
   3) Density of the molecules
   4) Potential energy of the molecules

7. The strength of intermolecular force in molecular substances will increase as
   1) Density of the substances increases
   2) Density of the substances decreases
   3) Molecular polarity increases
   4) Molecular polarity decreases

8. The strength of intermolecular forces among similar nonpolar substances will increase with
   1) Decrease molecular size and increase distance between the molecules
   2) Decrease molecular size and decrease distance between the molecules
   3) Increase molecular size and increase distance between the molecules
   4) Increase molecular size and decrease distance between the molecules

9. Which of the following physical properties of a molecular substance is due mostly to the strength of its intermolecular forces?
   1) Ionization energy
   2) Boiling point
   3) Density
   4) Mass

10. Which set of properties are due to the strength of intermolecular forces between molecules?
    1) Vapor pressure and boiling point
    2) Boiling point and Molar density
    3) Molar mass and vapor pressure
    4) Vapor pressure and Molar density

11. Hydrogen bonding are formed between molecules when the molecules contain a hydrogen atom that is covalently bonded to an atom that has
    1) Small atomic radius and low electronegativity
    2) Large atomic radius and low electronegativity
    3) Small atomic radius and high electronegativity
    4) Large atomic radius and low electronegativity

12. Oxygen, Nitrogen, and Fluorine bond with hydrogen to form molecules. These molecules are attracted to each other by
    1) Ionic bonds
    2) Hydrogen bonds
    3) Electrovalent bonds
    4) Coordinate covalent bonds

13. Which kind of bonds are found in a sample of $H_2O(\ell)$?
    1) Covalent bonds, only
    2) Hydrogen bonds, only
    3) Both covalent and Hydrogen bonds
    4) Both ionic and hydrogen bonds

14. Hydrogen bonding are strongest between the molecules of
    1) $HCl(\ell)$
    2) $HBr(\ell)$
    3) $HI(\ell)$
    4) $HF(\ell)$

15. In which substance would the force of attraction between the molecules be considered hydrogen bonding?
    1) $O_2(g)$
    2) $NH_3(\ell)$
    3) $NaCl(s)$
    4) $CO_2(g)$

28. Intermolecular forces: Relating molecular polarity to physical properties

1. The abnormally high boiling point of HF as compared to HCl is primarily due to intermolecular forces of attraction called
   1) Network bonds
   2) Van der Waals forces
   3) Electrovalent forces
   4) Hydrogen bonding

2. At 298 K, the vapor pressure of H_2O is less than the vapor pressure of CH_3OH because H_2O has
   1) Larger molecules
   2) Smaller molecules
   3) Stronger intermolecular forces
   4) Weaker intermolecular forces

3. The relative high boiling point of water is primarily due to the presence of
   1) Hydrogen bonds
   2) Covalent bond
   3) metallic bonding
   4) Network solid bonding

4. Compare to the boiling point of H_2S, the boiling point of H_2O is higher because H_2O molecules
   1) Have less mass than H_2S molecules
   2) Have smaller van der wails forces than H_2S molecules
   3) Form stronger hydrogen bond bonds than H_2S
   4) Form stronger covalent bonds than H_2S

5. At STP, fluorine is a gas and iodine is a solid. This observation can be best explained by the fact that fluorine has
   1) Weaker intermolecular forces of attraction than iodine
   2) Stronger intermolecular forces of attraction than iodine
   3) Lower average kinetic energy than iodine
   4) Higher average kinetic energy than iodine

29. Boiling and Melting Points: Determining formula with highest and lowest boiling point

1. Which of the following compounds has the highest normal boiling point?
   1) $H_2O(\ell)$
   2) $H_2S(\ell)$
   3) $H_2Se(\ell)$
   4) $H_2Te(\ell)$

2. Which of these compounds would have the highest boiling point?
   1) HI
   2) HBr
   3) HCl
   4) HF

3. Which of these nonpolar substances at STP likely has the highest boiling point?
   1) I_2
   2) Br_2
   3) Cl_2
   4) F_2

4. Which of these noble gases elements has the highest boiling point?
   1) Ne
   2) Ar
   3) Kr
   4) Xe

5. Which hydrocarbon likely has the highest boiling point?
   1) C_2H_6
   2) CH_4
   3) C_4H_{10}
   4) C_3H_8

6. Which of the followings has the lowest boiling point?
   1) He
   2) Xe
   3) Ne
   4) Kr

7. Which of the following substance has the lowest normal boiling point?
   1) C_5H_{10}
   2) C_4H_8
   3) C_3H_6
   4) C_2H_4

8. Which of these halogens has the lowest melting point?
   1) $Br_2(s)$
   2) $I_2(s)$
   3) $Cl_2(s)$
   4) $F_2(s)$

Topic 4: Chemical bonding

30. Lewis electron-dot diagrams: Recognizing Lewis electron-dot for neutral atoms and ions

1. Which is the correct electron-dot diagram of a sulfur atom in the ground state?

1) S: 2) ·S: 3) ·S: 4) :S:

2. Which Lewis electron-dot symbol represents an atom of argon in the ground state?

1) Ar: 2) ·Ar: 3) :Ar: 4) ·Ar:

3. Electron configuration of atom X is $2-8-8-2$. What is the correct electron-dot symbol for X?

1) X: 2) ·X: 3) ·X: 4) :X:

4. Which electron-dot symbol is correctly drawn for the atom it represents?

1) Al·   2) S·   3) ·B·   4) Li·

5. The X in the Lewis electron-dot diagram : X : could represent which element?

1) F   2) He   3) Si   4) Ca

6. Which is the correct electron-dot symbol for a chloride ion, Cl-?

1) : Cl :⁻   2) Cl · -   3) : Cl :⁻   4) Cl

7. Which diagram correctly represents the Lewis electron-dot diagram for oxygen ion?

1) : O : ²⁻   2) O : ²⁻   3) O :²⁻   4) : O : ²⁻

8. Which electron-dot symbol is correct for a B^{3+} ion?

1) B   2) B^{3+} 3) · B : ³⁺   4) : B : ³⁺

9. The Lewis electron-dot symbol for a magnesium ion is

1) Mg^{2+} 2) Mg :²⁺   3) : Mg : ²⁺   4) : Mg :²⁻

10. An ion of atom X has 37 protons and 36 electrons. What is the correct Lewis electron-dot diagram for this ion?

1) X ⁻   2) X⁺   3) : X :⁻   4) : X :⁺

11. Atom Y has a nuclear charge of +33 and 36 electrons. What is the correct Lewis electron-dot symbol for this atom?

1) · Y : ³⁺   2) · Y : ³⁻   3) : Y :³⁺   4) : Y : ³⁻

Copyright ©2015 E3 Scholastic Publishing. All Rights Reserved.   SurvivingChem.com   205

31. Lewis electron-dot diagrams. Recognizing Lewis electron-dot in bonds and molecules

1. In the Lewis electron-dot diagram $\overset{..}{H:Cl:}$, the dots represents

    1) Valence electrons of H atom only   3) Valence electron for both H and C atom

    2) Valence electrons of Cl atom only   4) All the electrons found in H and C atoms

2. Which electron-dot formula represents ionic bonding between two atoms?

1) $\overset{xx}{\underset{xx}{x}} Br \overset{x}{} \overset{..}{\underset{..}{Br}} :$ 2) $H \overset{x}{} \overset{..}{\underset{..}{Br}} :$ 3) $Na^+ \left[\overset{xx}{\underset{xx}{x}} F \overset{x}{x} \right]^-$ 4) $H \overset{xx}{\underset{xx}{x}} F \overset{x}{x}$

3. Which Lewis electron-dot diagram represents a compound that contains both ionic and covalent bonds?

1) $Ca^{2+} \left[\begin{array}{c} :\overset{..}{O}: \\ :\overset{..}{O}:\overset{..}{S}:\overset{..}{O}: \\ :\overset{..}{O}: \end{array} \right]^{2-}$ 2) $K^+ [:\overset{..}{\underset{..}{Br}}:]^-$ 3) $\begin{array}{c} H:\overset{..}{S}: \\ H \end{array}$ 4) $:\overset{..}{\underset{..}{Br}} \overset{..}{\underset{..}{Br}}:$

4. Which electron-dot symbol represents a nonpolar molecule?

1) $\begin{array}{c} H \\ H:\overset{..}{C}:\overset{..}{\underset{..}{Cl}}: \\ H \end{array}$ 2) $H:\overset{..}{\underset{..}{Cl}}:$ 3) $\begin{array}{c} H \\ H:\overset{..}{C}:H \\ H \end{array}$ 4) $\begin{array}{c} H:\overset{..}{O}: \\ H \end{array}$

5. Which is a Lewis electron-dot for a polar substance?

1) $H:H$ 2) $H:\overset{..}{\underset{..}{Cl}}:$ 3) $\begin{array}{c} H \\ H:C:H \\ H \end{array}$ 4) $:\overset{..}{F}:\overset{..}{\underset{..}{F}}:$

32. Lewis electron-dot symbols: Determining correct dot symbols

1. Which Lewis electron – dot diagram is correct for a hydrogen molecule?

1) $H \bullet H$ 2) $H \overset{\bullet}{\bullet} H$ 3) $\overset{..}{\underset{..}{:}} H \overset{\bullet}{\bullet} H \overset{..}{\underset{..}{:}}$ 4) $\overset{..}{\underset{..}{:}} H \bullet H \overset{..}{\underset{..}{:}}$

2. A diatomic chlorine molecule is correctly shown in which Lewis electron-dot diagram?

1) $:\overset{..}{\underset{..}{Cl}}: \overset{..}{\underset{..}{Cl}}:$ 2) $:\overset{..}{\underset{..}{Cl}}: :\overset{..}{\underset{..}{Cl}}:$ 3) $\cdot\overset{..}{\underset{..}{Cl}}: \overset{..}{\underset{..}{Cl}}\cdot$ 4) $:\overset{..}{\underset{..}{Cl}}: :\overset{..}{\underset{..}{Cl}}:$

3. Which is the correct electron-dot structure for hydrogen chloride?

1) $H:Cl$ 2) $:\overset{..}{\underset{..}{H}}:Cl$ 3) $:H:\overset{..}{\underset{..}{Cl}}:$ 4) $H:\overset{..}{\underset{..}{Cl}}:$

4. Carbon dioxide is correctly represented by which Lewis electron-dot diagram?

1) $:O::C::O:$ 2) $:O::C::O:$ 3) $O::C::O$ 4) $:\overset{\cdot}{O}::C::\overset{\cdot}{O}:$

5. Which electron-dot is correct for barium fluoride ?

1) $Ba^{2+} 2 \left[:\overset{..}{\underset{..}{F}}: \right]^-$ 2) $\left[:\overset{..}{Ba}: \right]^{2+} 2 F^-$ 3) $Ba^{2+} 2 \left[:F \right]^-$ 4) $:\overset{..}{Ba}:^{2+} 2 \left[:\overset{..}{\underset{..}{F}}: \right]$

Survivingchem.com

Topic 5: Chemical Formulas and Chemical Equations

1. Chemical formula: Recalling Concept Facts and Definitions

1. A chemical formula is used to represent symbols for
   1) Mixtures   2) Isotopes   3) Isomers   4) Pure substances

2. A chemical formula can be used to represent compositions of
   1) Elements, only
   2) Compounds, only
   3) Elements and compounds
   4) Compounds and mixtures

3. Which list includes only types of chemical formulas?
   1) Combustion, synthesis, and decomposition
   2) Empirical, molecular, and structural
   3) Empirical, molecular, and substitution
   4) structural, combustion, and synthesis

4. A chemical formula is an expression of
   1) Qualitative composition, only
   2) Quantitative composition, only
   3) Both qualitative and quantitative composition
   4) Neither qualitative nor quantitative composition

5. Which information can be obtained from a chemical formula?
   1) The type of atom in the formula, only
   2) The type of atom, and the number of each atom
   3) The number of neutrons in formula
   4) The mass number of the formula

2. Number of atoms in formulas: Determining correct number of atoms in a given formula

1. What is the total number of hydrogen atoms in the formula NH_4OH?
   1) 1   2) 2   3) 4   4) 5

2. In the formula Na_2SO_4, how many sulfur atoms are in the formula?
   1) 0   2) 1   3) 2   4) 4

3. How many atoms of hydrogen are there in the formula $(NH_4)_3PO_4$?
   1) 4   2) 7   3) 12   4) 3

4. What is the total number of moles of sulfur atoms in 1 mole of $Fe_2(SO_4)_3$?
   1) 1   2) 12   3) 3   4) 4

5. What is the total number of nitrate ions found in the formula $NaNO_3$?
   1) 1   2) 2   3) 3   4) 4

6. In the compound, $Ca_3(PO_4)_2$, what is the total number of phosphate ions the formula?
   1) 3   2) 2   3) 8   4) 4

7. How many atoms of oxygen are in the formula $Al(ClO_3)_3 \cdot 6H_2O$?
   1) 6   2) 9   3) 10   4) 15

8. In the formula $NH_4Cl. 3H_2O$, how many atoms of hydrogen are there?
   1) 4   2) 6   3) 9   4) 10

9. What is the total number of atoms in the formula $CaSO_4$?
   1) 3   2) 4   3) 5   4) 6

10. What is the total number of atoms in the formula $Al_2(SO_4)_3$?
    1) 17   2) 9   3) 14   4) 10

11. What is the total number of atoms in one formula unit of $MgSO_4 \cdot 7H_2O$?
    1) 27   2) 13   3) 16   4) 20

12. The total number of atoms in the hydrate $CuSO_4 \cdot 3H_2O$ is
    1) 9   2) 12   3) 15   4) 24

13. How many different kinds of atoms are present in NH_4NO_3?
    1) 7   2) 9   3) 3   4) 4

Topic 5: Chemical formulas and Chemical Equations

3. Ratio of atoms or ions in formulas: Determining ratio of composition in formulas

1. In the compound Al_2S_3, the mole ratio of aluminum to sulfur is
   1) 2 : 3   2) 3 : 2   3) 13 : 16   4) 27 : 16

2. What is the simplest ratio of carbon to hydrogen atoms in the formula C_4H_{10}?
   1) 4 : 10   2) 2 : 5   3) 1 : 5   4) 10 : 4

3. What is the ratio of sodium ion to phosphate ion in the formula Na_3PO_4 ?
   1) 4 : 3   2) 3 : 4   3) 1 : 3   4) 3 : 1

4. In a sample of solid $Ba(NO_3)_2$, the ratio of barium ions to nitrate ions is
   1) 1 : 1   2) 1 : 2   3) 1 : 3   4) 1 : 6

5. What is the ratio of ammonium ion to sulfate ion in the formula $(NH_4)_2SO_4$?
   1) 2 : 1   2) 1 : 2   3) 8 : 4   4) 4 : 1

6. The ratio of nitrogen to hydrogen in a molecule of ammonia is
   1) 1 : 1   2) 2 : 1   3) 1 : 3   4) 3 : 1

7. In the compound Al_2O_3, the ratio of aluminum to oxygen is
   1) 2 grams of aluminum to 3 grams of oxygen
   2) 3 grams of aluminum to 2 grams of oxygen
   3) 2 moles of aluminum to 3 moles of oxygen
   4) 3 moles of aluminum to 2 moles of oxygen

8. What is the ratio of lithium to sulfur in the formula Li_2S?
   1) 2 moles of lithium to 1 mole of sulfur
   2) 1 mole of lithium to 2 moles of sulfur
   3) 2 molecule of lithium to 1 molecule of sulfur
   4) 1 molecule of lithium to 2 molecule of sulfur

4. Types of chemical formulas: Recalling definitions and facts

1. A type of formula showing the simplest ratio in which atoms are combined is called
   1) A molecular formula   3) A structural formula
   2) An empirical formula   4) A condensed formula

2. A formula showing a true composition of a substance is the
   1) Molecular formula   3) Structural formula
   2) Empirical formula   4) Binary formula

3. Which is likely to show how atoms in a compound are bonded together?
   1) A molecular formula   3) A structural formula
   2) An empirical formula   4) An electron formula

4. A compound with just two atoms is classified as
   1) A ternary compound   3) A binary compound
   2) A polyatomic compound   4) A monatomic compound

5. In compounds, the sum of charges in all formulas must equal
   1) 3   2) 2   3) 1   4) 0

5. Empirical formula: Determining and recognizing empirical formulas

1. Which formula is an empirical formula?
   1) CH
   2) C_2H_2
   3) C_2H_4
   4) C_4H_8

2. Which formula is an empirical formula?
   1) C_2H_6
   2) C_4H_{10}
   3) H_2O
   4) H_2O_2

3. An example of an empirical formula is
   1) C_4H_{10}
   2) $C_6H_{12}O_6$
   3) $HC_2H_3O_2$
   4) CH_2O

4. Which formula is an empirical formula?
   1) H_2CO_3
   2) $H_2C_2O_4$
   3) CH_3COOH
   4) CH_2OHCH_2OH

5. Which represents an empirical formula and a molecular formula?
   1) P_2O_5
   2) N_2O_4
   3) C_3H_6
   4) $C_6H_{12}O_6$

6. Which compound has the same molecular and empirical formula?
   1) C_2H_4
   2) C_3H_6
   3) CH_4
   4) H_2O_2

7. Which formula is both an empirical formula and a molecular formula for a known substance?
   1) $C_6H_{12}O_6$
   2) $C_{12}H_{22}O_{11}$
   3) P_4H_{10}
   4) P_2O_2

6. Empirical and molecular formulas: Relating empirical to molecular formula

1. What is the empirical formula of a compound whose molecular formula is P_4H_{10} ?
   1) PO
   2) PO_2
   3) P_2O_5
   4) P_8O_{20}

2. What is the empirical formula of a compound with the molecular formula of C_6H_{10}?
   1) C_2H_5
   2) C_3H_5
   3) C_5H_3
   4) $C_{12}H_{20}$

3. What is the empirical formula of $C_{12}H_{22}O_{11}$?
   1) $C_{12}H_{22}O_{11}$
   2) $C_6H_{11}O_{11}$
   3) $C_3H_6O_3$
   4) $C_{22}H_{48}H_{22}$

4. The molecular formula of a compound is represented by X_3Y_6. What is the empirical formula of this compound?
   1) X_3Y
   2) X_2Y
   3) XY_2
   4) XY_3

5. The empirical formula of a compound is CH_3. The molecular formula of this compound could be
   1) CH_4
   2) C_2H_2
   3) C_2H_3
   4) C_2H_6

6. Which of the following molecular formulas could have the empirical formula C_2H_3 ?
   1) C_5H_6
   2) C_4H_6
   3) C_8H_{20}
   4) CH_3

7. Which compound has the empirical formula CH ?
   1) CH_4
   2) C_2H_4
   3) C_6H_6
   4) C_3H_8

8. Which molecular compound has the empirical formula of CH_2O ?
   1) CH_3COOH
   2) CH_3OH
   3) CH_3CH_2OH
   4) HCOOH

9. Which two compounds have the same empirical formula?
   1) C_2H_2 and C_2H_4
   2) CH_2 and C_3H_8
   3) HO and H_2O
   4) NO_2 and N_2O_4

10. Which molecular formula is correctly paired with its empirical formula?
    1) CO_2 and CO
    2) C_2H_2 and C_4H_4
    3) PO_2 and P_2O_4
    4) P_4O_{10} and PO_5

Topic 5: Chemical formulas and Chemical Equations

7. Formulas of binary ionic compounds: Determining correct formula from name

1. Which is the correct formula for potassium hydride?
   1) KH_2 2) KH 3) KOH 4) $K(OH)_2$

2. Which formula correctly represents the compound aluminum iodide ?
   1) AlI 2) AlI_3 3) Al_3I 4) Al_3I_3

3. What is the correct chemical formula for cesium oxide?
   1) CsO_2 2) C_2O_3 3) CsO 4) Cs_2O

4. Which formula is correct for magnesium sulfide?
   1) MgS 2) Mg_2S_2 3) MnS 4) Mn_2S_2

5. Which is the formula for calcium nitride?
   1) CaN 2) Ca_2N_3 3) Ca_3N_3 4) Ca_3N_2

8. Formulas of compounds with polyatomic ion: Determining correct formula from name

1. Which formula is correct for sodium nitrate?
   1) $NaNO_2$ 2) $NaNO_3$ 3) $Na(NO)_2$ 4) $Na(NO)_3$

2. Which formula is correct for magnesium phosphate?
   1) Mg_2PO_7 2) $MgPO_4$ 3) $Mg_2(PO_4)_3$ 4) $Mg_3(PO_4)_2$

3. Which is the correct formula for ammonium oxide?
   1) NH_4O 2) NH_2O 3) $(NH_4)_2O$ 4) $(NH_4)_2O_2$

4. Which is the correct formula for ammonium sulfate?
   1) NH_4SO_4 2) $NH_4(SO_4)_2$ 3) $(NH_4)_2(SO_4)_2$ 4) $(NH_4)_2SO_4$

5. Which is the correct formula for zinc carbonate?
   1) $ZnCO_3$ 2) $Zn_2(CO_3)_2$ 3) $ZnCO_6$ 4) $ZnCO$

9. Formulas of compounds with multiple oxidation numbers: Determining correct formula

1. What is the correct formula for lead(II) chloride?
   1) $PbCl$ 2) Pb_2Cl 3) Pb_2Cl2 4) $PbCl_2$

2. The formula for lead(II) oxide is
   1) PbO 2) PbO_2 3) Pb_2O 4) Pb_2O_3

3. The correct formula for the compound platinum(IV) nitride is ?
   1) PtN 2) Pt_3N_4 3) Pt_4N_3 4) Pt_4N

4. The correct formula for manganese(IV) sulfide is
   1) Mn_4S 2) MnS_2 3) Mn_4S_2 4) Mn_4S_4

5. Which formula is correct for copper(II) chlorate?
   1) Cu_2Cl 2) $CuCl_2$ 3) Cu_2ClO_3 4) $Cu(ClO_3)_2$

6. Which formula correctly represents lead(II) thiosulfate?
   1) $Pb_2(S_2O_3)_2$ 2) $Pb_2S_4O_6$ 3) PbS_2O_3 4) $PbSO_3$

7. Which formula is correct for nitrogen(IV) oxide?
   1) NO_2 2) N_2O 3) N_2O_2 4) N_4O_2

8. Which is the correct formula for phosphorous(IV) chloride?
   1) P_5Cl 2) PCl 3) PCl_5 4) P_5Cl_5

Copyright © 2015 E3 Scholastic Publishing. All Rights Reserved.   Survivingchem.com

10. Mixed formula writing

1. Which formula represents nickel(II) dichromate?
   1) $Ni_2Cr_2O_7$ 2) $NiCrO_7$ 3) $NiCr_2O_7$ 4) $Ni(Cr_2O_7)_2$

2. The formula for calcium cyanide is
   1) $CaCN_2$ 2) $CaSCN_2$ 3) $Ca(CN)_2$ 4) $Ca(SCN)_2$

3. The correct formula for potassium oxide is
   1) PO_2 2) P_2O 3) KO_2 4) K_2O

4. Which is the correct formula for iron(II) sulfide?
   1) FeS 2) Fe_5O_3 3) Fe_2S_3 4) $Fe_2(SO_4)_2$

5. Which is a correct formula for a compound with IUPAC name of Nickel(III) hypochlorite?
   1) $NiCl_3$ 2) Ni_3ClO 3) $NiClO_3$ 4) $Ni(ClO)_3$

6. The correct formula for manganese(VII) oxide will be
   1) Mn_7O_2 2) Mg_2O_7 3) Mn_2O_7 4) Mn_7O_2

7. Which formula is correct for ammonium carbonate?
   1) NH_4CO_3 2) $(NH_4)_2CO_3$ 3) $(NH_4)_3CO_3$ 4) $(NH_4)_3(CO)_3$

8. Which formula is correct for antimony(V) oxide?
   1) SbO_3 2) Sb_2O 3) Sb_2O_5 4) Sb_5O_2

9. Which formula is correct for sodium hydrogen carbonate?
   1) $NaHCO_3$ 2) $NaHC$ 3) Na_3HCO_3 4) $NaCO_3$

10. Which formula correctly represents chromium(VI) sulfide?
    1) Cr_6S_2 2) Cr_2S_6 3) CrS_3 4) Cr_3S

11. Naming binary compounds. Determining name from binary compound formula

1. What is the correct IUPAC name for the formula, LiN?
   1) Lithium nitride
   2) Lithium nitrite
   3) Lithium(I) nitride
   4) Lithium(I) Nitrite

2. Which name is correct for $BaBr_2$?
   1) Barium bromite
   2) Barium bromate
   3) Barium bromide
   4) Barium bromium

3. The name of the compound Na_3P is
   1) Sodium(III) phosphide
   2) Sodium(III) phosphate
   3) Sodium phosphide
   4) Sodium phosphate

4. The correct name for FrO is
   1) Francium oxide
   2) Francium(II) oxide
   3) Fluorine oxygen
   4) Fluorine(II) oxygen

12. Naming compounds containing polyatomic ions: Determining correct name from formula

1. What is the correct IUPAC name for $Mg(NO_3)_2$?
   1) Magnesium(II) nitrate
   2) Magnesium(II) nitrite
   3) Magnesium nitrate
   4) Magnesium nitride

2. What is the correct name for the compound with the formula $AlPO_4$
   1) Aluminum(IV) phosphate
   2) Aluminum phosphate
   3) Aluminum(III) phosphite
   4) Aluminum phosphite

3. The correct name for the compound with the IUPAC formula of NH_4Cl is
   1) Nitrogen chlorate
   2) Ammonium chloride
   3) Nitrate chloride
   4) Ammonium chlorite

13. Naming compounds containing an atom with multiple oxidation numbers atom

1. What is the correct name for the compound $CrPO_4$?
   1) Chromium(II) phosphate
   2) Chromium(III) phosphate
   3) Chromium(II) phosphide
   4) Chromium(III) phosphide

2. The correct IUPAC name of the compound with a formula of PbO_2 is
   1) Lead(I) oxide
   2) Lead(II) oxide
   3) Lead(III) oxide
   4) Lead(IV) oxide

3. Which formula is correct for $V(NO_3)_2$?
   1) Vanadium(I) nitrate
   2) Vanadium(II) nitrate
   3) Vanadium(III) nitrate
   4) Vanadium(IV) nitrate

4. What is the correct IUPAC name for Co_2O_3?
   1) Cobalt(II) oxide
   2) Cobalt(III) oxide
   3) Copper(II) oxide
   4) Copper(III) oxide

 Survivingchem.com

14. Naming compounds (Mixed problems) : Determining correct name from a given formula

1. What is the correct name for the compound with the formula of K_2SO_4?
   1) Potassium sulfide
   2) Potassium sulfite
   3) Potassium Sulfate
   4) Potassium(IV) sulfide

2. The correct IUPAC name for the formula MnO_2 is
   1) Manganese oxide
   2) Manganese (I) oxide
   3) Manganese(II) oxide
   4) Manganese(IV) oxide

3. What is the IUPAC name for the compound with the formula of Ca_3P_2?
   1) Calcium phosphide
   2) Calcium(II) phosphide
   3) Calcium Phosphate
   4) calcium(II) phosphate

4. The compound with the formula of $Cu(ClO_2)_2$ is
   1) Copper(I) Chlorite
   2) Copper(II) chlorite
   3) Copper(I) chlorate
   4) Copper(II) chlorate

5. The correct name for $NaClO_4$ is sodium
   1) Chloride
   2) Chlorate
   3) Perchlorate
   4) chlorite

6. The correct name of the compound with the formula Au_2O is
   1) Gold(I) oxide
   2) Gold(II) oxide
   3) Gold(II) Oxide
   4) Gold(IV) Oxide

7. What is the correct IUPAC name for the compound MgI_2 ?
   1) Manganese iodide
   2) Manganese(II) iodide
   3) Magnesium iodide
   4) Magnesium(II) iodide

15. Binary compounds: Recognizing formulas and names of binary compound

1. Which formula is a binary compound?
   1) KOH   2) $NaClO_3$ 3) Al_2S_3 4) $Bi(NO_3)_3$

2. Which of the following formulas represents a binary compound?
   1) NH_4NO_3 2) CH_4 3) $MgSO_4$ 4) CH_3COOH

3. Which formula contains just two elements?
   1) $Ca(ClO)_2$ 2) $CaSO_4$ 3) $CaCl_2$ 4) $Ca(OH)_2$

4. Which substance is a binary compound?
   1) Barium
   2) Beryllium
   3) Barium hydroxide
   4) Beryllium hydride

5. Which substance is a binary compound?
   1) Potassium chlorite
   2) Potassium chloride
   3) Potassium hydroxide
   4) Potassium cyanide

6. Which of the following compounds is composed of just two elements?
   1) Lithium hydroxide
   2) Magnesium sulfate
   3) Aluminum oxide
   4) Ammonium chloride

7. The correct name for a binary compound of sodium could be sodium
   1) Nitride
   2) Nitrite
   3) Nitrate
   4) Nitrous

8. Which substance is a binary compound?
   1) Aluminum
   2) Ammonia
   3) Aluminum chlorite
   4) Ammonium chloride

9. Which compound is a binary compound?
   1) Water
   2) Glucose
   3) Silver nitrate
   4) silver nitrite

10. Which substance is a binary substance?
   1) Carbon
   2) Potassium
   3) Carbon monoxide
   4) Potassium hydroxide

16. Miscellaneous questions on bonding

1. Elements in which group of the Periodic Table usually form oxides with a general formula of M_2O_3 ?
   1) 1   2) 3   3) 13   4) 14

2. Element X reacts with iron to form two different compounds with formulas FeX and Fe_2X_3. In which Group on the Periodic Table does element X belongs?
   1) Group 8   2) Group 2   3) Group 13   4) Group 16

3. Which Group on the Periodic Table contains elements that react with oxygen to form compounds with the general formula of X_2O?
   1) Group 1   2) Group 2   3) Group 14   4) Group 18

4. What is the simplest ratio of nitrogen to oxygen atom in the compound nitrogen (IV) oxide ?
   1) 1 : 2   2) 2 : 1   3) 2 : 4   4) 4 : 2

5. In which compound is the ratio of metal to nonmetal ions 1 to 2 ?
   1) Calcium bromide
   2) Calcium oxide
   3) Calcium phosphide
   4) Calcium sulfide

6. A compound is made up of iron and oxygen only. The ratio of iron ion to oxide ion is 2 : 3 in this compound. The IUPAC name for this compound is
   1) Triiron dioxide
   2) Iron (II) oxide
   3) Iron (III) oxide
   4) Iron trioxide

     Survivingchem.com

17. Chemical equations: Recalling Concept Facts and Definitions

1. The starting substances in chemical reactions are called
   1) Products
   2) Coefficients
   3) Reactants
   4) Activated complex

2. In a chemical reaction, the stable substances that are formed at the end of the reaction are called
   1) Products
   2) Coefficients
   3) Reactants
   4) Activated complex

3. What is conserve during chemical reactions?
   1) Energy, only
   2) Matter, only
   3) Both matter and energy
   4) Neither matter nor energy

4. If equation is balanced properly, both sides of the equation must have the same number of
   1) Atoms
   2) Coefficients
   3) Molecules
   4) Moles of molecules

5. Given a balanced chemical equation, it is always possible to determine
   1) Whether a reaction will or will not take place
   2) The conditions necessary for the reaction to take place
   3) The relative number of moles taking place in the reaction
   4) The physical state of the products and reactants

6. The coefficients in front of the substances in a balanced chemical equations always indicate
   1) The amount of energy released or absorbed
   2) The number of moles of substance
   3) The mass of the substances
   4) The number of electrons

7. Given the balanced equation representing a reaction:

   $$H^+(aq) \ + \ OH^-(aq) \ \rightarrow \ H_2O(\ell) \ + \ 55.8 \ kJ$$

   In this reaction there is conservation of

   1) Mass, only
   2) Mass and energy, only
   3) Mass and charge, only
   4) Mass, charge, and energy

18. Types of chemical reaction reactions: Recalling Concept Facts and Definitions

1. Which is a type of chemical reaction?
   1) Fission   2) Fusion   3) Crystallization   4) Synthesis

2. Which process is a type of chemical reaction?
   1) Dissolving   2) Combustion   3) Melting   4) Alpha decay

3. Which list is composed only of types of chemical reactions?
   1) Synthesis, decomposition, single replacement
   2) Decomposition, evaporation, and double
   3) Synthesis, decomposition, freezing
   4) Decomposition, melting, combustion

4. In which type of chemical reactions would two separate atoms of iodine joined to form a molecule of iodine?
   1) Decomposition
   2) Synthesis
   3) Single replacement
   4) Double replacement

5. In which type of chemical reaction would a molecule of hydrogen peroxide separates into water and oxygen?
   1) Combustion
   2) Synthesis
   3) Decomposition
   4) Single replacement

6. Which type of reaction always involves ions exchange?
   1) Decomposition
   2) Synthesis
   3) Single replacement
   4) Double replacement

19. Types of chemical reactions

1. Given the equation: $SO_2(g) + O_2(g) \rightarrow SO_3(g)$
    What type of reaction is shown above?

    1) Synthesis
    2) Decomposition
    3) Single replacement
    4) Double replacement

2. Given the equation: $Mg(s) + 2HCl(aq) \rightarrow MgCl_2(aq) + H_2(g)$

    What type of equation is shown above?
    1) Synthesis
    2) Double replacement
    3) Combustion
    4) Single replacement

3. Given the equation: $KCl + NaNO_3 \rightarrow KNO_3 + NaCl$

    What type of reaction is represented by the equation
    1) Combustion
    2) Synthesis
    3) Single replacement
    4) Double replacement

4. Given the equation : $CH_4 + O_2 \rightarrow CO_2 + H_2$

    This reaction represents
    1) combustion
    2) synthesis
    3) single replacement
    4) double replacement

5. The reaction: $N_2(g) + H_2(g) \rightarrow NH_3(g)$ is best described as a
    1) synthesis
    2) decomposition
    3) single replacement
    4) double replacement

6. Given the chemical equation : $KClO_3(s) \rightarrow KCl(s) + O_2(g)$.

    What type of reaction is represented by the above equation?
    1) Combustion
    2) Decomposition
    3) Synthesis
    4) Neutralization

7. Which equation represents a double replacement reaction?
    1) $2Na + 2H_2O \rightarrow 2NaOH + H_2$
    2) $CaCO_3 \rightarrow CaO + CO_2$
    3) $LiOH + HCl \rightarrow LiCl + H_2O$
    4) $CH_4 + 2O_2 \rightarrow CO_2 + 2H_2O$

8. Which chemical equation is showing a combustion reaction?
    1) $H_2(g) + I_2(g) \rightarrow 2 HI(g)$
    2) $2Zn(s) + 2HNO_3(aq) \rightarrow Zn(NO_3)_2 + H_2$
    3) $NaCl(aq) + KI(aq) \rightarrow NaI(aq) + KCl(aq)$
    4) $2C_2H_6(g) + 7O_2(g) \rightarrow 4CO_2(g) + 6H_2O(g)$

9. A single replacement reaction is shown in which equation?
    1) $Ca(OH)_2 + HCl \rightarrow CaCl_2 + H_2O$
    2) $Ca + 2H_2O \rightarrow H_2 + Ca(OH)_2$
    3) $2H_2O_2 \rightarrow 2H_2O + O_2$
    4) $2H_2 + O_2 \rightarrow 2 H_2O$

10. Which of the following equations is showing a decomposition reaction?
    1) $(NH_4)_2CO_3 \rightarrow 2NH_3 + CO_2 + H_2O$
    2) $4NH_3 + 5O_2 \rightarrow 4NO + 6H_2O$
    3) $NH_3 + H_2O \rightarrow NH_4OH$
    4) $N_2 + 3H_2 \rightarrow 2NH_3$

20. Balanced equations: Determining which equation demonstrates conservation

1. Which of these equations demonstrates conservation of matter and charge?
   1) $2CO + O_2 \rightarrow CO_2$
   2) $2CO + O_2 \rightarrow 2CO_2$
   3) $2H_2 + O_2 \rightarrow H_2O$
   4) $2H_2 + 2O_2 \rightarrow 2H_2O$

2. Which of these equations is correctly balanced?
   1) $Fe(s) + O_2(g) \rightarrow Fe_2O_3(s)$
   2) $Fe(s) + O_2(g) \rightarrow 2Fe_2O_3(s)$
   3) $2Fe(s) + 2O_2(g) \rightarrow Fe_2O_3(s)$
   4) $4Fe(s) + 3O_2(g) \rightarrow 2Fe_2O_3(s)$

3. Which of these equations shows conservation of atoms?
   1) $KBr \rightarrow K + Br_2$
   2) $2 KClO_3 \rightarrow 2KCl + 2O_2$
   3) $CuCO_3 \rightarrow CuO + CO_2$
   4) $CaCO_3 \rightarrow CO_2 + 2CaO$

4. Which is a correctly balanced equation for a reaction between hydrogen and oxygen?
   1) $H_2(g) + O_2(g) \rightarrow H_2O(g) + heat$
   2) $H_2(g) + O_2(g) \rightarrow 2H_2O(g) + heat$
   3) $2H_2(g) + 2O_2(g) \rightarrow H_2O(g) + heat$
   4) $2H_2(g) + O_2(g) \rightarrow 2H_2O(g) + heat$

5. Which equation is correctly balanced?
   1) $CaO + 2H_2O \rightarrow Ca(OH)_2$
   2) $NH_3 + 2O_2 \rightarrow HNO_3 + H_2O$
   3) $Ca(OH)_2 + 2H_2PO_4 \rightarrow Ca_3(PO_4)_2 + 3H_2O$
   4) $Cu + H_2SO_4 \rightarrow CuSO_4 + H_2O + SO_2$

21. Balanced equations: Predicting missing reactant or product

1. Given the incomplete equation:
   $$4Fe + 3O_2 \rightarrow 2X$$
   Which compound is represented by X?
   1) FeO
   2) Fe_2O_3
   3) Fe_3O_2
   4) Fe_3O_4

2. Given the balanced equation:
   $$2Na + 2H_2O \rightarrow 2X + H_2$$
   What is the correct formula for the product represented by the letter X?
   1) NaO
   2) Na_2O
   3) $NaOH$
   4) Na_2OH

3. Given the incomplete equation:
   $$2N_2O_5 \rightarrow$$
   Which set of products completes and balances the incomplete equation?
   1) $2N_2 + 3O_2$
   2) $2N_2 + 2O_2$
   3) $4NO_2 + O_2$
   4) $2NO + 2O_2$

4. Given the incomplete reaction:
   $$Ca + \underline{\hspace{1cm}} \rightarrow H_2 + CaCl_2$$
   Which is the correct formula and coefficient for the substance that completes and balances the
   equation?
   1) HCl
   2) $2HCl$
   3) HCl_2
   4) $2HCl_2$

5. Given the incomplete equation:
   $$4NH_3 + 3O_2 \rightarrow 2N_2 + XH_2O$$
   What is the number of moles of water, X, in the equation?
   1) 6
   2) 4
   3) 3
   4) 1

22. Balancing equation: Determining coefficients and sums of coefficient

1. Given the unbalanced equation :

    _____Fe_2O_3 + _____CO → _____Fe + _____CO_2

    When the equation is correctly balanced using the smallest whole-number coefficients, what is the coefficient of CO ?
    1) 1   2) 2   3) 3   4) 4

2. Given the unbalanced equation:

    _____Al + _____$CuSO_4$ → _____ $Al_2(SO_4)_3$ + _____Cu

    When the equation is balanced using the smallest whole-number coefficients, what is the coefficient of Al ?
    1) 1   2) 2   3) 3   4) 4

3. Given the unbalanced equation:

    ___ $Mg(ClO_3)_2(s)$ → _____ $MgCl_2(s)$ + _____$O_2(g)$

    What is the coefficient of O_2 when the equation is balanced correctly using the smallest whole-number coefficients?
    1) 1   2) 2   3) 3   4) 4

4. When the equation

    _____Na + _____H_2O → _____H_2 + _____$NaOH$

    Is correctly balanced using the smallest whole number coefficients, what is the coefficient of H_2O ?
    1) 1   2) 2   3) 3   4) 4

5. When the equation

    ___SiO_2 + _____ C → _____SiC + _____CO

    Is correctly balanced using the smallest whole-number coefficients, the sum of all coefficients is
    1) 6   2) 7   3) 8   4) 9

6. Given the unbalanced equation:

    _____H_2O_2 → _____H_2O + _____O_2

    What is the sum of all coefficients when the equation is balanced correctly using the smallest whole- number coefficients?
    1) 5   2) 9   3) 3   4) 4

7. Given the unbalanced equation:

    __$Ca(OH)_2$ + __ $(NH_4)_2SO_4$ → ___$CaSO_4$ + ___NH_3 +__H_2O

    What is the sum of all coefficients when the equation is correctly balanced using the smallest whole-number coefficients?
    1) 5   2) 7   3) 9   4) 11

8. When the equation

    ___C_2H_4 + _____O_2 → _____ CO_2 + ___H_2O

    is correctly balanced using the smallest whole-number, what is the coefficient of O_2?
    1) 1   2) 2   3) 3   4) 4

9. Given the unbalanced equation:

    ___ $C_3H_8(g)$ + ___$O_2(g)$ → __$CO_2(g)$ + __$H_2O(g)$

    When the equation is balanced correctly using the smallest whole-number coefficients, the sum of all coefficients is
    1) 12   2) 13   3) 24   4) 26

10. Given the unbalanced equation:

    ___C_5H_8 + _____O_2 → __ CO_2 + ___ H_2O

    When the equation is correctly balanced using the smallest whole-number coefficients, what is the coefficient of C_5H_8 ?
    1) 1   2) 5   3) 6   4) 10

  Survivingchem.com

Topic 6: Mole : Mathematics of formulas and equations

1. Mole interpretation: Interpret ting quantity of mole in formulas

1. Which quantity can correctly be represented by the symbol "Ar" ?
   1) 1 gram of atoms
   2) 10 grams of atoms
   3) 1 mole of atoms
   4) 10 moles of atoms

2. Which quantity best describe the formula "N_2"?
   1) 2 grams of atoms
   2) 2 moles of atoms
   3) 1 Liter of atoms
   4) 1 mole of atoms

3. Which quantity of particles is correctly represented by the formula "CO_2" ?
   1) 1 mole of molecules
   2) 3 moles of molecules
   3) 1 mole of atoms
   4) 44 moles of atoms

4. In a sample of oxygen gas at STP., which represents the greatest number of molecules?
   1) One molecule
   2) One liter
   3) One gram
   4) One mole

5. Which sample of water, H_2O, contains the greatest number of water molecules?
   1) One mole of H_2O
   2) Two moles of H_2O
   3) One gram of H_2O
   4) Two grams of H_2O

2. Chemical formulas: Determining mole of atoms in formulas

1. How many different types of atoms are present in the formula $(NH_4)_2HPO_4$
   1) 2   2) 4   3) 5   4) 16

2. How many different types of atoms are in the formula $Ba(OH)_2 \cdot 8H_2O$?
   1) 3   2) 2   3) 3   4) 8

3. What is the total number of moles of nitrogen atoms in the formula NH_4NO_3?
   1) 1   2) 2   3) 3   4) 4

4. How many moles of oxygen atoms are present in the formula $Be_3(PO_4)_2$?
   1) 4   2) 8   3) 6   4) 12

5. What is the total number of moles of hydrogen in 1 mole of $(NH_4)_2HPO_4$?
   1) 5   2) 7   3) 8   4) 9

6. How many moles of oxygen atoms are present in one mole of $CaSO_4 \cdot 3H_2O$?
   1) 7   2) 4   3) 3   4) 5

7. What is the total number of atoms in one mole of $Mg(ClO_4)_2$?
   1) 13   2) 3   3) 8   4) 11

8. The total number of atoms in one mole of $BaCl_2.2H_2O$ is
   1) 6   2) 7   3) 8   4) 9

9. What is the total number of moles of hydrogen atoms in 2 mole of $(NH_4)_2SO_4$?
   1) 8   2) 4   3) 16   4) 2

10. The total number of oxygen atoms in 0.5 mole of $CaCO_3 \cdot 7H_2O$ is
    1) 10   2) 2   3) 5   4) 4

11. What is the total number of moles of atoms in 2 moles of H_2SO_4?
    1) 14   2) 7   3) 12   4) 6

12. What is the total number of atoms in the 0.5 mole of formula $Na_2S_2O_3$?
    1) 7.0   2) 6   3) 14   4) 3.5

13. How many moles of hydrogen atoms are there in 2.5 moles of $(NH_4)_2CO_3 \cdot 5H_2O$?
    1) 8   2) 32.5   3) 45   4) 37.5

Topic 6: Moles and Stoichiometry - Mathematics of formulas and equations

3. Formula mass: Determining mass of 1 mole of a substance

1. What is the gram atomic mass of Ca?
   1) 20
   2) 40
   3) 18
   4) 2

2. What is the mass of one mole of gold?
   1) 11 g
   2) 79 g
   3) 197g
   4) 80 g

3. What is the mass in grams of 1 mole of Co?
   1) 27
   2) 28
   3) 12
   4) 59

4. What is the mass of 1 mole of H_3PO_4?
   1) 82
   2) 98
   3) 24
   4) 30

5. What is the formula mass of $Ca(OH)_2$?
   1) 29 g
   2) 74 g
   3) 34 g
   4) 57 g

6. The gram formula mass of $(NH_4)_3PO_4$ is
   1) 149 g
   2) 120 g
   3) 404 g
   4) 300 g

7. The formula mass of $C_3H_5(OH)_3$ is
   1) 48 g/mole
   2) 58 g /mole
   3) 74 g/mole
   4) 92 g/mole

8. What is the gram formula mass of $CuSO_4 \cdot 3H_2O$?
   1) 214 g
   2) 250 g
   3) 294 g
   4) 178 g

9. What is the mass of 1 mole of $(NH_4)_2CO_3 \cdot 4H_2O$?
   1) 154g
   2) 216 g
   3) 168 g
   4) 26 g

10. What is the molar mass of $Ba(OH)_2 \cdot 8H_2O$?
    1) 452 g/mol
    2) 187 g/mol
    3) 242 g/mol
    4) 315 g/mol

4. Mole calculation: Calculation of moles from mass

1. What is the total number of moles represented by 46 grams of Na?
   1) 23 moles
   2) 2.0 moles
   3) 0.5 moles
   4) 1 mole

2. The total number of moles in 28 grams of Fe is
   1) 0.5
   2) 1
   3) 2
   4) 2.5

3. The number of moles of the element lead that will have a mass of 311 grams is equal to
   1) 2 moles
   2) 1.5 moles
   3) 0.67 moles
   4) 1.0 mole

4. A student measured 56 grams of Fe_2O_3 for a laboratory experiment. How many moles of Fe_2O_3 do this mass represents?
   1) 1.00
   2) 0.50
   3) 0.35
   4) 2.00

5. The number of moles of H_2SO_4 that weighs 245 grams is equal to
   1) 0.4 mol
   2) 1 mol
   3) 2.5 mol
   4) 3 mol

6. How many moles of moles is represented by 184 grams of $C_3H_5(OH)_3$?
   1) 1
   2) 0.5
   3) 1.5
   4) 2

7. How many moles is represented by 286 grams of $Na_2CO_3 \cdot 10H_2O$?
   1) 0.2 moles
   2) 0.5 moles
   3) 1 mole
   4) 2 moles

8. Which set up is correct for calculating the number of moles in $Al(ClO_3)_3 \cdot 6H_2O$ in 576 grams of this substance?
   1) 576 x 384
   2) 6 x 576
   3) $\frac{384}{576}$
   4) $\frac{576}{384}$

 Survivingchem.com

5. Mass calculation: Calculation of mass from moles

1. What is the total mass of 2 moles of Ar?
   1) 18 g   2) 36 g   3) 40 g   4) 80 g

2. What is the total mass of 0.75 moles of Zn?
   1) 48 grams   2) 85 grams   3) 23 grams   4) 30 grams

3. What is the mass of 0.5 moles of O_2?
   1) 8 g   2) 64 g   3) 16 g   4) 32 g

4. The total mass of 0.25 moles of H_2 gas?
   1) 2 g   2) 0.5 g   3) 8 g   4) 4 g

5. What is the mass of 1 mole of $CaCO_3$?
   1) 20 g   2) 40 g   3) 80 g   4) 100 g

6. What is the total mass in grams of 3 moles of $Al_2(CrO_4)_3$?
   1) 134   2) 402   3) 1206   4) 1530

7. What is the mass of 0.3 moles of $Ca(C_2H_3O_2)_2$?
   1) 47   2) 190   3) 950   4) 38

8. What is the total mass of 0.5 moles of $CuSO_4 \cdot 5H_2O$?
   1) 250 g   2) 500 g   3) 125 g   4) 213 g

9. The total number of grams in 1.3 moles of $Na_2CO_3 \cdot 10H_2O$?
   1) 286 grams   2) 372 grams   3) 220 grams   4) 429 grams

10. What is the total mass in grams of 0.1 moles of $C_6H_{12}O_6$?
    1) 18 g   2) 180 g   3) 24 g   4) 2.4 g

11. Which set up is correct for calculating the mass of 0.3 moles of $Ca(OH)_2$?
    1) $\dfrac{0.3}{74}$ 2) $\dfrac{74}{0.3}$ 3) 0.3 x 74   4) 0.3 x 58

12. The mass in grams of two moles of $(NH_4)_2CO_3$ is equal to
    1) 96 x 2   2) 108 x 2   3) $\dfrac{96}{2}$ 4) $\dfrac{2}{96}$

6. Percent composition: Calculation of percent composition from formulas

1. The percent composition by mass of Fluorine in F_2 is
   1) 50 %   2) 100 %   3) 19 %   4) 8 %

2. The approximate percent composition of oxygen in SO_3 is
   1) 20 %   2) 40 %   3) 60 %   4) 80 %

3. What is the percent composition of nitrogen in the compound NH_4NO_3?
   1) 35 %   2) 29 %   3) 18 %   4) 5.7 %

4. In the formula $Mg(CN)_2$, what is the approximate percent by mass of carbon?
   1) 16 %   2) 32 %   3) 24%   4) 48 %

5. What is the approximate percent by mass of hydrogen in the formula $C_3H_5(OH)_3$?
   1) 6.5 %   2) 4.8 %   3) 8.7 %   4) 3.6 %

6. What is the percent by mass of phosphorous in the compound $Ca_3(PO_4)_2$?
   1) 20 %   2) 10 %   3) 80 %   4) 14 %

7. Which set up correct for calculating the percent by mass of carbon in the compound $HC_2H_3O_2$?
   1) $\dfrac{12}{60}$ x 100   2) $\dfrac{60}{24}$ x 100   3) $\dfrac{24}{60}$ x 100   4) $\dfrac{60}{12}$ x 100

8. The percent by mass of magnesium in the formula $Mg(ClO_3)_2$ is equal to
   1) $\dfrac{190}{24}$ x 100   2) $\dfrac{190}{48}$ x 100   3) $\dfrac{48}{190}$ x 100   4) $\dfrac{24}{190}$ x 100

9. What is the approximate percent composition by mass of $CaBr_2$ (formula mass = 200 g/mole) ?
   1) 20 % calcium and 80 % bromine   3) 30 % calcium and 70 % bromine
   2) 25 % calcium and 75 % bromine   4) 35 % calcium and 65 % bromine

10. What is the approximate percent composition of $CaCO_3$?
    1) 48 % Ca, 12 % C, and 40 % O   3) 40 % Ca, 12 % C, and 48 % O
    2) 12 % Ca, 48 % C, and 40 % O   4) 40 % Ca, 48 % C, and 12 % O

11. Which formula contains the greatest percent by mass of oxygen?
    1) NO   2) NO_2 3) N_2O 4) N_2O_2

12. Which formula has the least percent composition by mass of carbon?
    1) CH_4 2) C_2H_2 3) C_2H_6 4) C_3H_8

13. Which compound has the greatest composition of sulfur by mass?
    1) $Fe_2(SO_4)_3$ 2) $FeSO_4$ 3) $Fe_2(SO_3)_3$ 4) $FeSO_3$

14. In which compound does manganese has the least percent composition by mass?

    1) Manganese(II) oxide   3) Manganese(II) chloride

    2) Manganese(III) oxide   4) Manganese(III) chloride

15. Which compound of gold will produce the greatest mass of gold?

    1) Gold(I) oxide   3) Gold(I) sulfide

    2) Gold(III) oxide   4) Gold(III) sulfide

7. Percent composition of hydrates. Calculating percent composition of water in hydrates

1. A student measured 8.24 g sample of a hydrated salt and heated it until it has a constant mass of 6.20 g. What is the percent by mass of water in the hydrated salt?
   1) 14.1 %   2) 24.8 %   3) 32.9 %   4) 75.2 %

2. A hydrated salt is a solid that includes water molecules within its crystal structure. A student heated a 9.10 gram sample of an unknown hydrated salt to a constant mass of 5.41 gram. This mass represents the mass of the anhydrous compound. What percent by mass of water did the salt contain?
   1) 3.69 %   2) 16.8 %   3) 40.5 %   4) 59.5 %

3. During an experiment to determine the percent by mass of water in a hydrated crystal, a student found the mass of a hydrated compound to be 4.10 grams. After heating to constant mass, the mass was 3.70 g. What is the percent by mass of water in this crystal?
   1) 9.8 %   2) 90 %   3) 11%   4) 0.40 %

4. A 10.0 gram sample of a hydrate was heated until all water of hydration was driven off. The mass of the anhydrous product remaining was 8.00 grams. What is the percent of water in the hydrate?
   1) 12.5   2) 20.0   3) 25.0   4) 80.0

5. The following data was obtained by a student during an experiment to determine the percent by mass of water in a hydrate compound.

Mass of evaporated dish + hydrated compound	32.5 g
Mass of evaporated dish	25.3 g
Mass of evaporated dish + anhydrous compound	30.8 g

   What is the percent composition of water in the hydrate?

   1) 12 %   2) 76 %   3) 5 %   4) 24%

6. A hydrated salt was heated in a crucible until the anhydrous compound that remained has a constant mass. The following data were recorded during this lab experiment.

DATA

Mass of crucible	17.2 g
Mass of hydrate + crucible	22.0 g
Mass of anhydrous + crucible	20.4 g

   What is the percent composition of water in the hydrated compound?
   1) 33 %   2) 67 %   3) 7 %   4) 23 %

7. A student determining the percent by mass of water in a hydrated sample of salt obtained the following data:

Mass of hydrate	6.25 g
Mass of sample after 1st heating	5.45 g
Mass of sample after 2nd heating	5.10 g

   The correct expression for obtaining the percent by mass of water in the sample is

   1) $\dfrac{5.42}{6.25}$ x 100   2) $\dfrac{5.10}{6.25}$ x 100   3) $\dfrac{0.8}{6.25}$ x 100   4) $\dfrac{1.15}{6.25}$ x 100

8. Molecular formulas: Determining molecular formula from molecular mass and empirical formula

1. What is the molecular formula of a compound with a molecular mass of 56 g and an empirical formula of CH_2?
   1) CH_2 2) C_2H_4 3) C_3H_6 4) C_4H_8

2. What is the molecular formula of a compound with a molecular mass of 78 g/mol and an empirical formula of CH?
   1) C_3H_3 2) C_4H_4 3) C_6H_6 4) C_4H_{10}

3. A compound has a molecular mass of 284 g and an empirical formula of P_2O_5. What is the molecular formula of this compound?
   1) P_4O_{10} 2) P_5O_2 3) P_2O_5 4) $P_{10}O_4$

4. A compound has an empirical formula of HCO_2 and a mass of 90 g/mole. What is the molecular formula of this compound?
   1) HCO 2) $H_2C_2O_4$ 3) $H_4C_4O_8$ 4) $H_6C_6O_{12}$

5. A compound has an empirical formula of CH_2Br and a molecular mass of 188 grams per mole. What is the molecular formula of this compound?
   1) CH_2Br 2) $C_2H_4Br_2$ 3) $C_3H_6Br_3$ 4) $CHBr_2$

9. Ratio of composition: Determining ratio by mass of atoms in a formula

1. What is the ratio by mass of sulfur to oxygen in the formula SO_4?
   1) 1 : 1 2) 1 : 2 3) 2 : 1 4) 1 : 4

2. What is the ratio by mass of carbon to hydrogen in CH_4?
   1) 1 : 4 2) 3 : 1 3) 1 : 3 4) 1 : 6

3. What is the approximate ratio by mass of carbon to hydrogen in the formula C_5H_{10}?
   1) 1 : 2 2) 6 : 1 3) 1 : 6 4) 1 : 5

4. What is the approximate ratio by mass of hydrogen to oxygen in the formula H_2O?
   1) 2 : 1 2) 2 : 1 3) 1 : 8 4) 1 : 8

5. What is the approximate ratio by mass of Lithium to chloride in the gram formula mass of LiCl?
   1) 3 : 17 2) 1 : 5 3) 1 : 1 4) 1 : 2

6. The ratio by mass of carbon to hydrogen to oxygen in 1 mole of $C_6H_{12}O_6$ is
   1) 6 : 1 : 8 2) 3 : 1 : 4 3) 1 : 2 : 1 4) 2 : 6 : 2

7. Acetic acid has a formula of $HC_2H_3O_2$. What is the ratio by mass of hydrogen to carbon to oxygen in this formula?
   1) 1 : 2 : 2 2) 2 : 3 : 3 3) 1 : 6 : 8 4) 1 : 2 : 4

8. What is the ratio by mass of hydrogen to carbon to oxygen in the formula CH_3OH?
   1) 4 : 1 : 1 2) 1 : 3 : 1 3) 4 : 3 : 2 4) 1 : 3 : 4

9. In magnesium oxide formula, what is the ratio by mass of magnesium to oxygen ?
   1) 3 : 2 2) 1 : 1 3) 2 : 1 4) 3 : 4

10. When the formula for calcium bromide is correctly written, the ratio by mass of calcium to bromine is
   1) 1 : 2 2) 1 : 1 3) 4 : 1 4) 1 : 4

 Survivingchem.com

Topic 6: Mole and Stoichiometry - Mathematics of formulas and equations

10. Mole Ratio in chemical equation: Determining mole ratio in balanced equations

1. In the reaction:

    $$Fe_2O_3 + 3CO \rightarrow 2Fe + 3CO_2$$

    What is the mole ratio of Fe_2O_3 to Fe in the reaction?

    1) $1 : 1$ 2) $3 : 1$ 3) $1 : 2$ 4) $2 : 3$

2. In the reaction below:

    $$4Al + 3O_2 \rightarrow 2Al_2O_3$$

    The mole ratio of Al reacted to Al_2O_3 produced is

    1) $2 : 1$ 2) $2 : 4$ 3) $1 : 1$ 4) $2 : 3$

3. Given the reaction:

    $$N_2 + 3H_2 \rightarrow 2NH_3$$

    What is the mole ratio of N_2 reacted to NH_3 produced?
    1) $1 : 1$ 2) $1 : 2$ 3) $1 : 6$ 4) $1 : 3$

4. Given the reaction:

    $$2C_2H_6 + 7O_2 \rightarrow 4CO_2 + 6H_2O$$

    What is the moles ratio of CO_2 produced to moles of C_2H_6 consumed?

    1) 1 to 1 2) 2 to 1 3) 3 to 2 4) 7 to 2

5. Given the combustion reaction

    $$2C_2H_2(g) + 5O_2(g) \rightarrow 4CO_2(g) + 2H_2O(l)$$

    What is the mole ratio C_2H_2 to O_2 reacted?

    1) $4 : 5$ 2) $1 : 1$ 3) $5 : 2$ 4) $2 : 5$

6. Given the reaction:

    $$3Cu + 8HNO_3 \rightarrow 3Cu(NO_3)_2 + 2NO + 4H_2O$$

    The mole ratio of NO produced to HNO_3 reacted is

    1) $4 : 1$ 2) $2 : 3$ 3) $1 : 4$ 4) $2 : 3$

11. Mole – Mole problems: Determining mole of a substance in a chemical reaction

1. Given the reaction:

    $$C_3H_8 + 5O_2 \rightarrow 3CO_2 + 4H_2O$$

    How many moles of oxygen are required to produce 1.5 moles of CO_2?

    1) 1.5 2) 2.5 3) 3.0 4) 5.0

2. In the reaction

    $$2K + S \rightarrow K_2S$$

    What is the total number of moles of sulfur that will react with 4 moles of potassium?

    1) 0.5 moles 2) 1.0 mole 3) 2.0 moles 4) 4.0 moles

3. Given the reaction

    $$2C_2H_6(g) + 7O_2(g) \rightarrow 4CO_2(g) + 6H_2O(l)$$

    How many moles of CO_2 are produced from the combustion of one mole of C_2H_6?
    1) 1 2) 2 3) 3 4) 4

11. Continues

4. In the reaction below:

$$4NH_3 + 5O_2 \rightarrow 4NO + 6H_2O$$

What is the total number of moles of NO produced when 2 moles of O_2 is completely consumed?

1) 2.0 moles   2) 2.4 moles   3) 1.6 moles   4) 8.0 moles

5. Given the reaction:

$$6CO_2 + 6H_2O \rightarrow C_6H_{12}O_6 + 6O_2$$

What is the total number of moles of water needed to make 1.75 moles of $C_6H_{12}O_6$?

1) 10.5   2) 6   3) 7.5   4) 1.75

6. Given the reaction:

$$4Fe + 3O_2 \rightarrow 2Fe_2O_3$$

To produce 3 moles of Fe_2O_3, how many moles of Fe must be reacted?

1) 3 moles   2) 6 moles   3) 4 moles   4) 1.5 moles

7. In the balanced chemical reaction equation below:

$$C_3H_8 + 5O_2 \rightarrow 3CO_2 + 2H_2O$$

What is the total number of moles of CO_2 produced from reacting 0.25 moles of C_3H_8?

1) 11   2) 5   3) .8   4) 0.75

8. Given the reaction

$$2Al + 3H_2SO_4 \rightarrow 3H_2 + Al_2(SO_4)_3$$

How many moles of H_2SO_4 are needed to react completely with 7.50 moles of Al?

1) 2.5 moles   2) 5.0 moles   3) 9.0 moles   4) 22.5 moles

9. Given the reaction below:

$$Mg(s) + 2H_2O(\ell) \rightarrow Mg(OH)_2(aq) + H_2(g)$$

The number of moles of water needed to react with 3 moles of magnesium is

1) 6 moles   2) 3 moles   3) 0.50 moles   4) 4 moles

10. Given a balanced chemical equation below:

$$3Cu + 2H_3PO_4 \rightarrow Cu_3(PO_4)_2 + 3H_2$$

How many moles of copper are needed to react with 5 moles of phosphoric acid?

1) 10.0 moles   2) 5.00 moles   3) 15.0 moles   4) 7.50 moles

12. Volume – volume problems: Determining volume of a substance in a chemical reaction

1. According to the reaction below:

$$2SO_2(g) \quad + \quad O_2(g) \quad \rightarrow \quad 2SO_3(g)$$

What is the total number of liters of $O_2(g)$ that will react completely with 89.6 liters of SO_2 at STP?

1) 1.0 L   2) 0.500 L   3) 22.4 L   4) 44.8 L

2. Given the reaction:

$$C_2H_4 \quad + \quad 3O_2 \quad \rightarrow \quad 2CO_2 \quad + \quad 2H_2O$$

How many liters of CO_2 are produced when 15 liters of O_2 are consumed?

1) 10 L   2) 15 L   3) 30 L   4) 45 L

3. Given the reaction:

$$2C_2H_6(g) \quad + \quad 7O_2(g) \quad \rightarrow \quad 4CO_2(g) \quad + \quad 6H_2O(g)$$

What is the total number of liters of $CO_2(g)$ produced by the complete combustion of 1 liter of $C_2H_6(g)$?

1) 1 L   2) L   3) 0.5 L   4) 4 L

4. In the balanced chemical reaction equation below:

$$C_3H_8(g) \quad + \quad 5O_2(g) \quad \rightarrow \quad 3CO_2(g) \quad + \quad 2H_2O(g)$$

What is the total volume of $H_2O(g)$ formed when 8.0 liters of $C_3H_8(g)$ is completely oxidized at STP?

1) 32.0 L   2) 22.4 L   3) 8.00 L   4) 4.00 L

13. Mass - mass problems: Determining mass of a substance in a chemical reaction

1. Given the reaction:

$$Mg \quad + \quad 2HCl \quad \rightarrow \quad MgCl_2 \quad + \quad H_2$$

What is the total number of grams of Mg consumed when 1 g of H_2 is produced?

1) 6.0 g   2) 12 g   3) 3.0 g   4) 24 g

2. Given the reaction:

$$4Al(s) \quad + \quad 3O_2(g) \quad \rightarrow \quad 2Al_2O_3(s)$$

What is the minimum number of grams of O_2 gas required to produce 102 grams of Al_2O_3?

1) 32.0 g   2) 192 g   3) 96.0 g   4) 48.0 g

3. Given the balanced equation below:

$$3Cu \quad + \quad 8HNO_3 \quad \rightarrow \quad 3Cu(NO_3)_2 \quad + \quad 2NO \quad + \quad 4H_2O$$

The total number of grams of Cu needed to produce 188 grams of $Cu(NO_3)_2$

1) 64   2) 128   3) 32   4) 124

4. According to the reaction:

$$2C_2H_2 \quad + \quad 5O_2 \quad \rightarrow \quad 4CO_2 \quad + \quad 2H_2O$$

How many grams of CO_2 is produced from reacting 80 grams of C_2H_2?

1) 160 g   2) 251 g   3) 320 g   4) 176 g

Survivingchem.com

Topic 7: Solutions

1. Solution: Recalling Concept Facts and Definitions

1. Which must be a mixture of two or more substances?
   1) Solid 　　　 2) Liquid 　　　 3) Gas 　　　 4) Solution

2. All aqueous mixtures must contain
   1) Water 　　　 2) Sodium chloride 　　　 3) Oxygen 　　　 4) Sand

3. A small quantity of salt is stirred into a liter of water until it dissolves. The water in the mixture is
   1) The solute 　　2) Dispersed material 　3) A precipitate 　　4) The solvent

4. The process of recovering a salt from a solution by evaporating the solvent is known as
   1) Decomposition 　　2) Crystallization 　　3) Reduction 　　4) Filtration

5. In a true solution, the dissolved particles
   1) Are visible to the eyes 　　　　　　3) Are always solids
   2) Will settle out on standing 　　　　4) Cannot be removed by filtration

6. Aqueous solutions are best described as a
   1) Homogenous compounds 　　　　3) Heterogeneous compounds
   2) Homogeneous mixtures 　　　　　4) Heterogeneous mixtures

7. When sample X is passed through a filter paper and a white residue, Y, remains on the paper and a clear liquid, Z, passes through. When Z is vaporized, another white residue remains. Sample X is best classified as
   1) An element 　　　　　　　　　　3) A heterogeneous mixture
   2) A compound 　　　　　　　　　　4) A homogeneous mixture

8. An aqueous solution of copper sulfate is poured into a filter paper cone. What passes through the filter paper?
   1) Only the solvent 　　　　　　　3) Both solvent and solute
   2) Only the solute 　　　　　　　　4) Neither the solvent nor solute

9. One similarity between all solutions and compounds is that both
   1) Are always heterogeneous 　　　3) Have definite ratio of composition
   2) Are always homogeneous 　　　　4) Are composed of two or more substances

10. A solution
    1) Separate on standing 　　　　　3) Can be cloudy
    2) May have color 　　　　　　　　4) Can be heterogeneous

2. Solute and solvents: Determining solutes and solvent of a solution

1. In an aqueous solution of potassium fluoride, the solute is
   1) K^+ only 　　2) Cl^- only 　　3) K^+Cl^- 　　4) H_2O

2. A small of $LiNO_3$ is dissolved in H_2O to make a solution. In this solution
   1) $LiNO_3$ is the solute 　　　　　3) H_2O is the solute
   2) $LiNO_3$ is the solvent 　　　　　4) H_2O is the precipitate

3. What happens when $KI(s)$ is dissolved in water?
   1) I^- ions are attracted to the oxygen atoms of water
   2) K^+ ions are attracted to the oxygen atoms of water
   3) K^+ ions are attracted to the hydrogen atoms of water
   4) No attractions are involved, the crystal just falls apart

4. Which diagram best illustrates the molecule-ions attractions that occur when $NaF(s)$ is added to water?

3. Solubility factors: Recalling definitions and facts

1. The solubility of a salt in a given volume of water depends largely on the
   1) Surface area of the salt crystals
   2) Pressure on the surface of the water
   3) Rate at which the salt and water are stirred
   4) Temperature of the water

2. Which change will have the least effect on the solubility of a solid?
   1) Increase in temperature
   2) Increase in surface area
   3) Decrease in temperature
   4) Decrease in pressure

3. A change in pressure has the greatest effect on the solubility of a solution that contains a
   1) Solid in a liquid
   2) Gas in a liquid
   3) Liquid in a liquid
   4) Liquid in a solid

4. Which change will increase the solubility of a gas in water?
   1) Increase in pressure and increase in temperature
   2) Increase in pressure and decrease in temperature
   3) Decrease in pressure and increase in temperature
   4) Decrease in pressure and decrease in temperature

5. As temperature of water increases, the solubility of all gases
   1) Decrease, and the solubility of all solids increase
   2) Increase, and the solubility of all solids decrease
   3) Decrease, and the solubility of all solids also decrease
   4) Increase, and the solubility of all solids also increase

4. Solubility Factors: Relating change in solubility to type of solute

1. As water temperature increases, the solubility of which substance will increase?
   1) Nitrogen   2) Sodium chloride   3) Oxygen   4) Carbon dioxide

2. Which substance increases its solubility in water when the water temperature is changed from 30°C to 50°C?
   1) $NaNO_3$ 2) NH_3 3) Cl_2 4) CH_4

3. As the temperature of water increases, the solubility of which substance will decrease?
   1) SO_2 2) $CaCl_2$ 3) NaCl   4) NH_4Cl

4. A decrease in water temperature will increase the solubility of
   1) $C_6H_{12}O_6(s)$ 2) $NH_3(g)$ 3) $KCl(s)$ 4) $Br_2(l)$

5. As the pressure of a system is changed from 1 atm to 2 atm, the solubility of which substance will be most affected by this change?
   1) $HCl(l)$ 2) $HCl(g)$ 3) $LiCl(s)$ 4) $LiCl(l)$

6. At standard pressure, water at which temperature will contain the most dissolved NH_4Cl particles?
   1) 5°C   2) 10°C   3) 15°C   4) 20°C

7. At which temperature would 100 g $H_2O(l)$ contain the most dissolved oxygen?
   1) 10°C   2) 20°C   3) 30°C   4) 40°C

8. At which temperature would water contain the least amount of dissolved $CO(g)$ at 1 atm?
   1) 50°C   2) 60°C   3) 300 K   4) 350 K

9. Under which conditions would carbon dioxide be most soluble in water?
   1) 10°C and 1 atm   2) 10°C and 2 atm   3) 20°C and 1 atm   4) 20°C and 2 atm

10. Under which two conditions would water contain the least number of dissolved $NH_3(g)$ molecules?
    1) 101.3 kPa and 273 K
    2) 101.3 kPa and 546 K
    3) 60 kPa and 273 K
    4) 60 kPa and 546 K

     Survivingchem.com

5. Descriptions of solutions: Recalling definitions and facts

1. Which term best describes a solution containing all the dissolved solute that can be dissolved in a given amount of solute?
   1) Unsaturated solution
   2) Supersaturated solution
   3) Saturated solution
   4) Hydrated solution

2. A solution that contains a small amount of solute in a large amount of water can be best described as
   1) Dilute
   2) Supersaturated
   3) Concentrated
   4) Saturated

3. A solution containing less dissolved solute than can be dissolved in a given amount of solute is called
   1) An unsaturated solution
   2) A supersaturated solution
   3) A saturated solution
   4) A dehydrated solution

4. A solution containing a large amount of solute in a small amount of solvent is best described as
   1) Dilute
   2) Supersaturated
   3) Concentrated
   4) Saturated

5. A solution in which equilibrium exists between dissolved and undissolved particles is also a
   1) Saturated solution
   2) Concentrated solution
   3) Supersaturated solution
   4) Dilute solution

6. Soluble and insoluble compounds: Using the Solubility Guideline Table F

1. Based on Reference Table F, which substance is most soluble?
   1) AgI   2) $CaSO_4$ 3) $PbCl_2$ 4) $(NH_4)_2CO_3$

2. According to Reference Table F, which of these compounds is soluble in water at STP?
   1) $ZnSO_4$ 2) $BaSO_4$ 3) $ZnCO_3$ 4) $NaCO_3$

3. At STP, aqueous solution of which salt will have the most dissolved ion?
   1) LiCl   2) AgCl   3) $CaSO_4$ 4) $AgSO_4$

4. Which of these compounds will be the best electrolyte?
   1) $Ba(OH)_2$ 2) $BaCO_3$ 3) $BaCl_2$ 4) $Ba(NO_3)_2$

5. Based on Reference Table F, which of these substances is insoluble?
   1) NH_4Cl 2) $PbCl_2$ 3) NaCl   4) $CaCl_2$

6. Which of the following substances is insoluble?
   1) $BaCO_3$ 2) Na_2CO_3 3) $BaCl_2$ 4) $CaCl_2$

7. At STP, which aqueous solution will contain the least amount of dissolved ions?
   1) $NaNO_3$ 2) Na_2SO_4 3) $Pb(NO_3)_3$ 4) $PbSO_4$

8. According to Table F, which chromate salt is least soluble?
   1) Potassium chromate
   2) Calcium chromate
   3) Ammonium chromate
   4) Lithium chromate

9. Which of these salts is soluble in water?
   1) Lithium phosphate
   2) Lead (II) phosphate
   3) Magnesium sulfide
   4) Silver sulfide

10. Based on Reference Table F, which saturated solution will contain the highest concentration of iodide ion?
    1) Lead iodide
    2) Iron(II) iodide
    3) Silver iodide
    4) Mercury(II) iodide

11. Which of these compounds will form a saturated solution that is most dilute?
    1) Ammonium chloride
    2) Potassium iodide
    3) Sodium nitrate
    4) Calcium carbonate

7. Saturated solution – Using the Solubility Curve Table G: Determining amount of solute

1. What is the maximum number of grams of NH_4Cl needed to form a saturated solution in 100 g of water at 65°C?
   1) 30   2) 60   3) 100   4) 120

2. How many grams of KCl must be dissolved in 100 g of H_2O at 60°C to make a saturated ?
   1) 30 g   2) 45 g   3) 56 g   4) 90 g

3. According to Reference Table G, approximately how many grams of HCl are needed to saturated 100 grams of H_2O at 50°C?
   1) 50   2) 116   3) 58   4) 42

4. What is the approximate amount of $NaNO_3$ needed to saturate 50 grams of water that is at 10°C?
   1) 80 grams   2) 100 grams   3) 40 grams   4) 50 grams

5. According to Reference Table G, approximately how many grams of KNO_3 are needed to form a saturated solution of the salt in 50 grams of H_2O at 20°C?
   1) 70   2) 50   3) 35   4) 17

6. How many grams of KCl must be dissolved in 200 g of H_2O to make a saturated solution at 60°C?
   1) 30 g   2) 45 g   3) 56 g   4) 90 g

7. What amount of KI is needed to make a saturated solution in 200 g of water at 20°C?
   1) 290 g   2) 145 g   3) 150 g   4) 145

8. A saturated solution of $KClO_3$ was made in 200 g of water that is at 50°C. What is the approximate amount of the solute that was dissolved in the water?
   1) 20 g   2) 30 g   3) 40 g   4) 60 g

9. What is the total number of grams of KCl needed to saturate exactly 300 grams of water at 10°C?
   1) 60   2) 70   3) 80   4) 90

10. How many grams of sodium chloride are needed to form a saturated solution in 300 g of water at 90°C?
    1) 40 g   2) 80 g   3) 120 g   4) 160 g

11. According to Reference Table G, what is the approximate amount of potassium chlorate needed to form a saturated solution in 100 g of water at 10°C?
    1) 135 g   2) 30 g   3) 25 g   4) 5 g

12. What is the maximum grams of ammonia that must be dissolved in 200 g of H_2O at 20°C to form a saturated ammonia solution ?
    1) 400 g   2) 110 g   3) 27.5 g   4) 55 g

13. A saturated solution of ammonium chloride prepared with 100 grams of water at 80°C will contain how many grams of the solute?
    1) 15 g   2) 38 g   3) 52 g   4) 66 g

14. According to Reference Table G, which solution is a saturated solution at 30°C?
    1) 12 grams of $KClO_3$ in 100 grams of water   3) 30 grams of NaCl in 100 grams of water
    2) 12 grams of $KClO_3$ in 200 grams of water   4) 30 grams of NaCl in 200 grams of water

15. Which is a saturated solution?
    1) 40 g NH_4Cl in 100 g of water at 50°C   3) 52 g KCl in 100 g of water at 80°C
    2) 2 g SO_2 in 100 g water at 10°C   4) 120 g KI in 100 g water at 20°C

8. Saturated solution – Using the solubility curves: Determining how much more salt is needed to form a saturated solution

1. A solution contains 14 grams of KCl in 100 grams of water at 40°C. What is the maximum amount of KCl that must be added to make this a saturated solution?
   1) 14 g   2) 20 g   3) 25 g   4) 54 g

2. How many more grams of KNO_3 must be added to a solution containing 90 g of the solute in 100g of water at 60°C?
   1) 10 g   2) 15 g   3) 30 g   4) 105 g

3. An unsaturated solution of $NaNO_3$ contains 70 grams of $NaNO_3$ dissolved in 100 g of water at 20°C. How many more grams of $NaNO_3$ are needed to make this a saturated solution?
   1) 70 g   2) 95 g   3) 30 g   4) 18 g

4. A saturated solution of HCl is to be prepared. How many more grams of HCl are needed in a solution containing 100 grams of the solute in 200 grams of water at 20°C to make this a saturated solution?
   1) 44 g   2) 72 g   3) 144 g   4) 100 g

5. What amount of potassium chloride must be added to a solution made by dissolving 80 g of the solute in 200 grams of H_2O at 60°C to produce a saturated solution?
   1) 45 g   2) 160 g   3) 100 g   4) 120 g

6. A student dissolved only 40 grams of NaCl in 80 grams of water that is at 90°C. To make this a saturated solution, the student must add to the solution
   1) 10 grams of NaCl   3) 10 g of H_2O
   2) 20 grams of NaCl   4) 20 g of H_2O

7. A student found a potassium iodide solution that was prepared by dissolving 120 grams of the salt in 100 g of water at 10°C. To make a saturated solution of this substance, the student must add
   1) 15 grams of potassium iodide   3) 20 g of potassium iodide
   2) 15 grams of water   4) 20 g of water

9. Saturated solution – Using the Solubility Curve Table: Determine the amount of solute that precipitated (re-crystallized)

1. A saturated solution of KNO_3 is prepared with 100 grams of water at 70°C. According to Reference Table G, what amount of KNO_3 will precipitate if the solution is cooled to 50°C ?
   1) 215 g   2) 55g   3) 135 g   4) 20 g

2. One hundred grams of water is saturated with NH_4Cl at 50°C. If the temperature of the solution is decreased to 10°C, what amount of the solute will precipitate?
   1) 5 g   2) 17 g   3) 30 g   4) 50 g

3. When the temperature of a saturated solution of $KClO_3$ that is made with 100 g of H_2O is cooled from 25° C to 10°C, some salt crystals reformed at the bottom of the beaker. How many grams of the $KClO_3$ salt is at the bottom of the beaker?
   1) 5 g   2) 10 g   3) 15 g   4) 20 g

4. A test tube contains a saturated solution of KNO_3 that was prepared with 100 grams of H_2O at 60°C. If the test tube is cooled to 30°C, what will be found at the bottom of the test tube?
   1) 30 grams of KNO_3 3) 57 g of KNO_3
   2) 30 g of H_2O 4) 57 g of H_2O

5. A test tube containing a saturated solution is cooled from 30°C to 10°C. If the test tube contains a saturated solution of sodium nitrate made with 100 g of water, what will be found at the bottom of the test tube?
   1) 15 grams of water   3) 15 grams of sodium nitrate
   2) 20 grams of water   4) 20 grams of sodium nitrate

10. Descriptions of solutions - Using Solubility Curve Table G: Determine type of solution

1. A solution containing 85 g of KNO_3 in 100 grams of H_2O at 50°C is considered to be
   1) unsaturated   2) supersaturated   3) saturated

2. A solution containing 75 grams of KNO_3 in 100 grams of water at 50°C is considered to be
   1) unsaturated   2) supersaturated   3) saturated

3. A solution containing 90 grams of KNO_3 in 100 grams of water at 50 °C is considered to be
   1) unsaturated   2) supersaturated   3) saturated

4. Based on Reference Table G, a solution of $NaNO_3$ that contains 120 g of solute dissolved in 100 gram of H_2O at 50 °C is best described as
   1) saturated   2) unsaturated   3) supersaturated

5. A solution containing 10 grams of NH_3 in 100 grams of water 90°C is best classified as
   1) supersaturated   2) saturated   3) unsaturated

6. A solution of KCl contains 90 grams of the solute in 200 grams of water at 60°C. This solution can be best classified as
   1) unsaturated   2) supersaturated   3) saturated

7. Which best describes a solution of NH_3 that contains 120 g of the solute in 200 g of water at 25°C?
   1) Unsaturated   2) Supersaturated   3) Saturated

8. A solution containing 10 grams of $KClO_3$ in 50 grams of water at 65°C is best described as
   1) unsaturated   2) supersaturated   3) saturated

9. If 70 grams of KI is dissolved in 50 g of H_2O at 10°C, what will be the best description of this solution?
   1) Unsaturated   2) Supersaturated   3) Saturated

10. Based on Reference Table G, a solution of SO_2 that contains 15 grams of the solute dissolved in 100 g of H_2O at 10°C is best described as
    1) saturated and dilute   3) unsaturated and concentrated
    2) saturated and concentrated   4) supersaturated and concentrated

11. A solution containing 100 grams of $NaNO_3$ in 100 g at 40°C is best described as
    1) unsaturated and dilute   3) unsaturated and concentrated
    2) saturated and concentrated   4) supersaturated and concentrated

12. A solution of NaCl containing 35 g of the salt dissolved in 100 grams of water at 90°C is best described as
    1) saturated and dilute   3) saturated and concentrated
    2) supersaturated and dilute   4) unsaturated and dilute

13. A solution containing 140 grams of potassium iodide in 100 grams of water at 20°C is best classified as
    1) unsaturated and dilute   3) saturated and dilute
    2) unsaturated and concentrated   4) supersaturated and concentrated

11. Degree of solubility – Using the Solubility Curve Table G: Determine which solute is most (or least) soluble, dilute, or concentrated

1. According to Table G, which of these substances is most soluble at 60°C?
   1) NaCl   2) KCl   3) $KClO_3$ 4) NH_4Cl

2. A saturated solution of which compound will be the least concentrated solution in 100 g of water at 40°C?
   1) SO_2 2) NaCl   3) $KClO_3$ 4) NH_4Cl

3. Based on Reference Table G, which of these substances is least soluble at 50°C?
   1) $KClO_3$ 2) NH_3 3) NaCl   4) $NaNO_3$

4. Which of these saturated solution is the most dilute at 20°C?
   1) KI(aq)   2) KCl(aq)   3) $NaNO_3$(aq)   4) NaCl(aq)

5. Which saturated salt solution is most concentrated at 60°C?
   1) $NaNO_3$(aq)   2) $KClO_3$(aq)   3) KNO_4(aq)   4) KCl(aq)

12. The solubility Curve Table G: Miscellaneous questions

1. According to Reference Table G, which solution at equilibrium contains 50 grams of solute per 100 grams of H_2O at 75°C?
   1) An unsaturated solution of KCl   3) A saturated solution of KCl
   2) An unsaturated solution of $KClO_3$ 4) A saturated solution of $KClO_3$

2. Based on Reference Table G, which salt solution could contain 40 grams of solute per 100 grams of water at 40°C?
   1) A saturated solution of $KClO_3$ 3) An Unsaturated solution of NaCl
   2) A saturated solution of HCl   4) An unsaturated solution of NH_4Cl

3. A solution contains 100 grams of a nitrate salt dissolved in 100 grams of water at 50°C. The solution could be a
   1) supersaturated solution of nano3   3) supersaturated solution of kno3
   2) saturated solution of nano3   4) saturated solution of kno3.

4. A solution is formed by dissolving 45 grams of NH_4Cl in 100 grams of H_2O at 70°C. Which statement correctly describes this solution?
   1) NH_4Cl is the solute, and the solution is saturated
   2) NH_4Cl is the solute, and the solution in unsaturated
   3) NH_4Cl is the solvent, and the solution is saturated
   4) NH_4Cl is the solvent, and the solution is unsaturated

5. According to Reference Table G, which is the best description of a system prepared by dissolving 30 grams of NH_3(g) in 100 grams of water at 20°C?
   1) A saturated solution of NH_3 with no excess NH_3(g)
   2) A saturated solution of NH_3 in contact with excess NH_3(g)
   3) An unsaturated solution of NH_3 with no excess NH_3(g)
   4) An unsaturated solution of NH_3 in contact with excess NH_3(g)

6. A student adds solid KCl to water in a flask. The flask is sealed with a stopper and thoroughly shaken until no more solid KCl dissolves. Some KCl is still visible in the flask. The solution in the flask is
   1) saturated and is at equilibrium with the solid kCl
   2) saturated and is not at equilibrium with the solid kCl
   3) unsaturated and is at equilibrium with the solid kCl
   4) unsaturated and is not at equilibrium with the solid kCl

13. The Solubility Curve Table G: Relating change in solubility to temperature change

1. Which of these compounds has the greatest change in solubility between 30°C and 50°C?
   1) KNO_3 2) KCl   3) $NaNO_3$ 4) NaCl

2. The solubility of which compound is least affected by the change in temperature of water?
   1) NH_3 2) HCl   3) $NaNO_3$ 4) NaCl

3. According to Reference Table G, what change will cause the solubility of $KNO_3(s)$ to increase?
   1) Increase in pressure   3) Increase in temperature
   2) Decrease in pressure   4) Decrease in temperature

4. According to Reference Table G, how does a decrease in temperature from 40°C to 20°C affect the solubility of $NH_3(g)$ and that of NH_4Cl?
   1) The solubility of NH_3 increases, and the solubility of NH_4Cl increases
   2) The solubility of NH_3 decreases, and the solubility of NH_4Cl increases
   3) The solubility of NH_3 increases, and the solubility of NH_4Cl decreases
   4) The solubility of NH_3 decreases, and the solubility of NH_4Cl decreases

5. Based on Reference Table G, which is true of the solubility of KCl, NaCl, NH_3 and NH_4Cl at 60°C and 36°C?
   1) KCl, NaCl and NH_4Cl have the same solubility at 60°C
   2) KCl, NaCl and NH_4Cl have the same solubility at 36°C
   3) KCl, NaCl, and NH_3 have the same solubility at 60°C
   4) KCl, NaCl, and NH_3 have the same solubility at 36°C

14. Molarity and parts per million concentration: Definitions and facts

1. Molarity is defined as
   1) Moles of solute per kilogram of solvent   3) Volume of solvent
   2) Moles of solute per liter of solution   4) Mass of a solution

2. Molarity (M) of a solution is equal to the
   1) $\dfrac{\text{Number of grams of solute}}{\text{Liter of solution}}$ 3) $\dfrac{\text{Number of grams of solute}}{\text{Liter of solvent}}$
   2) $\dfrac{\text{Number of moles of solute}}{\text{Liter of solvent}}$ 4) $\dfrac{\text{Number of moles of solute}}{\text{Liter of solution}}$

3. Parts per million concentration of a solution can be as expressed as
   1) $\dfrac{\text{Grams of solvent}}{\text{Grams of solute}} \times 1\,000\,000$ 3) $\dfrac{\text{Grams of solute}}{\text{Grams of solvent}} \times 1\,000\,000$
   2) $\dfrac{\text{Grams of solvent}}{\text{Grams of solution}} \times 1\,000\,000$ 4) $\dfrac{\text{Grams of solute}}{\text{Grams of solution}} \times 1\,000\,000$

4. Which unit can be used to express solution concentration?
   1) J/mol   2) L/mol   3) mol/L   4) mol/s

15. Molarity concentration calculation: Calculation of concentration from moles or mass(g) and volume(l) of solute using equation:

1. What is the molarity of a NaOH solution if 0.5 L of the solution contains 0.5 moles of NaOH?
   1) 1.0 M   2) 2.0 M   3) 0.25 M   4) 0.5 M

2. What is the molarity of an H_2SO_4 solution if 2 liters of the solution contains 4 moles of H_2SO_4?
   1) 0.5 M   2) 2 M   3) 8 M   4) 80 M

3. What is the concentration of a solution of 10.0 moles of copper(II) nitrate dissolved in 5.00 liters of the solution?
   1) 0.50 M   2) 5.00 M   3) 10.0 M   4) 2.00 M

4. A 0.25 liter of potassium chloride solution contains 0.75 moles of KCl. What is the concentration of this solution?
   1) 0.33 M   2) 0.75 M   3) 3.0 M   4) 6.0 M

5. A solution of NaCl contains 1.8 moles of the solute in 600 ml of solution. What is the concentration of the solution?
   1) 333 M   2) 0.003 M   3) 3 M   4) 0. 05 M

6. What is the molarity of a solution of NH_4Cl if 500 ml of the solution contains 1 mole of NH_4Cl?
   1) 1 M   2) 2 M   3) 5 M   4) 6 M

7. A 250 milliliters of solution that contains 0.25 moles of solute will have a molarity concentration of
   1) 1.0 mol/L   2) 0.025 mol/L   3) 0.50 mol/L   4) 0.75 mol/L

8. What is the molarity of a solution that contains 20 grams of $CaBr_2$ in 0.50 liter of solution?
   1) 0.50 M   2) 0.20 M   3) 5.0 M   4) 10 M

9. What is the molarity of a solution that contains 40 grams of NaOH in 0.50 liter of solution?
   1) 1.0 M   2) 0.5 M   3) 0.25 M   4) 2.0 M

10. What is the concentration of a solution of KNO_3 (molecular mass = 101 g/mole) that contains 50.5 g of KNO_3 in 2.00 liters of solution?
    1) 25.25 M   2) 2.00 M   3) 0.500 M   4) 0.25 M

11. What is the concentration of a solution of HNO_3 if 1.7 L of the solution contains 31.5 grams of HNO_3?
    1) 0.29 M   2) 18.5 M   3) 0.05 M   4) 33.2 M

12. A student dissolved 48 grams of $(NH_4)_2CO_3$ in 2000 ml of water. What will be the molarity of this solution?
    1) 1 M   2) 2 M   3) 0.25 M   4) 0.5 M

13. A student prepared a solution of sodium nitrate by adding 17 grams of the solute to 0.5 L of water. What is the concentration of this solution?
    1) 0.4 M   2) 0.2 M   3) 2 M   4) 4 M

14. Which preparation produces a 2.0 M solution of $C_6H_{12}O_6$?
    1) 90 grams of $C_6H_{12}O_6$ dissolved in 500 mL of solution
    2) 90 grams of $C_6H_{12}O_6$ dissolved in 1000 mL of solution
    3) 180 grams of $C_6H_{12}O_6$ dissolved in 500 mL of solution
    4) 180 grams of $C_6H_{12}O_6$ dissolved in 1000 mL of solution

16. Molarity Concentration calculation: Calculating moles or mass (grams) from
molarity (M) and volume (L) of solution

1. How many moles of solute are contained in 0.2 L of a 1 M solution?
    1) 1   2) 0.2   3) 0.25   4) 0.50

2. What is the total number of moles of solute in 0.250 L of a 2 .0 M solution of NaCl?
    1) 1.0 mole   2) 2.0 moles   3) 1.25 moles   4) 0.5 moles

3. How many moles of KNO_3 are required to make 0.50 liter of a 2 molar solution of KNO_3?
    1) 1.0   2) 2.0   3) 0.50   4) 4.0

4. What is the total number of moles of solute in 2230 ml of 3.0 M NaOH solution
    1) 1.5 moles   2) 3.0 moles   3) 6.7 moles   4) 0.743 moles

5. What is the total number of moles in 500 ml of a 3.0 M solution of potassium iodide solution?
    1) 1.0   2) 1.5   3) 3.0   4) 3.5

6. What is the total number of grams of HI (formula mass = 128 grams /mole) in 1 liter of 1.00 M HI solution?
    1) 1.0 gram   2) 0.500 gram   3) 64 grams   4) 128 grams

7. How many grams of ammonium chloride, NH_4Cl, are contained in 0.500 L of a 2.0 M solution?
    1) 10 g   2) 26.5 g   3) 53.5 g   4) 107 g

8. What is the total number of grams of KCl in .250 liter of 0.200 molar solution?
    1) 3.7 g   2) 7.46 g   3) 14.9 g   4) 37 g

9. How many grams of H_2SO_4 are contained in 500 ml of a 0.2 M solution?
    1) 19.6 g   2) 49 g   3) 100 g   4) 9.8 g

10. A 1 M solution contains 20 grams of solute in 500 ml of solution. What is the mass of 1 mole of the solute?
    1) 10 g   2) 20 g   3) 40 g   4) 80 g

17. Molarity concentration calculation: Calculation of volume from
molarity (M) and moles (or mass) of solute

1. How many liters of a 0.5 M sodium hydroxide solution would contain 1 mole of solute?
    1) 0.5 L   2) 1.0 L   3) 2.0 L   4) 4.0 L

2. How many liters of 1.5 M $Ca(NO_3)_2$ solution would contain 0.45 moles of the $Ca(NO_3)_2$ solute?
    1) 0.3 L   2) 0.67 L   3) 1.95 L   4) 243 L

3. How many milliliters of a 0.1 M KNO_3 solution would contain .02 moles of the solute?
    1) 100 ml   2) 1000 ml   3) 500 ml   4) 200 ml

4. What is the total volume of a 2.5 molar HCl solution that contains 90 grams of HCl in 1 L of solution?
    1) 1 L   2) 2 L   3) 2.5 L   4) 3 L

5. What is the total number of liters of 1 M solution of $C_6H_{12}O_6$ that contains 360 grams of the solute?
    1) 1 L   2) 2 L   3) 0.5 L   4) 0.25 L

 Survivingchem.com

18. Parts Per Million concentration calculation: Calculation of ppm from
mass of solute and grams of solution

1. What is the concentration of $O_2(g)$, in parts per million, in a solution that contains 0.008 grams of $O_2(g)$ dissolved in 1000 grams of $H_2O(\ell)$?
   1) 0.8 ppm
   2) 80 ppm
   3) 8 ppm
   4) 800 ppm

2. A 3000 grams solution contains 1.5 grams of dissolved NaCl salt. What is the concentration of this solution in ppm?
   1) 5.0×10^2
   2) 2.0×10^4
   3) 4.5×10^{-3}
   4) 4.5×10^3

3. A 500 gram of oxygen solution contains .05 grams of dissolved oxygen. The concentration of this solution expressed in parts per million is closest to
   1) 1.0×10^4 ppm
   2) 1.0×10^2 ppm
   3) 1.0×10^{-4} ppm
   4) 2.5×10^7 ppm

4. What is the concentration in parts per million of a solution containing 20 grams of $C_6H_{12}O_6$ in 80.0 grams of H_2O?
   1) 2.50×10^5 ppm
   2) 2.00×10^5 ppm
   3) 4.00×10^6 ppm
   4) 5.00×10^6 ppm

5. What is the concentration in parts per million of a solution containing 333 grams of $NaNO_3$ in 700 grams of H_2O?
   1) 2.10×10^6 ppm
   2) 3.10×10^6 ppm
   3) 4.75×10^5 ppm
   4) 3.22×10^5 ppm

6. A student prepared a $CaCl_2(s)$ solution by adding 1.0 gram of the salt to a 1000 gram of $H_2O(\ell)$. The concentration of this solution is
   1) 1.00×10^{-4} ppm
   2) 1.00×10^4 ppm
   3) 1.00×10^{-3} ppm
   4) 1.00×10^3 ppm

19. Parts Per Million Concentration calculation: Calculation of mass(g) of solute from
ppm and grams of solution

1. What is the total mass of solute in 1000 grams of a solution having a concentration of 5 parts per million?
   1) 0.005 g
   2) 0.05 g
   3) 0.5 g
   4) 5 g

2. How many grams of KNO_3 are needed to be dissolved in water to make 100 grams of a 250 ppm solution?
   1) 2.5×10^{-1} g
   2) 2.5×10^{-2} g
   3) 2.5×10^{-3} g
   4) 2.5×10^{-4} g

3. How many grams of NaCl are needed to be dissolved in water to make 2000 grams of a 100 ppm solution?
   1) 2 g
   2) 0.05 g
   3) 0.2 g
   4) 0.5 g

4. A 500 gram $C_6H_{12}O_6$ solution has a concentration of 300 ppm. How many grams of $C_6H_{12}O_6(s)$ is in this solution?
   1) 1.5×10^{-1} g
   2) 1.5×10^1 g
   3) 4.5×10^{-1} g
   4) 4.5×10^1 g

20. Vapor pressure and boiling: Recalling definitions and facts

1. As the temperature of a liquid increases, its vapor pressure
    - 1) Decreases
    - 2) Increases
    - 3) Remains the same

2. As water in a sealed container is cooled from 20°C to 10°C, its vapor pressure
    - 1) Decreases
    - 2) Increases
    - 3) Remains the same

3. When the vapor pressure of a liquid is equal to the atmospheric pressure, the liquid will
    - 1) Freeze
    - 2) Melt
    - 3) Boil
    - 4) Condense

4. Given the diagram below.

   Liquid A is confined in a container. The equilibrium vapor pressure of liquid A depends on the
    - 1) Amount of vapor in the container
    - 2) Size of the confining container
    - 3) Amount of liquid in the container
    - 4) Temperature of liquid A

5. The vapor pressure of H_2O is less than that of CS_2. The best explanation for this is that H_2O has
    - 1) Larger molecules
    - 2) A larger molecular mass
    - 3) Stronger ionic bonds
    - 4) Stronger intermolecular forces

21. Vapor pressure and boiling: Determining vapor pressure and temperature.

1. According to Reference Table H, what is the vapor pressure of propanone at 50°C?
    - 1) 101.3 kPa
    - 2) 33 kPa
    - 3) 50 kPa
    - 4) 82 kPa

2. A sample of a pure liquid is boiling at a temperature of 150°C. The atmospheric pressure is 65 kPa. The vapor pressure of the liquid is
    - 1) 10 kPa
    - 2) 65 kPa
    - 3) 150 kPa
    - 4) 101.3 kPa

3. According to Reference Table H, which sample has the highest vapor pressure?
    - 1) Water at 70°C
    - 2) Propanone at 65°C
    - 3) Ethanol at 75°C
    - 4) Ethanoic acid at 110°C

4. The normal boiling point of ethanol is closest to
    - 1) 80°C
    - 2) 100°C
    - 3) 200°C
    - 4) 90°C

5. Which sample of water has the lowest vapor pressure?
    - 1) 100 ml at 50°C
    - 2) 200 ml at 30°C
    - 3) 300 ml at 40°C
    - 4) 400 ml at 20°C

6. The vapor pressure of a liquid is 0.92 atm at 60°C. The normal boiling point of the liquid could be
    - 1) 35°C
    - 2) 45°C
    - 3) 55°C
    - 4) 65°C

7. A liquid has a vapor pressure of 90 kPa at 75°C and a vapor pressure of 120 kPa at 90°C. At standard atmospheric pressure, the liquid will boil
    - 1) At 75°C
    - 2) At 90°C
    - 3) Above 75°C but below 90°C
    - 4) Above 90°C but below 100°C

22. Effect of solute on physical properties of water: Recalling d concept facts

1. The depression of the freezing point is dependent on
   1) The nature of the solute
   2) The concentration of dissolved particles
   3) Hydrogen bonding
   4) The formula of the solute

2. When a solute is dissolved in water, the effect on the boiling and the freezing point depends largely on
   1) Nature of the solute
   2) The formula mass of the solute
   3) The number of dissolved particles
   4) The density of the solute

3. As a solute is added to a solvent, what happens to the freezing point and the boiling point of the solution?
   1) The freezing point decreases and the boiling point decreases
   2) The freezing point decreases and the boiling point increases
   3) The freezing point increases and the boiling point decreases
   4) The freezing point increases and the boiling point increases

4. What occurs as a salt dissolves in water?
   1) The number of ions in the solution decreases, and the freezing point decreases
   2) The number of ions in the solution decreases, and the freezing point increases
   3) The number of ions in the solution increases, and the freezing point decreases
   4) The number of ions in the solution increases, and the freezing point increases

5. At standard pressure when NaCl is added to water, the solution will have a
   1) Higher freezing point and a lower boiling point than water
   2) Higher freezing point and a higher boiling point than water
   3) Lower freezing point and a higher boiling point than water
   4) Lower freezing point and a lower boiling point than water

6. As ethylene glycol (antifreeze) is added to water, the boiling point of the water is
   1) Elevated, and the freezing point is depressed
   2) Elevated, and the freezing point is elevated
   3) Depressed, and the freezing point is depressed
   4) Depressed, and the freezing point is elevated

7. As the concentration of ions in a solution is increased by addition of more solute, the conductivity of the solution
   1) Decreases, and the vapor pressure of the solution decreases
   2) Decreases, and the vapor pressure of the solution increases
   3) Increases, and the vapor pressure of the solution increases
   4) Increases, and the vapor pressure of the solution decreases

8. When a 1M solution of aqueous solution is diluted with water, the freezing point of the water
   1) Decreases and the boiling point decreases
   2) Decreases and the boiling point increases
   3) Increases and the boiling point decreases
   4) Increases and the boiling point increases

9. What happens when water is added to aqueous solution of glucose?
   1) Boiling point is elevated, and the freezing point is depressed
   2) Boiling point elevated, and the freezing point is elevated
   3) Boiling point is depressed, and the freezing point is depressed
   4) Boiling point is depressed, and the freezing point is elevated

10. As water is added to a solution, the number of dissolved ions in the solution
    1) Increases, and the concentration of the solution remains the same
    2) Decreases, and the concentration of the solution increases
    3) Remains the same, and the concentration of the solution decreases
    4) Remains the same, and the concentration of the solution remains the same

11. As water is added to a 0.10 M NaCl aqueous solution, the conductivity of the resulting solution
    1) Decreases because the concentration of the ions decreases
    2) Decreases because the concentration of the ion remains the same
    3) Increases because the concentration of the ions decreases
    4) Increases because the concentration of the ion remains the same

23. Effect of solute on boiling and freezing points of water:
Determining which solute has the least or greatest effect

1. Which 1 M solution has the lowest freezing point?
   1) $KCl(aq)$ 2) $C_6H_{12}O_6(aq)$ 3) $C_2H_5OH(aq)$ 4) $C_{12}H_{22}O_{12}(aq)$

2. Which 1 M solution will produce the greatest increase in boiling point of water?
   1) $CH_3OH(aq)$ 2) $C_2H_4(OH)_2(aq)$ 3) $CuCl_2(aq)$ 4) $C_6H_{12}O_6(aq)$

3. Which 0.1 M solution has the highest boiling point?
   1) $NaCl(aq)$ 2) $MgCl_2(aq)$ 3) $LiCl(aq)$ 4) $CsCl(aq)$

4. Which solution containing 1 mole of solute dissolved in 500 grams of water has lowest freezing point?
   1) $NaOH$ 2) $NaNO_3$ 3) $NaCl$ 4) Na_2SO_4

5. Which 1 M solution has the lowest boiling point?
   1) $KNO_3(aq)$ 2) $K_2SO_4(aq)$ 3) $Ca(OH)_2(aq)$ 4) $C_6H_{12}O_6(aq)$

6. A 0.5 M aqueous solution of which substance will have the highest freezing point?
   1) C_2H_5OH 2) $CaSO_4$ 3) KCl 4) KOH

24. Effect of concentration on boiling and freezing points of water:

Determining which concentration has the least or greatest effect

1. Which concentration of CH_3OH solution has the lowest freezing point?
   1) 0.0001 M   2) 0.001 M   3) 0.0002 M   4) 0.002 M

2. Which concentration of NaOH has the lowest freezing and highest boiling temperatures?
   1) 2.0 M   2) 1.5 M   3) 1.0 M   4) 0.1 M

3. A $LiNO_3$ solution of which concentration will boil at the lowest temperature?
   1) .1 M   2) .2 M   3) .3 M   4) .4 M

4. A 1000 grams sample of water will have the highest boiling point when it contains
   1) 1×10^{17} dissolved particles   3) 1×10^{21} dissolved particles
   2) 1×10^{19} dissolved particles   4) 1×10^{23} dissolved particles

5. Which solution will freeze at the lowest temperature?
   1) 1 mole of sugar in 500 g of water   3) 2 moles of sugar in 500 g of water
   2) 1 mole of sugar in 1000 g of water   4) 2 moles of sugar in 1000 g of water

6. Of the following solutions, the one that will boil at the highest temperature contains 1 mole of NaCl dissolved in
   1) 250 g of H_2O 3) 750 g of H_2O
   2) 500 g of H_2O 4) 1000 g of H_2O

7. Which sugar solution will freeze at the highest temperature?
   1) 1 mole of sugar in 500 grams of water   3) 2 moles of sugar in 500 grams of water
   2) 1 mole of sugar in 1000 grams of water   4) 2 moles of sugar in 1000 grams of water

25. Effect of solutes and concentration on boiling and freezing points.

Determination which solute and which concentration has the least and greatest effect

1. Which solution will have the lowest freezing point?
   1) 1 M NaCl   2) 1 M KCl   3) 1 M $CaCl_2$ 4) 1 M $C_6H_{12}O_6$

2. Which of the following solutions will have the highest boiling point?
   1) 0.1 M KCl   2) 0.2 M KCl   3) 0.1 M $CaCl_2$ 4) 0.2 M $CaCl_2$

3. Which of the preparation of solutions will have the lowest freezing point?
   1) 0.2 M KOH   2) 0.2 M NaOH   3) 0.2 M $Mg(OH)_2$ 4) 0.2 M $CH_2(OH)_2$

4. Which solution will boil at the highest temperature?
   1) 2 M Na_2SO_4 2) 1 M Na_2SO_4 3) 2 M $NaNO_3$ 4) 2 M $NaNO_3$

5. Which solution will boil at the lowest temperature?
   1) 0.1 M $C_6O_{12}O_6$ 2) 0.1 M LiBr   3) 0.2 M $C_6H_{12}O_6$ 4) 0.2 M LiBr

6. Which preparation will produce a solution with the lowest freezing point?
   1) .1 moles of HCl in 1000 g of water   3) .2 moles of H_2SO_4 in 1000 g of water
   2) .1 moles of HCl in 2000 g of water   4) .2 moles of H_2SO_4 in 2000 g of water

7. Which preparation will produce the greatest increase in the boiling point of water?
   1) 0.3 moles of $CaCl_2$ in 100 g of water   3) 0.3 moles of KCl in 100 g of water
   2) 0.3 moles of $CaCl_2$ in 1000 g of water   4) 0.3 moles of KCl in 1000 g of water?

8. Which of the following solutions, each containing a nonvolatile solute, will boil t the highest temperature?
   1) 1 mole of electrolyte dissolved in 1000 g of H_2O
   2) 2 moles of electrolyte dissolved in 1000 g of H_2O
   3) 1 mole of nonelectrolyte dissolved in 1000 g of H_2O
   4) 2 moles of nonelectrolyte dissolved in 1000 g of H_2O

9. Which solute, when added to 1000 grams of water, will produce a solution with the highest boiling point?
   1) 29 g of NaCl   3) 31 g of $C_2H_6O_2$
   2) 58 g of NaCl   4) 62 g of $C_2H_6O_2$

10. Which of the given solutes dissolved in 1000 g of H_2O will produce a solution with the lowest freezing temperature?
    1) 10 g of Li_2SO_4 3) 10 g of Ag_2SO_4
    2) 10 g of $SrSO_4$ 4) 10 g of $BaSO_4$

11. Which solute preparations will produce a solution with the highest boiling point?
    1) 55 g $CaCl_2$ dissolved in 1000 g H_2O 3) 21 g $CaCl_2$ dissolved in 500 g of H_2O
    2) 55 g $CaCl_2$ dissolved in 2000 g of H_2O 4) 21 g $CaCl_2$ dissolved in 200 g of H_2O

12. Which of the following preparations will produce a solution with the highest freezing point?
    1) 1 g NaOH in 10 g of water   3) 1 g HCl in 100 g of water
    2) 2 g NaOH in 10 g of water   4) 2 g HCl in 100 g of water

Topic 8:   Acids, Bases, and Salts

1. Arrhenius theory of acids and bases: Recalling Concept Facts and Definitions

1. Which is a characteristic of aqueous solution of an acid?
    1) It conducts electricity
    2) It turns litmus blue
    3) It forms OH⁻
    4) It turns phenolphthalein pink

2. Which is a characteristic of aqueous solution of a base?
    1) It turns phenolphthalein pink
    2) It does not conduct electricity
    3) It turns blue litmus red
    3) It reacts with a metal

3. When placed in a basic solution, litmus will turn
    1) red and phenolphthalein colorless
    2) red and phenolphthalein pink
    3) blue and phenolphthalein colorless
    4) blue and phenolphthalein pink

4. In a solution of acid, litmus will be
    1) red and phenolphthalein colorless
    2) red and phenolphthalein pink
    3) blue and phenolphthalein colorless
    4) blue and phenolphthalein pink

5. A solution of a base in the presence of an phenolphthalein will
    1) turn pink
    2) turn blue
    3) turn red
    4) stay colorless

6. Which property is of an acid but not of a base?
    1) A solution of an acid is an electrolyte
    2) A solution of an acid has effect on acid – base indicators
    3) A solution of an acid contains more H⁺ than OH⁻ ions
    4) A solution of an acid turns litmus blue

7. Which statement describes characteristics of an Arrhenius base?
    1) It changes blue litmus to red and has a pH less than 7
    2) It changes blue litmus to red and has a pH greater than 7
    3) It changes red litmus to blue and has a pH less than 7
    4) It changes red litmus to blue and has a pH greater than 7

8. When a solution of an acid is tested with a pH paper, the result will be a pH
    1) above 7, and the solution will conduct electricity
    2) above 7, and the solution will not conduct electricity
    3) below 7, and the solution will conduct electricity
    4) below 7, and the solution will not conduct electricity

9. When a solution of a base is tested with a pH paper, the result will be a pH
    1) above 7, and the solution will conduct electricity
    2) above 7, and the solution will not conduct electricity
    3) below 7, and the solution will conduct electricity
    4) below 7, and the solution will not conduct electricity

2. Properties of acids and bases: Recalling Concept Facts

1. Which ion is the only ion produced by all Arrhenius bases in water?
   1) NO_3^- 2) Cl^- 3) OH^- 4) H^+

2. Which ion is produced by all Arrhenius acids as the only positive ion in solutions?
   1) OH^+ 2) NH_4^+ 3) SO_4^{2+} 4) H_3O^+

3. Which ion is produce by a base when it is dissolved in water?
   1) Hydroxide ion   3) Ammonium ion
   2) Hydrogen ion   4) Hydronium ion

4. When a base is dissolved in water, it produces
   1) OH^- as the only negative ions in solution
   2) NH_4^+ as the only positive ions in solution
   3) CO_3^{2-} as the only negative ions in the solution
   4) H^+ as the only positive ions in solution

5. In solutions, Arrhenius acids have
   1) only hydroxide ions
   2) only hydrogen ions
   3) hydrogen ions as the only negative ions
   4) hydrogen ions as the only positive ions

6. According to Arrhenius theory, when an acid dissolves in water it produces
   1) hydrogen ion as the only negative ion in the solution
   2) hydrogen ion as the only positive ion in the solution
   3) hydroxide ion as the only negative ion in the solution
   4) hydroxide ion as the only positive ion in the solution

7. According to Arrhenius theory, when a base dissolves in water it produces
   1) hydronium ions as the only negative ion in the solution
   2) hydronium ions as the only positive ion in the solution
   3) hydroxide ions as the only negative ion in the solution
   4) hydroxide ions as the only positive ion in the solution

8. A sample of acidic solution contains
   1) neither OH^- nor H_3O^+
   2) equal number of OH^- ion to H_3O^+ ion
   3) a smaller amounts of H_3O^+ ions than OH^- ions
   4) larger amounts of H_3O^+ ions than OH^- ions

9. What are the relative ion concentrations of a basic solution?
   1) More OH^- ions than H^+ ions
   2) Fewer OH^- ions than H^+ ions
   3) H^+ ions but no OH^- ions
   4) An equal number of H^+ ions and OH^- ions

10. Unlike an acid solution, an aqueous solution of a base
    1) contains only OH^- ions
    2) contains only H_3O^+ ion
    3) contains less OH^- than H^+
    4) contains more OH^- than H^+

 Survivingchem.com

3. Arrhenius Acids : Determining formula of acids

1. Which is a formula of Arrhenius acid?
   1)NaCl   2) HCl   3) CCl_4 4) H_2O

2. Which substance is an acid?
   1)LiF   2) HBr   3) $Mg(OH)_2$ 4) CH_3CHO

3. According to Arrhenius theory, which list of compounds includes only acids?
   1) HNO_3, H_2SO_4, and $C_6H_{12}O_6$
   2) H_2PO_4, HCO_3, and NH_4Cl
   3) LiOH, HNO_3, and CH_3OH
   4) HCl, H_2CO_3, and HNO_3

4. Arrhenius Base: Determining formula of Bases

1. Which substance is a base?
   1) $HC_2H_3O_2$ 2) $Ca(OH)_2$ 3) C_2H_5OH 4) NH_4Cl

2. Which species is classified as an Arrhenius base?
   1) PO_4^{3-} 2) CH_3OH 3) CO_3^{2-} 4) LiOH

3. According to Arrhenius theory, which list of compounds includes only bases?
   1) KOH, $Ca(OH)_2$, and CH_3OH
   2) LiOH, $Ca(OH)_2$, and $C_2H_4(OH)_2$
   3) KOH, NaOH, and LiOH
   4) NaOH, $Ca(OH)_2$, and CH_3COOH

5. Salts: Determining formula of salts

1. Which compound is a salt?
   1) KOH   2) KNO_3 3) HOH   4) HCl

2. Which formula is a formula of a salt?
   1) NaOH   2) $NaC_2H_3O_2$ 3) HCOOH   4) CH_3COOH

3. Which of the following is a salt?
   1) $Ca(NO_3)_2$ 2) NH_3 3) $HC_2H_3O_2$ 4) CCl_4

4. Which list of compounds includes only salts?
   1) HNO_3, $NaNO_3$, and $Ca(NO_3)_2$
   2) C_2H_5OH, CH_3COOH, and $CaCl_2$
   3) CH_3OH, NaOH, and NaCl
   4) $Ba(NO_3)_2$, Na_2SO_4, and $MgCl_2$

6. Formula of acids and bases: Determining formulas of acids or bases based on properties

1. Which aqueous solution contains OH- ions as the only negative ion in the solution?
    1) $NH_4Cl(aq)$ 2) $NH_3(aq)$ 3) $H_2SO_4(aq)$ 4) $HCl(aq)$

2. Which substance will produce hydrogen ion as the only positive charge in a solution?
    1) H_2CO_3 2) LiF   3) LiOH   4) NH_3

3. Which solution will contain more hydroxide ions than hydrogen ions?
    1) $CaCl_2$ 2) C_2H_5OH 3) $Mg(OH)_2$ 4) CH_3Cl

4. In which aqueous solution would there be a greater concentration of OH- ions than H+ ions?
    1) $CH_3COOH(aq)$ 2) $C_{12}H_{22}O_{11}(aq)$ 3) $NH_4C_2H_3O_2(aq)$ 4) $NH_3(aq)$

5. If 1 mole of each of the following substances were dissolved in 1 L of water, which solution would contain the highest concentration of H_3O^+ ions?
    1) KBr   2) NaCl   3) CH_3COOH 4) $Ba(OH)_2$

6. Which aqueous solution can turn red litmus blue?
    1) $KOH(aq)$ 2) $CH_3OH(aq)$ 3) $HNO_3(aq)$ 4) $KCl(aq)$

7. Which compound when dissolved in water will turn blue litmus red?
    1) CH_3OH 2) HBr   3) $C_6H_{12}O_6$ 4) $Ca(OH)_2$

8. Water containing phenolphthalein will change from colorless to pink with the addition of
    1) HOH   2) $Ca(OH)_2$ 3) HCl   4) NaCl

9. In which 0.01 M aqueous is phenolphthalein pink?
    1) $CH_3OH(aq)$ 2) $HNO_3(aq)$ 3) $CH_3COOH(aq)$ 4) $LiOH(aq)$

10. In which solution would a phenolphthalein solution remains colorless?
    1) $Sr(OH)_2$ 2) $Ca(OH)_2$ 3) NH_4OH 4) HCl

11. A compound whose water solution conducts electricity and have a pH of 9 could be
    1) HCl   2) LiCl   3) NH_3 4) C_2H_5OH

12. Which aqueous solution would have a pH of 3?
    1) $H_2O(\ell)$ 2) $KOH(aq)$ 3) $CH_3OH(aq)$ 4) $HNO_3(aq)$

13. Which solution could have a pH of 10 ?
    1) NH_4OH 2) NaCl   3) $NaNO_3$ 4) Na_2SO_4

14. Which of these 1 M solutions will have the highest pH?
    1) LiOH   2) LiCl   3) HCl   4) $NaNO_3$

15. A solution of which substance would react with a metal to produce hydrogen gas?
    1) KNO_3 2) $LiNO_3$ 3) NaOH   4) H_3PO_4

16. Which substance would react with an active metal to produce salt and hydrogen gas
    1) HCl   2) KCl   3) NH_3 4) NH_4OH

7. Properties of acids and bases: Determining properties of a solution based on formula

1. In a 0. 1 M HNO_3 solution, litmus will be
   1) blue and phenolphthalein will be colorless
   2) red and phenolphthalein will be colorless
   3) blue and phenolphthalein will be pink
   4) red and phenolphthalein will be pink

2. A solution of LiOH is classified as
   1) Arrhenius base, with a pH below 7
   2) Arrhenius base, with a pH above 7
   3) Arrhenius acid, with pH below 7
   4) Arrhenius acid, with pH above 7

3. Both HNO_3(aq) and CH_3COOH(aq) can be classified as
   1) Arrhenius acids that turn blue litmus red
   2) Arrhenius acids that turns red litmus blue
   3) Arrhenius bases that turn blue litmus red
   4) Arrhenius bases that turn red litmus blue

4. The aqueous solution of $Ca(OH)_2$ contains
   1) equal molar of hydroxide and hydronium ions
   2) more hydronium than hydroxide ion
   3) more of hydroxide than hydronium ions
   4) neither hydronium nor hydroxide ion

5. The pH of aqueous solution of HCl will be
   1) exactly 7, and litmus will be red
   2) above 7, and litmus will be blue
   3) below 7, and litmus will be red
   4) below 7, and litmus will be colorless

6. Which are true of aqueous solution of $Mg(OH)_2$?
   1) It contains more OH^- ion than H^+ ion, and is a nonelectrolyte
   2) It contains more OH^- ion that H^+ ion, and is an electrolyte
   3) It contains more H^+ than OH^-, and is a nonelectrolyte
   4) It contains more H^+ than OH^-, and is an electrolyte

7. In aqueous solution of NH_3, phenolphthalein is
   1) pink because the nh_3 solution contain greater amount of h^+ than oh^-
   2) pink because the nh_3 solution contains greater amount of oh^- than h^+
   3) colorless because the nh_3 solution contains greater amount of h^+ than oh^-
   4) colorless because the nh_3 solution contains greater amount of oh^- than h^+

8. Which is true of NaOH?
   1) It is a base that contains equal concentration of OH^- and H_3O^+ ions in solutions
   2) It is a base that contains greater concentration of OH^- ions than H_3O^+ ions in solutions
   3) It is an acid that contains equal concentration of OH^- and H_3O^+ ions in solutions
   4) It is an acid that contains greater concentration of OH^- ions than H_3O^+ ions in solutions

9. Which is true of LiOH(aq) but not of HNO_3(aq)?
   1) LiOH(aq) conducts electricity
   2) LiOH(aq) have pH above 7
   3) LiOH(aq) contains both H^+ and OH^- ions
   4) LiOH(aq) change color of indicators

10. Which is true of a solution of CH_3COOH but not of $Ca(OH)_2$?
    1) CH_3COOH solution contains both hydronium ion and hydroxide ion
    2) CH_3COOH solution is an electrolyte
    3) CH_3COOH contains more hydronium ion than hydroxide ion
    4) CH_3COOH can change color of indicators

8. Electrolytes: Recalling Concept Facts and Definitions

1. A substance that conducts electrical current when dissolved in water is called
   1) a catalyst
   2) a metalloid
   3) a nonelectrolyte
   4) an electrolyte

2. Water solutions conducts electrical current because the solution contains mobile
   1) ions
   2) molecules
   3) atoms
   4) electrons

3. Which list contains types of substances that electrolytes?
   1) Soluble salts, sugar, and acids
   2) Soluble salts, alcohols, and bases
   3) Soluble salts, acids and bases
   4) Acids, bases, and alcohols

9. Electrolytes: Determining formulas and names of compounds that are electrolytes

1. Which species can conduct electrical current?
   1) NaOH(s)
   2) $CH_3OH(aq)$
   3) $H_2O(s)$
   4) HCl(aq)

2. Which 0.1 M solution contains electrolytes?
   1) $C_6H_{12}O_6(aq)$
   2) $CH_3COOH(aq)$
   3) $CH_3OH(aq)$
   4) $CH_3OCH_3(aq)$

3. Which compound is classified as an electrolyte?
   1) H_2O
   2) $C_{12}H_{22}O_{11}$
   3) CH_3OH
   4) $Ca(OH)_2$

4. An example of a nonelectrolyte is
   1) $C_6H_{12}O_6(aq)$
   2) $K_2SO_4(aq)$
   3) NaCl(aq)
   4) HCl(aq)

5. Which compound is a nonelectrolyte?
   1) NH_3
   2) CH_4
   3) KBr
   4) HCl

6. According to Reference Table F, which saturated salt solution would be the best electrolyte?
   1) AgCl(aq)
   2) $PbCl_2(aq)$
   3) $NH_4Cl(aq)$
   4) $HgCl_2(aq)$

7. Which salt will form a saturated solution with the highest electrical conductivity?
   1) Potassium nitrate
   2) Silver bromide
   3) Lead sulfate
   4) Potassium carbonate

8. In the diagram below, which solution will cause the light bulb to glow?

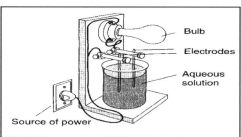

   1) $C_6H_{12}O_6(aq)$
   2) LiOH(aq)
   3) $CO_2(aq)$
   4) $C_2H_5OH(aq)$

 <u>Survivingchem.com</u>

10. pH: Determining pH of acids and bases

1. Which indicate a pH of an acidic solution?
   1) 4   2) 7   3) 9   4) 14

2. Which pH indicates a strongest acid solution?
   1) 3   2) 8   3) 2   4) 9

3. A basic solution will have a pH of
   1) 11   2) 7   3) 2   4) 1

4. Which pH of a solution indicates the strongest base?
   1) 6   2) 7   3) 8   4) 9

5. Which pH represents a neutral solution?
   1) 10   2) 8   3) 5   4) 7

11. pH: Determining pH of a solution based on given characteristics properties of the solution.

1. In a solution, litmus is blue. The pH of the solution could be
   1) 8   2) 6   3) 4   4) 2

2. Phenolphthalein has a pink color in a solution which has a pH of
   1) 1   2) 5   3) 7   4) 11

3. An aqueous solution turns litmus red. The pH of the solution could be
   1) 14   2) 11   3) 8   4) 5

4. When phenolphthalein is added to a solution, the solution stays colorless. What could be the pH of this solution?
   1) 2   2) 7   3) 9   4) 11

5. What will be the pH of a solution that conducts electricity but contains equal number of H^+ to OH^- ions?
   1) 1   2) 5   3) 7   4) 10

12. pH: **Determining properties of a solution based on its pH**

1. Which is true of a solution that has a pH of 4?
    1) Litmus will be blue
    2) Litmus will be red
    3) Phenolphthalein will pink
    4) Phenolphthalein will be red

2. An aqueous solution with a pH of 10 turns litmus
    1) blue, and phenolphthalein will be pink
    2) blue, and phenolphthalein will stay colorless
    3) red, and phenolphthalein will turn pink
    4) red, and phenolphthalein will stay colorless

3. Which is true concerning the relative concentration of OH- to H+ ions in a solution with a pH of 3?
    1) The solution contains more OH^- than H^+ ions
    2) The solution contains more H^+ than OH^- ions
    3) The solution contains equal number of OH^- to H^+ ions
    4)   The solution contains no H^+ and no OH^- ions

4. A solution with a pH of 11 contains
    1) more H^+ than OH^-
    2) more OH^- than H^+
    3) equal number of H^+ and OH^-
    4) neither H^+ nor OH^-

5. A solution with a pH of 13 is a(n)
    1) electrolyte that will turn litmus red
    2) electrolyte that will turn litmus blue
    3) nonelectrolyte that will turn litmus red
    4) nonelectrolyte that will turn litmus red

6. When tested, a solution turns red litmus to blue. This indicates that the solution contains more
    1) H_3O^+ than OH^- ions, and has a pH above 7
    2) H_3O^+ than OH^- ions, and has a pH below 7
    3) OH^- than H_3O^+ ions, and has a pH above 7
    4) OH^- than H_3O^+ ions, and has a pH below 7

7. An indicator is used to test a water solution with a pH of 12. Which indicator color could be observed?
    1) Colorless with litmus
    2) Red with litmus
    3) Colorless with phenolphthalein
    4) Pink with phenolphthalein

13. H+ and OH- concentration: Determining solution concentration of the ions

1. What is the OH- ion concentration of a solution with H+ concentration of 1.0×10^{-3} M?
   1) 1.0×10^{-3} M
   2) 1.0×10^{-11} M
   3) 1.0×10^{-7} M
   4) 1.0×10^{-14} M

2. What is the H^+ concentration of a solution that has an OH^- ion concentration of 1.0×10^{-6} M ?
   1) 1.0×10^{-8} M
   2) 1.0×10^{-6} M
   3) 1.0×10^{-1} M
   4) 1.0×10^{-14} M

3. The concentration of hydronium ions in a solution is 1.0×10^{-12} M at 298 K. What is the hydroxide ion concentration in the same solution?
   1) 1.0×10^{-14} M
   2) 1.0×10^{-7} M
   3) 1.0×10^{-9} M
   4) 1.0×10^{-2} M

4. What is the hydrogen ion concentration of a solution that has hydroxide ion concentration of 1.0×10^{-9} moles per liter at 25°C?
   1) 1×10^{-9} M
   2) 1×10^{-7} M
   3) 1×10^{-5} M
   4) 1×10^{-14} M

5. What is the H^+ concentration of a solution with OH^- concentration of 0.0000001 M?
   1) 0.01 mole per liter
   2) 0.001 mole per liter
   3) 0.0000001 mole per liter
   4) 0.000001 mole per liter

6. What is the hydroxide concentration of a solution with hydronium ion concentration of 0.0001 M?
   1) 1.0×10^{-10} M
   2) 1.0×10^{-4} M
   3) 1.0×10^{10} M
   4) 1.0×10^{4} M

14. H+ and OH- concentrations: Relating pH to ion concentration

1. A solution has H_3O^+ concentration of 1.0×10^{-9} M. What is the pH of this solution?
   1) 1   2) 5   3) 9   4) 10

2. What is the pH of a solution with H^+ ion concentration of 0.001 M?
   1) 1   2) 4   3) 3   4) 11

3. What is the pH of a solution with OH^- ion concentration of 1.0×10^{-2} M?
   1) 12   2) 10   3) 8   4) 2

4. What is the H^+ concentration of a solution with a pH of 8?
   1) 1.0×10^{8} M
   2) 1.0×10^{-8} M
   3) 1.0×10^{6} M
   4) 1.0×10^{-6} M

5. A solution with a pH of 13 will have H₃O+ concentration of
   1) 1.0×10^{-1} M
   2) 1.0×10^{-10} M
   3) 1.0×10^{-14} M
   4) 1.0×10^{-13} M

6. What is the hydroxide ion concentration of a solution with a pH of 1?
   1) 1.0×10^{-1} M
   2) 1.0×10^{-10} M
   3) 1.0×10^{-13} M
   4) 1.0×10^{-6} M

7. What is the OH- ion concentration with a pH of 11?
   1) 1.0×10^{-11} M
   2) 1.0×10^{11} M
   3) 1.0×10^{-3} M
   4) 1.0×10^{3} M

15. Properties of solutions: Relating ions concentration of a solution to properties

1. Which is true of a solution with H^+ concentration of 1.0 x 10^{-3} M?
    1) It is acidic and will turn litmus blue
    2) It is acidic that will turn litmus red
    3) It is basic and will turn litmus blue
    4) it is basic and will turn litmus red

2. A solution with H_3O^+ concentration of 1.0 x 10^{-11} M will be
    1) basic with a pH of 11
    2) basic with a pH of 3
    3) acidic with a pH of 11
    4) basic with a pH of 3

3. An aqueous solution with a hydrogen ion concentration of 1.0 x 10^{-9} M will turn litmus
    1) blue and phenolphthalein pink
    2) blue and phenolphthalein colorless
    3) red and phenolphthalein pink
    4) red and phenolphthalein colorless

4. A solution with H^+ concentration of 1.0 x 10^{-5} moles/L is
    1) acidic because it contains more H^+ than OH^-
    2) acidic because it contains more OH^- than H^+
    3) basic because it contains more H^+ than OH^-
    4) basic because it contains more OH^- than H^+

5. Which is true of a solution with an OH^- concentration of 1.0 x 10^{-4} M?
    1) It is acidic with a pH of 11
    2) It is acidic with pH of 4
    3) It is basic with pH of 11
    4) It is basic with pH of 4

6. In a solution with hydroxide ion concentration of 1.0 x 10^{-10} M,
    1) phenolphthalein is pink and litmus is red
    2) phenolphthalein is pink and litmus blue
    3) phenolphthalein is colorless and litmus is red
    4) phenolphthalein is colorless and litmus blue

7. An aqueous solution has OH^- concentration of 1.0 x 10^{-7} moles per liter. Which is true of this solution?
    1) It is acidic with pH below 7
    2) It is basic with pH above 7
    3) It is neutral with pH above 7
    4) It is neutral with pH of 7

8. Which hydrogen ion concentration could be of a solution that turns litmus red?
    1) 1.0 x 10^{-2} M
    2) 1.0 x 10^{-7} M
    3) 1.0 x 10^{-9} M
    4) 1.0 x10^{-11} M

9. An aqueous solution turns red litmus blue. What would be the hydroxide ion concentration of this solution?
    1) 1.0 x 10^{-4} mole/L
    2) 1.0 x 10^{-12} mole/L
    3) 1.0 x 10^{-7} mole/L
    4) 1.0 x 10^{-9} mole/L

10. A solution contains equal molar concentration of OH^- and H^+ ions. What would be the concentration of each of the ions in this solution?
    1) 1.0 x 10^{-7} M
    2) 1.0 x 10^{-1} M
    3) 1.0 x 10^{-10} M
    4) 1.0 x 10^{-14} M

16. Effect of adding an acid or a base to a solution: Recalling Concept Facts

1. As aqueous solution becomes more acidic, the hydroxide ion concentration of the solution
   1) increases   2) decreases   3) remains the same

2. As a solution becomes more basic, the hydrogen ion concentration in the solution
   1) increases   2) decreases   3) remains the same

3. As an acidic solution is added to a basic solution, the H$^+$ ion concentration in the solution
   1) increases   2) decreases   3) remains the same

4. As a basic solution is added to an acidic solution, the OH$^-$ ion concentration of the solution
   1) increases   2) decreases   3) remains the same

5. As a solution of a base is added to an acidic solution, the pH of the solution
   1) increases   2) decreases   3) remains the same

6. Which substance, if added to water, will increase the OH$^-$ concentration of water?
   1) NaCl   2) KNO$_3$ 3) LiOH   4) HNO$_3$

7. Hydronium ion concentration of an acidic solution will decrease with the addition of which substance?
   1) KNO$_3$ 2) K$_2$SO$_4$ 3) KOH   4) KCl

8. The pH of a solution will decrease with the addition of which compound?
   1) CH$_3$COOH   2) NH$_3$ 3) NaOH   4) CaCl$_2$

9. A student observed that the pH of a solution increases with the addition of substance X to the solution. Which compound could substance X be?
   1) Ammonia   3) Nitric acid
   2) Ammonium chloride   4) Sodium chloride

10. As CH$_3$COOH is added to water, the H$^+$ concentration of the water solution
    1) decreases, and the pH increases   3) increases, and the pH increases
    2) decreases, and the pH decreases   4) increases, and the pH decreases

11. When a solution of NaOH is added to water solution, the H$^+$ concentration will
    1) increase, and OH$^-$ concentration will increase
    2) increase, and OH$^-$ concentration will decrease
    3) decrease, and OH$^-$ concentration will decrease
    4) decrease, and OH$^-$ concentration will increase

12. As NH$_4$OH is added to HCl solution, the pH of the solution
    1) decreases as the OH$^-$ ion concentration increases
    2) decreases as the OH$^-$ ion concentration decreases
    3) increases as the OH$^-$ ion concentration increases
    4) increases as the OH$^-$ ion concentration decreases

13. When a solution of sulfuric acid is added to a solution of sodium hydroxide, the concentration of hydrogen ions in the solution
    1) decreases, and the pH increases
    2) increases, and the pH decreases
    3) decreases, and the pH decreases
    4) increases, and the pH increases

14. When a solution of ammonia is added to a solution of hydrochloric acid, the pH of the solution
    1) increases as OH$^-$ ion concentration increases
    2) increases as OH$^-$ ion concentration decreases
    3) decreases as H$^+$ ion concentration increases
    4) decreases as H$^+$ ion concentration decreases

17. Alternate theory of acids and bases: Recalling Concept Facts and Definitions

1. According to an alternate theory, an acid is any species that can
   1) donate a proton
   2) donate an electron
   3) accept a proton
   4) accept an electron

2. According to an alternate theory, a base in an acid-base reaction is any species that can
   1) donate a proton
   2) donate an electron
   3) accept a proton
   4) accept an electron

3. According to an "alternate theory" of acids and bases, H_2O will act as a base in a reaction if it
   1) donates OH^- to another species in the reaction
   2) donates H^+ ion to another species in the reaction
   3) accepts OH^- ion from another species in the reaction
   4) accepts H^+ ion from another species in the reaction

4. According to an "alternate theory" of acids and bases, H_2O will act as an acid in a reaction if it
   1) donates OH^- to another species in the reaction
   2) donates H^+ ion to another species in the reaction
   3) accepts OH^- ion from another species in the reaction
   4) accepts H^+ ion from another species in the reaction

18. Reaction of acids with metals: Determining which metal will react

1. According to Reference Table J, which metal will react with hydrochloric acid to produce hydrogen gas?
   1) Ag   2) Hg   3) Cu   4) Ni

2. Under standard conditions, which metal will react spontaneously with 1 M HNO_3?
   1) Mg   2) Ag   3) Hg   4) Au

3. Which of these metals will not produce a reaction with sulfuric acid?
   1) Ca   2) Au   3) Zn   4) Li

4. According to Reference Table J, which reaction will not occur under STP?
   1) Sn(s)   +   2HCl(aq) $\rightarrow$ H_2(g)   + $SnCl_2$(aq)
   2) Cu(s)   +   2HCl(aq) $\rightarrow$ H_2(g)   + $CuCl_2$(aq)
   3) Ba(s)   +   2HCl(aq) $\rightarrow$ H_2(g)   + $BaCl_2$(aq)
   4) Pb(s)   +   2HCl(aq) $\rightarrow$ H_2(g)   + $PbCl_2$(aq)

5. Which equation is showing a reaction that is likely to occur under standard conditions?
   1) Au(s)   +   2HBr(aq) $\rightarrow$ H_2(g)   + $AuBr_2$(aq)
   2) Cu(s)   +   2HBr(aq) $\rightarrow$ H_2(g)   + $CuBr_2$(aq)
   3) Hg(s)   +   2HBr(aq) $\rightarrow$ H_2(g)   + $HgBr_2$(aq)
   4) Cr(s)   +   2HBr(aq) $\rightarrow$ H_2(g)   + $CrBr_2$(aq)

19. Neutralization: Recalling Concept Facts and Definitions

1. What type of reaction occurs when equal molar of an acid and an a base are combined?
   1) Combustion
   2) Neutralization
   3) Single replacement
   4) Hydrolysis

2. Which reaction occurs when equal molar of H^+ and OH^- reacted?
   1) Decomposition
   2) Hydrolysis
   3) Esterification
   4) Neutralization

3. What are the two reactants in a neutralization reaction?
   1) Acid and salt
   2) Base and Salt
   3) Acid and base
   4) Salt and water

4. What substances are produced in a neutralization reaction?
   1) Water and salt
   2) Water and Hydrogen gas
   3) Salt and Hydrogen gas
   4) Sugar and salt

5. Which substances are always produced in a reaction between an acid and a base?
   1) Water
   2) Hydrogen gas
   3) Oxygen gas
   4) A Precipitate

20. Neutralization: Determining neutralization reaction equation

1. Which equation represents a neutralization reaction?
   1) $Ca(OH)_2 \rightarrow Ca^{2+} + 2OH^-$
   2) $CaCl_2 \rightarrow Ca^{2+} + 2Cl^-$
   3) $H^+ + OH^- \rightarrow HOH$
   4) $H^+ + F^- \rightarrow HF$

2. Which equation represents a neutralization reaction?
   1) $2\,Na + 2H_2O \rightarrow 2\,NaOH + H_2$
   2) $NaOH + HCl \rightarrow NaCl + HCl$
   3) $Zn + CuSO_4 \rightarrow ZnSO_4 + Cu$
   4) $AgNO_3 + NaCl \rightarrow AgCl + NaNO_3$

3. Which balanced equation represents a neutralization reaction?
   1) $Mg + NiCl_2 \rightarrow MgCl2 + Ni$
   2) $2KClO_3 \rightarrow 2KCl + 3\,O_2$
   3) $BaCl_2 + Cu(NO_3)_2 \rightarrow Ba(NO_3)_2 + CuCl_2$
   4) $H_2SO_4 + 2LiOH \rightarrow Li_2SO_4 + 2H_2O$

4. Which equation is showing a neutralization reaction?
   1) $H^+(aq) + OH^-(aq) \rightarrow H_2O(\ell)$
   2) $Ag^+(aq) + I^-(aq) \rightarrow AgI(s)$
   3) $Zn(s) + Cu^{2+}(aq) \rightarrow Zn^{2+}(aq) + Cu(s)$
   4) $2H_2(g) + O_2(g) \rightarrow 2H_2O(\ell)$

5. In which reaction are equal moles of H+ and OH- ions reacting?
   1) $CaO + H_2O \rightarrow Ca(OH)_2$
   2) $2HCl + Zn \rightarrow ZnCl_2 + H_2$
   3) $H_2SO_4 + CaCO_3 \rightarrow CaSO_4 + H_2O + CO_2$
   4) $HNO_3 + KOH \rightarrow KNO_3 + H_2O$

21. Salts : Determining names and formulas of salt formed in acid-base reactions

1. Given the neutralization reaction :
   $$H_2SO_4 + KOH \rightarrow HOH + K_2SO_4$$
   Which compound is a salt?

   1) KOH   2) H_2SO_4 3) K_2SO_4 4) HOH

2. Given the neutralization reaction below:
   $$HCl + LiOH \rightarrow LiCl + H_2O$$
   Which compound is a salt?

   1) H_2O 2) LiCl   3) LiOH   4) HCl

3. In the neutralization reaction:
   $$HC_2H_3O_2 + NH_4OH \rightarrow NH_4C_2H_3O_2 + H_2O$$
   The salt is

   1) NH_4OH 2) $HC_2H_3O_2$ 3) $NH_4C_2H_3O_2$ 4) H_2O

4. What is the formula of a salt produced from a reaction between KOH and HCl?
   1) KH   2) K_2H 3) KCl   4) KCl_2

5. What is the formula of a salt produced in the neutralization reaction between NaOH and HNO_3?
   1) $NaNO_3$ 2) $Na(NO_3)_2$ 3) H_2O 4) NaH

6. What is the formula of the salt produced by the reaction between magnesium hydroxide with sulfuric acid?
   1) HOH   2) $MgSO_3$ 3) $MgSO_4$ 4) MgH

7. What is the name of a salt produced by a reaction of calcium hydroxide with sulfuric acid?
   1) Calcium thiosulfate   3) Calcium sulfide
   2) Calcium sulfate   4) Calcium sulfite

8. What is the name of a salt produced by the reaction of barium hydroxide with phosphoric acid?
   1) Barium phosphide   3) Barium phosphate
   2) Barium hydride   4) Barium oxide

9. What is the name of a salt that is produced in a reaction between acetic acid and potassium hydroxide?
   1) Potassium acetate   3) Potassium acetic
   2) Potassium hydride   4) Potassium chloride

10. A reaction between which two substances will produce H_2O and a salt with the formula of $LiClO_3$?
    1) LiCl and H_2O 3) LiOH and HCl
    2) LiCl and $HClO_3$ 4) LiOH and $HClO_3$

11. Which two substances can react to produce H_2O and a salt with the formula of K_3PO_4?
    1) KOH and H_3PO_4 3) K_3P and H_2O
    2) K_2O and H_3PO_4 4) KOH and H_2O

12. Which two compounds could react to produce water and sodium carbonate?
    1) Sodium and water
    2) Sodium and carbon dioxide
    3) Sodium hydroxide and hydrochloric acid
    4) Sodium hydroxide and carbonic acid

22. Titration: Determining molarity or volume of a solution

1. If 50 milliliters of 0.50 M HCl is used to completely neutralize 25 milliliters of KOH solution, what is the molarity of the base?
    1) 1.0 M   2) 0.25 M   3) 0.50 M   4) 2.5 M

2. In a titration experiment, 20 ml of 1.0 M HCl neutralized 10 ml of NaOH solution of unknown concentration. What was the concentration of the base?
    1) 2.5 M   2) 2.0 M   3) 1.5 M   4) 0.50 M

3. If 100 mL of a 0.75 M HNO_3 is required to exactly neutralize 50 ml of NaOH, what is the concentration of the base?
    1) 0.25 M   2) 0.75 M   3) 1.0 M   4) 1. 5M

4. A 1.5 milliliters sample of HCl solution was needed to neutralized 6.0 milliliters of 0.50 M LiOH solution. What is the molarity of the acid?
    1) 1.0 M   2) 3.0 M   3) 0.5 M   4) 2.0 M

5. If 20 ml of a 2.0 M KOH is exactly neutralized by 10 ml of HCl, the molarity of the HCl is
    1) 0.50 M   2) 2.0 M   3) 4.0 M   4) 1.0 M

6. How many milliliters of 0.20 M KOH solution are needed to exactly neutralize 20 milliliters of 0.50 HCl solution?
    1) 50 ml   2) 25 ml   3) 10 ml   4) 4.0 ml

7. How much volume of a 0.01 M NaOH can be used to completely neutralized 25 ml of 0.20 M HNO_3?
    1) 50 ml   2) 10 ml   3) 25 ml   4) 500 ml

8. A 20 milliliters NaOH solution is used to titrate a 40 milliliters of 0.1 M HCl solution. What is the concentration of the NaOH solution?
    1) 80 M   2) 0.2 M   3) 4. 0 M   4) 2 M

9. What volume of a 4.0 molar solution of HCl is needed to completely neutralize a 60 ml of 3.2 molar NaOH solution?
    1) 24 ml   2) 48 ml   3) 60 ml   4) 75 ml

10. How many ml of a 0.4 M nitric acid are required to neutralize 200 ml of a 0.16 M potassium hydroxide?
    1) 30   2) 80   3) 200   4) 500

11. How many milliliters of a 1.5 M H_2SO_4 are needed to neutralize a 35 ml sample of a 1.5 M KOH solution?
    1) 17.5 ml   2) 35 ml   3) 52.5 ml   4) 3.0 ml

12. How many milliliters of a 2.5 M NaOH solution are needed to completely neutralize 25 ml of a 1.0 M H_2SO_4 solution?
    1) 10 ml   2) 50 ml   3) 20 ml   4) 8 ml

13. How many milliliters of a 3.0 M HCl are neutralized by 60 ml of a 0.5 M of $Ca(OH)_2$?
    1) 40 ml   2) 30 ml   3) 20 ml   4) 60 ml

1. Kinetics: Recalling Concept Facts and Definitions

1. Kinetic is the study of
   1) nuclear changes
   2) electrical currents
   3) organic compounds
   4) rates of reaction

2. Which term refers to the speed at which chemical reactions occur?
   1) Energy
   2) Rate
   3) Equilibrium
   4) Mechanism

3. Which term correctly defines a pathway in which a reaction occurs?
   1) Rate
   2) Equilibrium
   3) Activation
   4) Mechanism

4. The type of energy that is needed to start a chemical reaction is the
   1) kinetic energy
   2) activation energy
   3) potential energy
   4) ionization energy

5. A substance in a reaction that increases the rate of the reaction is called
   1) an isotope
   2) an activated complex
   3) a catalyst
   4) a precipitate

6. What will change when a catalyst is added to a chemical reaction?
   1) Activation energy
   2) Energy of reaction
   3) Potential energy of reactants
   4) Potential energy of products

7. In order for any chemical reaction to occur, there must always be
   1) a bond that breaks in a reactant particle
   2) effective collision between reacting particles
   3) a reacting particle with a high charge
   4) a reacting particle with high kinetic energy

8. For collision to be effective, reacting particles must collide with
   1) sufficient kinetic energy only
   2) proper orientation only
   3) sufficient kinetic energy and proper orientation
   4) sufficient potential energy and proper orientation

9. Two particles collide with proper orientation. The collision will be effective if the particles have
   1) high activation energy
   2) high electronegativity
   3) sufficient potential energy
   4) sufficient kinetic energy

10. As the number of effective collisions between reacting particles increase, the rate of reaction

   1) decreases   2) increases   3) remains the same

2. Factors affecting reaction rate: Recalling Concept Facts

1. As the temperature of a reaction increases, the rate of the reaction
    1) increases   2) decreases   3) remains the same

2. When surface area of a reacting solid is increased, the rate at which the solid reacts will
    1) decrease   2) increase   3) remain the same

3. As the concentration of a reacting substance decreases, the rate of the reaction generally
    1) increases   2) decreases   3) remains the same

4. Adding a catalyst to a reaction will cause the rate of a reaction to
    1) increase   2) decrease   3) remain the same

5. As the temperature of a reaction decreases, the rate of the reaction will
    1) remain the same   2) increase   3) decrease

6. When compared to reactions of covalent substances, the rate of reactions for ionic solutions is usually
    1) faster   2) slower   3) remains the same

7. As the number of liters per mole of a reactant in a reaction decreases, the number of collisions between reacting particles
    1) remains the same   2) increases   3) decreases

8. Which conditions will increase the rate of a chemical reaction?
    1) Decreased temperature and decreased concentration
    2) Decreased temperature and increased concentration
    3) Increased temperature and decreased concentration
    4) Increased temperature and increased concentration

9. Increasing the concentration of a reaction
    1) increases the reaction rate because there will be less effective collisions between particles
    2) increases the reaction rate because there will be more effective collisions between particles
    3) decreases the reaction rate because there will be less effective collisions between particles
    4) decreases the reaction rate because there will be more effective collisions between particles

10. Increasing temperature will
    1) increase reaction rate because of an increase in frequency of effective collisions
    2) increase reaction rate because of a decrease in frequency of effective collisions
    3) decrease reaction rate because of an increase in frequency of effective collisions
    4) decrease reaction rate because of a decrease in frequency of effective collisions

11. Increasing temperature speeds up a reaction by increasing
    1) the effectiveness of collisions, only
    2) the frequency of collision, only
    3) both the effectiveness and the frequency of the collisions
    4) neither the effectiveness nor the frequency of the collisions

12. When pressure on a reaction that involve gases is increased, the rate of the reaction will
    1) decrease because there is a decrease in concentration
    2) decrease because there is an increase in concentration
    3) increase because there is a decrease in concentration
    4) increase because there is an increase in concentration

13. When the surface area of reacting particles is decreased, there will be
    1) an increase in reaction rate because of more collision
    2) an increase in reaction rate because of less collision
    3) a decrease in reaction rate because of more collision
    4) a decrease in reaction rate because of less collision

14. When a catalyst is added to a reaction, the reaction rate is increased because the catalyst
    1) increases activation energy   3) increases potential energy of the reactants
    2) decreases activation energy   4) decreases potential energy of the reactants

 Survivingchem.com

3. Reaction Rate: Determining factors that will change chemical reaction rate of reactions

1. Given the reaction,

$$A_2(g) \ + \ B_2(g) \ \rightarrow \ 2AB(g) \ + heat$$

   An increase in concentration of $A_2(g)$ increases the rate of the reaction because of
   - 1) a decrease in activation energy
   - 2) an increase in activation energy
   - 3) a decrease in frequency of collision
   - 4) an increase in frequency of collision

2. Given the reaction

$$A(s) \ + \ B(s) \ \rightarrow \ C(aq) \ + \ D(aq)$$

   Which change would increase the rate of this reaction?
   - 1) A decrease in temperature
   - 2) An increase in temperature
   - 3) A decrease in pressure
   - 4) An increase in pressure

3. Given the reaction

$$Mg(s) \ + \ HNO_3(aq) \ \rightarrow \ Mg(NO_3)_2(aq) \ + \ H_2(g)$$

   At which temperature will the reaction occurs at the greatest rate?
   - 1) 10°C
   - 2) 30°C
   - 3) 50°C
   - 4) 70°C

4. At which temperature would a reaction between zinc and hydrochloric acid occur at the slowest speed?
   - 1) 25°C
   - 2) 50°C
   - 3) 75°C
   - 4) 100°C

5. Given the reaction

$$Zn(s) \ + \ HCl(aq) \ \rightarrow \ ZnCl_2(aq) \ + \ H_2(g)$$

   The reaction will occur more rapidly when a 10 gram sample of zinc powder is used rather than 1 piece of zinc because zinc powder
   - 1) has more surface area
   - 2) has less surface area
   - 3) lower potential energy
   - 4) higher potential energy

6. Four aluminum samples are each reacted with separate 1 M copper sulfate solution under the same conditions of temperature and pressure. Which aluminum sample would react most rapidly?
   - 1) 1 gram of Al block
   - 2) 1 gram of Al ribbon
   - 3) 1 gram of Al Powder
   - 4) 1 gram of Al pellet

7. Given the reaction

$$CuSO_4(s) \ \rightarrow \ Cu^{2+}(aq) \ + \ SO_4^{2-}(aq)$$

   The $CuSO_4(s)$ dissolves more rapidly when it is powdered because the increased in surface area allows for
   - 1) increased exposure of solute to solvent
   - 2) increased solute solubility
   - 3) decreased exposure of solute to solvent
   - 4) decreased solute solubility

3. Continues

8. Which statement explains why the rate of a chemical reaction is increased when the surface area of the reactant is increased?
    1) This change increases the density of the reacting particle
    2) This change increases the concentration of the reactant
    3) This change exposes more reactant particles to a possible collision
    4) This change alters the reaction mechanism

9. Given the reaction

    $$A + B \;\rightarrow\; C + D$$

    The reaction will occur at the greatest rate if A and B represents

    1) ionic compounds in the solid phase
    2) nonpolar molecular compounds in the solid phase
    3) solutions of ionic compounds
    4) solutions of nonpolar molecular compounds

10. Based on the nature of the reactants in each equation, which reaction at 25°C will occur at the fastest rate?
    1) $KI(aq)$ + $AgNO_3(aq)$ $\rightarrow$ $AgI(s)$ + $KNO_3(aq)$
    2) $C(s)$ + $O_2(g)$ $\rightarrow$ $CO(g)$
    3) $2SO_2(g)$ + $O_2(g)$ $\rightarrow$ $2SO_3(g)$
    4) $NH_3(g)$ + $HCl(g)$ $\rightarrow$ $NH_4Cl(s)$

11. When added to a chemical reaction, a catalyst
    1) lowers the activation energy, and increases reaction rate
    2) lowers the activation energy, and decreases reaction rate
    3) raises the activation energy, and increases reaction rate
    4) raises the activation energy, and decreases reaction rate

12. Which will occur if a catalyst is added to a reaction mixture?
    1) The concentration of the reactants will decrease
    2) The concentration of the reactants will increase
    3) The activation energy will decrease
    4) The activation energy will increase

13. When a catalyst is added to a reaction, the speed of the reaction will increase because the catalyst provides
    1) alternate higher activation energy pathway for the reaction
    2) alternate lower activation energy pathway for the reaction
    3) alternate higher pressure environment for the reaction to occur
    4) alternate lower pressure environment for the reaction to occur

14. Changes in activation energy during a chemical reaction are represented by a
    1) cooling curve   3) heating curve
    2) ionization energy diagram   4) potential energy diagram

   Survivingchem.com

4. Energy and Chemical reaction: Recalling Concept Facts and Definitions

1. Exothermic chemical reactions
   1) absorbs heat energy
   2) release heat energy
   3) absorbs electrons
   4) release electrons

2. Which best describes all endothermic reactions?
   1) They always release heat
   2) They always absorb heat
   3) They always occur spontaneously
   4) They never occur spontaneously

3. In what type of reactions do the products of the reactions always have more energy than the reactants?
   1) Exothermic
   2) Redox
   3) Endothermic
   4) Neutralization

4. In which type of a reaction is the energy of reactants always greater than the energy of products?
   1) Exothermic
   2) Redox
   3) Endothermic
   4) Neutralization

5. Activation energy is need for reactions that are
   1) exothermic, only
   2) endothermic, only
   3) both exothermic and endothermic
   4) neither exothermic nor endothermic

6. In a chemical reaction, the difference between the potential energy of the products and the potential energy of the reactants is called
   1) activation energy
   2) kinetic energy
   3) activated complex
   4) heat of reaction

7. The heat of reaction (ΔH) is equal to
   1) heat of products − heat of reactants
   2) heat of products + heat of reactants
   3) heat of products x heat of reactants
   4) heat of products ÷ heat of reactants

8. Which statement correctly describes heats of reaction for all endothermic reactions?
   1) ΔH is negative because heat is absorbed
   2) ΔH is positive because heat is absorbed
   3) ΔH is negative because heat is released
   4) ΔH is positive because heat is released

9. In exothermic reactions,
   1) heat is released, and ΔH is negative
   2) heat is released, and ΔH is positive
   3) heat absorbed, and ΔH is negative
   4) heat is absorbed, and ΔH is positive

10. ΔH (heat of reaction) of a chemical reaction is always equal to
    1) entropy of the products minus entropy of the reactants
    2) entropy of the reactant minus entropy of the products
    3) potential energy of the products minus the potential energy of the reactants
    4) potential energy of the reactant minus the potential energy of the products

11. In endothermic reactions,
    1) the products have lower potential energy than the reactants, and ΔH is negative
    2) the products have lower potential energy than the reactants, and ΔH is positive
    3) the products have higher potential energy than the reactants, and ΔH is negative
    4) the products have higher potential energy than the reactants, and ΔH is positive

12. Which correctly describes all exothermic chemical reactions?
    1) ΔH is negative because the products have lower potential energy than the reactants
    2) ΔH is positive because the products have lower potential energy than the reactants
    3) ΔH is negative because products have higher potential energy than the reactants
    4) ΔH is positive because the products have higher potential energy than the reactants

5. Energy and chemical reaction: Relating energy to change in temperature of reactions

1. What type of a chemical reaction will cause an increase in the temperature of the surrounding in which the reaction is taking place?
   1) Exothermic, because heat will be released
   2) Exothermic because heat will be absorbed
   3) Endothermic because heat will be released
   4) Endothermic because heat will be absorbed

2. When an endothermic reaction occurs in a solution, the temperature of the solution
   1) increases because heat energy is given off by the reaction
   2) increases because heat energy is absorbed by the reaction
   3) decreases because heat energy is given off by the reaction
   4) decreases because heat energy is absorbed by the reaction

3. When an exothermic process occurs in water, the temperature of the water will
   1) increase because heat energy is given off by the reaction
   2) increase because heat energy is absorbed by the reaction
   3) decrease because heat energy is given off by the reaction
   4) decrease because heat energy is absorbed by the reaction

4. When a substance is dissolved in water, the temperature of the water increases. This process is best described as
   1) endothermic, with a release of energy
   2) endothermic, with an absorption of energy
   3) exothermic, with a release of energy
   4) exothermic with an absorption of energy

5. Salt A and salt B were each dissolved in separate beakers of water at 21°C. The temperature of salt A solution decreased, and the temperature of salt B solution increased.
   Based on these results, which conclusion is correct?
   1) The water gained energy from both salt A and salt B
   2) The water lost energy to both salt A and salt B
   3) The water gained energy from salt A and lost energy to salt B
   4) The water lost energy to salt A and gained energy from salt B

6. Solid X and solid Y were dissolved in separate 100 ml beakers of water. The water temperatures were recorded as shown in the table below.

	Salt X	Salt Y
Initial water temperature	40.3°C	40.3°C
Final water temperature	34.5°C	46.1°C

   Which statement is the best conclusion from the above information?
   1) The dissolving of only Salt X was exothermic
   2) The dissolving of only Salt Y was endothermic
   3) The dissolving of both Salt X and Salt Y was exothermic
   4) The dissolving of Salt X was endothermic and the dissolving of Salt Y was exothermic

 Survivingchem.com

6. Heat energy of reactions: Determining energy change and ΔH of a given reaction

1. Given the equation

    Mg   +   HCl → MgCl$_2$ + H$_2$ + heat

    Which is true of this reaction?
    1) It is exothermic in which heat is absorbed
    2) It is exothermic in which heat is released
    3) It is endothermic in which heat is absorbed
    4) It is endothermic in which heat is released

2. Given the reaction

    N$_2$(g)   +   O$_2$(g) + energy →   2NO(g)

    This equation shows that the formation of nitrogen monoxide is
    1) exothermic, because heat is absorbed
    2) exothermic, because heat is released
    3) endothermic, because heat is absorbed
    4) endothermic, because heat is released

3. Given the reaction

    AB   +   Heat   →   A   +   B

    The equation is showing that the reaction is
    1) endothermic, in which the products have less energy than the reactants
    2) endothermic, in which the products have more energy than the reactants
    3) exothermic, in which the products have less energy than the reactants
    4) exothermic, in which the products have more energy than the reactants

4. Given the reaction

    2CO(g)   +   O$_2$(g)   →   2CO$_2$(g)   +   energy

    Which is true of the heat of reaction (Δ H)?
    1) ΔH is positive because heat is absorbed
    2) ΔH is positive because heat is released
    3) ΔH is negative because heat is absorbed
    4) ΔH is negative because heat is released

5. Given the reaction:

    I   +   I   →   I$_2$ +   energy

    This reaction has
    1) +ΔH because the products have less energy than the reactants
    2) +ΔH because the products have more energy than the reactants
    3) -ΔH because the products have less energy than the reactants
    4) -ΔH because the products have more energy than the reactants

6. Given the equation

    2H$_2$O(ℓ)   +   energy →   2H$_2$(g)   +   O$_2$(g)

    Which statement is true concerning the potential energy of the products and of the reactants?
    1) The products have less energy than the reactants, and ΔH will be negative
    2) The products have more energy than the reactants, and ΔH will be positive
    3) The products have less energy than the reactants, and ΔH will be positive
    4) The products have more energy than the reactants, and ΔH will be negative

7. Heat Energy of reactions (ΔH): Determining energy change and ΔH value of a reaction

1. Given the reaction
$$X_2 \ + \ 2Y_2 \ \rightarrow \ 2XY_2 \ + \ 10 \text{ kJ}$$
The formation of 2 moles of XY_2
   1) releases 10 kJ of heat because the reaction is exothermic
   2) releases 10 kJ of heat because the reaction is endothermic
   3) absorbs 10 kJ of heat because the reaction is exothermic
   4) absorbs 10 kJ of heat, because the reaction is endothermic

2. Given the chemical change
$$2H_2O(\ell) \ + \ 572 \text{ kJ} \ \rightarrow \ 2\,H_2(g) \ + \ O_2(g)$$
This reaction
   1) is endothermic and releases 572 kJ of heat energy
   2) is endothermic and absorbs 572 kJ of heat energy
   3) is exothermic and releases 572 kJ of heat energy
   4) is exothermic and absorbs 572 kJ of heat energy

3. The reaction
$$A \ + \ B \ \rightarrow \ C \ + \ D \ + \ 30 \text{ kJ}$$
Has ΔH of
   1) +30 kJ because the reaction is endothermic
   2) +30 kJ because the reaction is exothermic
   3) -30 kJ because the reaction is endothermic
   4) -30 kJ because the reaction is exothermic

4. Given the reaction
$$2C(s) \ + \ 2H_2(g) \ + \ 227 \text{ kJ} \ \rightarrow \ C_2H_2(g)$$
The heat of reaction, ΔH, is
   1) +227 kJ because products have more energy than reactants
   2) +227 kJ because products have less energy that reactants
   3) -227 kJ because products have more energy than reactants
   4) -227 kJ because products have less energy than reactants

5. Given the reaction
$$N_2O_4(g) \ + \ 58 \text{ kJ} \ \rightarrow \ 2NO_2(g)$$
What is the approximate heat of formation of 1 moles of $NO_2(g)$
   1) -58 kJ   3) -29 kJ
   2) +58 kJ   4) +29 kJ

6. Given the reaction
$$N_2(g) \ + \ 3H_2(g) \ \rightarrow \ 2NH_3(g) \ + \ 91.8 \text{ kJ}$$
What is the heat of reaction, ΔH, for the formation of 4 moles of $NH_3(g)$
   1) -91.8 kJ   3) -183.6 kJ
   2) +91.8 kJ   4) +183.6 kJ

7. In the reaction
$$2CO(g) \ + \ O_2(g) \ \rightarrow \ 2CO_2(g) \ + \ 566 \text{ kJ}$$
Which is true of the heat of formation of $CO_2(g)$
   1) ΔH = + 283 kJ/mole   3) ΔH = + 566 kJ/mole
   2) ΔH = - 283 kJ/mole   4) Δ H = - 566 kJ/mole

Survivingchem.com

8. Heat energy of reactions – Using Reference Table I:

Interpreting equations from Table I based on ΔH value

1. According to Reference Table I , which gas is formed from its elements as a result of an endothermic reaction?
   1) CO_2 2) NO_2 3) H_2O 4) C_2H_6

2. Which of these gases, according to Reference Table I, is formed by a reaction that is exothermic?
   1) $NO_2(g)$ 2) $NO(g)$ 3) $C_2H_4(g)$ 4) $C_2H_6(g)$

3. According to Reference Table I, which substance is formed by a reaction that absorbs heat energy?
   1) $HI(g)$ 2) $H_2O(\ell)$ 3) $NH_3(g)$ 4) $H_2O(g)$

4. Based on Reference Table I, the formation of I mole of which substance releases the greatest amount of heat energy?
   1) C_2H_2 2) NO 3) C_2H_6 4) NH_3

5. The dissolving of which salt is accompanied by the release of heat?
   1) Ammonium chloride   3) Potassium nitrate
   2) Lithium bromide   4) Ammonium nitrate

6. According to Table I, which reaction is endothermic?
   1) $NaOH(s) \longrightarrow Na^+(aq) + OH^-(aq)$ 3) $CO(g) + O_2(g) \longrightarrow CO_2(g)$
   2) $NH_4Cl(s) \longrightarrow NH_4^+(aq) + Cl^-(aq)$ 4) $N_2(g) + H_2(g) \longrightarrow NH_3(g)$

7. In which reaction, according to Reference Table I, do the products have lower energy content than the reactants?
   1) $2C(s) + 3H_2(g) \longrightarrow C_2H_6(g)$ 3) $N_2(g) + O_2(g) \longrightarrow 2NO(g)$
   2) $2C(s) + H_2(g) \longrightarrow C_2H_2(g)$ 4) $N_2(g) + 2O_2(g) \longrightarrow 2NO_2(g)$

8. According to Reference Table I, when two moles of $H_2O(g)$ are formed from its elements,
   1) 484 kJ of heat is absorbed   3) 242 kJ of heat is absorbed
   2) 484 kJ of heat is released   4) 242 kJ of heat is released

9. According to Reference Table I, when 1 mole of $H_2O(g)$ is formed from its element,
   1) 484 kJ of heat is absorbed   3) 242 kJ of heat is absorbed
   2) 484 kJ of heat is released   4) 242 kJ of heat is released

10. Based on Reference Table I, the combustion of 1 mole of CH_4
    1) releases 890.4 kJ of heat   3) absorbs 485.2 kJ of heat
    2) absorbs 890.4 kJ of heat   4) releases 485.2 kJ of heat

11. According to Table I, the combustion of 2 moles of methane
    1) releases 890.4 kJ of heat   3) releases 1780.8 kJ of heat
    2) absorbs 485.2 kJ of heat   4) absorbs 1780.8 kJ of heat

12. According to Reference Table I, the formation of 2 moles of ethyne, C_2H_2,
    1) releases 227.4 kJ of heat   3) releases 454.8 kJ of heat
    2) absorbs 227.4 kJ of heat   4) absorbs 454.8 kJ of heat

13. According to Table I, what is the heat of reaction for the combustion of 1 mole of ethanol, CH_3OH?
    1) $\Delta H = -1452$ kJ/mole   3) $\Delta H = -726$ kJ/mole
    2) $\Delta H = +1452$ kJ /mole   4) $\Delta H = +726$ kJ/mole

14. According to Reference Table I, what is ΔH for the formation of 0.5 mole of $HI(g)$ from its elements?
    1) +26.5 kJ/mole   3) +53.0 kJ/mole
    2) +13.25 kJ/mole   4) +106.0 kJ/mole

9. Potential Energy Diagram: Determining correct energy diagram to a reaction given.

1. Which of the following potential energy diagrams best represents a reaction that is endothermic?

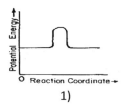
1)

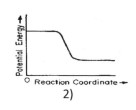
2)

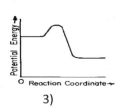
3)

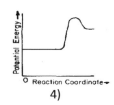
4)

2. Which energy diagram best represents a reaction in which the products have less potential energy contents than the reactants?

1)

2)

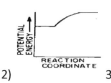
3)

4)

3. Which potential energy diagram best represents a reaction that has a negative heat of reaction (-ΔH)?

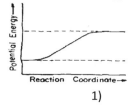
1)

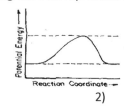
2)

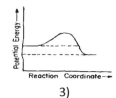
3)

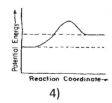
4)

4. Given the reaction and its ΔH value

$$C + D \rightarrow CD \quad \Delta H = +40 \text{ kJ/mole}$$

Which diagram best represents the potential energy change of this reaction?

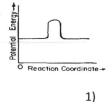
1)

2)

3)

4)

5. Given the reaction

$$A + B \rightarrow C + energy$$

Which diagram below best represents the Potential energy change for this reaction?

1)

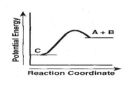
2)

3)

4)

9. Continues

6. Given the reaction
    XY   +   energy → X + Y
    Which potential energy diagrams best represents the energy change for this reaction?

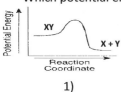
1)

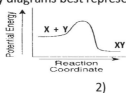
2)

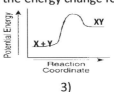
3)

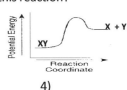
4)

7. According to Reference Table I, which diagram would correctly represent the potential energy change for the formation of NO(g) from its elements?

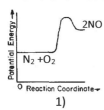
1)

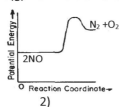
2)

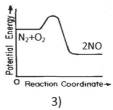
3)

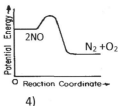
4)

8. According to Reference Table I, which diagram below best shows heat energy change for the formation of $H_2O(\ell)$ from its elements?

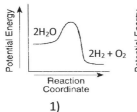
1)

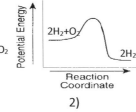
2)

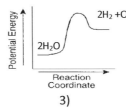
3)

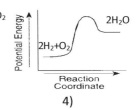
4)

10. Potential energy diagram: Interpreting and relating diagram to energy change

1. According to the potential energy diagram below

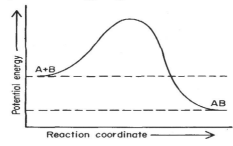

The reaction A + B →   AB can be best describe as

1) endothermic with a positive ▲H
2) endothermic with a negative ▲H
3) exothermic with a positive ▲H
4) exothermic with a negative ▲H

10. continues

2. Given the potential energy below

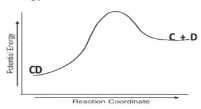

The reaction CD →   C + D is best described as

1) exothermic, because heat is released
2) exothermic, because heat is absorbed
3) endothermic, because heat is released
4) endothermic, because heat is absorbed

3. Given the potential energy below

Which is true of the formation of XY from its elements?

1) The product have more energy than the reactants, and the reaction has -▲H
2) The product have less energy than the reactants, and the reaction has -▲H
3) The product have more energy than the reactants, and the reaction has +▲H
4) The product have less energy than the reactants, and the reaction has +▲H

4. The diagram below represents energy change that occurs during the formation of a compound from its elements under standard conditions.

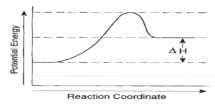

According to Reference Table I, the compound could be

1) $C_2H_6(g)$ 2) $HI(g)$ 3) $NH_3(g)$ 4) $CO_2(g)$

5. A potential energy diagram for a chemical reaction is given below.

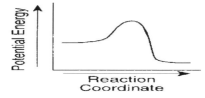

According to Reference Table I, which reaction could be represented by this potential energy diagram?

1) $2C_2(s)$ + $3H_2(g)$ → $C_2H_6(g)$
2) $2C(s)$ + $2H_2(g)$ → $C_2H_4(g)$
3) $N_2(g)$ + $O_2(g)$ → $2NO(g)$
4) $NH_4Cl(s)$ → $NH_4^+(aq)$ + $Cl^-(aq)$

11. Potential energy diagram: Identify and interpreting energy measurements

Answer questions 1 and 2 based on the potential energy diagram below.

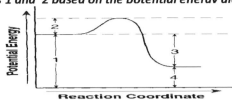

1. Which arrow represents the potential energy of the reactants?
    1) 1   2) 2   3) 3   4) 4

2. Heat of reaction, ΔH , is represented by which arrow?
    1) 1   2) 2   3) 3   4) 4

Answer questions 3 and 4 based on the diagram below.

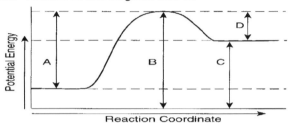

3. Energy of the activated complex is measured by which arrow in the above diagram?
    1) A   2) B   3) C   4) D

4. Which arrow represents the activation energy for the reverse reaction?
    2) A   2) B   3) C   4) D

Answer questions 5 through 7 based on the diagram below.

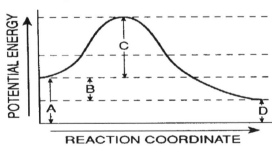

5. Activation energy for the forward reaction is represented by which arrow in the above diagram?
    1) A   2) B   3) C   4) D

6. Which measurement correctly represents the heat content of the products?
    1) A   2) B   3) C   4) D

7. ΔH of this reaction is measured by which arrow?
    1) A   2) B   3) C   4) D

11. Continues

Answers questions 8 through 10 on the potential energy diagram below.

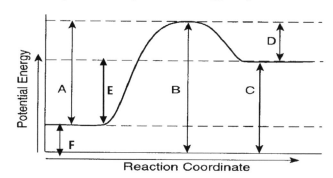

8. Which potential energy measurements will change if a catalyst is added to the reaction?

    1) A, B, and C   2) A, B, and E   3) B, C, and D   4) A, B, and D

9. Which arrow represents the difference between the potential energy of the products and that of the reactants?

    1) A   2) B   3) D   4) E

10. Potential energy of reactants for the reverse reaction can be determined by the length of arrow
    1) A   2) B   3) C   4) E

Base your answers to questions 11 and 12 on the potential energy diagram below

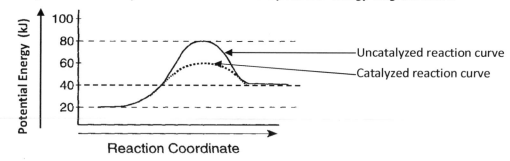

11. Which statement correctly describes the potential energy changes that occur in the forward uncatalyzed reaction?

    1) The activation energy is 40 kJ and a ΔH of +20 kJ

    2) The activation energy is 40 kJ and a ΔH of -20 kJ

    3) The activation energy is 60 kJ and a ΔH of +20 kJ

    4) The activation energy is 60 kJ and a ΔH of -20 kJ

12. Which reaction requires the lowest amount of activation energy?

    1) Forward uncatalyzed reaction

    2) Forward catalyzed reaction

    3) Reverse uncatalyzed reaction

    4) Reverse catalyzed reaction

13. What is the heat of reaction (ΔH) for the reverse catalyzed reaction?

    1) + 20 kJ
    2) − 20 kJ
    3) + 40 kJ
    4) − 40 kJ

12. Entropy: Recalling Concept Facts and Definitions

1. Entropy measures which of the followings about a chemical system?
   1) Activation energy of the system   3) Energy change of the system
   2) Intermolecular forces of the system   4) Disorder of the system

2. As a system becomes less random, its entropy
   1) decreases   2) increases   3) remains the same

3. As a chemical or physical system becomes more disorder, the entropy of the system
   1) increases   2) decreases   3) remains the same

4. As the temperature of a system increases, the entropy of the system
   1) remains the same   2) decreases   3) increases

5. As temperature of a chemical system decreases, the disorder of the system
   1) remains the same   2) increases   3) decreases

6. In which of the following forms would a substance has the highest entropy?
   1) Solid   2) Liquid   3) Gas   4) Aqueous

7. In which phase would particles of a substance be least random?
   1) Solid   2) Liquid   3) Gas   4) Aqueous

8. A system is most likely to undergo a reaction if the system after the reaction has
   1) lower energy and lower entropy   3) higher energy and higher entropy
   2) lower energy and higher entropy   4) higher energy and lower entropy

13. Entropy: Determining substance with highest or lowest entropy

1. Which sample of ammonia has the greatest entropy?
   1) $NH_3(g)$ 2) $NH_3(l)$ 3) $NH_3(s)$ 4) $NH_3(aq)$

2. Under the same temperature and pressure, which sample of carbon dioxide contains particles with the lowest entropy?
   1) $CO_2(g)$ 2) $CO_2(l)$ 3) $CO_2(s)$ 4) $CO_2(aq)$

3. AT STP, which of the following substances will have the greatest degree of randomness?
   1) $H_2O(s)$ 2) $H_2O(l)$ 3) $N_2(l)$ 4) $N_2(g)$

4. A sample of water at which temperature would have molecules with the greatest degree of entropy?
   1) $H_2O(l)$ at 25°C   3) $H_2O(l)$ at 15°C
   2) $H_2O(l)$ at 20°C   4) $H_2O(l)$ at 10°C

5. Which sample of a gas at 1 atm has particles with the least degree of disorder?
   1) $CH_4(g)$ at 30°C   3) $H_2S(g)$ at 40°C
   2) $CH_4(g)$ at 20°C   4) $H_2S(g)$ at 50°C

6. Which substance has the lowest entropy?
   1) $O_2(g)$ at 35°C   3) $O_2(g)$ at 320 K
   2) $CO(g)$ at 50°C   4) $CO(g)$ at 280 K

14. Entropy: Determining entropy change based on phase, temperature, or chemical change

1. Which phase change represents an increase in entropy?
    1) Liquid to gas
    2) Gas to solid
    3) Liquid to solid
    4) Gas to liquid

2. Which change will result in the particles becoming less random?
    1) Solid to liquid
    2) Solid to gas
    3) Liquid to gas
    4) Liquid to solid

3. Which change results in an increase in entropy?
    1) $H_2O(g) \rightarrow H_2O(l)$
    2) $H_2O(l) \rightarrow H_2O(s)$
    3) $H_2O(s) \rightarrow H_2O(l)$
    4) $H_2O(g) \rightarrow H_2O(s)$

4. In which system will there be a decrease in entropy as bromine undergoes a phase change?
    1) $Br_2(s) \rightarrow Br_2(l)$
    2) $Br_2(g) \rightarrow Br_2(l)$
    3) $Br_2(l) \rightarrow Br_2(g)$
    4) $Br_2(s) \rightarrow Br_2(g)$

5. Which process is accompanied by a decrease in entropy?
    1) Evaporation of water
    2) Condensing of steam
    3) Melting of ice
    4) Sublimation of ice

6. Which process is accompanied by an increase in randomness of the particles?
    1) Melting
    2) Condensing
    3) Freezing
    4) Crystallization

7. Which temperature change will result in particles of a substance becoming more random?
    1) 20 °C to 10°C
    2) 10°C to 0°C
    3) -5°C to 0°C
    4) 0°C to -5°C

8. Substance X is heated from one temperature to another. Which change in temperature of substance X is accompanied by a decrease in entropy of its particles?
    1) -10°C to -20°C
    2) 15°C to 20°C
    3) -10°C to -5°C
    4) 10°C to 15°C

9. In which chemical change would there be a change from a state of higher entropy to a state of lower entropy?
    1) $X_2(g) + Y_2(g) \rightarrow 2XY(g)$
    2) $X_2(g) + Y_2(g) \rightarrow 2XY(l)$
    3) $A(s) + B(l) \rightarrow AB(aq)$
    4) $A(l) + B(s) \rightarrow AB(g)$

10. Which chemical reaction is showing the substances in the reaction going from a state of lower entropy to a state of higher entropy?
    1) $H_2(g) + O_2(g) \rightarrow H_2O(l)$
    2) $H_2O(g) + O_2(g) \rightarrow H_2O(g)$
    3) $C(s) + O_2(g) \rightarrow CO_2(g)$
    4) $C_2H_2(g) \rightarrow 2C(s) + O_2(g)$

15. Equilibrium: Recalling Concept Facts and Definitions

1. Which changes can reach equilibrium?
   1) Chemical changes, only
   2) Physical changes, only
   3) Both physical and chemical changes
   4) Neither physical nor chemical changes

2. Equilibrium processes occur in
   1) reversible reactions that take place in an open system
   2) reversible reactions that take place in a closed system
   3) irreversible reactions that take place in an open system
   4) irreversible reactions that take place in a closed system

3. At equilibrium, the concentration of the products and of the reactants are
   1) equal
   2) constant
   3) increasing
   4) decreasing

4. At equilibrium, the rates at which the forward and the reverse processes are occurring are
   1) equal
   2) constant
   3) increasing
   4) decreasing

5. A chemical reaction has reached equilibrium when
   1) the forward and reverse reactions are occurring at equal rate
   2) the forward and reversible reactions are occurring at different rate
   3) the concentration of the substances are equal
   4) the concentration of the reactants have been used up

6. Which factor must be equal when a reversible chemical process reaches equilibrium?
   1) Mass of the reactant and mass of the products
   2) Rate of the forward reaction and rate of the reverse reaction
   3) Concentration of the reactants and the concentration of the products
   4) Activation energy of the forward reaction and the activation energy of the reverse reaction

7. A system is said to be in a state of dynamic equilibrium when the
   1) concentration of products is greater than the concentration of the reactants
   2) concentration of products is the same as the concentration of the reactants
   3) the rate at which products are formed is greater than the rate at which the reactants are formed
   4) the rate at which products are formed is the same as the rate at which the reactants are formed

8. Given the reaction at STP:

   $$N_2O_4(g) \leftrightarrow 2NO_2(g)$$

   Which statement correctly describes this system?

   1) The reaction is at equilibrium, and the concentration of N_2O_4 and NO_2 are equal
   2) The reaction is *not* at equilibrium, and the concentration of N_2O_4 and NO_2 are equal
   3) The reaction is at equilibrium, and the forward and reverse reaction rates are equal
   4) The reaction is *not* at equilibrium, and the forward and the reverse reaction rates are equal

9. Given the reaction

   $$AgCl(s) \leftrightarrow Ag^+(aq) + Cl^-(aq)$$

   When equilibrium is reached, which statement is accurate?

   1) The concentration of $AgCl(s)$, $Ag^+(aq)$ and $Cl^-(aq)$ are all equal
   2) The concentration of $AgCl(s)$, $Ag^+(aq)$ and $Cl^-(aq)$ are all constant
   3) The rate of dissolving of $AgCl(s)$ is greater than the rate of crystallization of $Ag^+(aq)$ and $Cl^-(aq)$
   4) The rate of crystallization of $Aq^+(aq)$ and $Cl^-(aq)$ is greater than the rate of dissolving of $AgCl(s)$

16. Physical equilibrium: Recalling Concept Facts and Definitions

1. Given the equilibrium phase change equation below
$$H_2O(s) \leftrightarrow H_2O(l)$$
   What is the temperature of the equilibrium mixture?
   1)   0°C   2) 373°C   3) 273°C   4) 100°C

2. Given the phase change equation
$$H_2O(g) \leftrightarrow H_2O(l)$$
   At 1 atm, at what temperature would equilibrium be reached?
   1) 273 K   2) 0 K   3) 373 K   4) 298 K

3. Solution equilibrium always exists in a solution that is
   1) unsaturated   2) saturated   3) concentrated 4) dilute

4. A sample of water in a sealed flask at 298 K is in equilibrium with its vapor. This is an example of a(n)
   1)   chemical equilibrium   3) solution equilibrium
   2)   phase equilibrium   4) energy equilibrium

5. Which equilibrium at 1 atm pressure is correctly associated with the Kelvin temperature at which it occurs?
   1)   Steam-water equilibrium at 273 K   3) Steam-water equilibrium at 373 K
   2)   Ice-water equilibrium at 0 K   4) Ice-water equilibrium at 373 K

6. Which of the followings is *not* an example of a physical equilibrium?
   1)   The equilibrium process for the synthesis and the decomposition of ammonia
   2)   The equilibrium process dissolving and crystallization of salt in a saturated solution
   3)   The equilibrium process for the evaporation and condensation of water at 373 K and 1 atm
   4)   The equilibrium process for the freezing and melting of water at 273 K and 1 atm

7. A liquid in a stoppered flask will be at equilibrium with its vapor when
   1)   only evaporation is occurring
   2)   only condensation is occurring
   3)   the rate of evaporation is greater than the rate of condensation
   4)   the rate of evaporation is equal to the rate of condensation

8. Which description applies to a system in a sealed flask that is half full of water?
   1)   Only evaporation occurs, but it eventually stops
   2)   Only condensation occurs, but it eventually stops
   3)   Neither evaporation nor condensation occurs
   4)   Both evaporation and condensation occur

9. A solution equilibrium is reached in a saturated solution when
   1)   dissolving stops occurring
   2)   crystallization stops occurring
   3)   both dissolving and crystallization stop occurring
   4)   dissolving occurs at the same rate as crystallization is occurring

10. Given the reaction
$$NaCl(s) \leftrightarrow Na^+(aq) + Cl^-(aq)$$

   Equilibrium is reached in the reaction when
   1) the rates of the forward and reverse reactions are constant
   2) the concentration of the reactants and the products are constant
   3) the energy of the reactants and the products are equal
   4) the entropy of the forward and the reverse reaction are equal

11. In the reaction
$$Pb(NO_3)_2(s) \leftrightarrow Pb^{2+}(aq) + NO_3^{-(aq)}$$
   Equilibrium is reached when the
   1) rate of dissolving of salt and the rate of crystallization of ions is constant
   2) concentration of $Pb(NO_3)_2(aq)$, $Pb^{2+}(aq)$, and $NO_3^-(aq)$ are constant
   3) rate of dissolving of salt is slower than the rate of crystallization of ions
   4) concentration of $Pb^{2+}(aq)$ is the same as the concentration of $Pb(NO_3)_2(s)$

17. Chemical equilibrium – Le Chatelier's Principle: Recalling Concept Facts

1. As the concentration of one or more reactants is increased in a reaction at equilibrium, the concentration of the products will
   1) increase   2) decrease   3) remains the same

2. As the concentration of the products is decreased in a reversible reaction that has reached equilibrium, the concentration of the reactants will
   1) increase   2) decrease   3) remains the same

3. Increasing temperature on equilibrium reactions favors
   1) exothermic reaction, only   3) both exothermic and endothermic reaction
   2) endothermic reaction, only   4) neither exothermic nor endothermic reaction

4. Decreasing temperature on a reversible reaction at equilibrium favors
   1) exothermic reaction and decrease its rate
   2) exothermic reaction and increase its rate
   3) endothermic reaction and decrease its rate
   4) endothermic reaction and increase its rate

5. When more heat is added to equilibrium reaction, the reaction will
   1) shift in the direction of exothermic reaction, and increase its rate
   2) shift in the direction of exothermic reaction, and decrease its rate
   3) shift in the direction of endothermic reaction, and increase its rate
   4) shift in the direction of endothermic reaction, and decrease its rate

6. Increasing pressure on equilibrium reaction will cause the reaction to speed up in the direction that will produce
   1) fewer substances that are on the side with greater number of moles
   2) more substances that are on the side with greater number of moles
   3) more substances that are on the side with lesser number of moles
   4) more of the reactants and the products equally

7. The addition of a catalyst to a system at equilibrium will increase the rate of
   1) forward reaction only
   2) reverse reaction only
   3) both the forward and reverse reactions
   4) neither the forward nor the reverse reaction

8. Which change will have the least effect on concentration of substances in equilibrium reaction?
   1) Adding a catalyst to the reaction
   2) Increasing temperature of the reaction
   3) Increasing pressure on the reaction
   4) Increasing concentration of the reactants

9. A reaction is at equilibrium. The rate of the forward reaction will increase with the addition of heat if the forward reaction
   1) is exothermic
   2) is endothermic
   3) both exothermic and endothermic
   4) neither exothermic nor endothermic

18. Le Chatelier's Principle – Changing concentration: Determining effect of reaction

1. Given the reaction at equilibrium:
    $$N_2(g) + 3H_2(g) \rightarrow 2NH_3(g)$$
    Increasing the concentration of $N_2(g)$ will cause
    1) An increase in the concentration of $H_2(g)$
    2) An increase in the rate of reverse reaction
    3) A decrease in the concentration of $H_2(g)$
    4) A decrease in the rate of forward reaction

2. The reaction below is at equilibrium:
    $$C(s) + O_2(g) \rightarrow CO_2(g)$$
    If the concentration of $C(s)$ is increased, the equilibrium point will shift
    1) right, and the concentration of $O_2(g)$ will increase
    2) right, and the concentration of $O_2(g)$ will decrease
    3) left, and the concentration of $O_2(g)$ will increase
    4) left, and the concentration of $O_2(g)$ will decrease

3. Given the equilibrium reaction
    $$A + B \rightarrow AB + heat$$
    If the concentration of B is increased, the rate of forward reaction will
    1) increase, and the concentration of AB will also increase
    2) increase, and the concentration of AB will decrease
    3) decrease, and the concentration of AB will also decrease
    4) decrease, and the concentration of AB will increase

4. Given the equilibrium reaction below
    $$N_2O_4 + 58.1\,kJ \rightarrow 2NO_2$$
    If the concentration of $NO_2(g)$ is increased
    1) the rate of forward reaction will increase, and equilibrium will shift to right
    2) the rate of forward reaction will increase, and equilibrium will shift to left
    3) the rate of reverse reaction will increase, and equilibrium will shift right
    4) the rate of reverse reaction will increase, and equilibrium will shift left

5. In the equilibrium reaction
    $$H_2(g) + I_2(g) \rightarrow 2HI(g)$$
    Increasing the concentration of $HI(g)$ will
    1) increase the concentration of $H_2(g)$, but decreases the concentration of $I_2(g)$
    2) increase the concentration of $H_2(g)$, and also increases the concentration of $I_2(g)$
    3) decrease the concentration of $H_2(g)$, but increases the concentration of $I_2(g)$
    4) decrease the concentration of $H_2(g)$, and also decreases the concentration of $I_2(g)$

6. Given the reaction at equilibrium
    $$SO_2(g) + NO_2(g) \rightarrow SO_3(g) + NO(g)$$
    As $NO(g)$ is removed from the system, the concentration of
    1) $SO_3(g)$ will increase
    2) $NO_2(g)$ will increase
    3) $SO_2(g)$ will increase
    4) $SO_2(g)$ and $NO_2(g)$ will both be equal

 Survivingchem.com

19. Le Chatelier's Principle – Changing Temperature: Determining effect of reaction

1. In the equilibrium reaction
$$2H_2(g) + O_2(g) \rightarrow 2H_2O(\ell) + energy$$

   As temperature is increased, the rate of reverse reaction will

   1) increase   2) decrease   3) remains the same

2. Given the reaction at equilibrium
$$2HBr(g) + 73\ kJ \rightarrow H_2(g) + Br_2(g)$$

   As the temperature decreases, the concentration of $H_2(g)$

   1) increases   2) decreases   3) remains the same

3. Given the equilibrium reaction below:
$$X_2(g) + 2Y_2(q) \rightarrow 2XY_2(g) + heat$$

   When the temperature is increased, the equilibrium will shift to the

   1) right, and the concentration of $XY_2(g)$ will increase
   2) right, and the concentration of $XY_2(g)$ will decrease
   3) left, and the concentration of $XY_2(g)$ will increase
   4) left, and the concentration of $XY_2(g)$ will decrease

4. Given the equilibrium reaction in a closed system:
$$N_2(g) + O_2(g) + 90.7\ kJ \rightarrow 2NO_2$$

   If the temperature of the reaction is increased, there will be an increase in the rate of

   1) forward reaction, and the concentration of NO_2 will also increase
   2) forward reaction, and the concentration of NO_2 will decrease
   3) reverse reaction, and the concentration of NO_2 will also increase
   4) reverse reaction, and the concentration of NO_2 will decrease

5. The reaction below is at equilibrium
$$2A(g) + B(g) + 42\ kJ \rightarrow C(g)$$

   As temperature increases, the rate of forward reaction

   1) decreases, and the concentration of $A(g)$ and $B(g)$ will also decrease
   2) decreases, and the concentration of $A(g)$ and $B(g)$ will increase
   3) increases, and the concentration of $A(g)$ and $B(g)$ will decrease
   4) increases, and the concentration of $A(g)$ and $B(g)$ will also increase

6. Given the reaction at equilibrium
$$2NO_2(g) \rightarrow N_2O_4(g) + energy$$

   As heat is removed from the reaction, the

   1) rate of reverse will decrease, and the concentration of NO_2 will increase
   2) rate of reverse will increase, and the concentration of NO_2 will also increase
   3) rate of forward will decrease, and the concentration of N_2O_4 will increase
   4) rate of forward will increase, and the concentration of N_2O_4 will also increase

7. Given the system at equilibrium
$$2NH_3(g) + 92\ kJ \rightarrow N_2(g) + 3H_2(g)$$

   Which statement is true of this reaction if the temperature is decreased?

   1) The equilibrium will shift left, and the concentration of $NH_3(g)$ will increase
   2) The equilibrium will shift right, and the concentration of $H_2(g)$ will increase
   3) The forward reaction will increase, and the concentration of $H_2(g)$ will increase
   4) The forward reaction will decrease, and the concentration of $NH_3(g)$ will decrease

20. Le Chatelier's Principle – Changing pressure: Determining effect on reaction

1. Given the reaction at equilibrium

   $H_2(g) + Cl_2(g) \leftrightarrow 2HCl(g)$

   As pressure is increased at constant temperature, the concentration of HCl

   1) decreases   2) increases   3) remains the same

2. The reaction below is at equilibrium

   $A(g) + 2B_2(g) + heat \leftrightarrow AB_2(g)$

   As pressure is increased at constant temperature, the rate of reverse reaction will

   1) increase   2) decrease   3) remains the same

3. Given the equation of a reaction at equilibrium

   $2CO(g) + O_2 \leftrightarrow 2CO_2(g)$

   If pressure is increased on this reaction, the rate of forward reaction will

   1) decrease, and the concentration of CO_2 will also decrease
   2) decrease, and the concentration of CO_2 will increase
   3) increase, and the concentration of CO_2 will decrease
   4) increase, and the concentration of CO_2 will also increase

4. Given the reaction below at equilibrium

   $W(g) + 3X(g) \leftrightarrow 2Y(g) + 3Z(g)$

   An increase in pressure at constant temperature will shift the equilibrium to the

   1) left, and the concentration of $W(g)$ will increase
   2) left, and the concentration of $W(g)$ will decrease
   3) right, and the concentration of $W(g)$ will increase
   4) right, and the concentration of $W(g)$ will decrease

5. Given the system at equilibrium

   $2Hg(\ell) + O_2(g) \leftrightarrow 2HgO(s)$

   Increasing pressure in this reaction will cause a(n)

   1) increase in the concentration of Hg
   2) increase in the rate of the reverse reaction
   3) shift in equilibrium point to right
   4) decrease in the rate of forward reaction

6. Given the reaction at equilibrium

   $2AB(g) \leftrightarrow A_2(g) + B_2(g)$

   As pressure is increased on this reaction,

   1) the rate of forward reaction will be greater than the rate of the reverse reaction
   2) the rate of reverse reaction will be greater than the rate of the forward reaction
   3) there will be a shift of equilibrium point to the left
   4) there will be no shift in equilibrium point

21. Le Chatelier's Principle – Adding catalyst: Determining effect on reaction

1. Given the reaction
   $$A(g) \; + \; B(g) \quad \leftrightarrow \quad 2AB(g)$$

   As a catalyst is added to the above reaction at equilibrium

   1) the rate of forward reaction alone will increase
   2) the rate of reverse reaction alone will increase
   3) the rate of forward and reverse reactions will increase equally
   4) the rate of forward and reverse reactions will decrease equally

2. Given the reaction
   $$N_2(g) \; + \; 3H_2(g) \quad \leftrightarrow \quad 2NH_3(g) \; + \; heat$$

   The addition of catalyst

   1) Increases the rate of exothermic reaction only
   2) Increases the rate of endothermic reaction only
   3) Increases the rate of exothermic reaction and decreases the rate of endothermic reaction
   4) Increases the both the rates exothermic and endothermic reactions equally

3. When a catalysts is added to the reaction below
   $$C(s) \; + \; O_2(g) \quad \leftrightarrow \quad CO_2(g)$$

   There will be no change in

   1) the rate of forward reaction
   2) the rate of reverse reaction
   3) the rate of exothermic reaction
   4) equilibrium concentrations of the substances

22. Le Chatelier's Principle: Determining a stress to equilibrium reactions

1. In the equilibrium reaction:
   $$A(g) \; + \; 2B(g) \quad \leftrightarrow \quad AB_2(g) \; + \; heat$$

   The rate of the forward reaction will increase if there is

   1) An increase in pressure
   2) An decrease in pressure
   3) An increase in temperature
   4) A decrease in concentration of $B(g)$

2. The reaction below is at equilibrium
   $$2Cl_2(g) \; + \; 2H_2O(g) \; + \; 31.2\,kJ \quad \leftrightarrow \quad HCl(g) \; + \; O_2(g)$$

   Which stress will cause the rate of reverse reaction to increase?

   1) Increase in temperature
   2) Increase $Cl_2(g)$ concentration
   3) Decrease in $HCl(g)$ concentration
   4) Decrease in $H_2O(g)$ concentration

22. Continues

3. Given the equilibrium reaction below
$$C_2(g) + D_2(g) \leftrightarrow 2CD(g) + energy$$
Which change will cause the equilibrium point to shift to the left?
   1) Increasing pressure
   2) Increasing the amount of $D_2(g)$
   3) Adding heat
   4) Addition of catalyst

4. Given the reaction below at equilibrium
$$2SO_2(g) + O_2(g) \leftrightarrow 2SO_3(g) + heat$$
Which change will shift the equilibrium to the right?
   1) Decreasing concentration of SO_3
   2) Decreasing pressure
   3) Decreasing concentration of O_2
   4) Increasing temperature

5. Given the system at equilibrium,
$$H_2(g) + F_2(g) \leftrightarrow 2HF(g) + Heat$$

   The concentration of $HF(g)$ may be increased by
   1) decreasing the concentration of $H_2(g)$
   2) decreasing the concentration of $F_2(g)$
   3) increasing the temperature
   4) increasing temperature

6. In the equilibrium reaction
$$C(s) + CO_2(g) + heat \leftrightarrow 2CO(g)$$
Which stress on the system would favor the rate of exothermic reaction to increase?
   1) An increase in the amount of $C(s)$
   2) An increase in the amount of $CO(g)$
   3) An increase in the amount of $CO_2(g)$
   4) An increase in pressure

7. The reaction below is at equilibrium
$$N_2 + O_2 + 182.6\ kJ \leftrightarrow 2NO$$
Which change to the reaction will cause an increase in the rate of the forward reaction?
   1) Adding more NO
   2) Removing heat
   3) Removing O_2
   4) Adding heat

8. Given the Haber reaction at equilibrium
$$N_2(g) + 3H_2(g) \leftrightarrow 2NH_3(g) + heat$$
Which stress on the system will decrease the production of $NH_3(g)$?
   1) Decreasing the temperature on the system
   2) Increasing the pressure on the system
   3) Increasing the concentration of $N_2(g)$
   4) Decreasing the concentration of $H_2(g)$

9. In the equilibrium reaction
$$2A(g) + 3B(g) \leftrightarrow A_2B_3(g) + Heat$$
Which change will NOT affect the equilibrium concentrations of $A(g)$, $B(g)$, and $A_2B_3(g)$?
   1) Adding more $A(g)$
   2) Adding a catalyst
   3) Increasing the temperature
   4) Increasing the pressure

10. Given the equilibrium reaction below:
$$SO_2(g) + NO_2(g) \leftrightarrow SO_3(g) + NO(g) + heat$$
Which stress will NOT shift the equilibrium point of this reaction?
   1) Increasing pressure
   2) Increasing $SO_2(g)$ concentration
   3) Decreasing heat
   4) Decreasing $NO(g)$ concentration

Topic 10: Organic Chemistry

1. Characteristics of Organic compounds: Recalling Concept Facts and Definitions

1. A compound that is classified as organic must contain
   1) carbon
   2) nitrogen
   3) oxygen
   4) hydrogen

2. Which type of bonds and solids are characteristics of organic compounds?
   1) Ionic bonds and ionic solids
   2) Ionic bonds and molecular solids
   3) Covalent bonds and ionic solids
   4) Covalent bonds and molecular solids

3. In general, which property do organic compounds share?
   1) High melting points
   2) High electrical conductivity
   3) High solubility in water
   4) Slow reaction rate

4. A characteristic of most organic compounds is that they have
   1) low boiling point
   2) high boiling point
   3) low solubility in nonpolar solvents
   4) high solubility in water

5. Organic compounds differ from ionic compounds in that organic compounds generally have
   1) low solubility in water and are nonelectrolyte
   2) low solubility in water and are electrolytes
   3) high solubility in water and are nonelectrolyte
   4) high solubility in water and are electrolytes

6. Compared with the rate of an inorganic reaction, the rate of organic reaction is usually
   1) faster, because organic compounds are ionic substances
   2) faster, because organic compounds are molecular substances
   3) slower, because organic compounds are ionic substances
   4) slower, because organic compounds are molecular substances

7. Which best explains why there are more organic compounds than inorganic compounds?
   1) The carbon atom readily forms covalent bonds with other carbon atoms
   2) The carbon atom readily forms ionic bonds with other carbon atoms
   3) The carbon atom readily combines with oxygen
   4) The carbon atom readily dissolves in water

8. A carbon atom in any organic compound can form a total
   1) 1 covalent bond
   2) 2 covalent bonds
   3) 3 covalent bonds
   4) 4 covalent bonds

9. The four single bonds of a carbon atom are directed in space toward the corner of a
   1) regular tetrahedron
   2) regular octahedron
   3) square planer
   4) trigonal bipyramid

10. A student investigated samples of four different substances in the solid phase. The table is a record of the behaviors observed (marked with an X) when each solid was tested.

Characteristic Tested	Substance A	Substance B	Substance C	Substance D
High Melting Point	X		X	
Low Melting Point		X		X
Soluble in Water	X			X
Insoluble in Water		X	X	
Decomposed under High Heat		X		
Stable under High Heat	X		X	X
Electrolyte	X			X
Nonelectrolyte		X	X	

Which substance has characteristics most like those of an organic compound?

1) A
2) B
3) C
4) D

2. Hydrocarbons: Recalling Concept Facts and Definitions

1. Which elements are found in all hydrocarbon compounds?
   1) Carbon and nitrogen
   2) Carbon and hydrogen
   3) Hydrogen and nitrogen
   4) Hydrogen and oxygen

2. A carbon atom in a hydrocarbon molecule can form
   1) single bond, only
   2) double bonds, only
   3) triple bonds, only
   4) either single, double, or triple bond

3. A series of hydrocarbons in which each member of a group differs from the preceding member by one carbon is called
   1) a periodic series
   2) a homologous series
   3) an actinide series
   4) a lanthanide series

4. Which list of compounds contains only hydrocarbon?
   1) Alkanes, alcohols, aldehydes
   2) Alkanes, alkenes, and alkynes
   3) Alkanes, alkenes, and halides
   4) Alkynes, amines, and alcohols

5. In a given homologous series of hydrocarbons, the boiling point generally increases as the size of the molecules increases. The best explanation for this statement is that in larger organic molecules
   1) the number of covalent bonds per molecule is greater
   2) the molecules are more symmetrical
   3) there more hydrogen bonding possible
   4) there are greater intermolecular forces

3. Saturated hydrocarbon: Recalling Concept Facts and Definitions

1. In saturated hydrocarbons, carbon atoms are bonded to each other by
   1) single covalent bonds
   2) double covalent bonds
   3) triple covalent bonds
   4) coordinate covalent bonds

2. The total number of electrons shared between two adjacent carbon atoms in a saturated hydrocarbon is
   1) 1
   2) 2
   3) 3
   4) 4

3. The number of pair of electrons needed to form a single covalent bond between two adjacent carbon atoms in a saturated hydrocarbon is
   1) 1
   2) 2
   3) 3
   4) 4

4. Which series of hydrocarbon contains saturated molecules?
   1) Alkyne series
   2) Alkene series
   3) Alkane series
   4) Alkyl series

5. Which general formula is possible for all saturated hydrocarbon molecules?
   1) C_nH_{2n}
   2) C_nH_{2n+2}
   3) C_nH_{2n-2}
   4) C_nH_{2n+6}

     Survivingchem.com

4. Unsaturated hydrocarbons: Recalling definitions and facts

1. The present of which type of bond between two adjacent carbon atoms is a characteristic of unsaturated hydrocarbons?
   1) A single covalent bond
   2) A single ionic bond
   3) A double covalent bond
   4) A double ionic bond

2. All unsaturated hydrocarbons must contain
   1) a triple or a double covalent bond
   2) a triple or a double ionic bond
   3) a single or a double ionic bond
   4) a coordinate or a hydrogen bond

3. Which series of hydrocarbons may contain unsaturated molecules?
   1) Alkane and benzene series
   2) Alkyl and alkene series
   3) Alkene and alkyne series
   4) Alkane and alkyne series

4. Which general formulas are possible for unsaturated hydrocarbon compounds?
   1) C_nH_{2n+2} and C_nH_{2n}
   1) C_nH_{2n+1} and C_nH_{2n+2}
   3) C_nH_{2n-2} and C_nH_{2n}
   4) C_nH_{2n-1} and C_nH_{2n-2}

5. Organic Prefixes: Relating name prefix to number of carbon

1. How many carbon atoms is in a molecule of pentane?
   1) 1   2) 3   3) 5   4) 7

2. Each molecule of butane will contain a total of how many carbon atoms?
   1) 2   2) 4   3) 6   4) 8

3. How many carbons atoms are in each molecule of octane?
   1) 8   2) 7   3) 10   4) 3

4. Which hydrocarbon consists of four carbon atoms?
   1) Propane   2) Butyne   3) Pentane   4) Heptyne

5. Which could be the name of a compound with the formula C_2H_2?
   1) Methane   2) Benzene   3) Butane   4) Ethyne

6. What is the correct name for a compound with a molecular formula of C_6H_{14}?
   1) Propane   2) Pentene   3) Heptane   4) Hexane

7. Given the organic structure below,

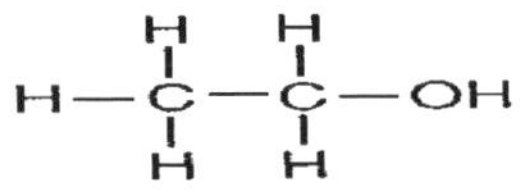

```
      H   H
      |   |
  H — C — C — OH
      |   |
      H   H
```

Which IUPAC name is possible for a compound with this structure?

   1) Methane   2) Ethanol   3) Propene   4) Butanol

8. Which could be the correct name for a hydrocarbon with the following structure?

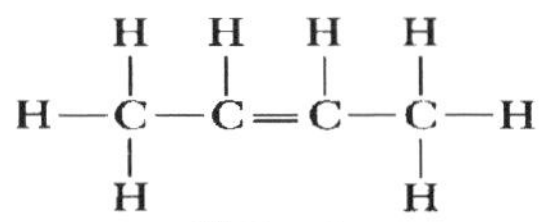

```
      H   H   H   H
      |   |   |   |
  H — C — C = C — C — H
      |           |
      H           H
```

   1) Hexane   2) Pentene   3) Ethene   4) Butene

6. Alkane hydrocarbon: Recalling Concept Facts and Definitions

1. Which bond type best describes molecules of compounds in the alkane series of hydrocarbons?
   1) They contain single ionic bonds
   2) They contain single covalent bonds
   3) They contain double covalent bond
   4) They contain double ionic bond

2. Which is true of all alkanes?
   1) They are saturated hydrocarbons
   2) They are unsaturated hydrocarbons
   3) They may contain halogens
   4) They may contain oxygen

3. The general formula for all alkane compounds is
   1) C_nH_{2n}
   2) C_nH_{2n-2}
   3) C_nH_{2n+2}
   4) C_nH_{2n+6}

4. All members of alkane hydrocarbon have IUPAC names ending with
   1) −yl
   2) −al
   3) −ene
   4) −ane

5. The total number of electrons shared between two adjacent carbon atoms in an alkane molecule is
   1) 1
   2) 2
   3) 3
   4) 4

6. The total number of pair of electrons found between two carbon atoms in a single bond is
   1) 1 pair
   2) 2 pairs
   3) 3 pairs
   4) 4 pairs

7. Each member in an alkane series of hydrocarbons, when considered in successive order, has one more carbon atom and how many more hydrogen atoms?
   1) 1
   2) 2
   3) 3
   4) 4

7. Alkane: Recognizing names and formulas of alkanes

1. Which two compounds belong to the alkane series of hydrocarbon?
   1) Methane and ethane
   2) Methane and ethene
   3) Ethane and ethene
   4) Ethene and ethyne

2. Which two IUPAC names are of compounds of alkane?
   1) Pentane and pentene
   2) Propene and methane
   3) Butane and butyne
   4) Hexane and nonane

3. Which two formulas are of compounds belonging to alkane series?
   1) C_4H_6 and C_4H_8
   2) $C_{11}H_{22}$ and $C_{11}H_{24}$
   3) C_2H_4 and C_4H_6
   4) C_8H_{18} and C_9H_{20}

4. Which set of formulas belong to substances from alkane hydrocarbon series of organic compounds?
   1) CH_3 and CH_4
   2) C_2H_2 and C_3H_4
   3) CH_4 and $C_{12}H_{26}$
   4) C_2H_6 and $C_{12}H_{24}$

5. Which set of structural formulas correctly represents members of alkane series?

8. Alkene hydrocarbon: Recalling Concept Facts and Definitions

1. Which best describes bonding in all alkene molecules?
   1) The must contain all single bonds
   2) They must contain one double bond
   3) They must contain one triple bond
   4) They must contain a double and a triple bond

2. Which formula correctly represents general formula for all alkene molecules?
   1) C_nH_{2n}
   2) C_nH_{2n+2}
   3) C_nH_{2n-2}
   4) C_nH_{2n+6}

3. What is the IUPAC name ending for all alkene compounds?
   1) –yl
   2) –yne
   3) –ene
   4) –ane

4. The number of electrons shared between two adjacent carbons in a double bond is
   1) 1
   2) 2
   3) 3
   4) 4

5. How many pairs of electrons are found between two double-bonded carbon atoms in an alkene molecule?
   1) 2
   2) 4
   3) 6
   4) 8

6. As the compounds in the alkene series are considered in other of increasing number of carbons, the ratio of carbon atoms to hydrogen atoms
   1) increases
   2) decreases
   3) remains the same

7. As the length of the chain of carbon atoms in molecules of alkene series increases, the number of double bonds per molecule
   1) increases
   2) decreases
   3) remains the same

8. Which are true of all alkenes?
   1) They contain all single bonds and are saturated hydrocarbons
   2) They contain one triple bond and are unsaturated hydrocarbons
   3) They contain one double bond and are saturated hydrocarbons
   4) They contain one double bond and are unsaturated hydrocarbons

9. Alkenes: Recognizing names and formulas of alkenes

1. Which two compounds belong to the alkene series of hydrocarbon?
   1) Pentane and pentene
   2) Ethane and ethyne
   3) Propene and butene
   4) Butene and propyne

2. Which set of IUPAC names are of compounds that are classified as alkenes?
   1) Methyl and ethyl
   2) Ethene and decene
   3) Ethane and pentene
   4) Ethyne and ethane

3. Which two formulas are of compounds belonging to the alkene series of hydrocarbons?
   1) C_2H_4 and $C_{11}H_{22}$
   2) C_2H_6 and C_3H_4
   3) C_3H_4 and C_3H_8
   4) C_3H_6 and C_3H_4

4. Which two formulas are of chemical substances belonging to the alkene homologous series?
   1) C_4H_6 and C_4H_{10}
   2) C_4H_6 and C_4H_8
   3) C_6H_{10} and C_7H_{14}
   4) C_6H_{12} and C_7H_{14}

5. Which set of structural formulas correctly represents members of the alkene series?

10. Alkyne hydrocarbon: Recalling Concept Facts and Definitions

1. Which best describes bonding in alkynes molecules?
   1) All singles covalent bonds
   2) All triple covalent bonds
   3) Single and triple covalent bonds
   4) Single and double covalent bonds

2. The general formula for all alkyne molecules is
   1) C_nH_{2n}
   2) C_nH_{2n+2}
   3) C_nH_{2n-2}
   4) C_nH_{2n+6}

3. Each member of alkyne series of hydrocarbon has an IUPAC name that ends with
   1) -yne
   2) -ol
   3) – ane
   4) –ene

4. In an alkyne molecule, how many electrons are shared between two carbon atoms held together with a triple bond?
   1) 1
   2) 2
   3) 4
   4) 6

5. How many pairs of electrons are found between two atoms in a triple bond?
   1) 4
   2) 3
   3) 8
   4) 6

6. As the length of chain of carbon atoms in alkyne molecules increase, the number of triple bonds per molecule
   1) increases
   2) decreases
   3) remains the same

7. Which are true of all alkynes?
   1) They contain all single bonds and are saturated hydrocarbons
   2) They contain one triple bond and are unsaturated hydrocarbons
   3) They contain one triple bond and are saturated hydrocarbons
   4) They contain one double bond and are unsaturated hydrocarbons

11. Alkynes: Recognizing names and formulas of alkynes

1. Which two IUPAC names are of compounds belonging to the alkyne series of hydrocarbons?
   1) Ethyl and ethyne
   2) Ethene and propanol
   3) Ethyne and octyne
   4) Ethyne and butonoate

2. Which two compounds are alkynes?
   1) Propyne and pentyne
   2) Ethane and pentyne
   3) Hexene and hexyne
   4) Hexane and hexyne

3. Which two molecules belong to the alkyne series of hydrocarbons?
   1) C_6H_6 and C_6H_7
   2) C_6H_{10} and C_7H_{12}
   3) C_3H_6 and C_3H_8
   4) C_3H_4 and C_4H_8

4. Which two formulas are alkynes?
   1) C_9H_{16} and C_8H_{14}
   2) C_8H_{16} and C_8H_{14}
   3) C_3H_6 and C_3H_8
   4) C_5H_{10} and C_6H_{12}

5. Which is a structural formula of an alkyne hydrocarbon?

Survivingchem.com

12. Alcohols: Recalling Concept Facts and Definitions
Recognizing names and formulas of alcohols

1. Which IUPAC name ending is common for all alcohol compounds?
   1) –al   2) –yl   3) –ol   4) -ioc

2. Which functional group is found in all alcohols?
   1) –OH   2) – COOH   3) –CHO   4) - O –

3. The general formula that represents members of alcohol compounds is

   1)   2) $R-C-O-R^1$ 3) $R-OH$ 4)

4. Which compound is an alcohol?
   1) Methanal   2) Methanoic   3) Octonone   4) Octanol

5. Which IUPAC name is of an alcohol?
   1) Ethanediol   2) Chloroethane   3) Propanone   4) Propaneamine

6. Which is a primary alcohol?
   1) Propanol   2) Pentanal   3) 2- butanol   4) 1,1, ethanediol

7. Which is an IUPAC name of a secondary alcohol?
   1) 1,2,-ethandiol   2) Propanol   3) 1,2,3-propanetriol 4) 2-butanol

8. The formula of which compound represents an alcohol?
   1) CH_3CHO 2) CH_3CH_2OH 3) CH_3COOH 4) CH_3COOCH_3

9. Which structure represents an alcohol?

   1)   2)   3)   4)

10. Which structure represents a secondary alcohol?

   1)   2)   3)   4)

11. An alcohol compound contains one –OH group that is bonded to an end carbon in a hydrocarbon chain. This alcohol should be classified as a
   1) secondary alcohol   3) trihydroxy alcohol
   2) primary alcohol   4) dihydroxy alcohol

12. An alcohol that contains two –OH functional groups is classified as a
   1) primary alcohol   3) dihydroxy alcohol
   2) monohydroxy alcohol   4) secondary alcohol

13. To be classified as a tertiary alcohol, the functional group –OH is bonded to a carbon that must be bonded to how many other carbon atoms?
   1) 1   2) 2   3) 3   4) 4

13. Halides: Recalling Concept Facts and Definitions

Recognizing names and formulas of halides

1. Which can be a functional group in a halide compound?
   1) An hydrogen atom
   2) A carbon atom
   3) A halogen atom
   4) An oxygen atom

2. Which group of atoms could bond to a hydrocarbon chain to form a halide compound?
   1) −OH
   2) − Cl
   3) −COOH
   4) − H

3. Which IUPAC name is of a halide compound?
   1) Bromoethane
   2) Ethanol
   3) Propanal
   4) Propane

4. The name of which compound belongs in the halide family?
   1) 2-pentene
   2) 2-pentyne
   3) 2-methylpropane
   4) 2-Iodopropane

5. The formula of which compound is a halide?
   1) $C_4H_8Cl_2$
   2) C_4H_8
   3) CH_3OH
   4) $HCOOH$

6. A formula of which compound is an organic halide?
   1) $CH_3CH_2NH_2$
   2) CH_3OCH_3
   3) $CH_3CH_2CH_2Br$
   4) HCl

7. Which organic structure represents an organic compound that is classified as a halide?

   1)
   ```
       H   Cl  Cl
       |   |   |
   H — C - C - C — H?
       |   |   |
       H   H   H
   ```

   2)
   ```
         O
         ‖
   H — C
         \
          OH
   ```

   3)
   ```
       H       H
       |       |
   H — C — O — C — H
       |       |
       H       H
   ```

   4)
   ```
   H — N — H
       |
       H
   ```

8. A structural formula of an organic compound is given below:

   This structure is of a halide because it contains

   1) Carbon atoms   2) Hydrogen atoms   3) Bromine atoms   4) Single bonds

14. Aldehydes: Recalling Concept Facts and Definitions

Recognizing names and formulas of aldehydes

1. Which correctly shows the functional group of all aldehydes?

1)   2)   3)   4)

2. Which IUPAC name ending is common for class of organic compound called aldehyde?

    1) –yl   2) –al   3) –ol   4) –one

3. Which is a name of an aldehyde?

    1) Methanal   2) Methanol   3) Ethane   4) Propanone

4. A compound of which IUPAC name represents an aldehyde?

    1) Pentane   2) Butanoic   3) Propanol   4) Hexanal

5. Which formula represents a member of the aldehyde family?

    1) CH_3CH_2OH 2) CH_3COOH 3) CH_3OCH_3 4) CH_3CHO

6. Which is a correct formula of an aldehyde?

    1) C_3H_7CHO 2) $C_3H_6(OH)_2$ 3) $C_6H_{12}O_6$ 4) C_2H_5COOH

7. A structure of an organic compound is shown below:

$$H-\underset{\underset{H}{|}}{\overset{\overset{H}{|}}{C}}-\overset{\overset{H}{|}}{C}=O$$

This structure is classified as an aldehyde because it contains

    1) = O atoms   2) - H atoms   3) -CHO group   4) C – C group

8. The structural formula of which compound represents an aldehyde?

15. Organic Acids: Recalling Concept Facts and Definitions

Recognizing names and formulas of organic acids

1. The general formula of organic acids is

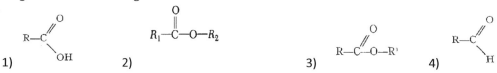

   1)   2)   3)   4)

2. Which will be the correct name ending for an organic acid?
   1) −ol   2) −ene   3) −ioc   4) −oate

3. Which is true of organic acids?
   1) They are nonelectrolyte   3) They are turn litmus blue
   2) They are weak electrolytes   4) They turn phenolphthalein pink

4. An organic acid will have which of the following properties in solutions?

   1) Produce OH⁻ ions in solutions   3) Produce OH⁺ ions in solutions
   2) Produce C⁻ ions in solutions   4) Produce H_3O^+ ions in solutions

5. Which compound is an organic acid?
   1) Methyl ethanoate   3) Hydrochloric acid
   2) Hexanoic acid   4) Sulfuric acid

6. The formula of which organic compound is classified as an acid?
   1) CH_3COCH_3 2) CH_3CH_2OH 3) CH_3COOH 4) $CH_2(OH)_2$

7. Which formula represents an organic acid?
   1) HCOOH   2) $CH_3COCH_2CH_3$ 3) CH_3CH_2CHO 4) CH_3NH_2

8. The structure of which compound is of an organic acid?

   1)   2)   3)   4)

9. Which is a structure of an organic acid?

   1)   2)   3)   4)

10. The structure   is classified as an organic acid because it contains

   1) −OH groups   2) −COOH group   3) − C − C − bonds   4) C = O bond

16. Ketones: Recalling concept definitions and facts

Recognizing names and formulas of ketones

1. Which structure best represents the general formula for ketones?

   1) R—OH
   2) 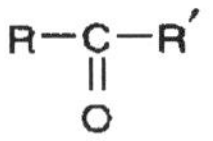 $R-\overset{\overset{\displaystyle}{||}}{\underset{O}{C}}-R'$
   3) R—O—R'
   4) 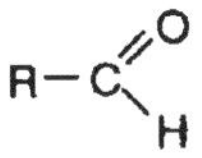 $R-\overset{\overset{\displaystyle O}{\diagup}}{C}{\diagdown}_H$

2. What is the IUPAC name ending for all ketones?
   1) –one   2) –ol   3) –oate   4) –al

3. The minimum number of carbon atoms a ketone may contain is
   1) 1   2) 2   3) 3   4) 4

4. An example of a ketone is
   1) octane   2) octanone   3) octanal   4) octanoate

5. Which is a ketone?
   1) Butanone   2) Butyne   3) 2-Butanol   4) 2-Butamide

6. Which formula represents a ketone?
   1) CH_3COOH 2) C_2H_5OH 3) CH_3COCH_3 4) CH_3COOCH_3

7. The molecular formula of which compound represents a ketone?
   1) $CH_3CHOHCH_3$ 2) CH_3CH_2COOH 3) $CH_3CH_2CH_2CHO$ 4) $CH_3CH_2CH_2COCH_3$

8. Which is a structural formula of a ketone?

   1) 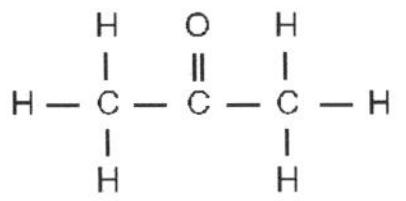
   2) 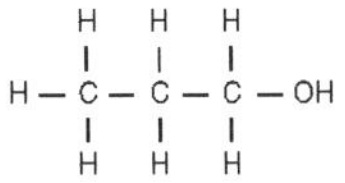
   3) 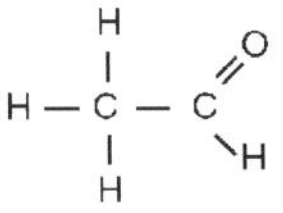
   4)

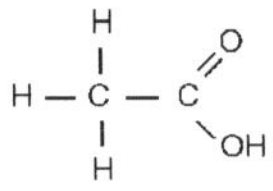

17. Ethers: Recalling concept definitions and facts
Recognizing names and formulas of ethers

1. Which general formula represents ether compounds?

   1) $R_1—O—R_2$ 2) R—CHO   3) R—OH   4) R—COOH

2. Which molecular formula is of a compound in the ether family?
   1) $CH_3COOCH_2CH_3$ 2) $CH_3CH_2CH_2COOH$ 3) $CH_3CH_2CH_2OH$ 4) $CH_3CH_2OCH_3$

3. Which formula is an ether?

   1) CH_3CH_2OH 2) $CH_3—O—CH_3$ 3) 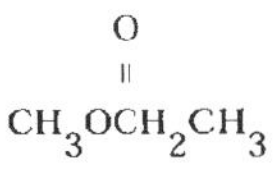 $CH_3OCH_2CH_3$ 4) 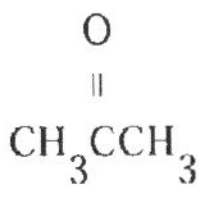 CH_3CCH_3 (with O double bonded)

4. Which structural formula represents an ether?

   1) 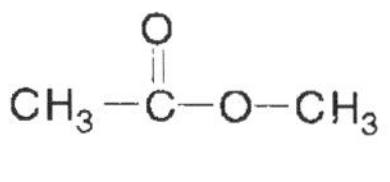 $CH_3—\overset{\overset{\displaystyle O}{||}}{C}—O—CH_3$ 2) 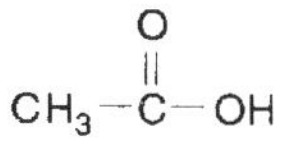 $CH_3—\overset{\overset{\displaystyle O}{||}}{C}—OH$ 3) $CH_3—O—CH_3$ 4) $CH_3—OH$

17. continues

5. The formula of which compound represents an ether?

1) 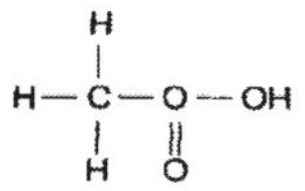 2) 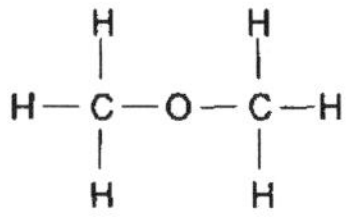 3) 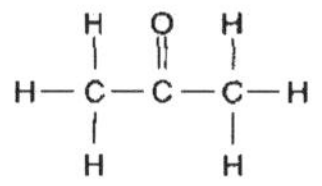 4)

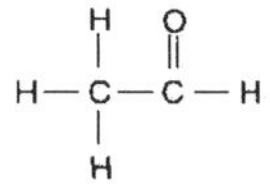

6. Which structure is of an ether?

1) 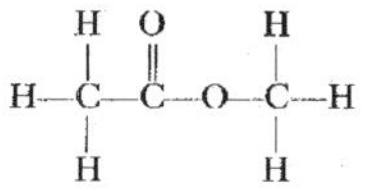 2) 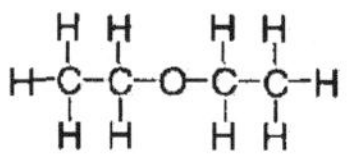 3) 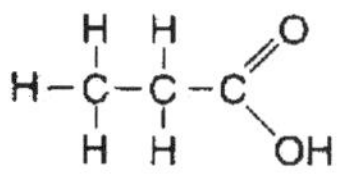 4

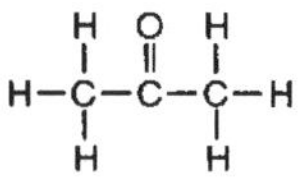

18. Esters : Recalling Concept Facts and Definitions
Recognizing names and formulas of esters

1. Which functional group represents esters?

1) 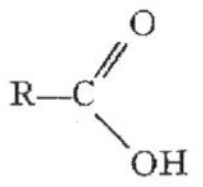 2) $R_1 - \overset{O}{\underset{||}{C}} - R_2$ 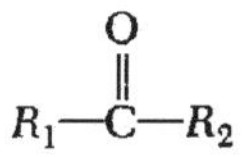 3) 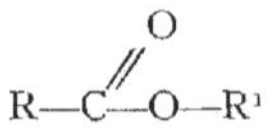 4)

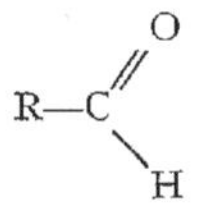

2. Which IUPAC name is of a compound that is an ester?
   1) Pentanone   2) Pentanoate   3) Ethanal   4) Ethanoic

3. Which formula correctly represents an ester?
   1) CH_3COOH 2) CH_3CHO 3) $CH_3COOCH_2CH_3$ 4) CH_3COCH_3

4. The formula of which compound is an ester?

1) CH_3CH_2OH 2) $CH_3 - O - CH_3$ 3) 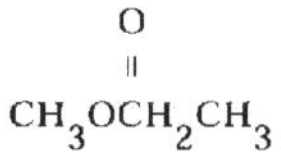 $CH_3OCH_2CH_3$ 4) 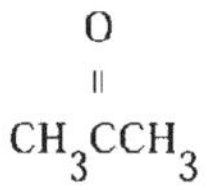 CH_3CCH_3

5. The structure of which compound is from class of compound called ester?

1) 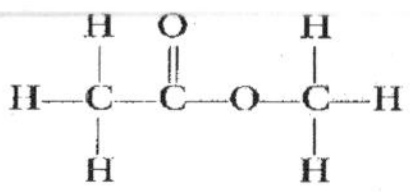 2) 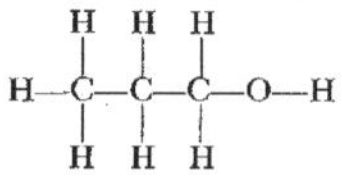 3) 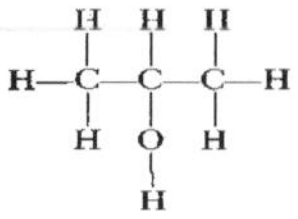 4)

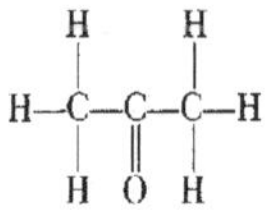

19. Amines and amides: Recalling definitions and facts

1. Which functional group correctly represents an amine?

   1) $-NH_3$ 2) $-OH$ 3) 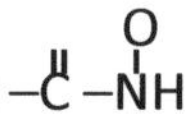 $-\overset{O}{\underset{||}{C}} - NH$ 4) $- N -$

2. Which general formula correctly represents amides?

   1) R-COOH   2) 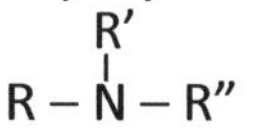 $R - \overset{R'}{\underset{|}{N}} - R''$ 3) 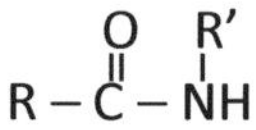 $R - \overset{O}{\underset{||}{C}} - \overset{R'}{\underset{|}{N}}H$ 4) R - O - R'

20. Names of organic compounds: Determining correct name from general formulas

1. Which compound is classified as a hydrocarbon?
   1) Chloroethane   2) Ethanol   3) Ethanoic acid   4) Ethane

2. Which compound is a hydrocarbon?
   1) Pentanone   2) Heptyne   3) Butanal   4) Hexanol

3. Which compound is a saturated hydrocarbon?
   1) Decyne   2) Decane   3) Ethene   4) Ethanol

4. Which compound is a saturated hydrocarbon?
   1) Chlorohexane   2) Hexanol   3) Hexene   4) Hexane

5. Which compound is an unsaturated hydrocarbon?
   1) Propene   2) Methanol   3) dibromoethane   4) Propane

6. Which of the following compounds would contain one double bond between two carbon atoms?
   1) Dimethyl ether   2) Heptene   3) Pentanol   4) Chloroethane

7. Which compound would have a triple bond between two adjacent carbon atoms?
   1) 1, 3- dimethyl butane   2) 3-octyne   3) 2-methyl propane   4) 2 –pentene

8. Which hydrocarbon is a member of organic compound class with the general formula C_nH_{2n-2}?
   1) Heptane   2) Benzene   3) Propyne   4) Butene

9. Which compound is a member of a hydrocarbon series with a general formula C_nH_{2n+2}?
   1) Propanal   2) Pentene   3) Pentane   4) Pentene

10. The compound belonging to a hydrocarbon series with a general formula C_nH_{2n} is
    1) 2-hexene   2) 2-methyl hexene   3) 2-Butyne   4) Butane

11. Which compound belongs to a class of organic compound with the general formula of R-OH?
    1) Propane   2) Propanol   3) Pentene   4) Pentanal

12. Then name of which compound is from a class of compound with the general formula R-CHO?
    1) Methanal   2) Methanol   3) Methane   4) Methanoic

13. The structural formula of which compound will contain the functional group   –COOH
    1) Methyl ethanoate   2) 2-pentanol   3) 2-pentanone   4) Butanoic acid

14. The structure of which compound contains the functional group $-\overset{\overset{\displaystyle O}{\|}}{C}-O-$
    1) Dimethyl ether   2) Propanone   3) Methyl Butanoate   4) Ethanoic acid

15. Which IUPAC name belongs to a class of organic with the general formula of R – O – R' ?
    1) Dimethyl ether   2) 2-hexanol   3) Pentanal   4) Ethanoic acid

16. The structure of which organic compound contains elements N and O?
    1) 1-butanamide   2) Butanamine   3) Methane butanoate   4) Butanal

21. Names of organic compounds: Determining correct name from molecular formula

1. Which compound has the formula C_6H_{10}?
   1) Hexane   2) Hexene   3) Hexyne   4) Hexanal

2. C_3H_8 is a molecular formula for
   1) Propene   2) Propanol   3) Propyne   4) Propane

3. What is the IUPAC name of a compound whose molecular formula is C_5H_8?
   1) 2-methyl pentane   2) 2-methyl pentene   3) Pentane   4) Pentyne

4. The formula $CH_3CH(CH_3)CH_2CH_2CH_3$ is a molecular formula for which compound?
   1) 2-methyl pentane   2) 2-methyl hexane   3) hexane   4) Pentane

5. Which compound has the molecular formula CH_3Cl?
   1) Ethane   2) Methane   3) Chloromethane   4) Chloroethane

6. Which IUPAC is correct for $CH_3CH_2CHBrCH_3$?
   1) 1-Bromobutane   2) 2-bromobutane   3) 3-bromobutane   4) Bromopropane

7. The molecular formula $CH_3CHCHCl_2$ represents the formula for which compound?
   1) 2-chloropropane   2) 3-chloropropane   3) Dichloropropane   4) Dichloropropene

8. Which organic compound is represented by the molecular formula C_4H_9OH?
   1) Butanol   2) Butanoic acid   3) Butane   4) Butanal

9. $CH_3CH(OH)CH_3$ is a formula for
   1) Propanol   2) 2-Propanol   3) 3-Propanol   4) methyl propanol

10. Which compound has the formula CH_3CH_2COOH ?
    1) Propanoic acid   2) Propanal   3) 2-propanol   4) 2- propanone

11. What is the IUPAC name of a compound with the formula CH_3COOCH_3?
    1) Methyl ethyl ether   2) Methyl ethanoate   3) Propanoic acid   4) Propanol

12. Which compound is represented by the formula CH_3OCH_3?
    1) Methyl methanoate   2) Ethanoate acid   3) Dimethyl ether   4) Diethyl ether

13. Which name is correct for a compound with a molecular formula $C_3H_6(OH)_2$?
    1) 2-propanol   2) 1-propanol   3) Propanetriol   4) Propanediol

14. The IUPAC name of a compound with the formula CH_3CH_2CHO is
    1) propanoic acid   2) propanone   3) propanol   4) propanal

15. The compound represented by the formula $CH_3COCH_2CH_3$ is
    1) 2-Butanone   2) 2-butanol   3) Dimethyl ether   4) Methyl ethanoate

16. The formula $CH_3CH_2NH_2$ is a molecular formula for
    1) ethanamine   2) ethanamide   3) propanamine   4) propanamide

17. The compound $CH_3CH_2COOCH_3$ is an example of an
    1) ether   2) alcohol   3) ester   4) acid

22. Names of organic compounds: Determining correct name given structural formula

1. Given the formula:

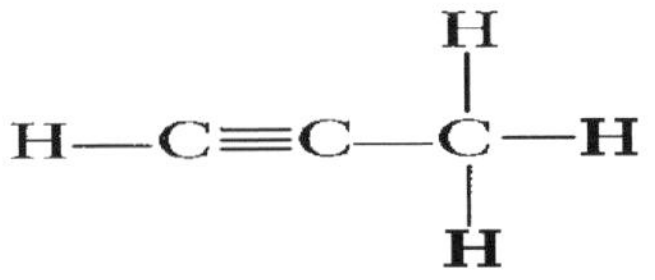

$$H—C≡C—\overset{\overset{\displaystyle H}{|}}{\underset{\underset{\displaystyle H}{|}}{C}}—H$$

What is the IUPAC name of this compound?
1) propene   2) 3-propene   3) 3-propyne   4) Propyne

2. Given the structural formula below:

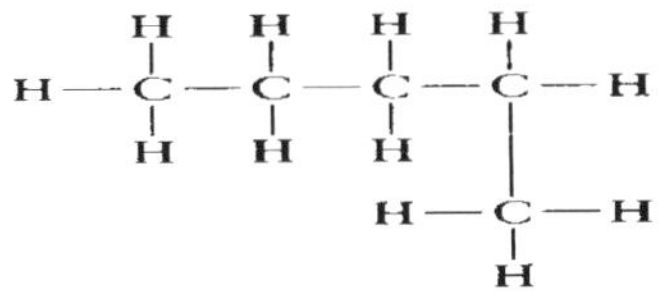

What is the IUPAC name for a compound with this structure?
1) Pentane   2) 1-methyl butane   3) 2-methyl butane   4) 4-methyl pentane

3. Which compound has the structural formula shown below?

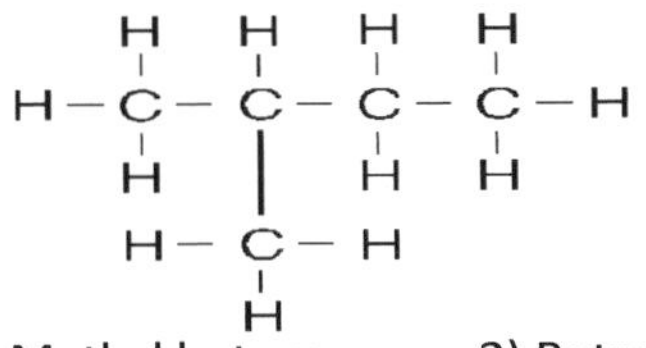

1) Methyl pentane   2) Methyl butane   3) Butane   4) Pentane

4. Given the structure below:

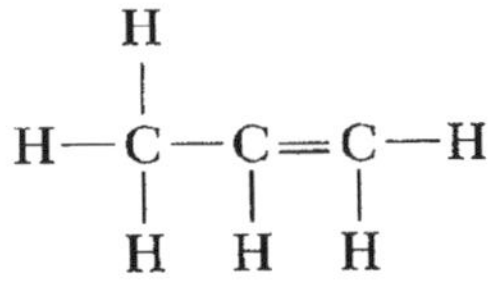

What is the correct name for this structure?
1) Propane   2) Propene   3) 3-propene   4) Propyne

5. Given the structure below:

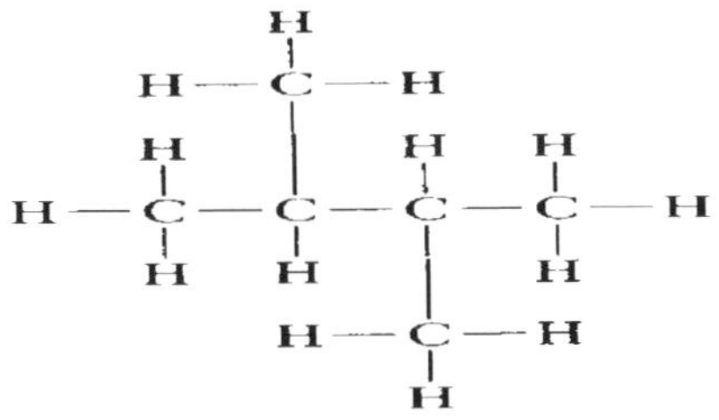

Which IUPAC name is correct for this structure?
1) Hexane   3) 2,3-dimethyl butane
2) 2,2-dimethyl hexane   4) Ethyl butane

22. Continues

6. What is the correct IUPAC name of the compound below?

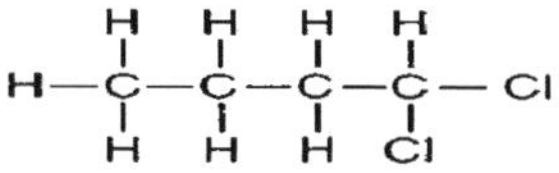

$$H-\overset{\overset{\displaystyle H}{|}}{\underset{\underset{\displaystyle H}{|}}{C}}-\overset{\overset{\displaystyle H}{|}}{\underset{\underset{\displaystyle H}{|}}{C}}-\overset{\overset{\displaystyle H}{|}}{\underset{\underset{\displaystyle H}{|}}{C}}-\overset{\overset{\displaystyle H}{|}}{\underset{\underset{\displaystyle Cl}{|}}{C}}-Cl$$

    1) Butane   2) 3,3-dichlorobutane   3) 1, 3-dichlorbutane   4) 1,1-dichlorobutane

7. What is the IUPAC name for the structural formula below?

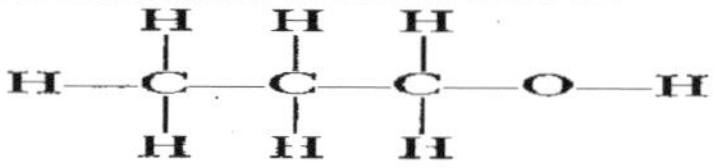

$$H-\overset{\overset{\displaystyle H}{|}}{\underset{\underset{\displaystyle H}{|}}{C}}-\overset{\overset{\displaystyle H}{|}}{\underset{\underset{\displaystyle H}{|}}{C}}-\overset{\overset{\displaystyle H}{|}}{\underset{\underset{\displaystyle H}{|}}{C}}-O-H$$

    1) Propanal   2) Propanol   3) 3-Propanol   4) 3-Propanal

8. What is the IUPAC name of the compound with the following structural formula?

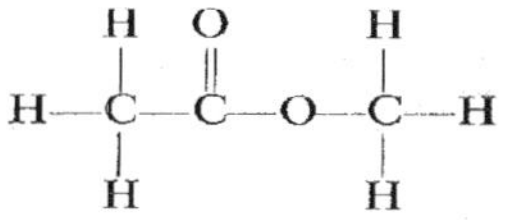

$$H-\overset{\overset{\displaystyle H}{|}}{\underset{\underset{\displaystyle H}{|}}{C}}-\overset{\overset{\displaystyle O}{||}}{C}-O-\overset{\overset{\displaystyle H}{|}}{\underset{\underset{\displaystyle H}{|}}{C}}-H$$

    1) Ethyl methanoate   2) Methyl ethanoate   3) Methyl ethyl ether   4) Propanoic acid

9. What is the correct IUPAC name for the alcohol with the structural formula shown below.

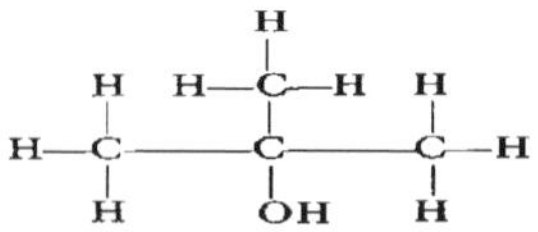

$$H-\overset{\overset{\displaystyle H}{|}}{\underset{\underset{\displaystyle H}{|}}{C}}-\overset{\overset{\displaystyle H-\overset{\overset{\displaystyle H}{|}}{\underset{\underset{\displaystyle}{}}{C}}-H}{}}{\underset{\underset{\displaystyle OH}{|}}{C}}-\overset{\overset{\displaystyle H}{|}}{\underset{\underset{\displaystyle H}{|}}{C}}-H$$

    1) 2-butanol   2) 2-Propanol   3) 2-methyl, 2-butanol   4) 2-methyl, 2-propanol

10. Given the structure below

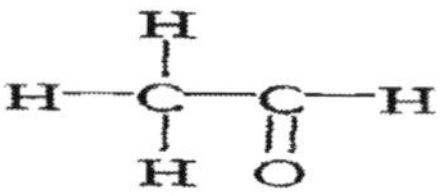

$$H-\overset{\overset{\displaystyle H}{|}}{\underset{\underset{\displaystyle H}{|}}{C}}-\overset{\overset{\displaystyle}{}}{\underset{\underset{\displaystyle O}{||}}{C}}-H$$

What is the correct IUPAC name for a molecule with the above structure?

    1) Ethanal   2) Ethanol   3) Ethene   4) Ethanoic acid

11. Which IUPAC name is correct for the structure given below?

$$H-\overset{\overset{\displaystyle H}{|}}{\underset{\underset{\displaystyle H}{|}}{C}}-\overset{\overset{\displaystyle H}{|}}{\underset{\underset{\displaystyle H}{|}}{C}}-\overset{\overset{\displaystyle OH}{\diagup}}{\underset{\underset{\displaystyle O}{\diagdown}}{C}}$$

    1) Propanol   2) Propanal   3) Propene   4) Propanoic acid

12. The structure below is best classified as an

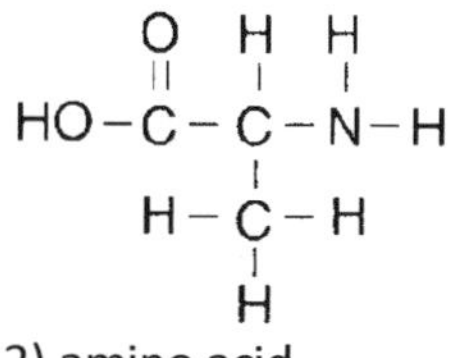

$$HO-\overset{\overset{\displaystyle O}{||}}{C}-\overset{\overset{\displaystyle H}{|}}{\underset{\underset{\displaystyle}{}}{C}}-\overset{\overset{\displaystyle H}{|}}{\underset{\underset{\displaystyle}{}}{N}}-H$$
$$\overset{\displaystyle}{\underset{\underset{\displaystyle H}{|}}{H-\overset{\overset{\displaystyle}{}}{\underset{\underset{\displaystyle}{}}{C}}-H}}$$

    1) amide   2) amino acid   3) organic acid   4) ester

Topic 10: Organic Chemistry

23. Molecular formulas: Determining molecular formula from bond type and name

1. Which formulas represent molecules of saturated hydrocarbons?
   1) C_5H_{12} and C_6H_{14} 2) C_5H_{10} and C_5H_8 3) C_4H_{10} and C_5H_8 4) C_4H_8 and C_4H_6

2. Which two formulas represent unsaturated hydrocarbons?
   1) C_2H_2 and C_2H_6 2) C_2H_2 and C_2H_4 3) C_2H_6 and C_3H_8 4) C_3H_4 and C_4H_{10}

3. Which is an unsaturated hydrocarbon?
   1) CH_2CHCl 2) CH_3CH_2Cl 3) $CH_3CH_2CH_3$ 4) CH_3CHCH_2

4. What is the correct formula for butyne?
   1) C_4H_{10} 2) C_4H_4 3) C_4H_6 4) C_4H_{10}

5. Which molecular formula is correct for hexene?
   1) C_6H_{10} 2) C_6H_{12} 3) C_6H_{14} 4) C_6H_6

6. Which condensed formula represents butane?
   1) $CH_3CH_2CH_2CH_2CH_3$ 2) $CH_3CH_2CH_2CH_3$ 3) CH_3CH_3 4) $CH_3CH_2CH_3$

7. The correct molecular formula for the compound with IUPAC name 2-methyl propane is
   1) $CH_3CH(CH_3)CH_3$ 2) $CH_3CH_2(CH_3)CH_2CH_3$ 3) $CH_3CH_2CH_2CH_3$ 4) $CH_3CH_2CH_3$

8. Chloropropane is correctly represented by which chemical formula?
   1) C_3H_5Cl 2) C_3H_6Cl 3) C_3H_7Cl 4) C_3H_8Cl

9. Which formula represents the compound 2-fluoropentane?
   1) $C_5H_{10}F$ 2) $C_5H_{11}F$ 3) $C_5H_{10}F_2$ 4) $C_5H_{11}F_2$

10. The formula for dibromobutane is
    1) C_4H_6Br 2) C_4H_9Br 3) $C_4H_6Br_2$ 4) $C_4H_8Br_2$

11. Which is the correct formula for butanol?
    1) $CH_3CH_2CH_2CH_2OH$ 2) $CH_3CH_2OCH_2CH_3$ 3) $CH_3CH_2CH_2COOH$ 4) $CH_3CH_2CH_2OH$

12. The correct formula for hexanol?
    1) $C_6H_{12}OH$ 2) $C_6H_{13}OH$ 3) C_6H_{12} 4) C_6H_{14}

13. Which formula is a dihydroxy alcohol?
    1) $Ca(OH)_2$ 2) $Al(OH)_3$ 3) $C_2H_4(OH)_2$ 4) $C_3H_5(OH)_3$

14. The condensed formula that represents methyl propanoate is
    1) $CH_3CH_2COOCH_3$ 2) CH_3CH_2CHO 3) CH_3COOH 4) CH_3CHO

15. Which chemical formula is correct for ethanal?
    1) C_2H_5CHO 2) CH_3CHO 3) C_2H_5COOH 4) CH_3COOH

16. Which best represents propanoic acid?
    1) C_2H_5COOH 2) C_3H_7COOH 3) C_2H_5CHO 4) C_3H_7CHO

17. The correct formula for dimethyl ether is
    1) CH_3COOCH_3 2) CH_3OCH_3 3) CH_3CH_3OH 4) CH_3COCH_3

24. Structural formulas: Determining structural formulas from bond types and names

1. Which structural formula correctly represents a hydrocarbon molecule?

2. Which is a correctly drawn structure for an organic compound?

3. Which structural formula represents a saturated hydrocarbon?

4. Which formula represents an unsaturated hydrocarbon?

5. The structure of which compound belongs to a hydrocarbon series with the general formula C_nH_{2n}?

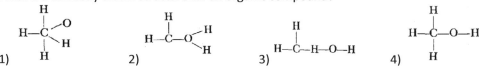

6. Which structural formula is of a compound of a hydrocarbon series with the general formula C_nH_{2n+2}

7. Which structure is correct for a compound with the general formula of C_nH_{2n-2}?

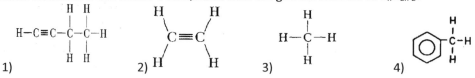

25. continues

8. Which structure correctly represents an organic compound with a molecular of formula C_3H_6?

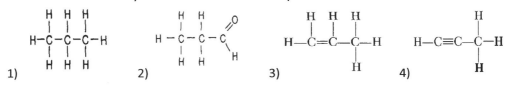

1)   2)   3)   4)

9. Which structure correctly represents a compound of an alkene?

1)   2) H—C≡C—Cl   3)   4)

10. Which structural formula represents a molecule of 2- butyne?

1)   2) H—C—C≡C—C—H   3)   4)

11. Which structure is correct for a compound with the IUPAC name of 2-methyl butane?

1)   2)   3)   4)

12. The structural formula that correctly represents 2-butene is

1) H—C=C—C=C—H   2)   3)   4)

13. Which structural formula represents 1.2-dibromopropane?

1)   2)   3)   4)

14. Which structure represents a compound with IUPAC name of 2-propanol?

1)   2)   3)   4)

25. Continues

15. What is the structural formula for 1,3-propanediol?

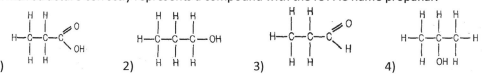

1)   2)   3)   4)

16. Which structure correctly represents a compound with the IUPAC name propanal?

1)   2)   3)   4)

17. Which structure is correct for ethanoic acid?

1)   2)   3)   4)

18   The correct structure for pentanone is

1)   2)   3)   4)

19. Which structural formula is correct for methyl ethyl ether?

1)   2)   3)   4)

20. A compound has an IUPAC of compound methyl ethanoate. Which structure correctly represents this compound?

1)   2)   3)   4)

25. Isomers: Recalling Concept Facts and definition

1. Two isomers must have the same
   1) percent composition
   2) arrangement of atoms
   3) physical properties
   4) chemical properties

2. Compounds that have the same molecular formula , but different molecular structures are called
   1) isotopes
   2) allotropes
   3) isomers
   4) electrovalent

3. 2-methyl butane and 2,2-dimethyl propane are isomers. Molecules of these two compounds have different
   1) molecular formulas
   2) number of carbon
   3) structural formulas
   4) number of covalent bonds

4. The compounds CH_3OCH_3 and CH_3CH_2OH are isomers because they have
   1) same molecular formula
   2) same structural formula
   3) different molecular formula
   4) different percentage composition

5. What is the minimum number of carbon atoms a hydrocarbon must have in other to have an isomer?
   1) 1   2) 2   3) 3   4) 4

6. As the number of carbon atoms in each successive member of a homologous series of hydrocarbon series increases, the number of possible isomers
   1) increases   2) decreases   3) remains the same

26. Isomers: Determining compound with most or least number of isomers

1. An alkene compound of which molecular formula will have the most number of isomers?
   1) C_2H_4 2) C_3H_6 3) C_4H_8 4) C_5H_{10}

2. Which alkane compound will have the most number of isomers?
   1) C_7H_{16} 2) C_6H_{14} 3) C_5H_{12} 4) C_4H_{10}

3. Which hydrocarbon molecular formula will have the least number of isomers?
   1) C_5H_8 2) C_4H_6 3) C_6H_{10} 4) C_7H_{12}

4. Which compound has no isomer?
   1) C_3H_7Cl 2) C_4H_9Cl 3) C_2H_5Cl 4) $C_5H_{11}Cl$

27. Isomers: Recognizing formulas that are isomers

1. The compound C_4H_9OH is an isomer of
   1) $C_3H_7COCH_3$ 2) $C_2H_5OC_2H_5$ 3) $C_3COOC_2H_5$ 4) CH_3COOH

2. Which compound is an isomer of butanoic acid, $CH_3CH_2CH_2COOH$?
   1) $CH_3CH_2CH_2CH_2OH$ 2) $CH_3CH_2CH_2CH_2COOH$ 3) $CH_3CH_2COOCH_3$ 4) $CH_3CH_2OCH_3$

3. Which two condensed formulas are isomers of each other?

   1) $CH_3CH_2CH(Cl)CH_3$ and $CH_3CH(Cl)CH_2CH_3$
   2) CH_2CH_2 and CH_3COCH_3
   3) $CH_3CH_2CH_3$ and CH_2CHCH_3
   4) $CH_3CH(OH)CH_3$ and $CH_3CH(OH)CH_2CH_3$

4. Which IUPAC name is an isomer of 3-hexene?
   1) 2-methyl hexene   2) 2-hexene   3) 3-heptene   4) 2-heptyne

27. cont.

5. Given the structure of a compound below:

```
      H   O   H
      |   ||  |
  H — C — C — C — H
      |       |
      H       H
```

Which compound represents an isomer

1)
```
      H       H
      |       |
  H — C — C — C — H
      |   ||  |
      H   O   H
```

2)
```
      H   O
      |   ||
  H — C — C — OH
      |
      H
```

3)
```
      H   H   H
      |   |   |
  H — C — C — C — H
      |   |   |
      H   OH  H
```

4)
```
      H   H   O
      |   |   ‖
  H — C — C — C
      |   |      \
      H   H       H
```

6. Which structural formula represents an isomer of the compound given below?

```
      H   OH  H
      |   |   |
  H — C — C — C — H
      |   |   |
      H   H   H
```

1)
```
      H   H       H
      |   |       |
  H — C — C — O — C — H
      |   |       |
      H   H       H
```

2)
```
      H   OH  OH
      |   |   |
  H — C — C — C — H
      |   |   |
      H   H   H
```

3)
```
      H
      |
  H — C — OH
      |
  H — C — OH
      |
  H — C — OH
      |
      H
```

4)
```
      H   H       O
      |   |       ‖
  H — C — C — C
      |   |       \
      H   H        OH
```

7. Which structural formula represents a compound that is an isomer of

```
      Br  H   H   H   H
      |   |   |   |   |
  H — C — C — C — C — C — H
      |   |   |   |   |
      Br  H   H   H   H
```

1)
```
      H   H   H   Br
      |   |   |   |
  H — C — C — C — C — H?
      |   |   |   |
      H   H   H   Br
```

2)
```
      Br  Br  Br
      |   |   |
  H — C — C — C — H
      |   |   |
      H   H   H
      |
  H — C — H
      |
      H
```

3)
```
          H
      Br — C — Br
          |
      H — C — H
          |
      H — C — H
          |
      H — C — H
          |
          H
```

4)
```
      H   Br  H   H
      |   |   |   |
  H — C — C — C — C — Br
      |   |   |   |
      H   H   H   H
```

8. Which formula is an isomer of pentane?

1)
```
              H   H
              |   |
  H — C ≡ C — C — C — H
              |   |
              H   H
```

2)
```
          H
      H — C — H
          |
      H   H   H
      |   |   |
  H — C — C — C — H
      |   |   |
      H   H   H
          |
      H — C — H
          |
          H
```

3)
```
      H   H   OH  H   H
      |   |   |   |   |
  H — C — C — C — C — C — H
      |   |   |   |   |
      H   H   H   H   H
```

4)
```
      H   H   H
      |   |   |
  H — C — C — C — H
      |   |   |
      H   |   H
          |
      H — C — H
          |
          H
```

9. Which compound is an isomer of 1-butene?

1)
```
      H   H   H     O
      |   |   |    ‖
  H — C — C — C — C
      |   |   |     \
      H   H   H      OH
```

2)
```
            H   H
            |   |
      H     C — C     H
       \   ⁄         ⁄
        C = C       C
       ⁄              \
      H                H
```

3)
```
            H   H
            |   |
  H     C = C — C — H
   \   ⁄            |
    C                H
   ⁄
  H
```

4)
```
      H   H   H   H
      |   |   |   |
  H — C — C = C — C — H
      |               |
      H               H
```

10. Which structure is an isomer of dimethyl ether?

1)
```
      H   H
      |   |
  H — C — C — OH
      |   |
      H   H
```

2)
```
      H   O
      |   ‖
  H — C — C — H
      |
      H
```

3)
```
      H   O
      |   ‖
  H — C — C — OH
      |
      H
```

4)
```
          H
          |
      H — C — OH
          |
      H — C — OH
          |
          H
```

28. Organic reaction: Recalling Concept Facts and Definitions

1. Unsaturated hydrocarbons can become saturated by which type of organic reaction?
   1) Esterification　　　2) Fermentation　　　3) Addition　　　4) Substitution

2. A common reaction of alkanes is
   1) addition　　　2) substitution　　　3) fermentation　4) neutralization

3. Alkenes and alkynes will undergo which type of organic reaction?
   1) Single replacement　　2) Substitution　　3) Addition　　　4) Fermentation

4. Which organic reaction involves the hydrolysis of a fat by a base?
   1) Saponification　　2) Esterification　　3) Polymerization　　4) Neutralization

5. The formation of large molecules from smaller molecules is an example of
   1) saponification　　2) decomposition　　3) substitution　　4) polymerization

6. By which organic reaction is ethanol produced from sugar?
   1) Addition　　　2) Fermentation　　　3) Saponification　　4) Combustion

7. Glycerol, a trihydroxy alcohol, is an organic product formed by this reaction?
   1) Esterification　　2) Polymerization　　3) Addition　　　4) Saponification

8. What type of organic reaction describes the burning of a hydrocarbon in the presence of oxygen?
   1) Addition　　　2) Decomposition　　3) Combustion　　4) Substitution

9. An alcohol and an organic acid are combined to form water and a compound with a pleasant odor. This reaction is an example of
   1) esterification　　2) fermentation　　3) polymerization　　4) saponification

10. Which reaction is used to produce polyethylene from ethylene?
    1) Addition polymerization　　　　3) Substitution
    2) Condensation polymerization　　4) Combustion

11. Carbon dioxide and water are two products formed from which organic reaction?
    1) Combustion　　　　3) Fermentation
    2) Esterification　　　4) Saponification

12. A halide of two attached halogen atoms is the only product formed from which reaction?
    1) Substitution　　　3) Addition
    2) Combustion　　　4) Polymerization

13. A halide and an acid are two products formed from
    1) combustion reaction　　　3) substitution reaction
    2) single replacement reaction　4) addition reaction

Topic 10: Organic Chemistry

29. Organic reactions: Determining formulas and names of reactants or products in organic reactions

1. Which compound will undergo a substitution reaction with bromine?
   1) Ethene   2) Ethane   3) Ethyne   4) Ethanol

2. Which organic compound will undergo an addition reaction?
   1) Chloropentane   2) Pentyne   3) Methane   4) Chloromethane

3. A compound of which formula would likely undergo a substitution reaction with Iodine (I_2)?
   1) C_3H_8 2) CH_3OH 3) C_3H_4 4) C_2H_4

4. Which compound would likely undergo an addition reaction with chlorine?
   1) C_4H_9OH 2) C_5H_{10} 3) C_2H_6 4) C_2H_2

5. The combustion of an alkane in the presence of oxygen produces
   1) CO_2 and H_2 2) CO and H_2 3) CO_2 and H_2O 4) CO and H_2O

6. Which compound is a likely product from fermentation of sugar?
   1) C_2H_2 2) C_2H_5OH 3) CH_3COOH 4) CH_3COOCH_3

7. A compound of which formula is likely formed from an addition reaction?
   1) C_2H_6 2) C_2H_5OH 3) $C_2H_4Cl_2$ 4) CH_3OCH_3

8. Which compound is likely formed from a substitution reaction
   1) C_4H_6 2) $C_4H_8Br_2$ 3) C_4H_9Br 4) C_4H_8

9. A reaction between fluorine and 2-methyl butane is likely to produce
   1) Butanone
   2) Pentane
   3) 2-methyl, 1-fluorobutane
   4) 2,2-difluorobutane

10. Which organic compound is likely produced as a result of condensation polymerization?
    1) 1,2 -dibromoproane
    2) 2,2-dimethyl propane
    3) Methyl propanoate
    4) Methanoic acid

11. In condensation polymerization, the two products formed are a polymer and
    1) water
    2) carbon dioxide
    3) an acid
    4) a base

12. What is a product of both fermentation reactions and saponification?
    1) An ester
    2) An acid
    3) A soap
    4) An alcohol

13. Which organic product is made up of monomers joined together in long chains?
    1) Protein
    2) Ester
    3) Ketone
    4) Acid

14. Which organic product is likely to form from addition polymerization of alkene monomers?
    1) Glycerol
    2) Polyethylene
    3) Dichloromethane
    4) Ethanol

15. A structure of which organic compound is formed from a saponification reaction?

16. A structure of which organic compound likely formed from a reaction between an organic acid and alcohol?

30. Organic reactions: Determining type of organic reaction from equation

1. Given the reaction below.
$$C_3H_8 + Cl_2 \rightarrow C_3H_7Cl + HCl$$
Which correctly identifies this reaction?
1) Addition　　2) Substitution　　3) Esterification　　4) Fermentation

2. Which type of reaction is represented by the equation
$$CH_4 + O_2 \rightarrow CO_2 + H_2O$$
1) Combustion　　2) Substitution　　3) Neutralization　　4) Fermentation

3. Given the reaction below:
$$C_4H_8 + Br_2 \rightarrow C_4H_8Br_2$$
What type of reaction is represented by the equation.
1) Combustion　　2) Substitution　　3) Polymerization　　4) Addition

4. Given the reaction below:
$$C_6H_{12}O_6 \rightarrow C_2H_5OH + CO_2$$
This reaction can be classified as
1) Saponification　　2) Fermentation　　3) Combustion　　4) Polymerization

5. The reaction below
$$CH_3COOH + CH_3OH \rightarrow CH_3COOCH_3 + H_2O$$
Is best classified as
1) Esterification　　2) Combustion　　3) Polymerization　　4) Saponification

6. Given the reaction
$$C_3H_8 + O_2 \rightarrow CO_2 + H_2O$$
This reaction is an example of
1) Fermentation　　2) Addition　　3) Substitution　　4) Combustion

7. Given an equation to organic reaction below:
$$C_5H_{12} + Cl_2 \rightarrow C_5H_{11}Cl + HCl$$

This reaction can be best classified as
1) Addition　　2) Substitution　　3) Polymerization　　4) Hydrogenation

8. Given the organic reaction:
$$CH_3CH_2COOH + OH-CH_2CH_3 \rightarrow CH_3CH_3COOCH_2CH_3 + H_2O$$
This reaction is an example of
1) Saponification　　2) Esterification　　3) Addition　　4) Neutralization

9. Which organic reaction is represented by the equation below?
$$n(CH_2=CH_2) \rightarrow (-CH_2-CH_2-)n$$

1) Condensation polymerization　　3) Esterification
2) Addition polymerization　　4) Substitution

10. An organic reaction is shown below:
$$CH_3CH_2CH_2OH + OHCH_2CH_2CH_3 \rightarrow CH_3CH_2CH_2OCH_2CH_2CH_3 + H_2O$$
Which type of a reaction is represented by the equation?
1) Condensation polymerization　　3) Addition polymerization
2) Saponification　　4) Fermentation

30. continues

11. What type of organic reaction is represented by the equation below?

$$H-C-C=C-C-H \quad + \quad H_2 \quad \rightarrow \quad H-C-C-C-C-H$$

1) Substitution   2) Saponification   3) Polymerization   4) Addition

12. Given the equation below:

$$H-C-C-C-H \quad + \quad F_2 \quad \rightarrow \quad H-C-C-C-H \quad + \quad HF$$

The reaction represented above is an example of
1) Substitution   2) Neutralization   3) Esterification   4) Addition

13. Which organic reaction is represented by the equation below:

$$H-C-C-OH \quad + \quad OH-C-H \quad \rightarrow \quad H-C-C-O-C-H \quad + \quad H_2O$$

1) Saponification   2) Esterification   3) Addition   4) Combustion

14. Which organic reaction is represent by the equation below?

$$C=C \quad + \quad Br_2 \quad \rightarrow \quad Br-C-C-Br$$

1) Fermentation   3) Addition
2) Combustion   4) Substitution

15. Given the organic reaction below:

$$H-C-C-C-OH \quad + \quad HO-C-C-C-H \quad \dashrightarrow \quad H-C-C-C-O-C-C-C-H \quad + \quad H_2O$$

The type of reaction represented above is
1) esterification   3) addition polymerization
2) saponification   4) condensation polymerization

16. What type of organic reaction is represented by the equation below?
Note: n and n are very large numbers equal to about 2000.

$$n \left(C=C \right) \longrightarrow \left(-C-C- \right)_n$$

1) Condensation polymerization   3) Condensation substitution
2) Addition polymerization   4) Addition substitution

31. Organic reactions: Determining missing reactant or product

1. Which formula is correct for the organic product produced in the reaction between C_3H_6 and Cl_2?
   1) C_3H_6Cl 2) C_3H_8Cl 3) $C_3H_6Cl_2$ 4) $C_3H_8Cl_2$

2. The reaction between C_5H_{12} and I_2 will produce HI and which organic compound?
   1) $C_5H_{11}I$ 2) $C_5H_{12}I$ 3) $C_5H_{12}I_2$ 4) $C_5H_{10}I_2$

3. Which formula correctly represents a compound formed from a reaction between C_2H_4 and Br_2?
   1) Bromoethene 3) Bromoethane
   2) 1,2-dibromoethane 4) 1,2-dibromoethene

4. Given the reaction

   $$CH_4 + Br_2 \rightarrow X + HBr$$

   Which formula correctly represents X?
   1) CH_4Br_2 2) CH_3Br_2 3) CH_3Br 4) CBr_4

5. Which structural formula represents a product formed from a reaction between Cl_2 and C_2H_4?

   1) 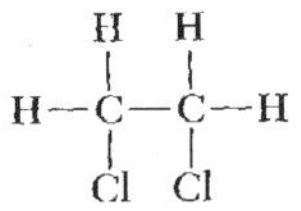
   2) 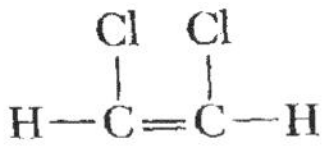
   3)
   4) 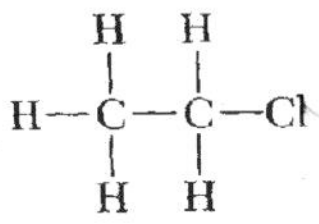

6. Given the equation

   $$C_2H_6 + F_2 \rightarrow X + HF$$

   What is the name of compound X produced?
   1) Ethene 2) Flouroethane 3) 1,2-difluoroethane 4) Fluropropane

7. In the reaction

   $$CH_3COOH + CH_3OH \rightarrow X + H_2O$$

   The organic product X can best be identified as
   1) Propanol 2) Propanone 3) Methyl Ethanoate 4) Methyl ethyl ether

8. A product of a reaction between a hydrocarbon and bromine is 1,2-dichlorobutane. The hydrocarbon reactant is
   1) C_5H_{10} 2) C_2H_4 3) C_3H_8 4) C_4H_8

9. Given the reaction below:

   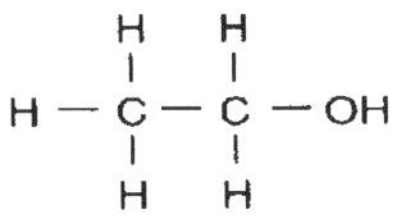 + X → 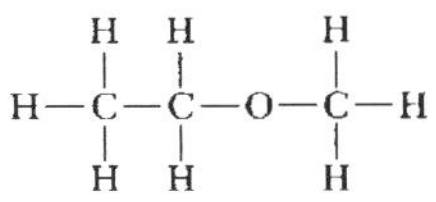 + H_2O

   Which structure is represented by X?

   1) 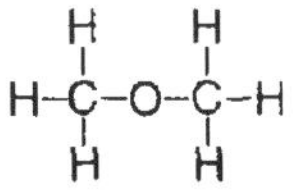
   2) 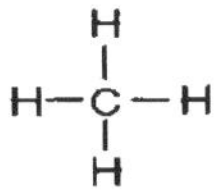
   3) 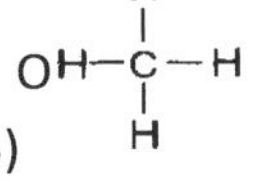
   4) 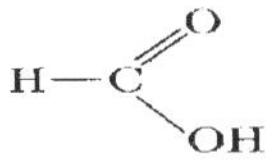

10. Given the organic reaction below:

    $$X + CH_3CH_3OH \rightarrow CH_3CH_2CH_2\overset{O}{\overset{\|}{C}}-OCH_2CH_3 + H_2O$$

    Which compound is represented by X?
    1) $CH_3CH_2\overset{O}{\overset{\|}{C}}-OH$ 2) $CH_3\overset{O}{\overset{\|}{C}}\text{-}H$ 3) $CH_3CH_2\overset{O}{\overset{\|}{C}}-H$ 4) CH_3CCH_3

Topic 11: Redox and electrochemistry

1. **Redox: Recalling Concept Facts and Definitions**

   1. A reaction that involve the losing and gaining of electrons is called
      1) fusion   2) neutralization   3) kinetics   4) redox

   2. A redox reaction always involves
      1) a change in oxidation number   3) the transfer of protons
      2) a change of phase   4) the formation of ions

   3. Which particles are gained and lost during a redox reaction?
      1) Protons   3) Neutrons
      2) Electrons   4) Positrons

   4. In all redox reactions, there is conservation of
      1) mass, but not charge   3) both mass and charge
      2) charge, but not mass   4) neither mass nor charge

   5. All redox reactions involve
      1) the gain of electrons, only   3) both the gain and the loss of electrons
      2) the loss of electrons   4) neither the gain nor the loss of electrons

   6. A redox reaction is a reaction in which
      1) only reduction occurs
      2) only oxidation occurs
      3) reduction and oxidation occur at the same time
      4) reduction and oxidation occur at different times

   7. Which statement correctly describes a redox reaction?
      1) The oxidation half-reaction and the reduction half-reaction occur simultaneously
      2) The oxidation half-reaction occurs before the reduction half-reaction
      3) The oxidation half-reaction occurs after the reduction half-reaction
      4) The oxidation half-reaction occurs spontaneously but the reduction half-reaction does not

   8. Which set includes only reactions that involve oxidation and reduction?
      1) Synthesis, decomposition, and double replacement
      2) Synthesis, decomposition, and single replacement
      3) Decomposition, single replacement, and double replacement
      4) Synthesis, single replacement, and double replacement

   9. A redox reaction always involves
      1) a transfer of protons
      2) a change in phase
      3) a change in oxidation number
      4) the formation of ions

   10. A charge an atom has or appears to have when it gains or loses electrons is called
      1) ionization number
      2) electronegativity number
      3) reduction number
      4) oxidation number

Survivingchem.com

Topic 11: Redox and electrochemistry

2. Oxidation Number: Recalling rules of assigning oxidation numbers

1. The sum of all oxidation numbers of atoms in a chemical formula must equal
   1) -1   2) 0   3) 1   4) 2

2. The oxidation number of elements in their free state must be always be a
   1) 0   2) 1   3) 2   4) 3

3. What oxidation number do elements in Group 1 tend to form when they bond with other elements in compounds?
   1) 0   2) +2   3) -1   4) +1

4. The alkaline earth metals in compounds tend to form oxidation number of a
   1) -2   2) +2   3) +1   4) 0

5. The most common oxidation number of halogen in a binary compound is
   1) 0   2) -1   3) +1   4) -2

3. Oxidation Numbers: Determining oxidation number of an element in a formula

1. The oxidation number of nitrogen in N_2 is
   1) +1   2) 0   3) +3   4) -3

2. What is the oxidation number of oxygen in OF_2?
   1) +1   2) +2   3) -1   4) -2

3. What is the oxidation number of calcium in CaH_2?
   1) 0   2) +1   3) +2   4) -2

4. The oxidation number of fluorine in MgF_2 is
   1) -1   2) 0   3) +1   4) 1-

5. The oxidation number of H in H_2O is
   1) +2   2) +1   3) 0   4) -1

6. What is the oxidation number of oxygen in hydrogen peroxide, H_2O_2?
   1) -1   2) +1   3) -2   4) +2

7. What is the oxidation number of oxygen in ozone, O_3?
   1) +1   2) 0   3) -2   4) -6

8. The oxidation number of hydrogen in BeH_2 is
   1) +1   2) -1   3) 0   4) +2

9. What is the oxidation of hydrogen in LiH?
   1) 0   2) +1   3) +2   4) -1

10. The oxidation number of nitrogen in Al_3N_2 is
    1) +3   2) +2   3) -3   4) -6

4. Oxidation numbers: Determining oxidation number of an element with multiple positive charges

1. The oxidation number of sulfur in the compound SO_3 is
   1) -3
   2) +3
   3) +6
   4) -6

2. What is the oxidation number of iodine in KIO_4?
   1) +1
   2) -1
   3) + 7
   4) -7

3. What is the oxidation number of nitrogen in HNO_3?
   1) +5
   2) +4
   3) -3
   4) -1

4. What is the oxidation number of Pt in K_2PtCl_6?
   1) -4
   2) +4
   3) -2
   4) +2

5. In $Na_2Cr_2O_7$, the oxidation number of chromium is
   1) +2
   2) +6
   3) +7
   4) +12

6. What is the oxidation number of carbon in $NaHCO_3$?
   1) -2
   2) +2
   3) -4
   4) +4

7. What are the two oxidation states of nitrogen in the compound NH_4NO_3?
   1) -3 and +5
   2) -3 and -5
   3) +3 and +5
   4) +3 and -5

8. Below, two compounds of chlorine are given:
   Compound A: Cl_2O Compound B: $HClO$
   Which is true of the oxidation number of chlorine in Compound A and B?
   1) Chlorine oxidation number is +2 in A, but a +1 in B
   2) Chlorine oxidation number is +1 in A, but a +2 in B
   3) Chlorine oxidation number is +2 in both A and B
   4) Chlorine oxidation number is +1 in both A and B

5. Oxidation number: Determining oxidation number of an element in ions

1. The oxidation number of sulfur in hydrogen sulfate ion, HSO_4^- is
   1) +1
   2) -2
   3) +6
   4) -4

2. What is the oxidation number of nitrogen in the ion NO_3^- ?
   1) +6
   2) -3
   3) +5
   4) -1

3. The oxidation number of hydrogen in the hydronium ion, H_3O^+ is
   1) +1
   2) -1
   3) 0
   4) +3

4. What is the oxidation number of S in the ion SO_4^{2-}
   1) -2
   2) -6
   3) +4
   4) +6

5. The oxidation number of phosphorous in a phosphate ion, PO_4^{3-} is
   1) +5
   2) -3
   3) +3
   4) +8

6. What is the oxidation number of nitrogen in ammonium ion, NH_4^+ ?
   1) -3
   2) +2
   3) +4
   4) +5

7. What is the oxidation number of Cr in the polyatomic ion, $Cr_2O_7^{2-}$?
   1) +7
   2) +6
   3) -2
   4) +2

8. In the ion O_2^{2-}, what is the oxidation number of O?
   1) -1
   2) +1
   3) -2
   4) 0

6. Oxidation numbers: Determining formula in which an atom has a certain oxidation number

1. In which compound does hydrogen have a negative oxidation number?
   1) NaH
   2) H_3PO_4
   3) NaOH
   4) H_2

2. In which substance does oxygen have a positive oxidation number?
   1) O_2
   2) OF_2
   3) H_2O_2
   4) H_2SO_4

3. Oxygen has an oxidation number of -2 in
   1) O_2
   2) Na_2O_2
   3) NO_2
   4) OF_2

4. In which compound does chlorine have an oxidation number of +5?
   1) $HClO_4$
   2) $HClO_2$
   3) $HClO$
   4) $HClO_3$

5. In which substance does bromine has oxidation number of +3?
   1) $KBrO$
   2) $KBrO_3$
   3) $KBrO_2$
   4) $KBrO_4$

6. In which compound does iodine have the highest oxidation number?
   1) KIO_3
   2) KIO
   3) KIO_2
   4) KI

7. In which formula does Nitrogen have a +3 charge?
   1) NO_2
   2) NO_2^-
   3) NO_3
   4) NO_3^-

8. In which substance does sulfur have a negative oxidation number?
   1) Na_2S
   2) S
   3) $CaSO_4$
   4) SO_2

9. In which substance does phosphorous have a +3 oxidation number?
   1) P_4O_{10}
   2) PCl_5
   3) $Ca_3(PO_4)_2$
   4) KH_2PO_3

10. Sulfur has an oxidation number of +6 in which two formulas?
    1) SO_3 and SO_4^{2-}
    2) H_2SO_4 and SO_2
    3) SO_2 and SO_4^{2-}
    4) HSO_4 and $S_2O_3^{2-}$

7. Redox reactions: Determining which equation represents a redox reaction

1. Which is a redox reaction?
   1) $Zn + 2HCl \rightarrow ZnCl_2 + H_2$
   2) $Zn(OH)_2 + 2HCl \rightarrow ZnCl_2 + 2H_2O$
   3) $NH_4^+ + OH^- \rightarrow NH_4OH$
   4) $H_3O^+ + OH^- \rightarrow H_2O + H_2O$

2. Which equation is an oxidation – reduction reaction?
   1) $2HCl + CaCO_3 \rightarrow CaCl_2 + H_2O + CO_2$
   2) $2HCl + FeS \rightarrow FeCl_2 + H_2S$
   3) $4HCl + MnO_2 \rightarrow MnCl_2 + H_2O + Cl_2$
   4) $HCl + KOH \rightarrow KCl + H_2O$

3. Which of the following equations is a redox reaction?
   1) $Ca^{2+} + SO_4^{2-} \rightarrow CaSO_4$
   2) $H+ + OH- \rightarrow H_2O$
   3) $Pb(NO_3)_2 + NaI \rightarrow 2NaNO_3 + PbI_2$
   4) $Cu + AgNO_3 \rightarrow Ag + Cu(NO_3)_2$

4. In which equation would there be a simultaneous losing and gaining of electrons?
   1) $NaCl + AgNO_3 \rightarrow NaNO_3 + AgCl$
   2) $HCl + Ca(OH)_2 \rightarrow CaCl_2 + 2H_2O$
   3) $2KClO_3 + MgI_2 \rightarrow Mg(ClO_3)_2 + 2KI$
   4) $2KClO_3 \rightarrow 2KCl + 3O_2$

5. Which equation represents oxidation – reduction reaction?
   1) $SO_2 + H_2O \rightarrow H_2SO_3$
   2) $SO_3^{2-} + 2H+ \rightarrow H_2SO_4$
   3) $O_2 + 2H_2 \rightarrow 2H_2O$
   4) $OH^- + H^+ \rightarrow H_2O$

6. Which equation is a redox reaction?
   1) $Mg + H_2SO_4 \rightarrow MgSO_4 + H_2$
   2) $Mg(OH)_2 + H_2SO_4 \rightarrow MgSO_4 + H_2O$
   3) $Mg^{2+} + 2OH^- \rightarrow Mg(OH)_2$
   4) $MgCl_2 + 6H_2O \rightarrow MgCl_2 \cdot 6H_2O$

7. Given the four equations below.
   I: $AgNO_3 + NaCl \rightarrow AgCl + NaNO_3$
   II: $Cl_2 + H_2O \rightarrow HClO + HCl$
   III: $CuO + CO \rightarrow CO_2 + Cu$
   IV4: $LiOH + HCl \rightarrow LiCl + H_2O$

   Which two equations represent redox reactions?
   1) I and II
   2) II and III
   3) III and I
   4) IV and II

8. Oxidation and Reduction: Recalling definitions and facts

1. Oxidation in a redox reaction involves a
   1) gain of protons
   2) loss of protons
   3) gain of electrons
   4) loss of electrons

2. In an oxidation-reduction chemical reactions, reduction is a
   1) gain of protons
   2) loss of protons
   3) gain of electrons
   4) loss of electrons

3. The oxidation number of oxidized substances in redox reactions always
   1) decreases   2) increases   3) remains the same

4. In redox chemical reactions, the oxidation number of a reduced species always
   1) increases   2) decreases   3) remains the same

5. The oxidation number of a reducing agent in a redox reaction always
   1) increases   2) decreases   3) remains the same

6. A reduced substance in oxidation and reduction reactions
   1) gains electrons and have a decrease in oxidation number
   2) gains electrons and have an increase in oxidation number
   3) loses electrons and have decreases in oxidation number
   4) loses electrons and have an increase in oxidation number

7. Which is true of a reducing agent in oxidation-reduction reactions?
   1) A reducing agent loses electrons, and is oxidized
   2) A reducing agent loses electrons, and is reduced
   3) A reducing agent gains electrons, and is oxidized
   4) A reducing agent gains electrons, and is reduced

8. Oxidizing agent is a species in a redox reaction that is
   1) reduced, because it has lost electrons
   2) reduced, because it has gained electrons
   3) oxidized, because it has lost electrons
   4) oxidized, because it has gained electrons

9. Oxidation and reduction:

1. Which change in oxidation number represents reduction?
   1) -4 to +1
   2) -1 to +2
   3) -1 to -2
   4) -3 to -2

2. Which change in oxidation number represents reduction?
   1) +1 $\rightarrow$ +2
   2) 0 $\rightarrow$ -1
   3) +2 $\rightarrow$ +4
   4) -1 $\rightarrow$ 0

3. Which of the following oxidation number change represents oxidation?
   1) 0 to +1
   2) -2 to -3
   3) 0 to -1
   4) +1 to 0

4. Which change in oxidation number represents oxidation?
   1) 0 to -1
   2) 0 to -2
   3) -2 to -1
   4) -2 to -3

9. Continues

5. Substance X can gain or lose electrons in an oxidation – reduction reaction. Which change in oxidation number is showing substance X losing the most number of electrons?
   1) -2 → 0
   2) -2 → -4
   3) -2 → +1
   4) -2 → +2

6. Which change in oxidation number represents the greatest number of electrons lost?
   1) -1 to +2
   2) +1 to +3
   3) -2 to -1
   4) +2 to -3

7. Which oxidation number change of a species in a redox reaction represents the least number of electrons gained?
   1) -1 to 0
   2) -1 to +2
   3) -1 to -2
   4) -1 to -3

8. In which oxidation number change would a species is a redox reaction gains the most number of electrons?
   1) +3 to -1
   2) +6 to +3
   3) 0 to +4
   4) +3 to +7

10. Oxidation and Reduction: Determining number of electrons lost and gained

1. How many electrons are gained by S^{+6} ion when it is reduced to S^{+2} atom?
   1) 1
   2) 2
   3) 3
   4) 4

2. What is the total number of electrons lost by Al atom as it becomes Al^{3+} ion?
   1) 1
   2) 2
   3) 3
   4) 4

3. Which change occurs when Sn^{2+} ion is oxidized to Sn^{4+}?
   1) Two electrons are lost
   2) Two electrons are gained
   3) Two protons are lost
   4) Two protons are gained

4. Which change occurs when N^{3+} is changes to N atom?
   1) Three neutrons are gained
   2) Three positrons are gained
   3) Three protons are gained
   4) Three electrons are gained

5. When Cr^{3+} ion becomes a Cr^{6+} ion, there will be a
   1) gain of 3 electrons
   2) loss of 3 electrons
   3) gain of 6 electrons
   4) loss of 6 electrons

6. Consider the oxidation number changes of Atom X and Atom Y below:

   Atom X: -2 → +1   Atom Y: +2 → +1

   Which is true of Atom X and atom Y?
   1) Atom X gains 3 electrons, Atom Y loses one electron
   2) Atom X gains 3 protons, Atom Y loses one proton
   3) Atoms X loses 3 electrons, Atom Y gains one electron
   4) Atoms X loses 3 protons, Atom Y gains one protons

Topic 11: Redox and electrochemistry

11. Half-reactions: Determining oxidation and reduction half-reaction equations

1. Which half-reaction equation correctly represents oxidation?
   1) $Mg + 2e^- \rightarrow Mg^{2+}$
   2) $Mg^{2+} + 2e^- \rightarrow Mg$
   3) $Mg^{2+} \rightarrow Mg + 2e^-$
   4) $Mg \rightarrow Mg^{2+} + 2e^-$

2. Which half-reaction correctly represents oxidation?
   1) $F_2 \rightarrow 2F^- + 2e^-$
   2) $F_2 + 2e^- \rightarrow 2F^-$
   3) $H_2 \rightarrow 2H^+ + 2e^-$
   4) $H_2 + 2e^- \rightarrow 2H^-$

3. Which half-reaction correctly shows reduction?
   1) $Sn^{2+} + 2e^- \rightarrow Sn^0$
   2) $Sn^{2+} \rightarrow Sn^{4+} + 2e^-$
   3) $Sn^{2+} + 2e^- \rightarrow Sn^{4+}$
   4) $Sn^{2+} \rightarrow Sn^0 + 2e^-$

4. Which half-reaction correctly represents oxidation?
   1) $3Ag + 3e^- \rightarrow 3Ag^-$
   2) $3Ag \rightarrow 3Ag^+ + 3e^-$
   3) $Au^{3+} + 3e^- \rightarrow Au$
   4) $Au^{3+} \rightarrow Au + 3e^-$

5. Which half-reaction equation correctly represents a reduction reaction?
   1) $Li^0 + e^- \rightarrow Li^+$
   2) $Na^0 + e^- \rightarrow Na^+$
   3) $Br_2^0 + 2e^- \rightarrow 2Br^-$
   4) $Cl_2^0 + e^- \rightarrow 2Cl^-$

6. Which half-reaction correctly represents a reduction reaction?
   1) $Nb^{5+} + 2e^- \rightarrow Nb^{3+}$
   2) $Nb^{3+} \rightarrow Nb^0 + 3e^-$
   3) $Mn^{7+} \rightarrow Mn^{4+} + 3e^-$
   4) $Mn^{4+} + 3e^- \rightarrow Mn^{7+}$

12. Half-reaction: Describing changes in half-reaction equations

1. Given the half reaction equation below

$$Fe^{3+} + 3e^- \rightarrow Fe$$

   Fe^{3+} is

   1) reduced by gaining 3 electrons
   2) reduced by losing 3 electrons
   3) oxidized by gaining 3 electrons
   4) oxidized by losing 3 electrons

2. Given the half-reaction equation below

$$Sn^{4+} + 2e^- \rightarrow Sn^{2+}$$

   Sn^{4+} is

   1) oxidized by gaining 2 electrons
   2) oxidized by losing 2 electrons
   3) reduced by gaining 2 electrons
   4) reduced by losing 2 electrons

3. In the half-reaction equation below:

$$Ca \rightarrow Ca^{2+} + 2e^-$$

   Which is true of calcium atom?

   1) It is oxidized by gaining 2 electrons
   2) It is oxidized by losing 2 electrons
   3) It is reduced by gaining 2 electrons
   4) It is reduced by losing 2 electrons

4. In the half-reaction equation below

$$P + 3e^- \rightarrow P^{3-}$$

   The phosphorous atom is
   1) oxidized, and becomes the oxidizing agent
   2) oxidized, and becomes the reducing agent
   3) reduced, and becomes the reducing agent
   4) reduced, and becomes the oxidizing agent

5. Consider the half-reaction equation below?

$$Li^0 \rightarrow Li + e^-$$

   The Li^0 is

   1) oxidized, and becomes the reducing agent
   2) reduced, and becomes the reducing agent
   3) oxidized, and becomes the oxidizing agent
   4) reduced, and becomes the reducing agent

6. Given the following half-reaction equation

$$Cl_2 + 2e^- \rightarrow 2Cl^-$$

   Each chlorine atom

   1) loses an electron, and its oxidation number increases
   2) loses an electron, and its oxidation number decreases
   3) gains an electron, and its oxidation number increases
   4) gains an electron, and its oxidation number decreases

7. In the half-reaction equation
$$Fe^{2+} \rightarrow Fe^{3+} + e^-$$

   Which is true of the Fe^{2+}?

   1) It gains an electron and becomes an ion with a greater charge
   2) It gains an electrons and becomes an ion with a smaller charge
   3) It loses an electrons and becomes an ion with a greater charge
   4) It loses an electrons and becomes an ion with a smaller charge

Topic 11: Redox and electrochemistry

13. Redox equations: Determining oxidized or reduced species from net ionic redox equation

1. Consider the oxidation-reaction reaction.
$$Co^0 + Cu^{2+} \rightarrow Co^{2+} + Cu^0$$
Which species is reduced?
   1) Co^0 2) Cu^0 3) Co^{2+} 4) Cu^{2+}

2. Given the redox reaction below
$$2Fe^{3+} + Sn^{2+} \rightarrow 2Fe^{3+} + Sn^{4+}$$
Which species is reduced?
   1) Fe^{3+} 2) Sn^{2+} 3) Fe^{2+} 4) Sn^{4+}

3. In the reaction below,
$$H_2 + 2Fe^{3+} \rightarrow 2H^+ + 2Fe^{2+}$$
Which species is gaining electrons?
   1) Fe^{+2} 2) H^+ 3) Fe^{3+} 4) H_2

4. Consider the following redox reaction:
$$Ni + Sn^{4+} \rightarrow Ni^{2+} + Sn^2$$
The species oxidized is
   1) Sn^{4+} 2) Sn^{2+} 3) Ni 4) Ni^{2+}

5. Given the redox reaction:
$$2Cr(s) + 3Sn^{2+}(aq) \rightarrow 2Cr^{3+}(aq) + 3Sn(s)$$
The species undergoing oxidation is
   1) $Sn^{2+}(aq)$ 2) $Cr(s)$ 3) $Sn(s)$ 4) $Cr^{3+\,(aq)}$

6. In the oxidation-reduction reaction below:
$$Zn + Ni^{2+} \rightarrow Zn^{2+} + Ni$$
Which species is losing electrons?
   1) Zn 2) Ni^{2+} 3) Zn^{2+} 4) Ni

7. In the oxidation-reduction reaction below:
$$2Fe^{3+} + S^{2-} \rightarrow 2Fe^{2+} + 2S^0$$
Which species acts as a reducing agent?
   1) Fe^{3+} 2) Fe^{2+} 3) S^0 4) S^{2-}

8. Consider the following equation.
$$Zn(s) + Cu^{2+}(aq) \rightarrow Zn^{2+}(aq) + Cu(s)$$
The reducing agent is
   1) $Cu^{2+}(aq)$ 2) $Zn(s)$ 3) $Cu(s)$ 4) $Zn^{2+(aq)}$

9. In the oxidation-reduction reaction below,
$$2Al + 3Ni^{2+} \rightarrow 2Al^{3+} + 3Ni$$
Which species acts as an oxidizing agent?
   1) Al 2) Al^{3+} 3) Ni 4) Ni^{2+}

14. Redox equations: Determining oxidized or reduced species from redox equation

1. In the redox reaction:
$$Ni + CuSO_4 \rightarrow NiSO_4 + Cu$$
   Which substance is oxidized?
   1) Ni   2) Cu   3) Ni^{2+} 4) Cu^{2+}

2. Given the oxidation-reduction reaction equation below:
$$Na + H_2O \rightarrow NaOH + H_2$$
   Which substance is oxidized?
   1) H_2 2) O^{2-} 3) H^+ 4) Na

3. In the reaction
$$2H_2O \rightarrow 2H_2 + O_2$$
   Which species is reduced?
   1) H_2 2) O^{2-} 3) H^+ 4) O_2

4. Given the redox reaction
$$Fe + 2AgCl \rightarrow 2Ag + FeCl_2$$
   The species oxidized is
   1) Fe^{3+} 2) Fe^0 3) Cl^- 4) Ag^+

5. Consider the redox reaction below:
$$2KBr + F_2 \rightarrow 2KF + Br_2$$

   Which substance is the oxidizing agent
   1) Br_2 2) K^+ 3) F_2 4) Br^-

6. Given the oxidation-reduction reaction.
$$C(s) + H_2O(g) \rightarrow CO(g) + H_2(g)$$
   The reducing agent in this reaction is
   1) C   2) H^+ 3) C^{2+} 4) H_2

7. In the redox reaction
$$3Ni(NO_3)_2 + 2Al \rightarrow 3Ni^0 + 2Al(NO_3)_3$$
   Which species is the oxidizing agent?
   1) Ni^{2+} 2) Al^0 3) Ni^0 4) Al^{3+}

8. In the redox reaction
$$CuO + CO \rightarrow CO_2 + Cu$$
   Which species is losing electrons?
   1) Cu   2) Cu^{2+} 3) C^{2+} 4) C_{4+}

9. Given the oxidation-reduction reaction below:
$$4HCl + MnO_2 \rightarrow MnCl_2 + H_2O + Cl_2$$
   Which of species in this reaction is gaining electrons?
   1) H^+ 2) Cl^- 3) Mn^{4+} 4) Mn^{2+}

10. Given the redox reaction
$$Ag + 2HNO_3 \rightarrow AgNO_3 + NO + H_2O$$
    Which substance is losing electrons?
    1) Ag^0 2) H^+ 3) Ag^+ 4) O^{2-}

15. Redox equation: Describing changes in redox reactions

1. In the reaction,

$$Mg \quad + \quad O_2 \quad \rightarrow \quad MgO$$

The O_2 is the

1) oxidizing agent, and is reduced
2) oxidizing agent, and is oxidized
3) reducing agent, and is reduced
4) reducing agent, and is oxidized

2. In the reaction,

$$Mg \quad + \quad ZnCl_2 \quad \rightarrow \quad MgCl_2 + \quad Zn$$

Which is true of the magnesium?

1) It is oxidized by losing electrons
2) It is oxidized by gaining electrons
3) It is reduced by losing electrons
4) It is reduced by gaining electrons

3. Given the reaction:

$$Pb \quad + \quad 2\,Ag^+ \quad \rightarrow \quad Pb^{2+} + \quad 2Ag$$

The lead atom is

1) reduced, and its oxidation number changes from +o to +2
2) reduced, and its oxidation number changes from +2 to 0
3) oxidized, and its oxidation number changes from 0 to +2
4) oxidized, and its oxidation number changes from +1 to 0

4. In the redox reaction:

$$4HCl \quad + \quad MnO_2 \quad \rightarrow \quad MnCl_2 \quad + \quad 2H_2O \quad + \quad Cl_2$$

The manganese is

1) oxidized, and its oxidation number changes from +2 to +4
2) oxidized, and its oxidation number changes from +4 to +2
3) reduced, and its oxidation number changes from +2 to +4
4) reduced, and its oxidation number changes from +4 to +2

5. Given the reaction:

$$2I^-(aq) \quad + \quad Br_2(\ell) \quad \rightarrow \quad 2Br^{-(aq)} \quad + \quad I_2(s)$$

As the reaction takes place

1) The I^- ion is oxidized, and its oxidation number decreases
2) The I^- ion is reduced, and its oxidation number decreases
3) The I^- ion is oxidized, and its oxidation number increases
4) The I^- ion is reduced, and its oxidation number increases

6. Given the reaction:

$$Zn(s) \quad + \quad 2HCl(aq) \quad \rightarrow \quad ZnCl_2(aq) \quad + \quad H_2(g)$$

Which is true of hydrogen in this reaction?

1) Hydrogen is reduced, and its oxidation number increases
2) Hydrogen is reduced, and its oxidation number decreases
3) Hydrogen is oxidized, and its oxidation number increases
4) Hydrogen is oxidized, and its oxidation number decreases

7. Given the oxidation-reduction reaction:

$$Co(s) \quad + \quad PbCl_2(aq) \quad \rightarrow \quad CoCl_2(aq) \quad + \quad Pb(s)$$

Which statement correctly describes the oxidation and reduction that occur?

1) $Co(s)$ is oxidized and $Cl^-(aq)$ is reduced
2) $Co(s)$ is oxidized and $Pb^{2+}(aq)$ is reduced
3) $Co(s)$ is reduced and $Cl^-(aq)$ is oxidized
4) $Co(s)$ is reduced and $Pb^{2+}(aq)$ is oxidized

16. Redox Reaction: Determining the correct oxidation and reduction equations

1. Given the oxidation-reduction reaction below
$$3Sn^{4+}(aq) + 2Cr(s) \rightarrow 3Sn^{2+}(aq) + 2Cr^{3+}(aq)$$
Which half-reaction correctly shows the oxidation that occurs?
   1) $Cr^{3+}(aq) + 3e^- \rightarrow Cr(s)$
   2) $Sn^{2+}(aq) + 2e^- \rightarrow Sn^{2+}(aq)$
   3) $Cr(s) \rightarrow Cr^{3+}(aq) + 3e^-$
   4) $Sn^{4+}(aq) \rightarrow Sn^{2+}(aq) + 2e^-$

2. In the redox reaction:
$$3Cu^{2+} + 2Al \rightarrow 3Cu + 2Al^{3+}$$
The oxidation half-reaction is
   1) $Cu^{2+} + 2e^- \rightarrow Cu$
   2) $Cu^{2+} \rightarrow Cu + 2e^-$
   3) $Al + 3e^- \rightarrow Al^{3+}$
   4) $Al \rightarrow Al^{3+} + 3e^-$

3. In the redox reaction given below:
$$Pb^{2+}(aq) + Sn^0(s) \rightarrow Pb^0(s) + Sn^{2+(aq)}$$
Which half-reaction equation is correct for the reduction that occurs?
   1) $Pb^{2+}(aq) + 2e^- \rightarrow Pb^0(s)$
   2) $Pb^0(s) + 2e^- \rightarrow Pb^{2+}(aq)$
   3) $Sn^0(s) \rightarrow Sn^{2+}(aq) + 2e^-$
   4) $Sn^{2+}(aq) \rightarrow Sn^0(s) + 2e^-$

4. Consider the redox reaction below:
$$Mn^0 + O_2 \rightarrow Mn^{4+} + 2O^{2-}$$
Which half-reaction is correct for the reduction that occurs?
   1) $O_2 \rightarrow 2O^{2-} + 4e^-$
   2) $O_2 + 4e^- \rightarrow 2O^{2-}$
   3) $Mn^0 + 4e^- \rightarrow Mn^{4+}$
   4) $Mn^0 \rightarrow Mn^{4+} + 4e^-$

5. Given the following redox reaction
$$Mg + 2HBr \rightarrow MgBr_2 + H_2$$
Which equation correctly represents the oxidation that occurs?
   1) $2H^+ \rightarrow H_2 + 2e^-$
   2) $Mg^0 \rightarrow Mg^{2+} + 2e^-$
   3) $2H^+ + 2e^- \rightarrow H_2$
   4) $Mg^0 + 2e^- \rightarrow Mg^{2+}$

6. In the oxidation-reduction reaction
$$2H_2O \rightarrow 2H_2 + O_2$$
Which half-reaction equation is correct for the reduction that occurs?
   1) $2H^+ + 2e^- \rightarrow 2H_2$
   2) $2H_2 + 2e^- \rightarrow 2H^+$
   3) $2O^{2-} + 2e^- \rightarrow O_2$
   4) $O_2 + 2e^- \rightarrow 2O^{2-}$

7. In the chemical reaction
$$2AgNO_3(aq) + Cu(s) \rightarrow Cu(NO_3)_2(aq) + 2Ag(s)$$
Which half-reaction equation correctly shows oxidation?
   1) $2Ag^+(aq) \rightarrow 2Ag(s) + 2e^-$
   2) $2Ag(s) \rightarrow 2Ag^+(aq) + 2e^-$
   3) $Cu(s) \rightarrow Cu^{2+}(aq) + 2e^-$
   4) $Cu^{2+}(aq) \rightarrow Cu(s) + 2e^-$

8. Given the following redox chemical reaction
$$2KClO_3 \rightarrow 2KCl + 3O_2$$
Which half-reaction equation correctly represents the reduction that occurs?
   1) $2O^{-2} \rightarrow O_2 + 4e^-$
   2) $O_2 + 4e^- \rightarrow 2O^{2-}$
   3) $Cl^{5+} \rightarrow Cl^- + 6e^-$
   4) $Cl^{5+} + 6e^- \rightarrow Cl^-$

17. Electrochemical cells – Voltaic and Electrolytic cells: Recalling Concept Facts and Definitions

1. What type of a chemical reaction occurs in all electrochemical cells?
   1) Neutralization
   2) Double replacement
   3) Redox
   4) Hydrolysis

2. What kind of reaction occurs in a voltaic cell?
   1) Non-spontaneous oxidation-reduction
   2) Spontaneous oxidation-reduction
   3) Non-spontaneous oxidation, only
   4) Spontaneous reduction, only

3. What kind of reaction occurs in operating an electrolytic cell?
   1) Non-spontaneous oxidation-reduction
   2) Spontaneous oxidation-reduction
   3) Non-spontaneous oxidation, only
   4) Spontaneous reduction, only

4. In a voltaic cell, electrical energy will be produced when
   1) only oxidation occurs
   2) only reduction occurs
   3) both oxidation and reduction occur
   4) neither oxidation nor reduction occurs

5. A voltaic cell differs from an electrolytic cell in that a voltaic cell uses
   1) spontaneous redox reaction to produce electrical energy
   2) non-spontaneous redox reaction to produce electrical energy
   3) electrical energy to force a spontaneous redox reaction to occur
   4) electrical energy to force a non-spontaneous redox reaction to occur

6. The redox reaction that occurs during the operation of a battery is best described as
   1) non-spontaneous and occurring in a chemical (voltaic) cell
   2) spontaneous and occurring in a chemical (voltaic) cell
   3) non-spontaneous and occurring in an electrolytic cell
   4) spontaneous and occurring in an electrolytic cell

7. Which is true of a voltaic cell but not of an electrolytic cell?
   1) Voltaic cells involve redox reaction
   2) Voltaic cells uses external energy source
   3) Voltaic cell is use in the electroplating of metallic surfaces
   4) Voltaic cells contains a salt bridge

8. An electrolytic cell is different from a voltaic cell because in an electrolytic cell a(n)
   1) redox reaction occurs
   2) spontaneous reaction occurs
   3) electrical current is produced
   4) electrical current causes a chemical reaction

9. Which is true of the anode in any electrochemical cell?
   1) The anode is the site for oxidation
   2) The anode is the site for reduction
   3) The anode is the site for both oxidation and reduction
   4) The anode is the site where protons are lost and gained

10. Which is true of the cathode in all electrochemical cells?
    1) The cathode is the site for oxidation
    2) The cathode is the site for reduction
    3) The cathode is the site for both oxidation and reduction
    4) The cathode is the site where protons are lost and gained

18. Salt bridge, anode and cathode: Recalling Concept Facts and Definitions

1. In voltaic cells, the function of the salt bridge is to
   1) permit the migration of ions
   2) permit the mixing of solutions
   3) prevent the migration of ions
   4) prevent the flow of ions

2. An electrochemical cell setup consists of two half cells connected by an external conductor and a salt bridge. The function of the salt bridge is to
   1) block a path for the flow of electrons
   2) block a path for the flow of ions
   3) provide a path for the flow of electrons
   4) provide a path for the flow of ions

3. In both the voltaic and the electrolytic cell, the anode is the electrode at which
   1) reduction occurs and electrons are lost
   2) reduction occurs and electrons are gained
   3) oxidation occurs and electrons are lost
   4) oxidation occurs and electrons are gained

4. What occurs when an electrolytic cell is used for silver-plating a spoon?
   1) A chemical reaction produces an electric current
   2) An electric current produces a chemical reaction
   3) An oxidation reaction takes place at the cathode
   4) A reduction reaction takes place at the anode

5. In a voltaic cells, the positive electrode is the
   1) anode, at which reduction occurs
   2) anode, at which oxidation occurs
   3) cathode, at which reduction occurs
   4) cathode, at which oxidation occurs

6. The negative electrode in a chemical (voltaic) cell is the
   1) cathode, where electrons are gained
   2) cathode, where electrons are lost
   3) anode, where electrons are gained
   4) anode, where electrons are lost

7. In an electrolytic cell, the positive electrode is the
   1) anode, at which reduction occurs
   2) anode, at which oxidation occurs
   3) cathode, at which reduction occurs
   4) cathode, at which oxidation occurs

8. The negative electrode in all electrolytic cells is the
   1) cathode, at which reduction occurs
   2) cathode, at which oxidation occurs
   3) anode, at which reduction occurs
   4) anode, at which oxidation occurs

19. Electrochemical cells: Describing diagrams or equations

1. Given the cell diagram below

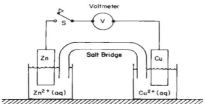

This cell is best described as

1) voltaic, that will absorb energy
2) voltaic, that will produce energy

3) an electrolytic, that will absorb energy
4) an electrolytic, that will produce energy

2. Given the cell diagram below.

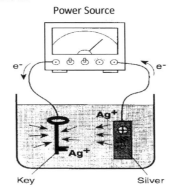

The reaction occurring in this cell is described as

1) non-spontaneous, taking place in a voltaic cell
2) spontaneous, taking place in a voltaic cell

3) non-spontaneous, taking place in an electrolytic cell
4) spontaneous, taking place in an electrolytic cell

3. Given the reaction;

$$Zn + Cu^{2+} \rightarrow Zn^{2+} + Cu$$

In which type of cell would this reaction most likely occur?

1) An electrolytic cell, because it is endothermic
2) An electrolytic cell, because it is exothermic

3) A voltaic cell, because it is endothermic
4) A voltaic cell, because it is exothermic

4. Consider the reaction below:

$$NaCl(aq) + electricity \rightarrow Na(s) + Cl_2(g)$$

This reaction would most likely occurs in

1) a voltaic cell, because it absorbs energy
2) a voltaic cell, because it produces energy

3) an electrolytic cell, because it absorbs energy
4) an electrolytic cell, because it produces energy

5. Given the reaction

$$2H_2O(\ell) + electricity \rightarrow 2H_2(g) + O_2(g)$$

This reaction can be best describe as

1) redox, and non-spontaneous
2) redox, and spontaneous

3) non-redox and spontaneous
4) non-redox and nonspontaneous

6. Given the reaction:

$$Mg(s) + FeSO_4(aq) \rightarrow Fe(s) + MgSO_4(aq)$$

The reaction would most likely occur in a(n)

1) voltaic cell, and will produce energy
2) voltaic cell, and will absorb energy

3) electrolytic cell, and will produce energy
4) electrolytic cell, and will absorb energy

20. Voltaic cell: Interpreting voltaic cell diagram

Answer questions 1 – 10 based on the electrochemical cell diagram below.

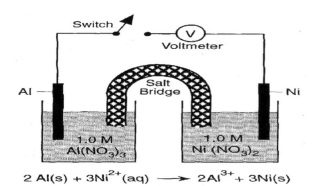

$$2\,Al(s) + 3Ni^{2+}(aq) \longrightarrow 2Al^{3+} + 3Ni(s)$$

1. The anode in this electrochemical cell is
    1) Al atoms   2) Ni atoms   3) Al^{3+} ions   4) Ni^{2+} ions

2. Which serves as the cathode in this chemical cell?
    1) Al   2) Ni   3) Al^{3+} 4) Ni^{2+}

3. When the switch is closed, which species will be oxidized in this electrochemical cell?
    1) Al^{3+} ions   2) Al atoms   3) Ni^{2+} ions   4) Ni atoms

4. Which particles in this electrochemical cell undergoes reduction?
    1) Al^{3+} 2) Al   3) Ni^{2+} 4) Ni

5. The loss of electrons occurs at
    1) aluminum electrode, because it is the anode   3) nickel electrode, because it is the anode
    2) aluminum electrode, because it is the cathode   4) nickel electrode, because it is the cathode

6. Which is true of the electrochemical cell when the switch is closed?
    1) Electrons will flow from Ni^{2+} to Ni   3) Electrons will flow from Ni to Al
    2) Electrons will flow from Al^{3+} to Al   4) Electrons will flow from Al to Ni

7. The salt bridge in the electrochemical cell connects
    1) Al atom to Ni atom   3) Ni atom to Ni^{2+} ion
    2) Al^{3+} ions to Ni^{2+} ions   4) Ni^{2+} ion to Al atom

8. Which equation correctly shows the oxidation that occurs in this cell?
    1) $Al + 3e^- \rightarrow Al^{3+}$ 3) $Ni^{2+} + 2e^- \rightarrow Ni$
    2) $Al \rightarrow Al^{3+} + 3e^-$ 4) $Ni^{2+} \rightarrow Ni + 2e^-$

9. When the switch is closed, which correctly shows the reduction process that takes place?
    1) $Al + 3e^- \rightarrow Al^{3+}$ 3) $Ni^{2+} + 2e^- \rightarrow Ni$
    2) $Al \rightarrow Al^{3+} + 3e^-$ 4) $Ni^{2+} \rightarrow Ni + 2e^-$

10. Which is true of this cell as the redox reaction is taking place?
    1) The mass of Al electrode will increase, and the mass of Ni electrode will decrease
    2) The mass of Al electrode will decrease, and the mass of Ni electrode will increase
    3) The mass of Al electrode will increase, and the mass of Ni electrode will remain the same
    4) The mass of Al electrode will remain the same, and the mass of Ni electrode will increase

21. Voltaic cells: Interpreting voltaic cell diagram

Answer questions 1 - 10 based on the cell diagram below.

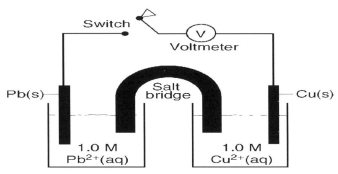

$$Pb(s) + Cu^{2+}(aq) \longrightarrow Pb^{2+}(aq) + Cu(s)$$

1. When the switch is closed, the species oxidized is
   1) $Cu^{2+}(aq)$ 2) $Pb^{2+}(aq)$ 3) Pb*(s)*   4) Cu*(s)*

2. The oxidizing agent in this reaction is
   1) Pb*(s)*   2) Cu*(s)*   3) $Pb^{2+}(aq)$ 4) $Cu^{2+}(aq)$

3. The anode in this electrochemical cell is the
   1) Cu atom, which is the positive electrode   3) Pb atom, which is the positive electrode
   2) Cu atom, which is the negative electrode   4) Pb atom, which is the negative electrode

4. The cathode in this electrochemical cell is the
   1) Cu atom, where electrons will be gained   3) Pb atom, where electrons will be gained
   2) Cu atom, where electrons will be lost   4) Pb atom, where electrons will be lost

5. When the switch is closed, reduction will occur at the
   1) Anode, which is the positive electrode   3) Cathode, which is the positive electrode
   2) Anode, which is the negative electrode   4) Cathode, which is the negative electrode

6. The salt bridge in the electrochemical diagram will connects
   1) Pb atom to Cu atom   3) Pb^{2+} ions to Cu atom
   2) Pb^{2+} ion to Cu^{2+} ion   4) Cu^{2+} ions to Pb atom

7. As the reaction occurs, the flow of electrons will be from
   1) Pb^{2+} to Cu^{2+} 3) Cu to Pb
   2) Pb to Cu   4) Cu^{2+} to Pb

8. Which half-reaction equation correctly represents what occurs at the anode of this cell?
   1) $Pb \longrightarrow Pb^{2+} + 2e^-$ 3) $Cu \longrightarrow Cu^{2+} + 2e^-$
   2) $Pb^{2+} + 2e^- \longrightarrow Pb$ 4) $Cu^{2+} + 2e^- \longrightarrow Cu$

9. Which correctly shows the half-reaction that occurs at the cathode of this cell?
   1) $Pb^{2+} + 2e^- \longrightarrow Pb$ 3) $Cu^{2+} + 2e^- \longrightarrow Cu$
   2) $Pb + 2e^- \longrightarrow Pb^{2+}$ 4) $Cu + 2e^- \longrightarrow Cu^{2+}$

10. Which is true in this electrochemical cell when the switch is closed?
    1) The mass of Cu will decrease   3) The mass of Pb will remain the same
    2) The mass of Pb will decrease   4) The mass of Cu will remain the same

22. Voltaic cell: Determining changes in voltaic cell reactions

Answer questions 1 – 10 based on the cell diagram below.

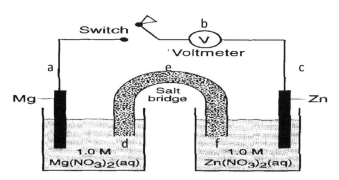

1. In the electrochemical diagram, the Mg serves as the
   1) cathode, where oxidation occurs
   2) cathode, where reduction occurs
   3) anode, where oxidation occurs
   4) anode, where reduction occurs

2. Zn in this electrochemical cell acts as the
   1) anode, and is the site for reduction
   2) cathode, and is the site for reduction
   3) anode, and is the site for oxidation
   4) cathode, and is the site for oxidation

3. Which is true of Mg in this cell?
   1) It is reduced by gaining electrons
   2) It is oxidized by losing electrons
   3) It is reduced by gaining protons
   4) It is oxidized by losing protons

4. The Zn electrode in this diagram is the
   1) anode, which is negative
   2) anode, which is positive
   3) cathode, which is negative
   4) cathode, which is positive

5. When the switch is closed, the Zn^{2+} in this reaction will be
   1) the anode
   2) the cathode
   3) oxidized
   4) reduced

6. Which change occurs with Mg in this cell?
   1) Mg is oxidized to Mg^{2+}
   2) Mg is reduced to Mg^{2+}
   3) Mg is oxidized to Zn
   4) Mg is reduced to Zn

7. Which is true of the Mg^{2+} ion in this cell?
   1) It is reduced
   2) It is oxidized
   3) It migrate across the salt bridge
   4) it migrate across the external conductor

8. In the given electrochemical diagram, the Zn^{2+} ions
   1) gain protons
   2) lose protons
   3) gains electrons
   4) lose electrons

9. When the switch is closed, which series of letters show the path and direction of Mg^{2+} ions?
   1) abc
   2) def
   3) cba
   4) fed

10. When the switch is closed, which letters show the path and direction of the electrons?
    1) abc
    2) def
    3) cba
    4) fed

Need Help? Study Book Pg 279 Set 31 – 32

23. Electrolytic cell diagram: Interpreting electrolytic diagrams

Answer questions 1 – 7 based on the cell diagram below.

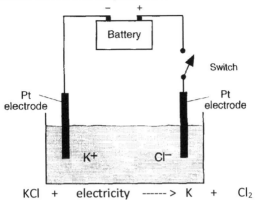

KCl   +   electricity   ------>   K   +   Cl₂

1. In the cell diagram above, the anode is the
   1) negative electrode, where oxidation occurs
   2) negative electrode, where reduction occurs
   3) positive electrode, where oxidation occurs
   4) positive electrode, where reduction occurs

2. The cathode in this diagram is the
   1) positive electrode, where oxidation occurs
   2) negative electrode, where oxidation occurs
   3) positive electrode, where reduction occurs
   4) negative electrode, where reduction occurs

3. What occurs when the switch is closed?
   1) K^+ ions migrate toward the anode, where they will gain electrons
   2) K^+ ions migrate toward the anode, where they will gain electrons
   3) K^+ ions migrate toward the cathode where they will lose electrons
   4) K^+ ions migrate toward the cathode, where they will gain electrons

4. When the switch is closed in this cell, the
   1) Cl^- ions migrate toward the cathode, where they will lose electrons
   2) Cl^- ions migrate toward the cathode, where they will gain electrons
   3) Cl^- ions migrate toward the anode, where they will lose electrons
   4) Cl^- ions migrate toward the anode, where they will gain electrons

5. Which equation best represents the reaction at the negative electrode?
   1) $K^+(aq) \longrightarrow K(s) + e^-$
   2) $K^+(aq) + e^- \longrightarrow K(s)$
   3) $2Cl^{-(aq)} \longrightarrow Cl_{2(g)} + 2e^-$
   4) $2Cl^-(aq) + 2e^- \longrightarrow Cl_2(g)$

6. The redox reaction that occurs in this cell is best described as
   1) spontaneous and endothermic
   2) spontaneous and exothermic
   3) non-spontaneous and endothermic
   4) non-spontaneous and exothermic

7. Which statement best describes the reaction that occurs in this cell?
   1) The reaction occurs in an electrolytic cell and requires the use of electrical energy
   2) The reaction occurs in an electrolytic cell, and produces electrical energy
   3) The reaction occurs in a voltaic cell, and requires the use of electrical energy
   4) The reaction occurs in a voltaic cell, and produces electrical energy

24. Electroplating cell diagram: Interpreting electroplating cell diagram.

Answer questions 1 – 10 based on the cell diagram below.

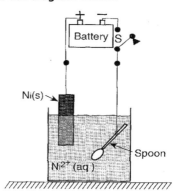

1. In this electroplating cell diagram, the substance or object oxidized is
   1) Ni atom   2) Ni^{2+} ions   3) the battery   4) the spoon

2. Which is reduced?
   1) Ni atom   2) Ni^{2+} ions   3) the battery   4) the spoon

3. The reducing agent in thee redox reaction that occurs in this cell is
   1) the spoon   2) the battery   3) Ni^{2+} 4) Ni

4. The Nickel bar in this diagram acts as the
   1) anode, and is positive
   2) anode, and is negative
   3) cathode, which is the positive electrode
   4) cathode, which is the negative electrode

5. Which statement best describes the spoon in this diagram?
   1) It acts as the anode, and is negative
   2) It acts as the anode, and is positive
   3) It acts as the cathode, and is negative
   4) It acts as the cathode, and is positive

6. In this electrolytic cell, the negative electrode is the
   1) cathode, at which reduction occur
   2) cathode, at which oxidation occurs
   3) anode, at which reduction occurs
   4) anode, at which oxidation occurs

7. The positive electrode in this electroplated diagram is the
   1) anode, where electron are lost
   2) anode, where electrons are gained
   3) cathode, where electrons are lost
   4) cathode, where electrons are gained

8. Which correctly shows the half-reaction at the cathode?
   1) Ni(s) + 2e$^-$ → Ni$^{2+}(aq)$
   2) Ni(s) → Ni$^{2+}(aq)$ + 2e$^-$
   3) Ni$^{2+}(aq)$ + 2e$^-$ → Ni(s)
   4) Ni$^{2+}(aq)$ → Ni(s) + 2e$^-$

9. Which correctly shows the reaction at the positive electrode?
   1) Ni(s) + 2e$^-$ → Ni$^{2+}(aq)$
   2) Ni(s) → Ni$^{2+}(aq)$ + 2e$^-$
   3) Ni$^{2+}(aq)$ + 2e$^-$ → Ni(s)
   4) Ni$^{2+}(aq)$ → Ni(s) + 2e$^-$

10. Which statement correctly describes what occurs in this cell when the switch is closed?
    1) The Ni(s) will be oxidized, and the spoon will lose mass
    2) The Ni(s) will be oxidized, and the spoon will gain mass
    3) The Ni(s) will be reduced, and the spoon will lose mass
    4) The Ni(s) will be reduced, and the spoon will gain mass

25. Electroplated diagram: Interpreting electroplating cell diagrams

Base your answers to questions 1 – 9 on the cell diagram below.

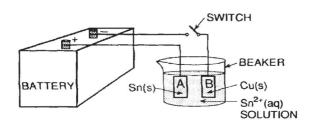

1. Which species are oxidized and reduced in this cell?
    1) Sn^{2+} is oxidized, and Sn is reduced
    2) Sn is oxidized, and Sn^{2+} is reduced
    3) Cu is oxidized, and Sn is reduced
    4) Sn is oxidized, and Cu is reduced

2. When the switch is closed, Sn^{2+} is
    1) oxidized, and Sn will be coated with Cu
    2) oxidized, and Cu will be coated with Sn
    3) reduced, and Sn will be coated with Cu
    4) reduced, and Cu will be coated with Sn

3. Which best explains why the mass of electrode B increases as a redox reaction occurs in this cell?
    1) Electrode B is oxidized
    2) Electrode B is losing electrons
    3) Electrode B is coated with more copper
    4) Electrode B is coated with tin

4. The battery in this cell acts as the
    1) external conduit
    2) external energy source
    3) reducing agent
    4) oxidizing agent

5. Electrode A in this diagram is the
    1) anode, where oxidation is occurring
    2) cathode, where reduction is occurring
    3) cathode, where oxidation is occurring
    4) anode, where reduction is occurring

6. Which statement is true of electrode B when the switch is closed in this cell diagram?
    1) B is the cathode, where oxidation is occurring
    2) B is the cathode, where reduction is occurring
    3) B is the anode, where oxidation is occurring
    4) B is the anode, where reduction is occurring

7. Which equation correctly shows the reaction at electrode A?
    1) $Sn(s) + 2e^- \rightarrow Sn^{2+}(aq)$
    2) $Sn^{2+}(aq) + 2e^- \rightarrow Sn(s)$
    3) $Sn(s) \rightarrow Sn^{2+}(aq) + 2e^-$
    4) $Sn^{2+}(aq) \rightarrow Sn(s) + 2e^-$

8. When the switch is closed, the half-reaction that occurs at electrode B is represent by which equation?
    1) $Sn(s) + 2e^- \rightarrow Sn^{2+}(aq)$
    2) $Sn^{2+}(aq) + 2e^- \rightarrow Sn(s)$
    3) $Sn(s) \rightarrow Sn^{2+}(aq) + 2e^-$
    4) $Sn^{2+}(aq) \rightarrow Sn(s) + 2e^-$

9. The redox reaction in this cell is
    1) spontaneous, occurring in an electrolytic cell
    2) spontaneous, occurring in a voltaic cell
    3) non-spontaneous, occurring in an electrolytic cell
    4) non-spontaneous, occurring in a voltaic cell

26. Redox reaction: Determining the most easily reduced and oxidized substances

1. According to Reference Table J, which of these ions is most easily reduced?
   1) Ca^{2+} 2) Cr^{3+} 3) Cu^{+} 4) Ag^{+}

2 . Based on Reference Table J, which ion is most easily reduced?
   1) Sr^{2+} 2) Mg^{2+} 3) Ca^{2+} 4) Ba^{2+}

3. According to Table J, which ion is most easily oxidized?
   1) Br- 2) Cl- 3) F- 4) I-

4. Based on Reference Table J, which metal is most easily oxidized?
   1) Ni 2) Zn 3) Cr 4) Co

5. Which metal will reduced Zn^{2+} to Zn ?
   1) Mn 2) Cr 3) H_2 4) Ag

27. Spontaneous redox: Determining reactions that are spontaneous

1. Based on Reference Table J, which reaction will take place spontaneously?
   1) Ni^{2+} + Pb*(s)* $\rightarrow$ Ni*(s)* + Pb^{2+}
   2) Au^{3+} + Al*(s)* $\rightarrow$ Au*(s)* + Al^{3+}
   3) Sr^{2+} + Sn*(s)* $\rightarrow$ Sr*(s)* + Sn^{2+}
   4) Fe^{2+} + Cu*(s)* $\rightarrow$ Fe*(s)* + Cu^{2+}

2. According to information from Reference Table J, which redox reaction occurs spontaneously?
   1) Cu*(s)* + $2H^{+}$ $\rightarrow$ Cu^{2+} + $H_2(g)$
   2) Mg*(s)* + $2H^{+}$ $\rightarrow$ Mg^{2+} + $H_2(g)$
   3) 2Ag*(s)* + $2H^{+}$ $\rightarrow$ $2Ag^{+}$ + $H_2(g)$
   4) 2Au*(s)* + $2H^{+}$ $\rightarrow$ $2Au^{+}$ + $H_2(g)$

3. Based on Reference Table J, which redox reaction will occur spontaneously?
   1) Br_2 + KI $\rightarrow$ KBr + I_2
   2) I_2 + KCl $\rightarrow$ KI + Cl_2
   3) Cl_2 + KF $\rightarrow$ KCl + F_2
   4) I_2 + KBr $\rightarrow$ KI + Br_2

4. Referring to the Activity Series on Reference Table J, which reaction will not occur spontaneously under standard conditions?
   1) Sn*(s)* + 2HF $\rightarrow$ SnF_2 + $H_2(g)$
   2) Mg*(s)* + 2HF $\rightarrow$ MgF_2 + $H_2(g)$
   3) Ba*(s)* + 2HF $\rightarrow$ BaF_2 + $H_2(g)$
   4) 2Cu*(s)* + 2HF $\rightarrow$ CuF_2 + $H_2(g)$

5. Which metal, according to Reference Table J, will react spontaneously with Al^{3+}?
   1) Co*(s)* 2) Cr*(s)* 3) Cu*(s)* 4) Ca*(s)*

  Survivingchem.com

Topic 12 : Nuclear Chemistry

1. Nuclear Decays and transmutations: Recalling Concept Facts and Definitions

1. Atoms of one element are converted to atoms of another element through the process of
   1) combustion
   2) oxidation
   3) transmutation
   4) polymerization

2. Which process converts an atom from one element to another when the nucleus of an atom is bombarded with high-energy particles?
   1) Artificial transmutation
   2) Addition polymerization
   3)) Natural transmutation
   4) Condensation polymerization

3. Spontaneous decay of elements with atomic number of 83 and above is through the process of
   1) artificial transmutation
   2) natural transmutation
   3) naturalization reactions
   4) oxidation-reduction reaction

4. Spontaneous decay of certain elements in nature occurs because these elements have
   1) disproportionate ratio of electrons to protons
   2) disproportionate ratio of neutrons to protons
   3) high reactivity with oxygen
   4) low reactivity with oxygen

5. Unstable atoms generally have
   1) more electrons than protons
   2) more protons than electrons
   3) more neutrons than protons
   4) more protons than neutrons

6. A beta or an alpha particle may be spontaneously emitted from
   1) a ground-state atom
   2) a stable nucleus
   3) an excited electron
   4) an unstable nucleus

7. The energy released by a nuclear reaction results primarily from
   1) breaking of bonds between atoms
   2) formation of bonds between atoms
   3) conversion of mass into energy
   4) conversions of energy into mass

8. A carbon-14 atom spontaneously decayed to form a nitrogen-14 atom. This change took place because
   1) a transmutation occurred without particle emission
   2) a transmutation occurred with particle emission
   3) nitrogen-14 has an unstable nucleus
   4) carbon-14 has a stable nucleus

9. Elements with no stable isotope generally have
   1) atomic number of 82 or less
   2) atomic number of 83 or more
   3) atomic mass of 82 or less
   4) atomic mass of 83 or more

10. Bombarding a nucleus with high-energy particles that changes it from one element to another is called
   1) a half-reaction
   2) a breeder reaction
   3) natural transmutation
   4) artificial transmutation

2. Nuclear decay and transmutation: Determining elements with stable isotopes

1. Element of which atomic number has no stable isotopes?
   1) 19
   2) 1
   3) 88
   4) 18

2. Which of these elements has no known stable isotope?
   1) Polonium
   2) Gold
   3) Xenon
   4) Iron

3. Which Group 18 element is naturally radioactive and has no known stable isotope?
   1) Ar
   2) Rn
   3) Xe
   4) Kr

4. Element with which atomic number has stable isotopes?
   1) 79
   2) 84
   3) 90
   4) 92

Topic 12: Nuclear Chemistry

3. Nuclear chemistry particles: Recalling Concept Facts and Definitions

1. A neutron has approximately the same mass as a(n)
   1) alpha particle   2) beta particle   3) electron   4) proton

2. Which product of nuclear decay has mass but no charge?
   1) gamma rays   2) positrons   3) alpha particles   4) beta particles

3. An electron has a charge identical to that of
   1) a positron   2) a beta particle   3) an alpha particle   4) a proton

4. Which nuclear decay particle is identical in mass and charge to a helium nucleus?
   1) An Alpha particle   2) A Beta particle   3) A Proton   4) A neutron

5. Which nuclear radiation is similar to high energy X-ray?
   1) Beta   2) Alpha   3) Gamma   4) Neutron

6. Which of these types of nuclear radiation has the greatest penetrating power?
   1) Alpha   2) Beta   3) Neutron   4) Gamma rays

7. Which type of radioactive emission have positive charge and weak penetrating power?
   1) Gamma rays   2) Neutrons   3) Beta particles   4) Alpha particles

8. Which particles has the least mass?
   1) A beta particle   2) An alpha particle   3) A Proton   4) A neutron

9. Which nuclear decay emission consists of energy only?
   1) Alpha particle   2) Beta particle   3) Gamma radiation   4) Positron

10. Alpha particles and beta particles differ in
    1) mass only   3) both mass and charge
    2) charge only   4) neither mass and charge

11. Which nuclear emission symbol has neither mass nor charge?
    1) α 3) $\beta+$
    2) $\beta-$ 4) γ

12. Which list of particles is in order of increasing mass?
    1) Proton $\rightarrow$ Beta $\rightarrow$ Alpha   3) Alpha $\rightarrow$ Beta $\rightarrow$ Proton
    2) Beta $\rightarrow$ Proton $\rightarrow$ Alpha   4) Proton $\rightarrow$ Alpha $\rightarrow$ Beta

13. Which list of particles is in order of decreasing charge?
    1) Beta $\rightarrow$ Neutron $\rightarrow$ Alpha   3) Gamma $\rightarrow$ Beta $\rightarrow$ Alpha
    2) Neutron $\rightarrow$ Positron $\rightarrow$ Alpha   4) Alpha $\rightarrow$ Positron $\rightarrow$ Gamma

14. Which list is showing the particles arranged in order of increasing penetrating power?
    1) Gamma $\rightarrow$ Beta $\rightarrow$ Alpha   3) Alpha $\rightarrow$ Beta $\rightarrow$ Gamma
    2) Beta $\rightarrow$ Gamma $\rightarrow$ Alpha   4) Gamma $\rightarrow$ Alpha $\rightarrow$ Beta

15. In which list can all particles be accelerated by an electric field?
    1) Alpha, beta, and neutrons   3) Alpha, protons, and neutrons
    2) Alpha, beta, and protons   4) Beta, protons, and neutrons

 Survivingchem.com

4. Decay modes of radioisotopes: Determining decay modes using Reference Table N

1. Which radioisotope is a beta emitter?
   1) Ne-19   2) Ca-37   3) Co-60   4) Fr-220

2. Which radioactive isotope is an alpha emitter?
   1) ^{226}Ra 2) ^{99}Tc 3) ^{90}Sr 4) ^{131}I

3. Which nuclide will emit a positron when decaying?
   1) Iron-53   2) Francium-220   3) Hydrogen-3   4) Cesium-137

4. Which isotope spontaneously decays and emits a particle with a charge of +2?
   1) ^{53}Fe 2) ^{137}Cs 3) ^{198}Au 4) ^{220}Fr

5. According to Reference Table N, the radioactive decay of which isotope will emit a particle with a charge of a +1?
   1) Phosphorous-32   2) Cobalt-60   3) Thorium-232   4) Iron-53

6. Which particle is spontaneously emitted in the nucleus of Calcium - 37?
   1) Alpha   2) Beta   3) Positron   4) Electron

7. When ^{226}Rn spontaneously decays, it releases a particle with a mass of
   1) 4   2) 0   3) 2   4) 1

8. Which notation of a radioisotope is correctly paired with the notation of its emission particle?
   1) $^{37}_{19}K$ and $^{0}_{-1}e$ 2) $^{222}_{86}Rn$ and $^{4}_{2}He$ 3) $^{16}_{7}N$ and $^{1}_{1}p$ 4) $^{99}_{43}Tc$ and $^{0}_{+1}e$

9. Which two radioisotopes have the same decay mode?
   1) ^{37}K and ^{42}K 2) ^{220}Fr and ^{222}Rn 3) ^{232}Th and ^{239}Pu 4) ^{233}U and ^{99}Tc

5. Separation emanations: Determining path of emission particles in an electric field

1. Which emanation is attracted toward a negatively charged electrode of an electric field?
   1) Alpha particle   2) Beta particle   3) Gamma rays   4) Neutron

2. Which nuclear emission moving through an electric field would be attracted toward a positive electrode?
   1) Proton   2) Gamma radiation   3) Beta Particle   4) Alpha particle

3. The path of which nuclear emission would not be affected when passing through an electric field?
   1) Positron   2) Gamma   3) Alpha   4) Beta

4) In the diagram below, the radiation from a radioactive source is being separated as it passes between electrically charged plates. What are the three types of radiation observed on the detector?

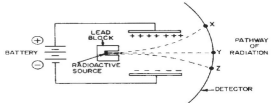

   1) X = Alpha, Y = Beta, Z = Gamma   3) X = Beta, Y = Gamma, Z = Alpha
   2) X = Gamma, Y = Beta, Z = Alpha   4) X = Gamma, Y = Alpha, Z = Beta

6. Alpha Decay - Natural Transmutation: Recalling Concept Facts

1. As an atom of a radioactive isotope emits an alpha particle, the mass number of the atom
   1) increases   2) decreases   3) remains the same

2. As a radioactive isotope emits an alpha particle, the atomic number of the atom
   1) Decreases   2) Increases   3) Remains the same

3. When a radioisotope undergoes an alpha decay, the number of protons of the atom will
   1) increase   2) decrease   3) remain the same

4. As a radioisotope undergoes releases alpha particle during a nuclear decay, the number of neutrons will
   1) decrease   2) increase   3) remain the same

5. When an alpha particle is emitted by an atom, the atomic number of the atom
   1) increases by 2   3) increases by 4
   2) decreases by 2   4) decreases by 4

6. As a radioactive isotope undergoes an alpha decay, the mass number of the atom
   1) increases by 2   3) decreases by 4
   2) increases by 4   4) remains unchanged

7. Compared to an atom before an alpha decay, the number of protons of the atom after alpha decay will be
   1) greater by 4   3) lesser by 2
   2) greater by 2   4) the same

7. Alpha decay: Recognizing alpha decay equations

1. Which nuclear decay equation correctly represents alpha decay?

   1) $^{116}_{49}\text{In} \rightarrow\ ^{116}_{50}\text{Sn} +\ ^{0}_{-1}\text{e}$ 3) $^{234}_{90}\text{Th} \rightarrow\ ^{234}_{91}\text{Pa} +\ ^{0}_{+1}\text{e}$

   2) $^{38}_{19}\text{K} \rightarrow\ ^{37}_{18}\text{Ar} +\ ^{1}_{1}\text{p}$ 4) $^{226}_{88}\text{Ra} \rightarrow\ ^{222}_{86}\text{Rn} +\ ^{4}_{2}\text{He}$

2. Which equation represents nuclear disintegration resulting in the release of an alpha particle?

   1) $^{27}_{13}\text{Al} +\ ^{4}_{2}\text{He} \rightarrow\ ^{30}_{15}\text{P} +\ ^{1}_{0}\text{n}$ 3) $^{37}_{18}\text{Ar} +\ ^{0}_{-1}\text{e} \rightarrow\ ^{37}_{17}\text{Cl}$

   2) $^{212}_{83}\text{Bi} \rightarrow\ ^{4}_{2}\text{He} +\ ^{208}_{81}\text{Ti}$ 4) $^{14}_{6}\text{C} \rightarrow\ ^{14}_{7}\text{N} +\ ^{0}_{-1}\text{e}$

3. A nuclear change resulting in a release of an alpha particle is shown in which equation?

   1) $^{252}_{98}\text{Cf} \rightarrow\ ^{248}_{96}\text{Cm} +\ ^{4}_{2}\text{He}$ 3) $^{220}_{87}\text{Fr} +\ ^{4}_{2}\text{He} \rightarrow\ ^{224}_{89}\text{Ac}$

   2) $^{19}_{10}\text{Ne} \rightarrow\ ^{19}_{11}\text{Na} +\ ^{0}_{-1}\text{e}$ 4) $^{228}_{89}\text{Ac} \rightarrow\ ^{228}_{88}\text{Ra} +\ ^{1}_{1}\text{p}$

4. Which nuclear equation below represents a decay with emission of an alpha particle?

   1) $^{218}_{85}\text{At} \rightarrow\ ^{218}_{86}\text{Rn} + \text{X}$ 3) $^{239}_{94}\text{Pu} \rightarrow\ ^{235}_{92}\text{U} + \text{X}$

   2) $^{1}_{1}\text{H} +\ ^{2}_{1}\text{H} \rightarrow \text{X}$ 4) $^{11}_{5}\text{B} + \text{X} \rightarrow\ ^{14}_{7}\text{N} +\ ^{1}_{0}\text{p}$

5. Which equation represents a nuclear decay with the released of an alpha particle?

   1) $^{239}_{93}\text{Np} \rightarrow\ ^{239}_{94}\text{Pu} + \text{X}$ 3) $^{32}_{15}\text{P} +\ ^{1}_{1}\text{p} \rightarrow\ ^{32}_{16}\text{S} + \text{X}$

   2) $^{228}_{90}\text{Th} \rightarrow\ ^{224}_{88}\text{Ra} + \text{X}$ 4) $^{37}_{18}\text{Ar} \rightarrow\ ^{37}_{17}\text{Cl} + \text{X}$

7. Beta decay - Natural transmutation: Recalling Concept Facts

1. As an atom of a radioactive isotope emits a beta particle, the mass number of the atom
   1) increases
   2) decreases
   3) remains the same

2. As a radioactive isotope emits a beta particle, the atomic number of the atom
   1) decreases
   2) increases
   3) remains the same

3. When a radioisotope undergoes a beta decay, the number of protons of the atom will
   1) increase
   2) decrease
   3) remain the same

4. As a radioisotope undergoes releases a beta particle during a nuclear decay, the number of neutrons
   1) decreases
   2) increases
   3) remains the same

5. When a beta particle is emitted by an atom, the atomic number of the atom will
   1) increase by 1
   2) decrease by 1
   3) increase by 1
   4) remain the same

6. As a radioactive isotope undergoes a beta decay, the mass number of the atom
   1) increases by 2
   2) increases by 1
   3) decreases by 1
   4) remains unchanged

7. Compared to an atom before a beta decay, the number of protons of the atom after the decay will be
   1) greater by 1
   2) greater by 2
   3) lesser by 2
   4) the same

8. Beta decay: Recognizing beta decay equations

1. Which nuclear equation correctly represents a decay with the emission of a beta particle?
   1) $^{214}_{82}Pb \rightarrow \ ^{214}_{83}Bi \ + \ ^{0}_{-1}e$
   2) $^{239}_{90}Pu \rightarrow \ ^{235}_{92}U \ + \ ^{4}_{2}He$
   3) $^{32}_{15}P \ + \ ^{0}_{-1}e \rightarrow \ ^{32}_{14}Si$
   4) $^{42}_{19}K \ + \ ^{1}_{0}n \rightarrow \ ^{43}_{18}Ar + \ ^{0}_{+1}e$

2. Which equation is showing a beta decay?
   1) $^{220}_{87}Fr \ + \ ^{4}_{2}He \ \rightarrow \ ^{224}_{89}Ac$
   2) $^{43}_{21}Sc \ \rightarrow \ ^{43}_{20}Ca \ + \ ^{0}_{+1}e$
   3) $^{198}_{79}Au \ \rightarrow \ ^{98}_{80}Hg \ + \ ^{0}_{-1}e$
   4) $^{42}_{19}K \ + \ ^{0}_{-1}e \ \rightarrow \ ^{42}_{18}Ar$

3. Which equation correctly represents a nuclear decay with a release of a beta particle?
   1) $^{116}_{49}In \rightarrow \ ^{116}_{50}Sn \ + \ ^{0}_{-1}e$
   2) $^{38}_{19}K \ \rightarrow \ ^{37}_{18}Ar \ + \ ^{1}_{1}p$
   3) $^{234}_{90}Th \ \rightarrow \ ^{234}_{91}Pa \ + \ ^{0}_{+1}e$
   4) $^{226}_{88}Ra \ \rightarrow \ ^{222}_{86}Rn \ + \ ^{4}_{2}He$

4. Which nuclear reaction is a beta decay?
   1) $^{218}_{85}At \ \rightarrow \ ^{218}_{86}Rn \ + \ X$
   2) $^{1}_{1}H \ + \ ^{2}_{1}H \rightarrow \ X$
   3) $^{239}_{94}Pu \ \rightarrow \ ^{235}_{92}U \ + \ X$
   4) $^{19}_{10}N \ \rightarrow \ ^{19}_{8}O \ + \ X$

5. Which transmutation resulted in the emission of a beta particle?
   1) $^{210}_{84}Po \ \rightarrow \ ^{206}_{82}Pb \ + \ X$
   2) $^{206}_{81}Ti \ \rightarrow \ ^{206}_{82}Pb \ + \ X$
   3) $^{53}_{26}Fe \ \rightarrow \ ^{53}_{25}Mn \ + \ X$
   4) $^{32}_{16}S \ + \ ^{1}_{0}n \ \rightarrow \ ^{32}_{15}P \ + \ X$

9. Positron emission: Recalling Concept Facts

1. As an atom of a radioactive isotope emits a positron, the mass number of the atom
   1) increases   2) decreases   3) remains the same

2. As a radioactive isotope emits a positron, the atomic number of the atom
   1) decreases   2) increases   3) remains the same

3. When a radioisotope undergoes a positron emission, the number of protons of the atom will
   1) increase   2) decrease   3) remain the same

4. As a radioisotope releases a positron during a nuclear decay, the number of neutrons will
   1) decrease   2) increase   3) remain the same

5. When a positron is emitted by an atom, the atomic number of the atom
   1) increases by 1   2) increases by 2   3) decreases by 1   4) remains the same

6. As a radioactive isotope undergoes a positron emission, the mass number of the atom
   1) increases by 2   2) increases by 1   3) decreases by 1   4) remains unchanged

10. Positron emission: Determining positron emission equations

1. Which nuclear transmutation involves a positron emission?

   1) $^{239}_{94}Pu \rightarrow ^{235}_{92}U + ^{4}_{2}He$

   2) $^{16}_{7}N \rightarrow ^{16}_{8}O + ^{0}_{-1}e$

   3) $^{38}_{19}K \rightarrow ^{37}_{18}Ar + ^{1}_{1}p$

   4) $^{11}_{6}C \rightarrow ^{11}_{5}B + ^{0}_{+1}e$

2. Which nuclear disintegration is accompanied by the emission of a positron?

   1) $^{13}_{7}N \rightarrow ^{13}_{6}C + ^{0}_{+1}e$

   2) $^{137}_{55}Cs \rightarrow ^{137}_{56}Ba + ^{0}_{-1}e$

   3) $^{24}_{11}Na + ^{0}_{+1}e \rightarrow ^{24}_{12}Mg$

   4) $^{249}_{98}Cf \rightarrow ^{245}_{96}Cm + ^{4}_{2}H$

3. Which nuclear reaction involves the emission of a positron?

   1) $^{9}_{4}Be + ^{1}_{1}H \rightarrow ^{6}_{3}Li + X$

   2) $^{234}_{90}Th \rightarrow ^{234}_{91}Pa + X$

   3) $^{18}_{9}F \rightarrow ^{18}_{8}O + X$

   4) $^{14}_{7}N + ^{1}_{0}n \rightarrow ^{14}_{6}C + X$

11. Artificial transmutation: Determining artificial transmutation equations

1. Artificial transmutation is represented by which balanced nuclear equation?

   1) $^{218}_{85}At \rightarrow ^{218}_{86}Rn + ^{0}_{-1}e$

   2) $^{1}_{1}H + ^{2}_{1}H \rightarrow ^{3}_{2}He$

   3) $^{239}_{94}Pu \rightarrow ^{235}_{92}U + ^{4}_{2}He$

   4) $^{11}_{5}B + ^{4}_{2}He \rightarrow ^{14}_{7}N + ^{1}_{0}n$

2. Which equation is an example of artificial transmutation?

   1) $^{1}_{0}n + ^{14}_{7}N \rightarrow ^{14}_{6}C + ^{1}_{1}H$

   2) $^{212}_{84}Po \rightarrow ^{208}_{82}Pb + ^{4}_{2}He$

   3) $^{38}_{19}K \rightarrow ^{37}_{18}Ar + ^{1}_{1}p$

   4) $^{2}_{1}H + ^{2}_{1}H \rightarrow ^{3}_{2}He$

3. Artificial transmutation is represented by which equation?

   1) $^{43}_{21}Sc \rightarrow ^{43}_{20}Ca + ^{0}_{+1}e$

   2) $^{235}_{92}U + ^{1}_{0}n \rightarrow ^{139}_{56}Ba + ^{94}_{36}Kr + 3^{1}_{0}n$

   3) $^{10}_{4}Be \rightarrow ^{10}_{5}B + ^{0}_{-1}e$

   4) $^{32}_{16}S + ^{1}_{0}n \rightarrow ^{32}_{15}P + ^{1}_{1}H$

12. Fission and Fusion - Nuclear energy: Recalling Concept Facts and Definitions

1. Which statement best describes what happens in a fission reaction?
   1) Light nuclei join to form heavier nuclei
   2) Heavy nuclei split into lighter nuclei
   3) Energy is converted to mass
   4) Electron is converted to energy

2. What is the primary result of a fission reaction?
   1) Conversion of mass to energy
   2) Conversion of energy to mass
   3) Binding together of two heavy nuclei
   4) Binding together of two lighter nuclei

3. Compared to ordinary chemical reaction, a fission reaction will
   1) absorb smaller amount of energy
   2) absorb larger amount of energy
   3) release smaller amount of energy
   4) release larger amount of energy

4. Which best describes what occurs in a fusion reaction?
   1) Light nuclei join to form heavier nuclei
   2) Heavy nuclei split into lighter nuclei
   3) Energy is converted to mass
   4) Electron is converted to energy

5. The energy released during fusion is converted from
   1) electrons
   2) nuclei
   3) mass
   4) gamma

6. A fission reaction is similar to a fusion reaction in that both reactions involve
   1) collision between nuclei of high atomic number
   2) collision between nuclei of low atomic number
   3) the conversion of energy to mass
   4) the conversion of mass to energy

7. Compared to fission reaction, a fusion reaction will
   1) release larger amount of energy
   2) release smaller amount of energy
   3) absorb larger amount of energy
   4) absorb smaller amount of energy

8. Which conditions are required for a fusion reaction to take place?
   1) low pressure and low temperature
   2) high pressure and low temperature
   3) low pressure and high temperature
   4) high pressure and high temperature

9. The fusion of hydrogen nuclei can be initiated by a fission reaction because the fission reaction provides a
   1) high temperature and high pressure
   2) high temperature and low pressure
   3) good supply of hydrogen nuclei
   4) good supply of neutrons

10. Which statement explains why fusion reactions are difficult to start?
    1) Positive nuclei attract each other
    2) Positive nuclei repel each other
    3) Negative nuclei attract each other
    4) Negative nuclei repel each other

11. A nuclear fission reaction and a nuclear fusion reaction are both similar because both reactions
    1) form heavy nuclides from light nuclides
    2) form light nuclides from heavy nuclides
    3) release large amount of energy
    4) absorbed a large amount of energy

12. One benefit of nuclear fission reaction is
    1) nuclear reaction meltdowns
    2) storage of waste materials
    3) biological exposure
    4) production of energy

13. The amount of energy released from a fission reaction is much greater than the energy from a chemical reaction because in a fission reaction
    1) energy is converted to mass
    2) ionic bonds are broken
    3) mass is converted to energy
    4) covalent bonds are broken

13. Fission and Fusion reactions: Determining fission and fusion reactions equations.

1. Which nuclear equation represents a fusion reaction?

   1) $^{14}_{7}N + ^{1}_{0}n \rightarrow ^{14}_{6}C + ^{1}_{1}H$

   2) $^{238}_{92}U + ^{4}_{2}He \rightarrow ^{241}_{94}Pu + ^{1}_{0}n$

   3) $^{2}_{1}H + ^{1}_{1}H \rightarrow ^{3}_{2}He$

   4) $^{235}_{92}U + ^{1}_{0}n \rightarrow ^{87}_{35}Br + ^{146}_{57}La + 3^{1}_{0}n$

2. Which equation represents nuclear fusion?

   1) $^{2}_{1}H + ^{3}_{1}H \rightarrow ^{4}_{2}He + ^{1}_{0}n$

   2) $^{238}_{92}U + ^{1}_{0}n \rightarrow ^{239}_{93}Np + ^{0}_{-1}e$

   3) $^{226}_{88}Ra \rightarrow ^{222}_{84}Rn + ^{4}_{2}He$

   4) $^{7}_{3}Li + ^{1}_{1}p \rightarrow ^{8}_{4}Be$

3. Fission reaction is represented by which nuclear equation?

   1) $^{238}_{92}U + ^{4}_{2}He \rightarrow ^{241}_{94}Pu + ^{1}_{0}n$

   2) $^{14}_{7}N + ^{1}_{0}n \rightarrow ^{14}_{6}C + ^{1}_{1}H$

   3) $^{235}_{92}U + ^{1}_{0}n \rightarrow ^{87}_{35}Br + ^{146}_{57}La + 3^{1}_{0}n$

   4) $^{2}_{1}H + ^{1}_{1}H \rightarrow ^{3}_{2}He$

4. Which nuclear equation represents fission reaction?

   1) $^{43}_{21}Sc \rightarrow ^{43}_{20}Ca + ^{0}_{+1}e$

   2) $^{235}_{92}U + ^{1}_{0}n \rightarrow ^{139}_{56}Ba + ^{94}_{36}Kr + 3^{1}_{0}n$

   3) $^{10}_{4}Be \rightarrow ^{10}_{5}B + ^{0}_{-1}e$

   4) $^{32}_{16}S + ^{1}_{0}n \rightarrow ^{32}_{15}P + ^{1}_{1}H$

14. Balancing nuclear equation: Determining missing particles in nuclear equations

1. In the nuclear equation:

   $$^{234}_{91}Pa \rightarrow X + ^{0}_{-1}e$$

   Which particle is represented by the X?

   1) $^{234}_{92}U$ 2) $^{234}_{93}Np$ 3) $^{235}_{92}U$ 4) $^{235}_{93}Np$

2. Given the nuclear equation below

   $$^{15}_{8}O \rightarrow X + ^{15}_{7}N$$

   Which particle is represented by X?
   1) Neutron   2) Alpha particle   3) Beta particle   4) Positron

3. Which particle is represented by X in the nuclear equation below?

   $$^{75}_{33}As + X \rightarrow ^{78}_{35}Br + ^{1}_{0}n$$

   1) $^{1}_{1}H$ 2) $^{1}_{0}n$ 3) $^{0}_{+1}e$ 4) $^{4}_{2}He$

4. Given the nuclear reaction:

   $$^{241}_{95}Am \rightarrow ^{237}_{93}Np + X$$

   Which particle is represented by X?
   1) Alpha   2) Beta   3) Positron   4) Proton

5. X in the equation below is

   $$X + ^{0}_{-1}e \rightarrow ^{37}_{17}Cl$$

   1) Chlorine-37   2) Argon-37   3) Sulfur-37   4) Phosphorous-37

15. Mixed nuclear reactions: Determining type of nuclear reactions

1. Which type of nuclear decay is accompanied by the released of a particle with a mass of 0?
   1) Fusion　　　　2) Alpha decay　　　3) Beta decay　　4) Artificial transmutation

2. Which nuclear reaction would cause the mass number of the atom to decrease by 4?
   1) Alpha decay　　　2) Beta decay　　　3) Fusion　　　4) Positron emission

3. A nuclear reaction occurs in which an unstable isotope is changed to a stable isotope. If the stable isotope has an atomic number that is one amu greater than that of the unstable isotope, what type of nuclear reaction took place?
   1) Beta decay　　　2) Alpha decay　　　3) Fusion　　　4) Fission

4. Which nuclear process is a type of natural transmutation?
   1) Alpha decay　　　2) Fission　　　　3) Fusion　　　　4) Artificial transmutation

5. Radioactive cobalt-60 is used in radiation therapy treatment. Cobalt-60 undergoes beta decay. This type of nuclear reaction is called
   1) nuclear fission　　　　　　　　3) artificial transmutation
   2) nuclear fusion　　　　　　　　4) natural transmutation

6. The change that is undergone by an atom of an element made radioactive by bombardment with high-energy particle is called a(n)r
   1) natural decay　　　　　　　　3) radioactive decay
   2) natural transmutation　　　　　4) artificial transmutation

7. Given the nuclear reaction

$$^{60}_{27}\text{Co} \rightarrow {}^{0}_{-1}\text{e} + {}^{60}_{28}\text{Ni}$$

   The reaction is an example of
   1) fission　　　　　　　　　　3) fusion
   2) natural transmutation　　　　4) artificial transmutation

8. Given the reaction

$$^{24}_{11}\text{Na} \rightarrow {}^{24}_{12}\text{Mg} + {}^{0}_{-1}\text{e}$$

   The reaction is best described as
   1) alpha decay　　　　　　　　3) beta decay
   2) fission　　　　　　　　　　4) artificial transmutation

9. The reaction

$$^{40}_{18}\text{Ar} + {}^{1}_{1}\text{H} \rightarrow {}^{40}_{19}\text{K} + {}^{1}_{0}\text{n}$$

   is an example of
   1) artificial transmutation　　　　3) nuclear fusion
   2) natural transmutation　　　　　4) nuclear fission

10. Given the nuclear equation below

$$^{121}_{53}\text{I} \rightarrow \text{X} + {}^{121}_{52}\text{Te}$$

   The reaction is best described as
   1) beta decay　　　　　　　　　3) positron emission
   2) artificial transmutation　　　　4) alpha decay

Topic 12: Nuclear Chemistry

16. Half-Life: Determining and interpreting half-life information, Using Reference Table N

1. What is the half-life of potassium – 42?
    1) 1.23 s   2) 12.4 h   3) 14.3 d   4) 27.5 s

2. Which of the following radioisotope has the longest half-life?
    1) Fr-220   2) K -37   3) Fe-53   4) K-42

3. Which radioisotope has the shortest half-life?
    1) ^{14}C   2) ^{3}H   3) ^{37}K   4) ^{32}P

4. Which radioisotope has a half-life that is less than 1 minute?
    1) K – 37   2) K – 42   3) Ca – 37   4) Ne - 19

4. Compared to K-37, the isotope of K-42 has a
    1) shorter half-life and the same decay mode
    2) longer half-life and the same decay mode
    3) shorter half-life and a different decay mode
    4) longer half-life and a different decay mode

5. Compared to Uranium – 238, uranium – 235 has a
    1) shorter half-life and the same decay mode
    2) shorter half-life and a different decay mode
    3) longer half-life and the same decay mode
    4) longer half-life and a different decay mode

17. Half-Life Problems: Determining length of time

1. What is the total number of hours required for potassium – 42 to undergo 2 half-life periods?
   1) 6.2 hours
   2) 12.4 hours
   3) 24.8 hours
   4) 37.2 hours

2. ^{131}I will go through 4 half-life periods in approximately how many days?
   1) 32 days
   2) 2 days
   3) 24 days
   4) 12 days

3. Sr-90 undergoes 2 half-life periods in approximately
   1) 14 years
   2) 28 years
   3) 30 years
   4) 56 years

4. The half-life of a radioisotope X is 30 days. In how many days will X undergo 3 half –life periods?
   1) 3 days
   2) 90 days
   3) 10 days
   4) 33 days

5. Exactly how much time elapse before 16 grams of potassium-42 decays, leaving 2 grams of the original isotope?
   1) 99.2 hours
   2) 24.8 hours
   3) 37.2 hours
   4) 49.6 hours

6. How many days are required for a 200 gram sample of Radon-222 to decay to 50.0 grams?
   1) 1.91
   2) 3.82
   3) 7.64
   4) 11.5

7. How long will it takes for ^{220}Fr to decay from 50 grams to 12.5 grams?
   1) 27.5 s
   2) 45 s
   3) 343.75 s
   4) 110 s

8. In how many years would a radioisotope with a half-life of 15 years decays from an original mass of 32 grams to 2 grams?
   1) 480 years
   2) 64 years
   3) 60 years
   4) 30 years

9. In approximately how many days would a 12 gram sample of Iodine -131 decays leaving only 3 grams of the original isotope remaining ?
   1) 1 x 8 days
   2) 2 x 8 days
   3) 3 x 8 days
   4) 4 x 8 days

10. The half-life of a radioisotope is 30 seconds. Which set up is correct for calculating the total length of time it takes for a 50 g sample of this isotope to decay to 3.125 g?
    1) 30 x 3.125
    2) 30 ÷ 3.125
    3) 30 x 4
    4) 30 ÷ 4

18. Half-life problems: Determining half-life

1. What is the half-life of Nitrogen–16?
   1) 16 s   2) 17.2 s   3) 7.2 s   4) 19 s

2. A radioisotope undergoes 2 half-life periods in 180 ms. What is the half-life of this radioisotope?
   1) 90 ms   2) 360 ms   3) 2 ms   4) 180 ms

3. In 6.20 h, a 100 gram sample of Ag-112 decays to 25.0 gram. What is the half-life of Ag-112?
   1) 1.60 h   2) 3.10 h   3) 6.20 h   4) 12.4 h

4. What is the half-life of ^{25}Na if 1.00 grams of a 16.00 grams sample of ^{25}Na remains unchanged after 237 seconds?
   1) 47.4 s   2) 59.3 s   3) 79.0 s   4) 118 s

5. After 32 days, 5 milligrams of an 80-gram sample of a radioactive isotope remains unchanged. What is the half-life of this element?
   1) 8 days   2) 16 days   3) 4 days   4) 2 days

6. A radioactive isotope of an element decays from 20 grams to 5 grams in 8 minutes. What is the half-life of this radioisotope?
   1) 15 minutes   2) 20 minutes   3) 10 minutes   4) 4 minutes

19. Half-life: Determining remaining mass

1. What is the total mass of a 50 grams sample of a radioisotope remaining after 3 half-life periods?
   1) 150 grams   2) 12.5 grams   3) 6.25 grams   4) 16.7 grams

2. How many grams of a 120 grams sample of cobalt-60 will remain after 2 half-life periods?
   1) 60 grams   2) 30 grams   3) 240 grams   4) 2 grams

3. What amount of a 48 g sample of K-37 will remain after 5 half-life periods?
   1) 1.5 g   2) 3.0 g   3) 5.1 g   4) 6.0 g

4. What is the mass of a 60.0 gram sample of N-16 remaining unchanged after 28.8 seconds?
   1) 30.0 g   2) 15.0 g   3) 7.50 g   4) 3.75 g

5. What total mass of a 32 g sample of ^{60}Co will remain unchanged after 21.16 years?
   1) 1.0 g   2) 2.0 g   3) 4.0 g   4) 8.0 g

6. Approximately how many grams of a 50 g sample of radium-226 will remain unchanged after 6400 years?
   1) 25 g   2) 128 g   3) 6.25   4) 3.13 g

7. A radioisotope of element X has a half-life of 1.5 days. How many grams of a 5 gram sample of this isotope will remain unchanged after 3.0 days?
   1) 1.25 grams   2) 2.5 grams   3) 7.5 grams   4) 4.5 grams

8. The half-life of a radioisotope is 20.0 minutes. What is the total amount of a 10 g sample of this isotope remaining after 1 hour minutes?
   1) 5.00 g   2) 3.33 g   3) 2.50 g   4) 1.25 g

20. Half-life problems: Determining original mass

1. After 4 half-life periods, 1.5 mg of a radioactive isotope remained. What was the mass of the original sample of the isotope?
   1) 6.0 mg   2) 3.0 mg   3) 12 mg   4) 24 mg

2. If 10.0 grams of P-32 remains after 3 half-life periods, what was the original mass of P-32?
   1) 60.0 g   2) 30.0 g   3) 20.0 g   4) 3.33 g

3. What was the original mass of ^{198}Au if only 4 grams of the isotope remained after about 8 days?
   1) 2 g   2) 4 g   3) 8 g   4) 32 g

4. A sample of iodine-131 decays to 1.0 g in 40 days. What was the mass of the original sample?
   1) 8.0 g   2) 16 g   3) 32 g   4) 4.0 g

5. A sample of ^{99}Tc decays to 0.5 grams in 1.49 x 10^6 years. What was the mass of the original sample?
   1) 64 g   2) 32 g   3) 128 g   4) 8 g

21. Half-life: Determining fraction remaining

1. What fraction of a radioactive substance will remain after 3 half-life periods?
   1) $^1/_2$ 2) $^1/_3$ 3) $^1/_4$ 4) $^1/_8$

2. What fraction of the radioactive waste Strontium-90 will remain unchanged after 5 half-life periods of decaying?
   1) $^1/_{32}$ 2) $^1/_{16}$ 3) $^1/_8$ 4) $^1/_5$

3. A radioactive element has a half-life of 2 days. Which fraction represents the amount of an original sample of this element remaining after 6 days?
   1) $^1/_6$ 2) $^1/_2$ 3) $^1/_3$ 4) $^1/_8$

4. If the half-life of a radioactive element is 2.5 years, what fraction of this element will remain unchanged after 15 years?
   1) $^1/_{32}$ 2) $^1/_2$ 3) $^1/_{16}$ 4) $^1/_{64}$

5. According to Reference Table N, what fraction of Rn-222 will remain unchanged after 3.82 days?
   1) $^1/_8$ 2) $^1/_4$ 3) $^1/_2$ 4) $^1/_3$

6. After 55 days of decaying, what fraction of a sample of Fr-220 will remain unchanged?
   1) ½   2) ¼   3) $^1/_8$ 4) $^1/_{16}$

7. Approximately what fraction of an original ^{60}Co sample remains unchanged after 21 years?
   1) $^1/_2$ 2) $^1/_4$ 3) $^1/_8$ 4) $^1/_{16}$

8. What fraction of a 10 gram sample of Cesium – 137 will remain unchanged after 90.7 years?
   1) $^1/_9$ 2) $^1/_2$ 3) $^1/_8$ 4) $^1/_3$

9. After 1.42 x 10^9 years, what fraction of a 6 gram sample of U-235 will remain unchanged?
   1) $^1/_2$ 2) $^1/_4$ 3) $^1/_6$ 4) $^1/_8$

10. Approximately what fraction of ^{99}Tc will remain unchanged after 8.52 x 10^5 years?
    1) $^1/_2$ 2) $^1/_8$ 3) $^1/_{16}$ 4) $^1/_4$

Topic 12: Nuclear Chemistry

22. Half-life problems: Using fraction remaining in half-life problems

1. In how many half-life periods would a sample of a radioisotope decays to $1/8$th its original mass?
   1) 1   2) 2   3) 3   4) 4

2. What is the total number of half-life periods it will take for any sample of Co-60 to decay to $1/16$th of its original mass?
   1) 1   2) 2   3) 3   4) 4

3. After 60 years, ½ of an original sample of a radioactive substance remained unchanged. What is the half-life of this radioactive substance?
   1) 10 years   2) 20 years   3) 30 years   4) 60 years

4. A sample of a radioisotope Cr-51 decays to $1/8$th in 84 days, what is the half-life of Cr-51?
   1) 14 days   2) 28 days   3) 56 days   4) 84 days

5. What is the half of sodium-22 if, after 13 years, only $1/32$th of an original sample of sodium-22 will remain unchanged?
   1) 13.0 years   2) 26.0 years   3) 2.6 years   4) 5.2 years

6. If the half-life of a radioactive O-15 is 122 seconds. How long will it take for a sample of this isotope to decay to $1/4$th its original mass?
   1) 61 s   2) 122 s   3) 244 s   4) 488 s

7. The half-life of the isotope ^{59}Fe is 44.5 days. In approximately how many days will it take for a 10 gram sample of ^{59}Fe to decay to $1/8$th its original mass.
   1) 133.5 days   2) 89.0 days   3) 44.5 days   4) 22.25 days

8. A radioisotope has a half-life of 16 years. In how many years would a given sample of this isotope decays leaving only $1/32$th of this isotope remaining?
   1) 8 years   2) 80 years   3) 2 years   4) 512 years

23. Half-Life problems: Determining correct radioisotope

1. According to Reference Table N, a 10 gram sample of which radioisotope will decay to the greatest extent in 28 days?
   1) ^{32}P   2) ^{85}Kr   3) ^{220}Fr   4) ^{131}I

2. Which radioisotope will decay the most over a period of 100 days?
   1) ^{32}P   2) ^{131}I   3) ^{198}Au   4) ^{222}Rn

3. Which 20 gram sample of a radioisotope will have the highest percentage remaining after 5000 years of decaying?
   1) Pu-239   2) Th-232   3) U-238   4) Tc-99

4. A sample of which radioisotope will decay the least over a period of 100 years?
   1) 5 g of Co-60   2) 5 g of H-3   3) 5 g of Kr-85   4) 5 g of Sr-90

5. Which radioisotope sample will have the greatest amount remaining after 10 years?
   1) 2.0 g of Au-198   2) 2.0 g of K-42   3) 4.0 g of P-32   4) 4.0 g of Co-60

6. According to Reference Table N, which radioisotope will retain only $1/8$th its original mass after approximately after 43 days?
   1) Phosphorous-32   2) Radon-222   3) Gold-198   4) Iron-53

7. Which of the following isotopes will have only ¼ of its original atoms remaining unchanged after approximately 14.4 seconds?
   1) ^{19}Ne   2) ^{16}N   3) ^{37}K   4) ^{220}Fr

                   Survivingchem.com

24. Half-Life: Interpreting half-life graphs

1. The graph below represents the decay of a radioisotope.

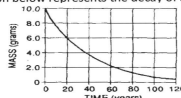

   What is the half-life of this radioisotope?

   1) 8 years　　　　2) 45 years　　　　3) 30 years　　　　4) 60 years

2. The graph below represents the decay of a radioactive material X into a stable decay product.

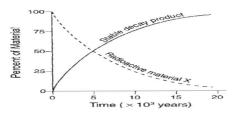

   What is the approximate half-life of radioactive material X?

   1) 5,000 years　　2) 50,000 years　　3) 10,000 years　　4) 1000,000 years

3. The graph below represents the decay of a radioisotope.

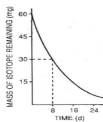

   According to Reference Table N, the decay of which radioisotope is represented by the graph?

   1) ^{42}k　　　　2) ^{42}P　　　　3) ^{131}I　　　　4) ^{198}Au

4. The graph below represents the decay of a radioactive material X into a stable decay product?

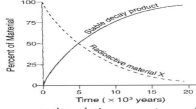

   Which graph best represents the relative percentages of the radioactive material X and its stable product after 15,000 years? (shaded area represents radioactive material while the non-shaded area represents stable products)

   1) 　　2) 　　3) 　　4)

25. Usages of radioisotopes: Recalling Concept Facts and Definitions

1. The course of a chemical reaction can be traced by using a
   1) polar molecule
   2) diatomic molecule
   3) stable isotope
   4) radioisotope

2. A radioisotope used to follow a chemical reaction is called
   1) tracer
   2) isomer
   3) calorimeter
   4) kinetics

3. A radioisotope is called a tracer when it is used to
   1) determine the age of animal skeletal remains
   2) determine the course of a chemical reaction
   3) kill cancerous tissue
   4) kill bacteria in food

4. Iodine-131 is used in diagnosing thyroid disorders because it is absorbed by the thyroid gland and
   1) has a very short half-life
   2) has a very long half-life
   3) emits alpha particle
   4) emits gamma radiation

5. Which procedure is based on the half-life of a radioisotope?
   1) Accelerating to increase kinetic energy
   2) Counting to determine a level of radioactivity
   3) Dating to determine age
   4) Radiating to kill cancer cells

6. Diagnostic injections of radioisotopes used in medicine normally have
   1) short half-lives and are quickly eliminated from the body
   2) short half-lives and are slowly eliminated from the body
   3) long half-lives and are quickly eliminated from the body
   4) long half-lives and are slowly eliminated from the body

26. Usages of radioisotopes: Determining isotope for common usage

1. Which nuclide is a radioisotope used in the study of organic reaction mechanism?
   1) Carbon-12   2) Carbon – 14   3) Uranium – 235   4) Uranium – 238

2. Which radioisotope is used in diagnoses of thyroid disorder?
   1) N-14   2) C-12   3) I-131   4) Fe-56

3. A radioisotope that is sometimes used in pinpointing brain tumor is
   1) Technetium – 99   2) Lead – 206   3) Uranium – 238   4) Carbon – 12

4. Diagnosing of blood disorder could be done using which radioisotope?
   1) ^{131}I   2) ^{56}Fe   3) ^{14}C   4) ^{206}Pb

5. A product is formed during a reaction between organic molecules. This reaction may be studied by using which of the following radioisotope?
   1) C-12   2) C-14   3) N-14   4) Fe-56

6. Geological dating can be done by comparing mineral remains of which two isotopes?
   1) U-238 and U-235
   2) U-238 and Co-60
   3) U-238 and Pb-206
   4) C-14 and Pb-206

7. Radioactive dating of the remains of organic materials can be done by comparing the ratio of which two isotopes?
   1) Uranium -235 to Uranium -238
   2) Carbon-14 to Carbon-12
   3) Nitrogen-14 to Nitrogen-16
   4) Hydrogen-2 to Hydrogen-3

Topic 13: Lab and measurements

Set A. Lab procedure, report and safety

1. Which of the following statements contained in a student's laboratory report is a conclusion?
 1) A gas is evolved   3) The gas is hydrogen
 2) The gas is insoluble in water 4) The gas burns in air

2. Which of the following statements in a student's laboratory report is an observation?
 1) Metal A will also react with an acid 3) Metal A is an alkali metal
 2) Metal A has luster   4) Metal A will be good for electrical wiring

3. During a laboratory activity, a student combined two solutions. In the laboratory report, the student wrote " A yellow color appeared." The statement represents the student's recorded
 1) conclusion   3) hypothesis
 2) observation   4) inference

4. A student investigated the physical and chemical properties of a sample of an unknown gas and then identified the gas. Which statement represents a conclusion rather than an experimental observation?
 1) The gas is colorless
 2) The gas is carbon dioxide
 3) When the gas is bubbled into limewater, the liquid becomes cloudy
 4) When placed in the gas, a flaming splint stops burning

5. Flame tests are used to identify
 1) polar molecules   3) nonmetal ions
 2) nonpolar molecules   4) metal ions

6. What is the safest method for diluting concentrated sulfuric acid with water?
 1) Add the acid to the water quickly 3) Add the acid to the water slowly while stirring
 2) Add the water to the acid quickly 4) Add the water to the acid slowly while stirring

7. A student wishes to prepare approximately 100 ml of an aqueous solution of 6 M HCl using 12 M HCl. Which procedure is correct?
 1) Adding 50 ml of 12 M HCl to 50 mL of water while stirring the mixture steadily
 2) Adding 50 ml of 12 M HCl to 50 ml of water, and then stir the mixture steadily
 3) Adding 50 ml of water to 50 mL of 12 M HCl while stirring the mixture steadily
 4) Adding 50 ml of water to 50 mL of 12 M HCl , and then stir the mixture steadily

8. Which activity is considered a proper laboratory technique
 1) heating the contents of an open test tube held vertically over a flame
 2) heating the content of a test tube that has been closed with a stopper
 3) adding water to a concentrated acids
 4) striking a match first before turning on the gas valve to light a Bunsen burner

Topic 13: Lab and measurements

Set B: Lab data, lab calculation, Percent error

1. A student determined the percentage of water of hydration in $BaCl_2 \cdot 2H_2O$ by using the data in the table below.

Quantity Measured	Value Obtained
Mass of $BaCl_2 \cdot 2H_2O$	3.80 grams
Mass of $BaCl_2$	3.20 grams
% of water calculated	15.79 %

The accepted percent of water of hydration is 14.75 %. What is the student's percent error?

    1) 1.04 %   2) 6.00 %   3) 6.59 %   4) 7.05 %

2. A student determined in the laboratory that the percent by mass of water in $CuSO_4 \cdot 5H_2O$ is 40.0%. If the accepted value is 36%, what is the percent error?

    1) 0.11 %   2) 1.1 %   3) 11 %   4) 4.0 %

3. A student calculated the percent by mass of water in a hydrate as 14.2 %. A hydrate is a compound that contains water as part of its crystal structure. If the accepted value is 14.7 %, the student's percent error was

    1) $\dfrac{0.5}{14.2} \times 100$ 2) $\dfrac{14.7}{14.2} \times 100$ 3) $\dfrac{0.5}{14.7} \times 100$ 4) $\dfrac{14.2}{14.7} \times 100$

4. A student found the boiling point of a liquid to be 80.4°C . If the liquid's actual boiling point is 80.6°C , the experimental percent error is equal to

    1) $\dfrac{80.6 - 80.4}{80.6} \times 100$ 3) $\dfrac{80.5 - 80.4}{80.5} \times 100$

    2) $\dfrac{80.6 - 80.4}{80.4} \times 100$ 4) $\dfrac{80.5 - 80.4}{80.4} \times 100$

5. A sample of water is being heated from 20°C to 30°C, and the temperature is recorded every 2 minutes. Which table would be most appropriate recording the data?

Time (min)	Temp (°C)
0	
2	
4	
6	
8	
10	

1)

Time (min)	Temp (°C)
20	
22	
24	
26	
28	
30	

2)

Temp (°C)	Time (min)
0	
2	
4	
6	
8	
10	

3)

Temp (°C)	Time (min)
20	
22	
24	
26	
28	
30	

4)

Topic 13: Lab and measurements

Set C. Significant figures

1. Which mass measurement contains four significant figures?
   1) 0.086 g   2) 0.431 g   3) 1003 g   4) 3870 g

2. Which measurement contains three significant figures?
   1) 0.03 g   2) 0.030 g   3) 0.035 g   4) 0.0351 g

3. Which volume measurement is expressed in two significant figures?
   1) 20 ml   2) 202 ml   3) 220 ml   4) 0.2 ml

4. Which measurement has the greatest number of significant figures?
   1) 44000 g   2) 404 g   3) 40.44 g   4) 0.40004 g

5. The volume measurement with the greatest number of significant figure is
   1) 0.0250 L   2) 0.2050 L   3) 0.00025 L   4) 2500 L

6. Which of these numbers has the least number of significant figures?
   1) 10.1   2) 0.10   3) 0.1001   4) 10

7. Which pressure measurement has the least number of significant figures?
   1) 84 kPa   2) 34.1 kPa   3) 70.88 kPa   4) 90 kPa

Set D: Significant figures in calculations

1. The mass of a solid is 3.60 g and its volume is 1.8 cm³. What is the density of the solid, expressed to the correct number of significant figures?
   1) 12 g/cm³   2) 2.0 g/cm³   3) 0.5 g/cm³   4) 0.50 g/cm³

2. Which quantity expresses the sum of 22.1 g + 375.66 g + 5400.132 g to the correct number of significant figures?
   1) 5800 g   2) 5798 g   3) 5797.9 g   4) 5797.892 g

3. The volume of a gas sample is 22 L at STP. The density of the gas is 1.35 g/ L. What is the mass of the gas sample, expressed to the correct number of significant figures?
   1) 30. g   2) 30.0 g   3) 16.7 g   4) 2.56 g

4. A student calculates the density of an unknown solid. The mass is 10.04 grams, and the volume is 8.21 cubic centimeters. How many significant figures should appear in the final answer?
   1) 1   2) 2   3) 3   4) 4

5. The density of a solid is 1.235 g/ml and its volume is 40.2 ml. A student calculating the mass of the solid should have how many significant figures in the final answer?
   1) 1   2) 2   3) 3   4) 4

Set E: Lab equipment

1. Which piece of equipment represents an Erlenmeyer's flask?

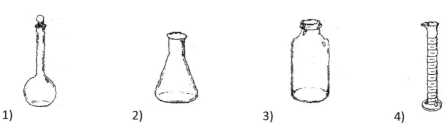

1) 2) 3) 4)

2. Which set of laboratory equipment would most likely be used with a crucible?

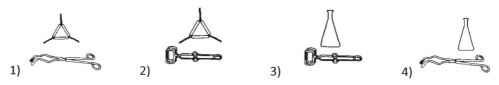

1) 2) 3) 4)

3. Which equipment represents a graduated cylinder?

1) 2) 3) 4)

4. The two lab equipments shown below are

1) Round bottom flask and a crucible   3) Evaporated dish and a beaker

2) Round bottom flask and a watch glass   4) Evaporated dish and a watch glass

5. The diagram to the right shows a laboratory setup that can be used in a titration.

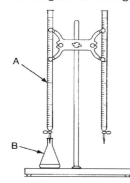

Which pieces of equipment are indicated by arrows A and B, respectively?

1) Burette and Erlenmeyer flask

2) Burette and volumetric flask

3) Pipet and Erlenmeyer flask

4) Pipet and volumetric flask

Topic 13: Lab and measurements

Set F: Lab measurements

1. The diagram below represents a portion of a 100-milliter graduated cylinder?

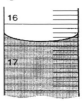

What is the reading of the meniscus?

1) 35.0 mL   3) 36.0 mL

2) 44.0 mL   4) 45.0 mL

2. The diagram below shows a portion of a buret.

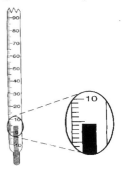

What is the meniscus reading in milliliters?

1) 16.00   3) 16.40

2) 17.00   4) 17.60

3. The diagram below represents a Celsius thermometer recording a certain temperature.

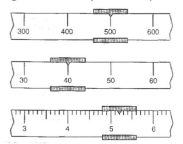

What is the correct reading of the thermometer?

1) 5°C   3) 4.3°C

2) 0.3°C   4) 4°C

4. The diagram below represents a portion of a triple beam balance.

If the beams are in balance with the riders in the positions shown, what is the total mass of the object?

1) 540.20 g   3) 540.52 g

2) 545.20 g   4) 545.52 g

5.

The diagram below represents a section of a buret containing acid used in acid-base titration

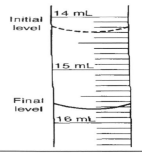

What is the total volume of acid that was used?

1) 1.10 mL

2) 1.30 mL

3) 1.40 mL

4) 1.45 mL

6. The diagram below shows the upper part of a laboratory burner.

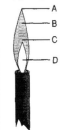

Which letter represents the hottest part of the burner flame?

1) A   3) C

2) B   4) D

Constructed Response

Concept by Concept

Set A: Types of Matter

Base your answers to questions 1 – 4 on the diagram below concerning the classification of matter.

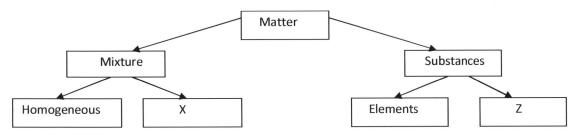

1. What type of substance is represented by Z?   1.

2. What type of mixture is represented by X?   2.

3. Identify one type of matter in the diagram that is composed of atoms of the same atomic number.   3.

4. Identify one type of matter in the diagram that can have varying ratio of composition.   4.

Set B: Composition of Matter

Base your answers to questions 5 - 8 on the pictures below.

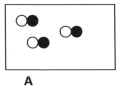

A

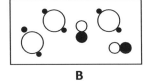

B

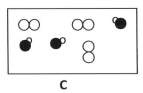

C

5. Contrast sample A and sample B in terms of compounds and mixtures. Include both sample A and B in your answer.   5.

6. Explain why sample C could represent a mixture of fluorine and hydrogen chloride.   6.

7. Explain, in terms of composition, why sample A represents a pure substance.   7.

8. Explain how the average kinetic energy of sample B can be equal to the average kinetic energy of sample C.   8.

Set C : Particle Arrangements of Matter

Base your answers to the following questions on the diagram of a molecule of nitrogen shown below.

     represents one molecule of nitrogen.

9. Draw a particle model that shows at least six molecules of nitrogen gas.

10. Draw a particle model that shows at least six molecules of liquid nitrogen.

11. Describe, in terms of particle arrangement, the difference between nitrogen gas and liquid nitrogen.

12. Good models should reflect the true nature of the concept being represented. What is the limitation of two-dimensional models.

Set D

Base your answers to questions 13 – 16 on the information below.

Given the heating curve where substance X starts as a solid below its melting point and is heated uniformly.

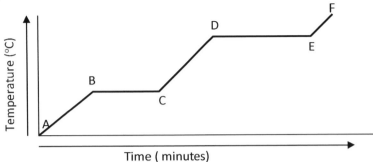

13. Describe, in terms of particle behavior or energy, what is happening to substance X during line segment BC.

13.

14. Using (●) to represent particles of substance X, draw at least five particles as they would appear in the substance at points F.

14.

15. Identify a line segment in which the average kinetic energy is increasing.

15.

16. Identify the process that takes place during line segment DE of the heating curve.

16.

17. How does the heating curve illustrates that the heat of vaporization is greater than the heat of fusion?

17.

Set E Phases of Matter and Temperature

Base your answers to questions 18 – 22 on the information below.

A substance is a solid at 15°C . A student heated a sample of the substance and recorded the temperature at one-minute intervals in the data table below.

Time (min)	0	1	2	3	4	5	6	7	8	9	10	11	12
Temperature (°C)	15	32	46	53	53	53	53	53	53	53	53	60	65

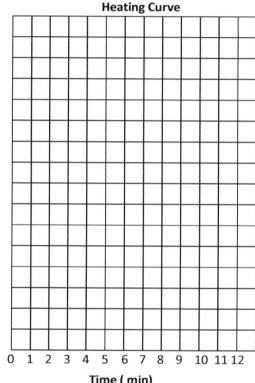

Heating Curve

18. On the grid , mark an appropriate scale on the axis labeled " Temperature (°C) ." An appropriate scale is one that allows a trend to be seen.

19 . Plot the data from the data table. Circle and connect the points

20. Based on the data table, what is the melting point of the substance?

20.

21. What is the evidence that the average kinetic energy of the particles of the substance is increasing during the first three minutes?

21.

22. The heat of fusion for this substance is 122 joules per gram. How many joules of heat are needed to melt 7.50 grams of this substance at its melting point?

22.

                   Survivingchem.com

Set F: Phases of Matter and Temperature

Base your answers to questions 23 through 26 on the information below.

The graph below shows a compound being cooled at a constant rate starting in the liquid phase at 75°C and ending at 15°C.

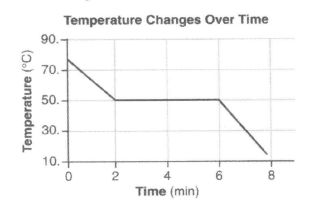

23. What is the freezing point of the compound,   23.

    in degree Celsius?

24. State what is happening to the average kinetic energy   24.
    of the particles of the sample between minute 2 and
    minute 6.

25. What Kelvin temperature is equal to 15°C?   25.

26. A different experiment was conducted with another sample   26.
    of the same compound starting in the solid phase.
    The sample was heated at a constant rate from 15°C to 75°C.
    On the graph above, draw the resulting heating curve.

Set K: Heat Transfer

Base your answers to questions 27 through 29 on the information below.

A student investigated heat transfer using a bottle of water. The student placed the bottle in a room at 20.5°C. The student measured the temperature of the water in the bottle at 7 a.m. and again at 3 p.m. The data from the investigation are shown in the table below.

Water Bottle Investigation Data

7 a.m.		3 p.m.	
Mass of Water (g)	Temperature (°C)	Mass of Water (g)	Temperature (°C)
800.	12.5	800.	20.5

27. Compare the average kinetic energy of the water molecules in the bottle at 7 a.m. to the average kinetic energy of the water molecules in the bottle at 3 p.m.

27.

28. State the direction of heat transfer between the surroundings and the water in the bottle from 7 a.m. to 3 p.m.

28.

29. Show a numerical setup for calculating the change in the thermal energy of the water in the bottle from 7 a.m. to 3 p.m.

29.

Set L: Gas Characteristics and Gas Laws

Base your answer to questions 35 through 37 on the information and diagrams below.

Cylinder A contains 22.0 grams of $CO_2(g)$ and Cylinder B contains $N_2(g)$. The volumes, pressures, and temperatures of the two gases are indicated under each cylinder.

Cylinder A   **Cylinder B**

$CO_2(g)$ $N_2(g)$

V = 12.3 L   V = 12.3 L
P = 1.0 atm   P = 1.0 atm
T = 300. K   T = 300. K

30. How does the number molecules of $CO_2(g)$ in Cylinder A compares to the number of molecules of $N_2(g)$ in Cylinder B. Your answer must include both $CO_2(g)$ and $N_2(g)$.

30.

31. The temperature of $CO_2(g)$ is increased to 450. K and the volume of cylinder A remains constant.
Show a correct numerical setup for calculating the new pressure of $CO_2(g)$ in Cylinder A.

31.

32. Calculate the new pressure of $CO_2(g)$ in Cylinder A based on your setup.

32.

Set M: Gas Laws

Answer questions 33 through 36
on the information below.

A rigid cylinder is fitted with a movable piston. The cylinder contains a sample of helium gas, He*(g)*, which has an initial volume of 125.0 milliliters and an initial pressure of 1.0 atmosphere, as shown below. The temperature of the helium gas sample is 20.0°C.

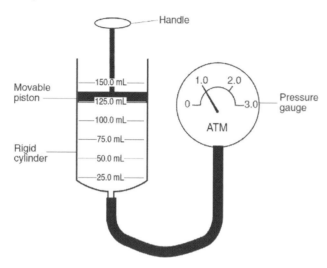

33. Express the initial volume of the helium gas sample, in liters.

33.

34. The piston is pushed further into the cylinder. In the space to the right, show a correct numerical setup for calculating the volume of the helium gas that is anticipated when the reading on the pressure gauge is 1.5 atmosphere. The temperature of the helium gas remains constant.

34.

35. Helium gas is removed from the cylinder and a sample of nitrogen gas, N₂*(g)*, is added to the cylinder. The nitrogen gas has a volume of 125.0 milliliters and a pressure of 1.0 atmosphere at 20.0°C. Compare the number of particles in this nitrogen gas sample to the number of particles in the original helium gas sample.

35.

36. Express 1.5 atmosphere in kilopascal (kPa).

36.

Survivingchem.com

Set A : Properties of Groups, Periodic Law

Write your answers here

1. In the 19th century, Dmitri Mendeleev predicted the existence of   1.
   a then unknown element X with a mass of 68. He also
   predicted that an oxide of X would have the formula X_2O.
   On the modern Periodic Table, what is the Group number
   and Period number of element X?

2. Explain, in terms of atomic structure, why the atomic radius   2.
   of iodine is greater than the atomic radius of fluorine.

3. Explain, in terms of electron configuration, why selenium   3.
   and sulfur have similar chemical properties?

4. Base your answer to the following question on the   4.
   information below
        Given: Samples of Na, Ar, As, Rb.

   Explain why Na and Rb share similar chemical characteristics.

Set B: Reactivity of elements, Trend in atomic size, Periodic trend

Base your answers to question 5 and 6 on the following information.

Potassium is a mineral that appears in abundance in all living plant and animal cells.
The human body uses it to promote regular heartbeat, help build muscles, help
contract muscles, regulate blood pressure, and control the water balance in the
body tissues and cells.

Calcium is a mineral that primarily functions in your body by making your bones and
teeth hard. The rest is in your blood and soft tissues; it helps your muscles contract
and your blood clot, and helps your nervous system work properly

Write your answers here.

5. According to your knowledge of atomic structure,   5.
   explain why the calcium atom is smaller than
   potassium atom.

6. Potassium and calcium are rarely found as pure element   6.
   in nature. They are usually combined with other
   substances. Explain why this is so.

Set C: Lewis electron-dot diagram, electronegativity, periodic trend

Base your answers questions 7 and 8 on the information below.

Fluorine is a Group 17 element. Fluorine is the most electronegative and reactive of all elements. It is a pale yellow, corrosive gas, which reacts with practically all organic and inorganic substances.

Write your answers here.

7. Draw the Lewis electron-dot structure for an atom of fluorine.

7.

8. What is the definition (or your interpretation) of the term "electronegativity"?

8.

9. Explain why the electronegativity of elements in Group 17 decreases from top to bottom down the group.

9.

Set D: Ionization energy, trend, properties of groups

A knowledge of the ionization energies of elements can be very useful in predicting the activity and type of reaction an element will have.

Write your answers here.

10. What does ionization energy quantitatively measure about an atom?

10.

11. Why do ionization energies decrease from the top to the bottom of a Group on the Periodic Table of Elements.

11.

12. Why do ionization energies increases from left to right across any Period.

12.

Set E: Reference Table S, Properties of elements: atomic radius (size), density, reactivity

Base your answers to questions 13 – 15 on the following information:

Given the elements: N , P, O, Se

Write answers here.

13. Which of these four elements has the smallest atomic radius?

13.

14. Which of these elements has the least mass*(g)* per volume (mL)?

14.

15. Which of these elements has the same chemical reactivity as sulfur?

15.

Set F: Properties of Groups, Phases at STP, conductivity, atomic size comparison

Base your answer to questions 16 through 19 on the information below.

A metal, M, was obtained from compound in a rock sample. Experiments have determined that the element is a member of Group 2 on the Periodic Table of the Elements.

Write answers here.

16. What is the phase of element M at STP.   16.

17. Explain, in terms of electrons, why element M is a good conductor of electricity.   17.

18. Explain why the radius of a positive ion of element M is smaller than the radius of an atom of element M.   18.

19. Using the element symbol M for the element, write the chemical formula for the compound that forms when element M reacts with Iodine?   19.

Set G: Graphing, data interpretation, electronegativity trend

The table below shows the electronegativity of selected elements of the Periodic Table.

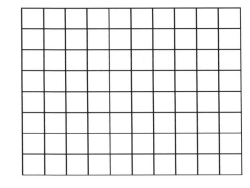

Electronegativity (y-axis)

Atomic Number (x-axis)

Element	Atomic Number	Electronegativity
Beryllium	4	1.6
Boron	5	2.0
Carbon	6	2.6
Fluorine	9	4.0
Lithium	3	1.0
Oxygen	8	3.4

20. On the grid, set up a scale for electronegativity on the y-axis. Plot the data by drawing a best-fit line.   Write answers here.

21. Using the graph, predict the electronegativity of Nitrogen.   21. _____

22. For these elements, state the trend in electronegativity in terms of atomic number.   22.

Set H: Physical and chemical properties of elements, Valence electrons.

Base your answers to questions 23 through 26 on the information below.

The table below lists physical and chemical properties of six elements at standard pressure that correspond to known elements on the Periodic Table. The elements are identified by the code letters, *D, E, G, J, L,* and *Q.*

Properties of Six Elements at Standard Pressure

Element D	Element E	Element G
Density 0.00018 g/cm³	Density 1.82 g/cm³	Density 0.53 g/cm³
Melting point –272°C	Melting point 44°C	Melting point 181°C
Boiling point –269°C	Boiling point 280°C	Boiling point 1347°C
Oxide formula (none)	Oxide formula E_2O_5	Oxide formula G_2O
Element J	**Element L**	**Element Q**
Density 0.0013 g/cm³	Density 0.86 g/cm³	Density 0.97 g/cm³
Melting point –210°C	Melting point 64°C	Melting point 98°C
Boiling point –196°C	Boiling point 774°C	Boiling point 883°C
Oxide formula J_2O_5	Oxide formula L_2O	Oxide formula Q_2O

23. What is the total number of elements in the "Properties of Six Elements at Standard Pressure" table that are solids at STP?

23.

24. An atom of element G is in the ground state. What is the total number of valence electrons in this atom?

24.

25. Letter Z corresponds to an element on the Periodic Table other than the listed elements. Elements G, Q, L, and Z are in the same group of the Periodic Table, as shown in the diagram below.

G
Q
L
Z

Based on the trend in melting points for elements G, Q, and L listed in the "Properties of Six Elements at Standard Pressure" table, estimate the melting point of element Z, in degree Celsius.

25.

26. Identify, by code letter, the element that is a noble gas in the "Properties of Six Elements at Standard Pressure" table.

26.

Set A: History of Atomic Models

John Dalton was an English scientist who proposed that atoms were hard, indivisible spheres. In the modern model, the atom has a different internal structure.

Write your answers here.

1. Identify one experiment that led scientists to develop the modern model of the atom.

1.

2. Describe this experiment.

2.

3. State one conclusion about the internal structure of the atom, based on this experiment.

3.

Set B: Atomic Model, Rutherford's Experiment

Base your answers to questions 4 through 6 on the information and diagram below.

One model of the atom states that atoms are tiny particles composed of a uniform mixture of positive and negative charges. scientists conducted experiment where alpha particles were aimed at a thin layer of gold atoms.

Most of the alpha particles passed directly through the gold atoms. A few alpha particles were deflected from their straight-line paths. An illustration of the experiment is shown below.

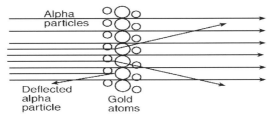

Write your answers here.

4. How should the original model be revised based on the results of this experiment?

4.

5. A few of the alpha particles were deflected. What does this evidence suggests about the structure of the gold atoms?

5.

6. Most of the alpha particles passed directly through the gold atoms undisturbed. What does this evidence suggest about the structure of the gold atoms?

6.

Set C: Subatomic particles

Base your answers to questions 7 through 9 on the information below.

In the modern model of the atom, each atom is composed
of three major subatomic (or fundamental) particles.

Write your answers here.

7. Name the subatomic particles contained in the nucleus.   7.

8. State the charge associated with each type of subatomic   8.
   particle contained in the nucleus of the atom.

9. What is the sign of the net charge of the nucleus?   9.

Set D: Isotopes, Atomic Mass Calculation

Base your answers to questions 10 through 12 on the data table below, which shows three isotopes of neon.

Isotope	Atomic Mass (atomic mass units)	Percent Natural Abundance
^{20}Ne	19.99	90.9 %
^{21}Ne	20.99	0.3 %
^{22}Ne	21.99	8.8 %

Write your answers here.

10. Based on the atomic mass and the natural abundances   10.
    shown in the data table show a correct numerical set-up
    for calculating the average atomic mass of neon.

11. Based on natural abundances, the average atomic   11.
    mass of neon is closest to which whole number?

12. In terms of atomic particles, state one difference   12.
    between these three isotopes of neon.

Set E: Electron Configuration, Subatomic Particles

Base your answers to questions 13 and 14 on the information below.

An atom has an atomic number of 9, a mass number of 19, and electron configuration of $2 - 6 - 1$.

13. Explain why the number of electrons in the second and   13.
    the third shells show that this atom is in an excited state.

14. What is the total number of neutrons in this atom?   14.

Set F: Subatomic Particles

Base your answers to questions 15 through 17 on the information below.

Two isotopes of potassium are K − 37 and K − 42.

Write your answers here.

15. Explain, in terms of subatomic particles, why K − 37 and K − 42 are isotopes of potassium.

    15.

16. How many valence electrons are in an atom of K − 42 in the ground state?

    16.

17. What is the total number of neutrons in the nucleus of a K − 37 atom.

    17.

Set G: Electron Transition

Base your answers to questions 18 and 19 on the diagram below, which shows bright-line spectra of selected elements.

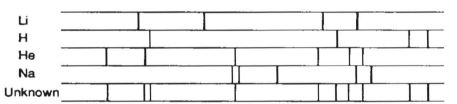

Write your answers here.

18. Explain, in terms of excited state, energy transition, and ground state, how a bright-line spectrum is produced.

    18.

19. Identify the two elements in the unknown spectrum.

    19.

Set H: Electron Configurations

Base your answers to questions 20 and 21 on the diagram below, which represents an atom of magnesium-26 in the ground state.

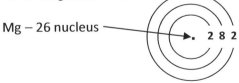

Mg − 26 nucleus

2 8 2

Write your answers here.

20. Write an appropriate number of electrons in each shell to represent a Mg − 26 atom in an excited state. Your answer may include additional shells.

    20.

21. What is the total number of valence electrons in an atom of Mg-26 in the ground state.

    21.

Set I: Atomic Structure, Lewis Electron-dot Diagrams

Base your answers to questions 22 through 57 on the information below.

Atomic Diagrams of Magnesium and Aluminum

Key	Element	Lewis Electron-Dot Diagram	Electron-Shell Diagram
• = electron	magnesium	Mg:	12 p / 11 n
	aluminum	Al:	13 p / 14 n

22. Identify one piece of information shown in the electron-shell diagrams that is not shown in the Lewis electron-dot diagrams.

22.

23. Determine the mass number of the magnesium atom represented by the electron-shell diagram.

23.

24. Based on the information given in the electron shell symbol, write the isotope symbol for the aluminum atom.

24.

25. Based on the information provided on the diagrams, draw Lewis electron – dot diagrams for the atom and for the ion of magnesium.

25. Atom　　　　　　　　Ion

26. Explain why Lewis electron-dot diagrams are generally more suitable than electron-shell diagrams for illustrating chemical bonding.

26.

Set A: Bonding

Base your answers to questions 1 and 2 on the balanced equation below.

$$2Na(s) \quad + \quad Cl_2(g) \quad \rightarrow \quad 2NaCl(s)$$

Write your answers here.

1. Explain, in terms of electrons, why the bonding in NaCl is ionic.   1.

2. Draw the Lewis electron-dot diagram for a molecule of chlorine, Cl_2.   2.

Set B: Bond and Molecular Polarities

Base your answers to questions 3 through 6 on the information below.

Each molecule listed below is formed by the sharing of electrons between atoms when atoms within the molecule are bonded together.

Molecule A: Cl_2

Molecule B: CCl_4

Molecule C: NH_3

Write your answers here.

3. Explain how the bonding in KCl is different from the bonding in molecules A, B, and C.   3.

4. Explain why NH_3 has stronger forces of attraction than Cl_2.   4.

5. Explain why CCl_4 is classified as a nonpolar molecule.   5.

6. Draw the Lewis electron-dot structures for the NH_3 molecule.   6.

Set C: Molecular Polarity

Base your answers to questions 7 through 8 on the information below.

When hydrogen bromide, a gas, is dissolved in water, the solution is called hydrobromic acid.

Write your answers here.

7. Is hydrogen bromide a polar or nonpolar molecule? Explain your answer?   7.

8. Draw the Lewis electron-dot diagram for hydrogen bromide.   8.

Set D: Molecular Polarity and Shapes

Base your answers to questions 9 through 11 on the information below.

Water is a polar molecule because it is bent and has a definite positive and negative side to it.

Write your answers here.

9. Draw the structure for a molecule of water, H_2O.

9 and 10:

10. *On your drawing,* indicate with a "+" the positive side and with " – " the negative side.

11. Describe one property of water that would change if water molecule were a straight molecule and nonpolar.

11.

Set E: Types and Properties of Substances

Base your answers to question 12 and 13 on the table and information below.

The table below shows some properties of three solids: X, Y, and Z

Properties	X	Y	Z
Melting Point (°C)	800	80	1200
Soluble in water	yes	no	no
Solid state conducts electricity	no	no	Yes
Liquid state conduct electricity	yes	no	yes

12. Classify solid X, Y, and Z as the followings:

Metallic, ionic, or molecular

12.   Solid X :_____

Solid Y: _____

Solid Z: _____

13. Explain, in terms of ions, why solid X would be able to conduct electricity when it dissolves in water.

13.

Set F: Intermolecular Forces and Electronegativity

Write your answers here.

14. Explain, in terms of intermolecular forces, why hydrogen has a lower boiling point than hydrogen bromide.

14.

15. Explain, in terms of electronegativity difference, why the bond in H – Cl is more polar than the bond in H – I.

15.

16. Explain, in terms of molecular polarity, why hydrogen chloride is more soluble than hydrogen in water under the same conditions of temperature and pressure.

16.

    Survivingchem.com

Set G: Lewis Electron-dot Diagrams, Bonding, Polarity

Base your answers to questions 17 through 20 on your knowledge of chemical bonding and on the Lewis electron-dot diagrams of H_2S, CO_2, and F_2 below.

$$H \cdot \ddot{S} \cdot \quad \ddot{O} :: C :: \ddot{O} \quad : \ddot{F} \cdot \ddot{F} :$$
$$H$$

17. Which atom, when bonded as shown, has the same   17.
     electrons configuration as an atom of argon?

18. Explain, in terms of structure and/or distribution of charge,   18.
     why CO_2 is a nonpolar molecule?

19. Explain, in terms of electronegativity, why a C = O bond   19.
     in CO_2 is more polar than F − F bond in F_2?

20. What is the total number of covalent bond in molecule of CO_2?   20.

21. What is the shape and molecular polarity of H_2S?   21.   Shape:

                                                                        Molecular Polarity:

Set A: Writing Formulas and Naming

Base your answers to questions 1 and 2 on the information below.

A scientist in a chemistry laboratory determined the molecular formula for two compounds containing nitrogen and oxygen to be NO_2 and N_2O_5.

Write your answers here.

1. Write the IUPAC name for the compound NO_2.   1.

2. Write the IUPAC name for the compound N_2O_5.   2.

Set B: Chemical Equation, Naming

Base your answers to questions 3 and 4 on the information and the equation below.

Antacids can be used to neutralize excess stomach acid.

Brand A antacids contains the acid-neutralizing agent magnesium hydroxide, $Mg(OH)_2$. It reacts with $HCl(aq)$ in the stomach according to the following balanced equation:

$$2HCl(aq) \ + \ Mg(OH)_2(aq) \ \rightarrow \ MgCl_2(aq) \ + \ 2H_2O(\ell)$$

Brand B antacids contains the acid-neutralizing agent sodium hydrogen carbonate.

3. Write the chemical formula for sodium hydrogen carbonate.   3.

4. What type of reaction is shown in the above balanced equation.   4.

Set C: Chemical Formulas, Nomenclature

5. What is the chemical formula for manganese(II) sulfide?   5.

6. What is the correct formula for ammonium dichromate?   6.

7. What is the correct IUPAC name for the formula BeO?   7.

8. Write the correct IUPAC name for the formula $Au(NO_3)_3$ 8.

9. Write the correct IUPAC name for the formula Y_2O?   9.

10. What is the total number of atoms in the formula $NaNO_3 \cdot 4H_2O$?   10.

11. What is the ratio of calcium ion to phosphate ion in the formula $Ca_3(PO_4)_2$.   11.

12. What is the ratio of ammonium ion to chlorate ion in the formula NH_4ClO_3?   12.

13. What is the correct empirical formula to the molecular formula $C_4H_{10}O_2$?   13.

Set D: Chemical Equation

Base your answers to the questions 14 through 16 on the information below.

Scientists discovered, and have confirmed, that sulfur dioxide (SO_2) and nitrogen oxides (NO_x) are the primarily causes of acid rain. In the US, about 2/3 of all SO_2 comes from electric power generator that relies on burning fossil fuels like coal.

When sulfur dioxides reaches the atmosphere, it oxidizes to first form sulfur trioxide SO_3. It then becomes sulfuric acid as it joins with water in the air and falls back down to earth. Acid rain causes acidification of lakes and streams. In addition, acid rain accelerates the decay of building materials and paints, including irreplaceable buildings, statues, and sculptures that are part of our nation's cultural heritage.

Write your answers here.

14. Write a balance chemical equation for the reaction between SO_2 and O_2 to form sulfur trioxide.

14.

15. Write a balance chemical equation for the reaction between water and sulfur trioxide to form sulfuric acid.

15.

16. Buildings and statues are often made of limestone which is composed of calcium carbonate. Write the formula for calcium carbonate.

16.

Set E. Types of Reactions, Balancing Equation

Answer questions 17 and 18 based on the equation and information below.

A neutralization reaction equation between nitric acid and calcium hydroxide is shown below.

___HNO_3 +   ___ $Ca(OH)_2$ $\rightarrow$ ___$Ca(NO_3)_2$ + H_2O

17. Balance the neutralization reaction equation above, using the smallest whole number coefficients.

18. What is the sum of all coefficients in the balanced equation ?

18.

Base your answers to questions 19 through 21 on the equation below.

___ C_2H_6 +   ___ O_2 $\rightarrow$ ___ CO_2 +   ___ H_2O

19. Balance the equation above, using the smallest whole number coefficients.

20. What is the sum of all coefficients when the equation is balanced.

20.

21. What type of a chemical reaction is represented by the equation?

21.

Set A: Moles of Atoms in Formulas.

	Write your answers here.
1. What is the total number of moles of oxygen atoms in 1 mole of the formula $MgSO_4 \cdot 7H_2O$	1.
2. What is the total number of moles of hydrogen in 2 moles of the formula NH_4HCO_3 ?	2.
3. What is the total number of moles of atoms in 0.5 moles of the formula $Al_2(CO_3)_3$?	3.

Set B. Mole Calculations, Empirical Formula

Base your answers to questions 4 through 6 on the formula of a compound below.

$$C_4H_{10}O_8$$

	Write your answers here.
4. Calculate the formula mass of the compound. Your work should include the correct numerical set up.	4.
5. Calculate the number of moles in 17.7 grams of the compound.	5.
6. What is the empirical formula for this compound	6.

Set C: Mole Calculation, Percent Composition

Base your answers to questions 7 through 9 on the information below.

Gypsum is a mineral that is used in the construction industry to make drywall (sheetrock). The chemical formula for this hydrated compound is $CaSO_4 \cdot 2H_2O$. A hydrated compound contains water molecules within the crystalline structures. Gypsum contains 2 moles of water for each 1 mole of calcium sulfate.

7. What is the gram-formula mass of $CaSO_4 \cdot 2H_2O$.   7.

8. Show a correct numerical setup for calculating the percent composition by mass of water in this compound and record your result.   8.

9. What is the IUPAC name for gypsum, $CaSO_4 \cdot 2H_2O$ 9.

Set D: Density, Mole Calculation

Base your answers to questions 10 through 12 on the information below.

The decomposition of sodium azide, $NaN_3(s)$, is used to inflate airbags.
On impact, $NaN_3(s)$ is ignited by an electrical spark, producing $N_2(g)$ and Na.
The $N_2(g)$ inflates the airbag.

Write your answers here.

10. An inflated airbag has a volume of 5.00×10^{-4} cm^3
    at STP. The density of $N_2(g)$ at STP is 0.00125g/cm^3.
    What is the total number of grams of $N_2(g)$ in the bag?

10.

11. What is the total number of moles present in a
    52.0 gram sample of NaN_3.
    (Grams-formula mass = 65.0 grams/mole)

11.

12. Balance the equation to the right using the
    smallest whole number coefficients.

12. ___ NaN_3 $\rightarrow$ ___ Na + ___N_2

Set E. Molar Mass Calculation, Nomenclature

Base your answers to questions 13 through 15 on the information below.

Sodium is essential ingredient in the human diet. The Federal Food and Drug
Administration recommends that the average adult daily requirement for
sodium is 2.4 grams. Sodium is ingested through consuming plants and animal
tissues, but another good source is table salt, sodium chloride.

Write and show work here.

13. What is the chemical formula for sodium chloride?

13.

14. What is the gram formula mass of a mole
    of sodium chloride?

14.

15. Based on your answer to previous question (#14),
    how many moles of table salt, sodium chloride
    would need to be consumed in order to ingest
    the 2.4 grams? [Show work]

15.

Set F: Percent composition

Given the formula: NH_4NO_3

16. What is the percent composition by mass of
    Nitrogen in the formula ? (Show setup and answer)

16.

17. What is the percent composition by mass of
    Oxygen in the formula? (show set up and work)

17.

Set G: Reaction Type, Mole Ratio in Chemical Equation

Base your answers to questions 18 through 20 on the balanced chemical equation below.

$$2H_2O \rightarrow 2H_2 + O_2$$

Show work and write your answers here.

18. What is the total number of moles of O_2 produced when 8 moles of H_2O is completely consumed?   18.

19. How does the balanced chemical equation show the Law of Conservation of Mass?   19.

20. What type of reaction does this equation represents?   20.

Set H: Balancing Equation, Mole Ratio in Equation

Base your answers to questions 21 and 22 on the balanced equation below.

$$4 Al(s) + 3O_2(g) \rightarrow 2Al_2O_3(s)$$

Show work and answer here

21. What is the total number of moles of $O_2(g)$ that must react completely with 8.0 moles of $Al(s)$ in order to form $Al_2O_3(s)$?   21.

22. What type of reaction is represented by the above Equation?   22.

Set I: Lab Data Interpretation and Calculation

Base your answers to questions 23 through 27 on the information below.

A hydrate is a compound that has water molecules within its crystal structure. The formula for the hydrate $CuSO_4 \cdot 5H_2O(s)$ shows that there are five moles of water for every one mole of $CuSO_4(s)$. When $CuSO_4 \cdot 5H_2O(s)$ is heated, the water within the crystals is released, as represented by the balanced equation below.

$$CuSO_4 \cdot 5H_2O(s) \rightarrow CuSO_4(s) + 5H_2O(g)$$

A student first masses an empty crucible (a heat-resistant container). The student then masses the crucible containing a sample of $CuSO_4 \cdot 5H_2O(s)$. The student repeatedly heat and masses the crucible and its contents until the mass is constant. The student's recorded experimental data and calculations are shown below.

Data and calculation before heating:

mass of $CuSO_4 \cdot 5H_2O(s)$ and crucible	21.37 g
− mass of crucible	19.24 g
mass of $CuSO_4 \cdot 5H_2O(s)$	2.13 g

Data and calculation after heating to a constant mass:

mass of $CuSO_4(s)$ and crucible	20.61 g
− mass of crucible	19.24 g
mass of $CuSO_4(s)$	1.37 g

Calculation to determine the mass of water:

mass of $CuSO_4 \cdot 5H_2O(s)$	2.13 g
− mass of $CuSO_4(s)$	1.37 g
mass of $H_2O(g)$	0.76 g

23. Identify the total number of significant figures recorded in the calculated mass of $CuSO_4 \cdot 5H_2O(s)$.

    23.

24. In the space to the right, use the student's data to show a correct numerical setup for calculating the percent composition by mass in the hydrate.

    24.

25. Explain why the sample in the crucible must be heated until the constant mass is reached.

    25.

26. How many moles of water is represented by the mass of $CuSO_4$ calculated by the student?

    26.

27. How many moles of water is represented by the mass of H_2O calculated by the student?

    27.

Set A: Solubility Factors

Base your answers to questions 1 and 3 on the information below.

When cola, a type of soda pop, is manufactured, $CO_2(g)$ is dissolved in it.

On the set of axes to the right.

1. Label one of them "Solubility" and the other "Temperature."

2. Draw a line to indicate the solubility of $CO_2(g)$ versus temperature.

3. A capped bottle of soda contains $CO_2(g)$ under high pressure. When the cap is removed, how does pressure affect the solubility of the dissolved $CO_2(g)$?

3.

Set B : Solubility Factors, Data Table Interpretation

Base your answer to questions 4 through 6 on the information and table below.

A student conducts an experiment to determine how the temperature of water affects the rate at which an antacid tablet dissolves in the water. The student has three antacid tablets of the same size and composition. The student drops one tablet into each of the three beakers containing 200. millimeters of water at different temperature and measures the time it takes for each tablet to completely dissolves. The results are shown in the table below.

Dissolving Data for Three Antacid Tablets

Beaker	Original temperature of water (°C)	Time for Tablet to Dissolve(s)
1	20.	40.
2	30.	25
3	40.	10

4. Describe the effect of water temperature on the rate of dissolving.

4.

5. The student had a 4th tablet and a Beaker 4 containing 200 milliliters of water at 25°C. Predict the possible time (in seconds) that it will take for the 4th antacid tablet to completely dissolve.

5.

6. Antacid tablet is solid. Indicate any other factor (other than temperature) that will affect the rate at which it will dissolve in water.

6.

Set C: Properties of Substances

Base your answers to questions 7 and 8 on the information below.

Naphthalene, a nonpolar substance that sublimes at room temperature, can be used to protect wool clothing from being eaten by moths.

7. Explain why naphthalene is NOT expected to dissolve in water.

7.

8. Explain, in terms of intermolecular forces, why naphthalene sublimes.

8.

Set D: The Solubility Curves

Base your answers to questions 9 through 11 on the information below.

A student uses 200 grams of water at 60°C to prepare a saturated solution of potassium chloride, KCl.

Write your answers here.

9. According to reference Table G, how many grams of KCl must be used to create this saturated solution.

9.

10. This solution is cooled to 10°C and the excess precipitate (settle) out. The resulting solution is saturated at 10°C. How many grams of KCl precipitated out of the original solution?

10.

11. Identify the solute in this solution?

11.

Set E. Solubility Guidelines – Using Reference Table F

According to Reference Table F, indicate in the space if the compound is "soluble" or "insoluble."

12. Ammonium chloride

12. _____

13. Calcium phosphate

13. _____

14. Sodium sulfide

14. _____

15. Silver bromide

15. _____

16. Barium sulfate

16. _____

Set F. Solubility Curves, Data Interpretation

Base your answers to questions 17 through 20 on the data table below, which shows the solubility of a solid solute.

Solubility Curve

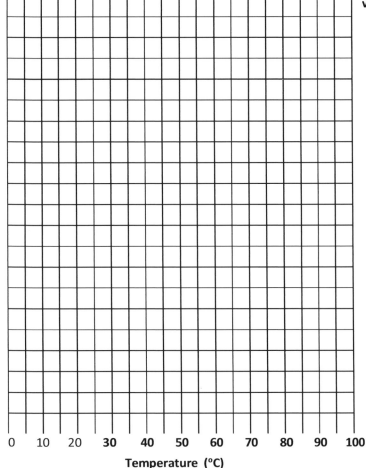

The solubility of the solute at various Temperature

Temperature (°C)	Solute per 100 g of $H_2O(g)$
0	18
20	20
40	24
60	29
80	36
100	49

17. On the grid provided, mark an appropriate scale on the axis labeled "Solute per 100 g of $H_2O(g)$.

18. On the same grid, plot the data from the data table. Circle and connect the points.

19. Based on the data table, if 15 grams of solute is dissolved in 100 grams of water at 40°C, how many more grams of solute can be dissolved in this solution to make a saturated at 40°C?

19.

20. According to Reference Table G, how many grams of $KClO_3$ must be dissolved in 100 grams of H_2O at 10°C to produce a saturated solution?

20.

Set G: Molarity Calculations

Base your answers to questions 21 and 22 on the information below.

A student is instructed to make 0.250 liter of a 0.200 M aqueous solution of $Ca(NO_3)_2$.

21. In order to prepare the described solution in the laboratory, two quantities must be measured accurately. One of these quantities is the volume of the solution. What other quantity must be measured to prepare this solution?

21.

22. Show a correct numerical setup for calculating the total number of moles of $Ca(NO_3)_2$ needed to make 0.250 liter of the 0.200 M calcium nitrate solution.

22.

23. Show a correct numerical setup for determining how many liters of a 1.2 M solution can be prepared with 0.50 mole of $C_6H_{12}O_6$.

23.

24. What is the concentration of a solution that contains 2 moles of solute in 1.2 L of solution.

24.

Set H: Heat Flow, Molecule-Ion Attraction

Given the balanced equation for the dissolving NH4Cl*(s)* in water:

$$NH_4Cl(s) \xrightarrow{H_2O} NH_4^+(aq) + Cl^-(aq)$$

25. A student is holding a test tube containing 5.0 milliliters of water. When a sample of $NH_4Cl(s)$ is placed in the test tube, the test tube feels colder to the student's hand. Describe the direction of heat flow between the test tube and the hand.

25.

26. Using the key to the right, draw at least two water molecules in the box showing the correct orientation of each water when it is near the Cl- ion in the aqueous solution

26.

Key	
• =	Hydrogen atom
◯ =	Oxygen atom
◉ =	Water molecule

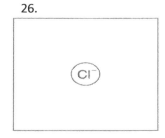

Set H: Type of Solution, Parts Per Million Calculation

Base your answers to questions 27 through 30 on the information below.

Scientists who study aquatic ecosystems are often interested in the concentration of dissolved oxygen in water. Oxygen, O_2, has a very low solubility in water, and therefore its solubility is usually expressed in units of milligrams per 1000. grams of water at 1.0 atmosphere pressure. The graph below shows a solubility curve of oxygen in water.

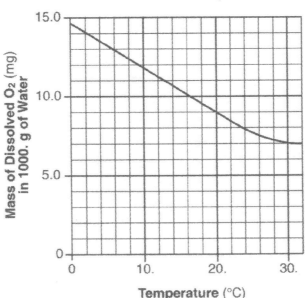

27. A student determines that 8.2 milligrams of oxygen is   27.
    dissolved in a 1000. gram sample of water at 15°C and
    1.0 atmosphere of pressure. In terms of saturation, what
    type of solution is this sample?

28. Explain, in terms of molecular polarity, why oxygen gas   28.
    has a low solubility in water. Your response must include
    both oxygen and water?

29. A student prepared a solution of oxygen by dissolving 6.0 mg 29.
    of oxygen in 1000 gram of water at 20°C. Determine how
    many more milligram of oxygen must be added to the
    solution to make it a saturated solution.

30. An aqueous solution has 0.007 gram of oxygen dissolved in   30.
    1000 grams of water. In the space to the right, calculate the
    dissolved oxygen concentration of this solution in parts per million.
    Your response should include both a correct numerical setup and
    · calculated result.

Set A: pH

Base your answers to question 1 and 2 on the information below.

Three bottles of liquids labeled 1,2, and 3 were found in a storeroom. One of the liquids is known to be drain cleaner. Drain cleaners contain KOH or NaOH. The pH of each liquid at 25°C was determined with a pH meter. The table below shows the test results.

pH Test Results

Bottle	pH of liquid
1	3.8
2	7.0
3	12.8

1. Explain, in terms of pH values, why thymol blue is not a suitable indicator to distinguish between the contents of bottle 1 and 2.

    1.

2. Explain how the pH results in this table enable a student to correctly concluded that bottle 3 contain the drain cleaner.

    2.

Set B: pH and H⁺ Concentration

Base your answers to questions 3 through 5 on the information below.

A truck carrying concentrated nitric acid overturns and spills its contents. The acid drains into a nearby pond. The pH of the pond water was 8.0 before the spill. After the spill, the pond water is 1,000 times more acidic.

3. What is the new pH of the pond water after the spill?   3.

4. What color would bromthymol blue be at this new pH?   4.

5. Name an ion in the pond water that has increased in concentration due to the spill.   5.

Set C: Indicators, Titration Calculation

Base your answer to the following questions on the information below.

A student titrates 60.0 mL of $HNO_3(aq)$ with 0.30 M NaOH(aq) . Phenolphthalein is used as the indicator. After adding 42.2 mL of NaOH(aq), a color change remains for 25 seconds, and the student stops the titration.

6. What color change does phenolphthalein undergo during this titration.   6.

7. What is concentration of the HNO_3 that was titrated?   7.

Set D: pH Interpretation

Base your answers to questions 8 through 10 on the information below.

A student was studying the pH difference in samples from two Adirondack streams. The student measured a pH of 4 in stream A and a pH of 6 in stream B.

8. Identify one compound that could be used to neutralize the sample from stream A.

8.

9. What is the color of bromthymol blue in the sample from stream A?

9.

10. Compare the hydronium ion concentration in stream A to the hydronium ion concentration in stream B.

10.

Set E. Titration, Significant Figures

Base your answers to questions 10 through 12 on the information below.

In a titration, 3.00 M NaOH*(aq)* was added to an Erlenmeyer flask containing 25.00 millimeters of HCl*(aq)* and three drops of phenolphthalein until one drop of NaOH*(aq)* turned the solution a light-pink color. The following data were collected by a student performing this titration.

Initial NaOH*(aq)* buret reading: 14. 45 milliliters
Final NaOH*(aq)* buret reading: 32.66 milliliters

Write answers here.

11. What is the total volume of NaOH*(aq)* that was used in the titration?

11.

12. Show a correct numerical setup for calculating the molarity of HCl*(aq)*.

12.

13. Based on the data given, what is the correct number of significant figures that should be shown in molarity of HCl*(aq)* ?

13.

Set F: Indicators

Indicate the color of the given indicators based on the pH of the solution.

14. Litmus in a solution with a pH of 11

14.

15. Bromthymol blue in a solution with a pH of 4

15.

16. Methyl orange in a solution with a pH of 3.5.

16.

Set G: Titration Calculation

> **Base your answers to questions 17 and 18 on the information and data table below.**
>
> Using burets, a student titrated a sodium hydroxide solution of unknown concentration with a standard solution of 0.10 M hydrochloric acid. The data are recorded in the table below.
>
> **Titration Data**
>
> | Solutions | HCl*(aq)* | NaOH*(aq)* |
> |---|---|---|
> | **Initial Buret Reading (mL)** | 15.50 | 5.0 |
> | **Final Buret Reading (mL)** | 25.00 | 8.80 |

17. Determine both the total volume of HCl*(aq)* and the total volume of NaOH*(aq)* used in the titration.

    17. Total volume of HCl*(aq)* used: _____mL
        Total volume of NaOH*(aq)* used: _____ mL

18. Show a correct numerical setup for calculating the molarity of the sodium hydroxide solution.

    18.

19. Calculate the molarity of the sodium hydroxide solution from your setup.

    19.

Set H: Electrolytes, Classification of Substances

> **Base your answers to questions 20 through 23 on the information and diagrams below.**
>
> Four beakers each containing 100 milliliters of aqueous solution of equal concentration at 25°C.

 KCl   CH₃OH   Ba(OH)₂   CH₃COOH

Write your answers here.

20. Which solutions contain electrolytes?

    20.

21. Which solution has the lowest pH?

    21.

22. Which solution is most likely to react with Arrhenius acid to form a salt and water?

    22.

23. Which solution has the lowest freezing point?

    23.

24. What causes some aqueous solution to have a low pH?

    24.

Set I: Graph Interpretation

Base your answers to questions 25 through 28 on the graph below. The graph shows the relationship between pH value and hydronium ion concentration for common aqueous solutions and mixtures.

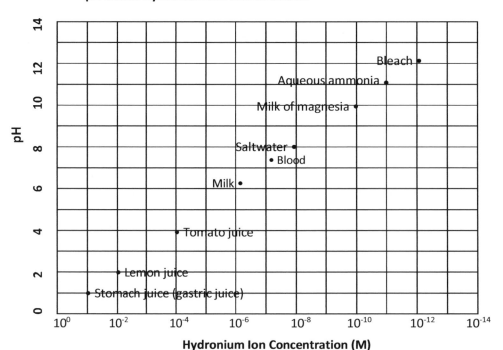

pH Versus Hydronium Ion Concentration

	Write your answers here.
25. According to this graph, which mixture is approximately 100 times more acidic than milk of magnesia?	25.
26. According to the graph, which mixture is approximately 10 times less acidic than aqueous ammonia?	26.
27. What color is thymol blue when added to milk of magnesia?	27.
28. What is the hydronium concentration of tomato juice?	28.

Set I: Properties of Acids and Bases

Base your answers to questions 29 through 30 on the information below.

A laboratory worker filled a bottle with a hydrochloric acid solution. Another bottle was filled with methanol, while a third bottle was filled with a sodium hydroxide solution. However, the worker neglected to label each bottle. After a few days, the worker could not remember which liquid was in each bottle.

The worker needed to identify the liquid in each bottle. The bottles were labeled A, B, and C. Using materials found in the lab (indicator, conductivity apparatus, and pieces of Mg metal), the worker tested samples of liquid from each bottle. The test results are shown in the table below.

Table of Tests and Results

Test Results

Test	Bottle A	Bottle B	Bottle C
Methyl orange indicator	Yellow	Yellow	Yellow
Bromthymol blue indicator	Blue	Green	Yellow
Electrical conductivity	Conductor	Nonconductor	Conductor
Reactivity with Mg metal	No reaction	No reaction	Reaction

29. Using the test results, state how the worker differentiated   29.
    the bottle that contained methanol from the other two bottles.

30. The worker concluded that bottle C contained hydrochloric acid.   31.
    Identify one test and state the corresponding test result that
    supports this conclusion.

31. If bottle C contains hydrochloric acid as concluded by the worker, 31.
    name one chemical substance that is produced in the reaction
    of the hydrochloric acid with the Mg metal?

32. Explain, in terms of pH, why the methyl orange indicator test   32.
    results were the same for each of the three liquids.

33. Identify another metal on Reference Table J that will also react   33.
    with the liquid is Bottle C .

  Survivingchem.com

Set A: Factors affecting reaction rate, Collision Theory

Base your answers to questions 1 through 3 on the information below.

A Student wishes to investigate how the reaction rate changes with a change in concentration of HCl(*aq*).

Given the equation.

$$Zn(s) \quad + \quad HCl(aq) \rightarrow H_2(g) \quad + \quad ZnCl_2(aq)$$

Write your answers here.

1. Describe the effect of increasing concentration of HCl(*aq*) on the reaction rate and justify your response in terms of Collision Theory.

    1.

2. Identify one other variable that might affect the rate and should be held constant during this investigation.

    2.

3. Identify the independent variable in this investigation .

    3.

Set B: : Solubility, Le Chatelier's Principle

Base your answers to questions 4 and 5 on the information below.

Given the equilibrium equation at 298 K

$$KNO_3(s) \quad + \quad 34.89 \text{ kJ} \quad \leftrightarrow \quad K^+(aq) \quad + \quad NO_3^-(aq)$$

4. The equation indicates that KNO_3 has formed a saturated solution. Explain , in terms of equilibrium, why the solution is saturated.

    4.

5. Describe, in terms of Le Chatelier's principle, why an increase in temperature increases the solubility of KNO_3.

    5.

Set C: Potential Energy Diagram

6. On the set of axes provided:
Sketch the potential energy diagram for an endothermic chemical reaction that shows the activation energy and the potential energy of the reactants and the potential energy of the products.

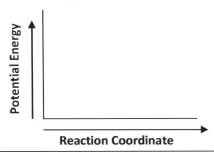

Set D: Le Chatelier's Principle

Base your answers to question 7 through 10 on the equilibrium chemical reaction below.

$$N_2(g) \quad + \quad 3H_2(g) \quad \leftrightarrow \quad 2NH_3(g) \quad + \quad 92.05 \text{ kJ}$$

Write your answers here.

7. State the effect on the number of moles of $N_2(g)$ if the temperature of the system is decreased.

   7.

8. State the effect on the number of moles of $H_2(g)$ if the pressure on the system is increased.

   8.

9. State the effect on the number of moles of $NH_3(g)$ if a catalyst is introduced into the reaction system.

   9.

10. State the effect on the number of moles of $N_2(g)$ if the number of moles of $H_2(g)$ is increased.

   10.

Set E: Collision Theory, Le Chatelier's Principle.

Base your answers to question 11 and 12 on the information and balanced equation below.

Given the equation for a reaction at equilibrium.

$$2 SO_2(g) \quad + \quad O_2(g) \quad \leftrightarrow \quad 2SO_3(g) \quad + \quad \text{energy}$$

11. Explain, in term of collision between molecules, why increasing the concentration of $O_2(g)$ produces a decrease in the concentration of $SO_2(g)$.

   11.

12. Explain, in terms of Le Chatelier's principle, why the concentration of $SO_2(g)$ increases when the temperature is increased.

   12.

Set F: Le Chatelier's Principle

Base your answer to question 13 on the information and equation below.

Human blood contains dissolved carbonic acid, H_2CO_3, in equilibrium with carbon dioxide and water. The equilibrium system is shown below.

$$H_2CO_3(aq) \quad \leftrightarrow \quad CO_2(aq) \quad + \quad H_2O(\ell)$$

13. Explain, using Le Chatelier's principle, why decreasing concentration of CO_2 decreases the concentration of H_2CO_3.

   13.

Set G: Potential Energy Diagram, Catalyst

Base your answers to questions 14 through 17 on the potential energy diagram and the equation below.

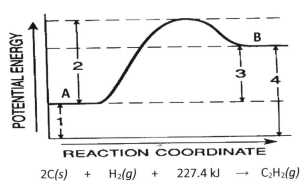

$$2C(s) \quad + \quad H_2(g) \quad + \quad 227.4\,kJ \quad \rightarrow \quad C_2H_2(g)$$

14. Describe how the potential energy diagram will change if a catalyst is added.

14.

15. If 682.2 Kilojoules are absorbed, how many moles of $C_2H_2(g)$ are produced.

15.

16. The letter B represents which chemical formula or formulas in the equation?

16.

17. What is the sign for the heat of reaction, ΔH?

17

Set H: Potential Energy Diagram, Effect of Catalyst

Base your answer to questions 18 through 20 on the potential energy diagram below.

18. Explain, in terms of the function of catalyst, why the curves on the potential energy diagram for the catalyzed and uncatalyzed reactions are different.

18.

19. What is the activation energy for the forward reaction with the catalyst?

19.

20. What is the heat of reaction for the reverse reaction without catalyst?

20.

Set I: Graphing, Reaction Rate

Base your answers to questions 21 through 23 on the information below.

An investigation was conducted to study the effect of the concentration of a reactant on the total time needed to complete a chemical reaction. Four trials of the same reaction were performed. In each trial the initial concentration of the reactant was different. The time needed for the chemical reaction to be completed was measured. The data for each of the four trials are shown in the data table below.

Reactant Concentration and Reaction Time

Trial	Initial Concentration (M)	Reaction Time (s)
1	0.020	11
2	0.015	14
3	0.010	23
4	0.005	58

Reaction Time Versus Initial Concentration

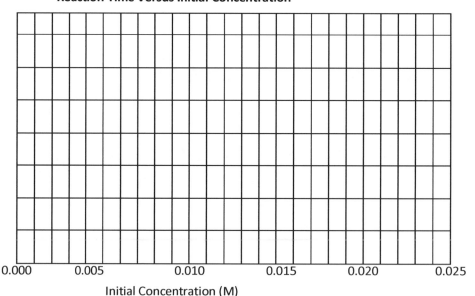

Reaction Time(s)

Initial Concentration (M)

21. On the grid, mark an appropriate scale on the axis labeled " Reaction Time*(s)*."
   An appropriate scale is one that allows a trend to be seen.

22. On the same grid, plot the data from the table. Circle and connect the points .

23. State the effect of the concentration of the   23.
   reactant on the rate of the chemical reaction.

24. In a different experiment involving the same   24.
   reaction, it was found that an increase in temperature
   increased the rate of the reaction. Explain this result
   in terms of collision theory.

Set J: Equilibrium, Le Chatelier's Principle, Collision Theory

Base your answers to questions 25 through 27 on the information below.

Nitrogen gas, hydrogen gas, and ammonia gas are in equilibrium in a closed container at constant temperature and pressure. The equation below represents this equilibrium.

$$N_2(g) + 3H_2(g) \leftrightarrow 2NH_3(g)$$

The graph below shows the initial concentration of each gas, the changes that occurs as a result of adding $H_2(g)$ to the system, and the final concentration when equilibrium is reestablished.

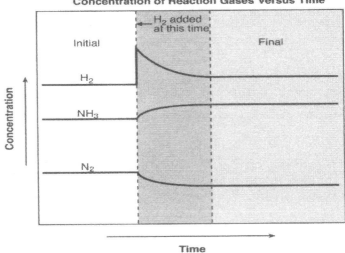

Concentration of Reaction Gases Versus Time

25. What information on the graph indicates that the system was initially at equilibrium?

25.

26. Explain, in terms of Le Chatelier's Principle, why the final concentration of $NH_3(g)$ is greater than the initial concentration of $NH_3(g)$

26.

27. Explain, in terms of collision theory, why the concentration of $H_2(g)$ begins to decrease immediately after more $H_2(g)$ is added to the system.

27.

Survivingchem.com

Set A: Drawing Organic Structure

Base your answer to the following question on the formula below:

$$CH_3CH_2CHCH_2$$

1. Draw the structural formula for this compound   1.

Set B: Drawing Hydrocarbon Structure, Isomers

Given the structural formula below.

```
        H   H   H   H
        |   |   |   |
    H — C — C — C — C — H
        |   |   |   |
        H   H   H   H
```

2. Draw the structural formula of an isomer of butane.

Set C: Bonding in hydrocarbon, organic reactions, reading comprehension

Base your answers to questions 3 through 5 on the information below.

Ethene (common name ethylene) is a commercially important organic compound. Millions of tons of ethene are produce by the chemical industry each year. Ethene is used in the manufacture of synthetic fibers for carpeting and clothing, and it is widely used in the making of polyethylene. Low-density polyethylene can be stretched into a clear, thin film that is used for wrapping food products and consumer goods. High-density polyethylene is molded into bottles for milk and other liquids. Ethene can also be oxidized to produce ethylene glycol, which is widely used in antifreeze for automobiles. The structural formula for ethylene glycol is:

```
        H   H
        |   |
    H — C — C — H
        |   |
        OH  OH
```

At standard atmosphere pressure, the boiling point of ethylene glycol is 198°C, compared to ethene that boils at -104°C.

3. Explain, in terms of bonding, why ethene is   3.
   an unsaturated hydrocarbon.

4. According to the information in the reading passage, state   4.
   two consumer products manufactured from ethene.

5. Identify the type of organic reaction by which ethene is   5.
   made into polyethylene.

Set D: Organic Reactions, Classes of Organic Compounds

Base your answers to questions 6 and 7 on the information below.

Many artificial flavorings are prepared using the type of organic reaction shown below.

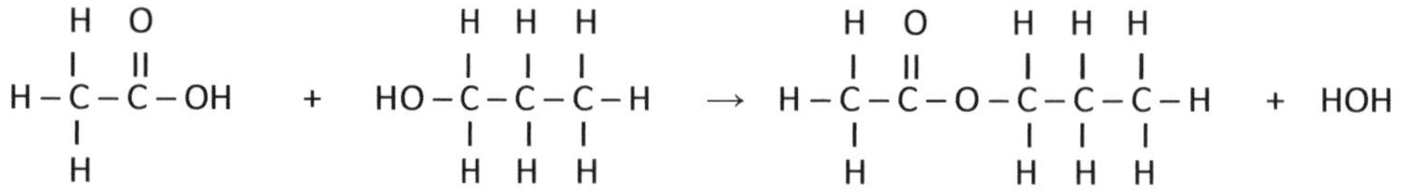

```
    H   O                      H   H   H               H   O     H   H   H
    |   ||                     |   |   |               |   ||    |   |   |
H – C – C – OH      +     HO – C – C – C – H    →   H – C – C – O – C – C – C – H     +    HOH
    |                         |   |   |               |         |   |   |
    H                         H   H   H               H         H   H   H

    Reactant 1             Reactant 2
```

6. Draw the structural formula of an isomer of Reactant 2.   6.

7. To what class of organic compounds does Reactant 1 belongs?   7.

8. To what class of organic compound does Reactant 2 belongs?   8.

9. What is the name of organic product formed in this reaction?   9.

Set E: Organic Reactions, Naming

Base your answers to questions 10 through 13 on the equation below, which represents an organic compound reacting with bromine.

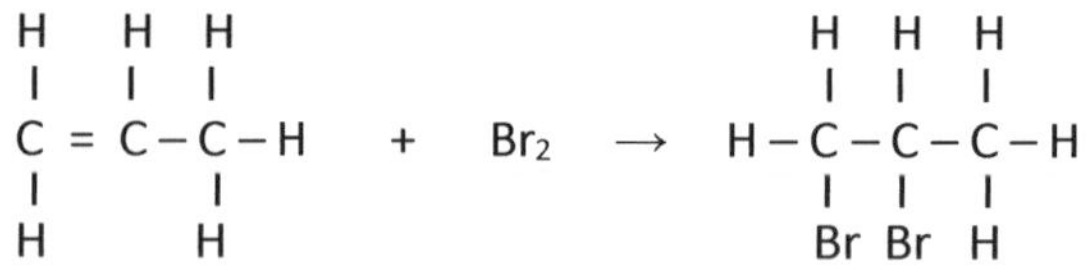

```
        H   H   H                              H   H   H
        |   |   |                              |   |   |
        C = C – C – H      +     Br₂     →   H – C – C – C – H
        |       |                              |   |   |
        H       H                              Br  Br  H
```

10. What is the gram-formula mass of the product   10.
     in this reaction?

11. What type of organic reaction is represented   11.
     by this equation?

12. What is the IUPAC name for the organic compound   12.
    that reacts with Br₂?

13. What is the IUPAC name of the organic product   13.
     that is formed in this reaction?

Set E: Organic Reaction, Balancing equation

Base your answers to questions and 15 on the information below.

Given the unbalance equation:

$$\underline{\hspace{1cm}} C_6H_{12}O_6 \xrightarrow{\text{enzyme}} \underline{\hspace{1cm}} C_2H_5OH \;+\; \underline{\hspace{1cm}} CO_2$$

14. Identify the type of reaction represented.   14.

15. What is the IUPAC name of the organic product?   15.

16. Balance the equation provided, using the smallest whole-number coefficients.

Set F: Organic Reaction, Naming Organic Compound

Base your answers to questions 17 and 19 on the incomplete organic reaction below, which shows a reaction between a hydrocarbon and a chlorine molecule.

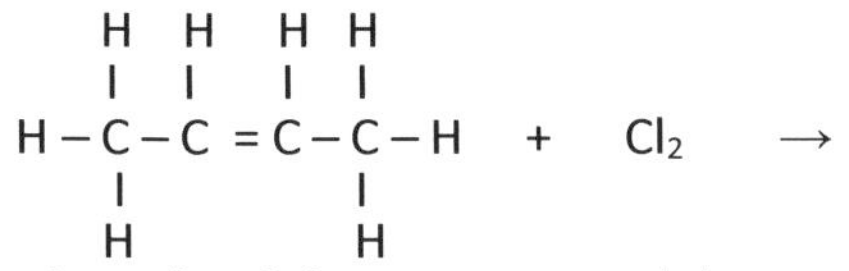

```
        H   H   H  H
        |   |   |  |
    H — C — C = C — C — H    +    Cl₂    →
        |           |
        H           H
```

17. To the right of the reactants and the arrow, draw the structural formula for the product of the reaction shown.

18. What is the IUPAC name of the hydrocarbon reactant?   18.

19. Draw an isomer of the organic compound that reacted with Cl_2?   19.

Set G: Organic Structure, Group Properties

Base your answers to questions 20 and 21 on the information below.

A thiol is very similar to an alcohol, but a thiol has a sulfur atom instead of an oxygen atom in the functional group. One of the compounds in a skunk's spray is 2-butene-1-thiol. The formula of this compound is shown below.

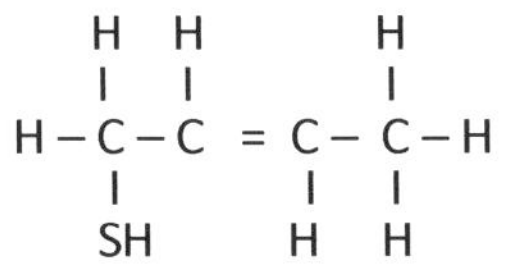

```
        H   H         H
        |   |         |
    H — C — C  =  C — C — H
        |         |   |
        SH        H   H
```

20. Explain, in terms of electron configuration,   20.
    why oxygen and sulfur atoms form compounds
    with similar molecular structures.

21. Explain, in terms of composition, why this compound   21.
    is a thiol.

SurvivingChem.com   **407**

Set H: Classes of Organic Compounds, Properties, Organic Reactions

Base your answers to questions 22 through 24 on the information below.

The hydrocarbon 2–methylpropane reacts with iodine as represented by the balanced equation below. At standard pressure,, the boiling point of 2–methylpropane is lower than the boiling point of 2–iodo–2–methylpropane.

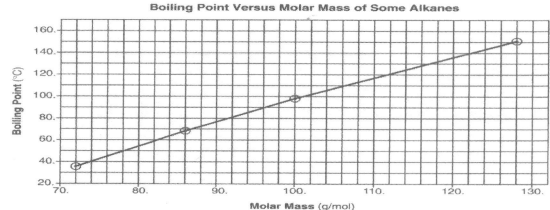

22. To which class of organic compound does this organic product belong?

22.

23. Explain, in terms of bonding, why the hydrocarbon 2-methylpropane is saturated.

23.

24. Explain the difference in the boiling points of 2-methylpropane and 2-iodo-2-methylpropane in terms of both molecular polarity and intermolecular forces.

24.   Molecular polarity:

        Intermolecular forces:

Set I: Graph Interpretation, Relating Intermolecular Forces to Boiling Points

Base your answers to questions 25 and 26 on the information below.

The graph below shows the relationship between boiling point and molar mass at standard pressure for pentane, hexane, heptane, and nonane

Boiling Point Versus Molar Mass of Some Alkanes

25. Octane has a molar mass of 114 grams per mole. According to this graph, what is the boiling point of octane at standard pressure?

25.

26. State the relationship between molar mass and the strength of intermolecular forces for the selected alkanes

26.

Set J: Hydrocarbons, Boiling Point

Base your answers to questions 27 through 30 on the information and diagram below, and on your knowledge of chemistry.

Crude oil is a mixture of many hydrocarbons that have different numbers of carbon atoms. The use of fractionating towers allows the separation of this mixture bases on the boiling points of the hydrocarbons.

To begin the separation process, the crude oil is heated to about 400°C in a furnace, causing many of the hydrocarbons of the crude oil to vaporize. The vaporized mixture is pumped into a fractionating tower that is usually more than 30 meters tall. The temperature of the tower is highest at the bottom. As vaporized samples of hydrocarbons travel up the tower, they cool and condensed. The liquid hydrocarbons are collected on trays and removed from the tower. The diagram below illustrates the fractional distillation of the crude oil and the temperature ranges in which the different hydrocarbons condensed.

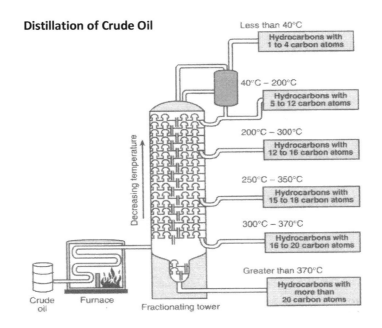

27. State the trend between the boiling point of the hydrocarbons contained in the crude oil and the number of carbon atoms in these molecules.

27.

28. Describe the relationship between the strength of the intermolecular forces and the number of carbon atoms in the different hydrocarbon molecules.

28.

29. Write the IUPAC name of one of the saturated hydrocarbon that leaves the fractionating tower at less than 40°C.

29.

30. How many hydrogen atoms are present in one molecule of octane.

30.

Survivingchem.com

Set A: Electrochemical Cells

Base your answers to questions 1 through 4 on the following information.

Aluminum is one of the most abundant metals in Earth's crust. The aluminum compound found in bauxite ore is Al_2O_3. Over one hundred years ago, it was difficult and expensive to isolate aluminum from bauxite ore. In 1886, a brother and sister team, Charles and Julia Hall, found that molten (melted) cryolite, Na_3AlF_6, would dissolve bauxite ore. Electrolysis of the resulting mixture caused the aluminum ions in the Al_2O_3 to be reduced to molten aluminum metal. This less expensive process is known as the Hall process.

1. Explain, in terms of electrical energy, how the operation of a voltaic cell differs from the operation of an electrolytic cell used in the Hall process. Include both voltaic cell and electrolytic cell in your answer.

   1.

2. Explain, in terms of ions, why molten cryolite conducts electricity.

   2.

3. Write a balance half-reaction equation for the reduction of Al^{3+} to Al

   3.

4. Write the oxidation state for each of the elements in cryolite.

   4.

Set B: Balancing Redox Equations

Base your answers to questions 5 and 6 on the unbalanced redox reaction below.

$$\_\_Cu(s) \ + \ \_\_ AgNO_3(aq) \ \rightarrow \ \_\_ Cu(NO_3)_2(aq) + \_\_ Ag(s)$$

5. Balance the redox equation using the smallest whole number coefficients.

6. Write half-reaction equations for oxidation and reduction that occur in the above reaction.

   6.   Oxidation half:

        Reduction half:

Set C: Writing Half-reactions Equation, Oxidation Numbers

Base your answers to questions 7 and 8 on the equation below.

$$4Al(s) \ + \ 3O_2(g) \ \rightarrow \ 2Al_2O_3(s)$$

7. Write a balance oxidation half-reaction equation for this reaction.

   7.

8. What is the oxidation number of oxygen in Al_2O_3?

   8.

Set D: Redox Reaction, Balancing Redox Equation, Writing Half-reaction

Base your answers to questions 9 through 14 on the following redox reaction, which occurs spontaneously.

$$Zn + Cr^{3+} \rightarrow Zn^{2+} + Cr$$

9. State what happens to the number of protons in a Zn atom when it changes to Zn^{2+} as the redox reaction occurs.

9.

10. Which half-reaction occurs at the anode?

10.

11. Which species loses electrons and which species gains electrons?

11. Loses: Gains;

12. Write the half-reaction for the oxidation that occurs.

12.

13. Write the half-reaction for the reduction that occurs.

13.

14. Balance the redox equation using the smallest whole-number coefficients.

14. __Zn + ___ $Cr^{3+} \rightarrow$ __ Zn^{2+} + __ Cr

Set E: Voltaic Cell

Base your answers to questions 15 through 17 on the diagram of the voltaic cell below.

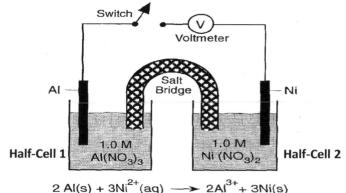

$$2\ Al(s) + 3Ni^{2+}(aq) \longrightarrow 2Al^{3+} + 3Ni(s)$$

15. Base on the given equation, write the balance half-reaction equation for the reaction that occurs in Half-Cell 1.

15.

16. What acts as the cathode in this voltaic cell?

16.

17. When the switch is closed, state the direction that electrons will flow though the wire.

17.

Set F: Voltaic Cell

Base your answers to questions 18 and 20 on the diagram of a voltaic cell and the balance ionic equation below.

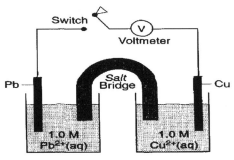

$$Pb(s) + Cu^{2+}(aq) \longrightarrow Pb^{2+}(aq) + Cu(s)$$

18. Explain the function of the salt bridge   18.
    in the voltaic cell.

19. What is the total number of moles of   19.
    electrons needed to completely reduce
    6.0 moles of $Cu^{2+}(aq)$ ions?

20. Identify the anode in the voltaic cell.   20.

Set G: Electrolytic Cell

Base your answers to questions 21 through 23 on the diagram and balance equation below, which represents the electrolysis of molten NaCl.

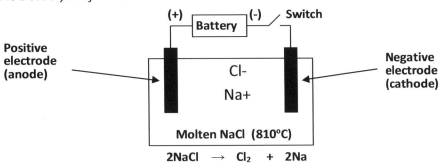

$$2NaCl \longrightarrow Cl_2 + 2Na$$

21. Write the balance half-reaction for the reduction   21.
    that occurs in this electrolytic cell.

22. What is the purpose of the battery in this   22.
    electrolytic cell?

23. When the switch is closed, which electrode   23.
    will attract the sodium ions?

Set H: Electroplating

Base your answers to questions 24 and 25 on the information below.

Electroplating is an electrolytic process used to coat metal objects with a more expensive and less reactive metal. The diagram below shows an electroplating cell that includes a battery connected to a silver bar and a metal spoon. The bar and spoon are submerged in AgNO₃*(aq)*.

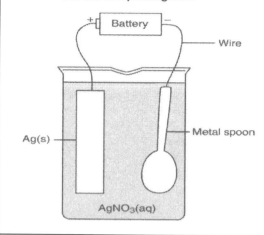

An Electroplating Cell

24. According to Reference Table F, explain why AgNO₃ is a better choice than AgCl for use in this electrolytic process.

25. Explain the purpose of the battery in this cell.

Set I: Voltaic Cell, Balancing Redox Equation

Base your answers to questions 26 through 28 on the diagram below.

The diagram below shows a voltaic cell with copper and aluminum electrodes immediately after the external circuit is completed.

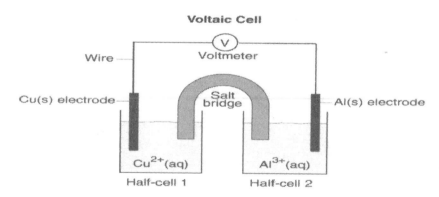

Voltaic Cell

25. Balance the redox equation using the smallest whole-number coefficients.

25. __Cu²⁺*(aq)* + __ Al*(s)* → __ Cu*(s)* + __ Al³⁺*(aq)*

26. As this voltaic cell operates, the mass of the Al*(s)* electrode decreases. Explain, in terms of particles, why this decrease in mass occurs.

26.

27. Explain the function of the salt bridge.

27.

Set A: Nuclear Equation, Half-life

Base your answers to questions 1 and 2 on the information below.

Uranium-238, a solid, is a naturally radioactive element found in the earth's crust.
As it decays one of the products is radon-222, which is a gas and is very radioactive.

1. Write a nuclear equation for the decay of Rn-222.

   1.

2. The half-life of Radon-222 is 3.82 days. How many grams of a 1.0 gram sample of radon-222 would remain after 7.64 days?

   2.

Set B: Balancing Nuclear Equation

Given the equation below:

$$^{58}_{29}Cu \longrightarrow {}^{58}_{28}Ni + X$$

3. What nuclear particle is represented by X?

   3.

Set C: Radioactive Dating, Balancing Nuclear Equation, Half-life

Base your answers to questions 4 through 6 on the information below.

The radioisotopes carbon-14 and nitrogen-16 are present in a living organism.
Carbon-14 is commonly used to date once-living organisms.

4. Explain why N-16 is a poor choice for radioactive dating of a bone.

   4.

5. Complete the nuclear equation for the decay of C-14. Include both the atomic number and the mass number of the missing particle.

   5. $^{14}_{6}C \longrightarrow {}^{0}_{-1}e + \underline{\hspace{1.5cm}}$

6. A sample of wood is found to contain $^1/_8$ as much C-14 as is present in the wood of a living tree. What is the age, in years, of this sample of wood?

   6.

Set D: Nuclear Reaction, Nuclear Energy

Base your answers to questions 7 through 9 on the nuclear equation shown below.

$$^{235}_{92}U \; + \; ^{1}_{0}n \; \rightarrow \; ^{142}_{56}Ba \; + \; ^{91}_{36}Kr \; + \; 3^{1}_{0}n \; + \; energy$$

7. State the type of nuclear reaction represented   7.
    by the equation.

8. The sum of the masses of the products is slightly   8.
    less than the sum of the masses of the reactants.
    Explain this loss of mass.

9. This process releases greater amount of energy than   9.
    an ordinary chemical reaction does. Name another type
    of nuclear reaction that releases greater energy than an
    ordinary chemical reaction.

Set E: Radioisotope Uses, Half-life, Writing Nuclear Equation

Base your answers to questions 10 and 11 on the information and Table below.

Some radioisotopes used tracers to make it possible for doctors to see the images
of internal body parts and observe their functions. The table below lists information
about three radioisotopes and their body part each radioisotope is used to study.

Medical uses of Some Radioisotopes

Radioisotope	Half-life	Decay Mode	Body Part
^{24}Na	15 hours	Beta	Circulatory system
^{59}Fe	44.5 days	Beta	Red blood cells
^{131}I	8.1 days	Beta	Thyroid

10. It could take up to 60. hours for a radioisotope to be   10.
    delivered to the hospital from the laboratory where
    it is produced. What fraction of an original sample
    of ^{24}Na remains unchanged after 60 hours?

11. Complete the equation for the nuclear decay of the   11. ^{59}Fe $\rightarrow$ _____ + _____
    radioisotope used to study red blood cells. Include both
    atomic number and the mass number for each missing
    particle.

Set F: Radioactivity, Usages of Radioisotope, Writing Nuclear Equation

Base your answers to questions 12 through 14 on the information below, the Reference Tables for Chemistry, and your knowledge of chemistry.

Radioactivity and radioactive isotopes have the potential for both benefiting and harming living organisms. One use of radioactive isotopes is in radiation therapy as a treatment for cancer. Cesium-137 is sometimes used in radiation therapy.
A sample of cesium-137 was left in an abandoned clinic in Brazil in 1987. Cesium-137 gives off a blue glow because of its radioactivity. The people who discovered the sample were attracted by the blue glow and had no idea of any danger. Hundreds of people were treated for overexposure to radiation, and four people died.

12. Suppose a 40-gram sample of iodine-131 and a 40-gram sample of cesium-137 were both abandoned in the clinic in 1987. Explain why the sample of iodine-131 would not pose as great a radiation risk to people as the sample of cesium-137 would.

12.

13. If 12.5 grams of the original sample of cesium-137 remained after 90.69 years, what was the mass of the original sample?

13.

14. Using Reference Table N, complete the equation provided in your answer booklet for the radioactive decay of $^{137}_{55}$Cs. Include both atomic number and mass number for each particle.

14. $^{137}_{55}$Cs $\rightarrow$ _____ + _____

Set G: Types of Nuclear Reactions

Identify the type of nuclear reaction represented by each equation below.

15. $^{2}_{1}$H + $^{1}_{1}$H $\rightarrow$ $^{3}_{2}$He

15.

16. $^{210}_{84}$Po $\rightarrow$ $^{4}_{2}$He + $^{206}_{82}$Pb

16.

17. $^{4}_{2}$He + $^{11}_{5}$B $\rightarrow$ $^{14}_{7}$N + $^{1}_{0}$n

17.

18. $^{214}_{83}$Bi $\rightarrow$ $^{214}_{84}$Po + $^{0}_{-1}$e

18.

Set H. Disintegration Series, Decay Mode

Base your answers to questions 19 through 22 on the information and graph below.

A U-238 atom decays to a Pb-206 atom through a series of steps. Each point on the graph below represents a nuclide and each arrow represents a nuclear decay mode.

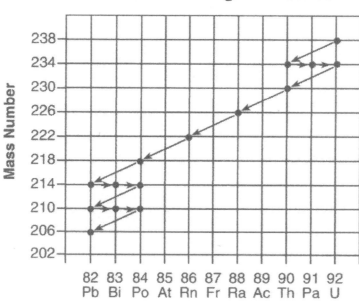

Uranium Disintegration Series

Mass Number (y-axis): 238, 234, 230, 226, 222, 218, 214, 210, 206, 202

Atomic Number and Chemical Symbol
82 83 84 85 86 87 88 89 90 91 92
Pb Bi Po At Rn Fr Ra Ac Th Pa U

19. Explain why the U-238 disintegration series   19.
    ends with the nuclide Pb-206.

20. Based on this graph, what particle is emitted   20.
    during the nuclear decay of a Po-218 atom ?

21. Based on this graph, what is the mass of the particle   21.
    emitted during the nuclear decay of Th-234?

22. Base on this graph, what is the decay mode of Bi-214?   22.

Set I: Graph, Completing Nuclear Equation, Stable Nuclide

Base your answers to questions 23 through 26 on the information below, which relates the numbers of neutrons and protons for specific nuclides of C, N, Ne, and S.

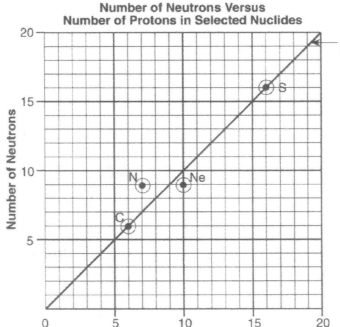

Number of Neutrons Versus
Number of Protons in Selected Nuclides

This line connects points where the neutron-to-proton ratio is 1:1

23. Based on your Reference Tables, complete the nuclear decay equation for Ne-19.

23. $^{19}_{10}\text{Ne} \rightarrow$ _____ + _____

24. Using the point plotted on the graph for nitrogen, what is the neutron-to-proton ratio of this nuclide?

24.

25. Explain, in terms of atomic particles, why S-32 is a stable nuclide.

25.

26. What is the mass number of the carbon isotope represented on the graph?

26.

Reference Tables for Physical Setting/CHEMISTRY
2011 Edition

Table A
Standard Temperature and Pressure

Name	Value	Unit
Standard Pressure	101.3 kPa 1 atm	kilopascal atmosphere
Standard Temperature	273 K 0°C	kelvin degree Celsius

Table B
Physical Constants for Water

Heat of Fusion	334 J/g
Heat of Vaporization	2260 J/g
Specific Heat Capacity of $H_2O(\ell)$	4.18 J/g•K

Table C
Selected Prefixes

Factor	Prefix	Symbol
10^3	kilo-	k
10^{-1}	deci-	d
10^{-2}	centi-	c
10^{-3}	milli-	m
10^{-6}	micro-	μ
10^{-9}	nano-	n
10^{-12}	pico-	p

Table D
Selected Units

Symbol	Name	Quantity
m	meter	length
g	gram	mass
Pa	pascal	pressure
K	kelvin	temperature
mol	mole	amount of substance
J	joule	energy, work, quantity of heat
s	second	time
min	minute	time
h	hour	time
d	day	time
y	year	time
L	liter	volume
ppm	parts per million	concentration
M	molarity	solution concentration
u	atomic mass unit	atomic mass

421

Formula	Name	Formula	Name
H_3O^+	hydronium	CrO_4^{2-}	chromate
Hg_2^{2+}	mercury(I)	$Cr_2O_7^{2-}$	dichromate
NH_4^+	ammonium	MnO_4^-	permanganate
$C_2H_3O_2^-$ CH_3COO^- } acetate		NO_2^-	nitrite
		NO_3^-	nitrate
CN^-	cyanide	O_2^{2-}	peroxide
CO_3^{2-}	carbonate	OH^-	hydroxide
HCO_3^-	hydrogen carbonate	PO_4^{3-}	phosphate
$C_2O_4^{2-}$	oxalate	SCN^-	thiocyanate
ClO^-	hypochlorite	SO_3^{2-}	sulfite
ClO_2^-	chlorite	SO_4^{2-}	sulfate
ClO_3^-	chlorate	HSO_4^-	hydrogen sulfate
ClO_4^-	perchlorate	$S_2O_3^{2-}$	thiosulfate

Table F
Solubility Guidelines for Aqueous Solutions

Ions That Form Soluble Compounds	Exceptions	Ions That Form Insoluble Compounds*	Exceptions
Group 1 ions (Li^+, Na^+, etc.)		carbonate (CO_3^{2-})	when combined with Group 1 ions or ammonium (NH_4^+)
ammonium (NH_4^+)		chromate (CrO_4^{2-})	when combined with Group 1 ions, Ca^{2+}, Mg^{2+}, or ammonium (NH_4^+)
nitrate (NO_3^-)			
acetate ($C_2H_3O_2^-$ or CH_3COO^-)		phosphate (PO_4^{3-})	when combined with Group 1 ions or ammonium (NH_4^+)
hydrogen carbonate (HCO_3^-)		sulfide (S^{2-})	when combined with Group 1 ions or ammonium (NH_4^+)
chlorate (ClO_3^-)		hydroxide (OH^-)	when combined with Group 1 ions, Ca^{2+}, Ba^{2+}, Sr^{2+}, or ammonium (NH_4^+)
halides (Cl^-, Br^-, I^-)	when combined with Ag^+, Pb^{2+}, or Hg_2^{2+}		
sulfates (SO_4^{2-})	when combined with Ag^+, Ca^{2+}, Sr^{2+}, Ba^{2+}, or Pb^{2+}		

*compounds having very low solubility in H_2O

Table G
Solubility Curves at Standard Pressure

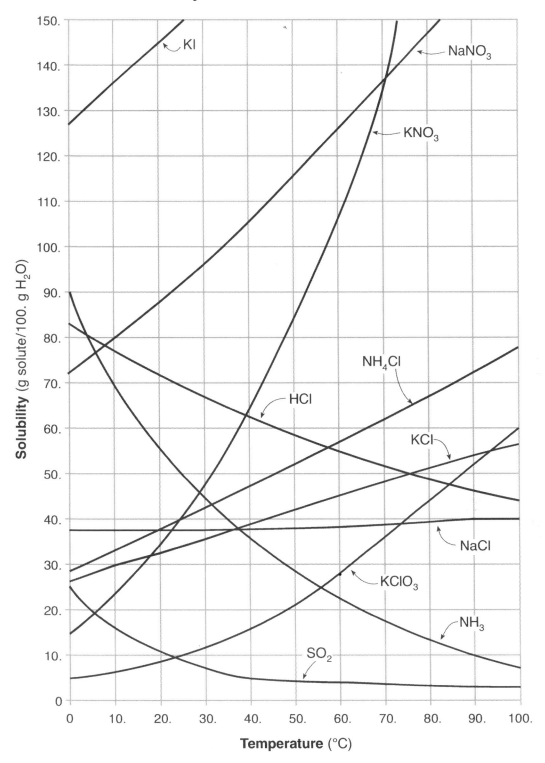

423

Table H
Vapor Pressure of Four Liquids

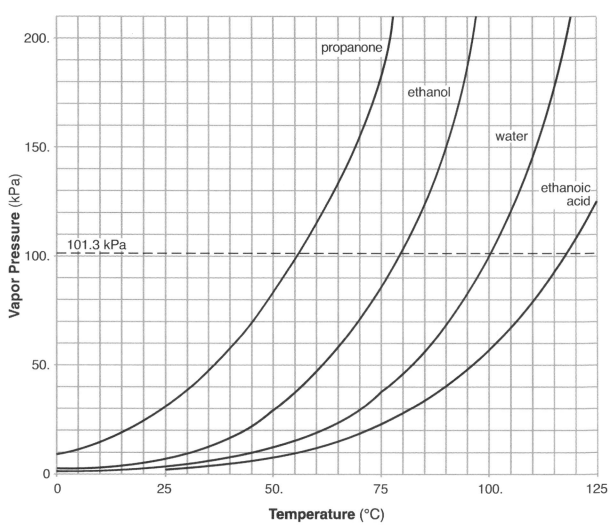

Table I
Heats of Reaction at 101.3 kPa and 298 K

Reaction	ΔH (kJ)*
$CH_4(g) + 2O_2(g) \longrightarrow CO_2(g) + 2H_2O(\ell)$	−890.4
$C_3H_8(g) + 5O_2(g) \longrightarrow 3CO_2(g) + 4H_2O(\ell)$	−2219.2
$2C_8H_{18}(\ell) + 25O_2(g) \longrightarrow 16CO_2(g) + 18H_2O(\ell)$	−10943
$2CH_3OH(\ell) + 3O_2(g) \longrightarrow 2CO_2(g) + 4H_2O(\ell)$	−1452
$C_2H_5OH(\ell) + 3O_2(g) \longrightarrow 2CO_2(g) + 3H_2O(\ell)$	−1367
$C_6H_{12}O_6(s) + 6O_2(g) \longrightarrow 6CO_2(g) + 6H_2O(\ell)$	−2804
$2CO(g) + O_2(g) \longrightarrow 2CO_2(g)$	−566.0
$C(s) + O_2(g) \longrightarrow CO_2(g)$	−393.5
$4Al(s) + 3O_2(g) \longrightarrow 2Al_2O_3(s)$	−3351
$N_2(g) + O_2(g) \longrightarrow 2NO(g)$	+182.6
$N_2(g) + 2O_2(g) \longrightarrow 2NO_2(g)$	+66.4
$2H_2(g) + O_2(g) \longrightarrow 2H_2O(g)$	−483.6
$2H_2(g) + O_2(g) \longrightarrow 2H_2O(\ell)$	−571.6
$N_2(g) + 3H_2(g) \longrightarrow 2NH_3(g)$	−91.8
$2C(s) + 3H_2(g) \longrightarrow C_2H_6(g)$	−84.0
$2C(s) + 2H_2(g) \longrightarrow C_2H_4(g)$	+52.4
$2C(s) + H_2(g) \longrightarrow C_2H_2(g)$	+227.4
$H_2(g) + I_2(g) \longrightarrow 2HI(g)$	+53.0
$KNO_3(s) \xrightarrow{H_2O} K^+(aq) + NO_3^-(aq)$	+34.89
$NaOH(s) \xrightarrow{H_2O} Na^+(aq) + OH^-(aq)$	−44.51
$NH_4Cl(s) \xrightarrow{H_2O} NH_4^+(aq) + Cl^-(aq)$	+14.78
$NH_4NO_3(s) \xrightarrow{H_2O} NH_4^+(aq) + NO_3^-(aq)$	+25.69
$NaCl(s) \xrightarrow{H_2O} Na^+(aq) + Cl^-(aq)$	+3.88
$LiBr(s) \xrightarrow{H_2O} Li^+(aq) + Br^-(aq)$	−48.83
$H^+(aq) + OH^-(aq) \longrightarrow H_2O(\ell)$	−55.8

*The ΔH values are based on molar quantities represented in the equations. A minus sign indicates an exothermic reaction.

Table J
Activity Series**

Most Active ↓	Metals	Nonmetals	Most Active ↓
	Li	F_2	
	Rb	Cl_2	
	K	Br_2	
	Cs	I_2	
	Ba		
	Sr		
	Ca		
	Na		
	Mg		
	Al		
	Ti		
	Mn		
	Zn		
	Cr		
	Fe		
	Co		
	Ni		
	Sn		
	Pb		
	H_2		
	Cu		
	Ag		
Least Active	Au		Least Active

**Activity Series is based on the hydrogen standard. H_2 is *not* a metal.

425

Table K
Common Acids

Formula	Name
$HCl(aq)$	hydrochloric acid
$HNO_2(aq)$	nitrous acid
$HNO_3(aq)$	nitric acid
$H_2SO_3(aq)$	sulfurous acid
$H_2SO_4(aq)$	sulfuric acid
$H_3PO_4(aq)$	phosphoric acid
$H_2CO_3(aq)$ or $CO_2(aq)$	carbonic acid
$CH_3COOH(aq)$ or $HC_2H_3O_2(aq)$	ethanoic acid (acetic acid)

Table L
Common Bases

Formula	Name
$NaOH(aq)$	sodium hydroxide
$KOH(aq)$	potassium hydroxide
$Ca(OH)_2(aq)$	calcium hydroxide
$NH_3(aq)$	aqueous ammonia

Table M
Common Acid–Base Indicators

Indicator	Approximate pH Range for Color Change	Color Change
methyl orange	3.1–4.4	red to yellow
bromthymol blue	6.0–7.6	yellow to blue
phenolphthalein	8–9	colorless to pink
litmus	4.5–8.3	red to blue
bromcresol green	3.8–5.4	yellow to blue
thymol blue	8.0–9.6	yellow to blue

Source: *The Merck Index*, 14th ed., 2006, Merck Publishing Group

Table N
Selected Radioisotopes

Nuclide	Half-Life	Decay Mode	Nuclide Name
^{198}Au	2.695 d	β^-	gold-198
^{14}C	5715 y	β^-	carbon-14
^{37}Ca	182 ms	β^+	calcium-37
^{60}Co	5.271 y	β^-	cobalt-60
^{137}Cs	30.2 y	β^-	cesium-137
^{53}Fe	8.51 min	β^+	iron-53
^{220}Fr	27.4 s	α	francium-220
^{3}H	12.31 y	β^-	hydrogen-3
^{131}I	8.021 d	β^-	iodine-131
^{37}K	1.23 s	β^+	potassium-37
^{42}K	12.36 h	β^-	potassium-42
^{85}Kr	10.73 y	β^-	krypton-85
^{16}N	7.13 s	β^-	nitrogen-16
^{19}Ne	17.22 s	β^+	neon-19
^{32}P	14.28 d	β^-	phosphorus-32
^{239}Pu	2.410×10^4 y	α	plutonium-239
^{226}Ra	1599 y	α	radium-226
^{222}Rn	3.823 d	α	radon-222
^{90}Sr	29.1 y	β^-	strontium-90
^{99}Tc	2.13×10^5 y	β^-	technetium-99
^{232}Th	1.40×10^{10} y	α	thorium-232
^{233}U	1.592×10^5 y	α	uranium-233
^{235}U	7.04×10^8 y	α	uranium-235
^{238}U	4.47×10^9 y	α	uranium-238

Source: *CRC Handbook of Chemistry and Physics*, 91st ed., 2010–2011, CRC Press

Table O
Symbols Used in Nuclear Chemistry

Name	Notation	Symbol
alpha particle	$_2^4\text{He}$ or $_2^4\alpha$	α
beta particle	$_{-1}^{0}\text{e}$ or $_{-1}^{0}\beta$	β^-
gamma radiation	$_0^0\gamma$	γ
neutron	$_0^1\text{n}$	n
proton	$_1^1\text{H}$ or $_1^1\text{p}$	p
positron	$_{+1}^{0}\text{e}$ or $_{+1}^{0}\beta$	β^+

Table P
Organic Prefixes

Prefix	Number of Carbon Atoms
meth-	1
eth-	2
prop-	3
but-	4
pent-	5
hex-	6
hept-	7
oct-	8
non-	9
dec-	10

Table Q
Homologous Series of Hydrocarbons

Name	General Formula	Examples	
		Name	Structural Formula
alkanes	C_nH_{2n+2}	ethane	H-C-C-H (with H atoms)
alkenes	C_nH_{2n}	ethene	C=C (with H atoms)
alkynes	C_nH_{2n-2}	ethyne	$H-C\equiv C-H$

Note: n = number of carbon atoms

427

Table R
Organic Functional Groups

Class of Compound	Functional Group	General Formula	Example
halide (halocarbon)	$-F$ (fluoro-) $-Cl$ (chloro-) $-Br$ (bromo-) $-I$ (iodo-)	$R-X$ (X represents any halogen)	$CH_3CHClCH_3$ 2-chloropropane
alcohol	$-OH$	$R-OH$	$CH_3CH_2CH_2OH$ 1-propanol
ether	$-O-$	$R-O-R'$	$CH_3OCH_2CH_3$ methyl ethyl ether
aldehyde	$\overset{\displaystyle O}{\overset{\|}{-C}}-H$	$\overset{\displaystyle O}{\overset{\|}{R-C}}-H$	$CH_3CH_2\overset{\displaystyle O}{\overset{\|}{C}}-H$ propanal
ketone	$-\overset{\displaystyle O}{\overset{\|}{C}}-$	$R-\overset{\displaystyle O}{\overset{\|}{C}}-R'$	$CH_3\overset{\displaystyle O}{\overset{\|}{C}}CH_2CH_2CH_3$ 2-pentanone
organic acid	$-\overset{\displaystyle O}{\overset{\|}{C}}-OH$	$R-\overset{\displaystyle O}{\overset{\|}{C}}-OH$	$CH_3CH_2\overset{\displaystyle O}{\overset{\|}{C}}-OH$ propanoic acid
ester	$-\overset{\displaystyle O}{\overset{\|}{C}}-O-$	$R-\overset{\displaystyle O}{\overset{\|}{C}}-O-R'$	$CH_3CH_2\overset{\displaystyle O}{\overset{\|}{C}}OCH_3$ methyl propanoate
amine	$-\overset{\|}{N}-$	$R-\overset{R'}{\overset{\|}{N}}-R''$	$CH_3CH_2CH_2NH_2$ 1-propanamine
amide	$-\overset{\displaystyle O}{\overset{\|}{C}}-\overset{\|}{N}H$	$R-\overset{\displaystyle O}{\overset{\|}{C}}-\overset{R'}{\overset{\|}{N}}H$	$CH_3CH_2\overset{\displaystyle O}{\overset{\|}{C}}-NH_2$ propanamide

Note: R represents a bonded atom or group of atoms.

Periodic Table of the Elements

KEY

Atomic Mass → 12.011	Selected Oxidation States ← −4, +2, +4
Symbol → **C**	
Atomic Number → 6	
Electron Configuration → 2-4	

Relative atomic masses are based on $^{12}C = 12$ (exact)

Note: Numbers in parentheses are mass numbers of the most stable or common isotope.

Period	Group 1	2	3	4	5	6	7	8	9	10	11	12	13	14	15	16	17	18
1	**H** 1; 1.00794; 1; +1 −1																	**He** 2; 4.00260; 2; 0
2	**Li** 3; 6.941; 2-1; +1	**Be** 4; 9.01218; 2-2; +2											**B** 5; 10.81; 2-3; +3	**C** 6; 12.011; 2-4; −4 +2 +4	**N** 7; 14.0067; 2-5; −3 −2 −1 +1 +2 +3 +4 +5	**O** 8; 15.9994; 2-6; −2	**F** 9; 18.9984; 2-7; −1	**Ne** 10; 20.180; 2-8; 0
3	**Na** 11; 22.98977; 2-8-1; +1	**Mg** 12; 24.305; 2-8-2; +2											**Al** 13; 26.98154; 2-8-3; +3	**Si** 14; 28.0855; 2-8-4; −4 +2 +4	**P** 15; 30.97376; 2-8-5; −3 +3 +5	**S** 16; 32.065; 2-8-6; −2 +4 +6	**Cl** 17; 35.453; 2-8-7; −1 +1 +5 +7	**Ar** 18; 39.948; 2-8-8; 0
4	**K** 19; 39.0983; 2-8-8-1; +1	**Ca** 20; 40.08; 2-8-8-2; +2	**Sc** 21; 44.9559; 2-8-9-2; +3	**Ti** 22; 47.867; 2-8-10-2; +2 +3 +4	**V** 23; 50.9415; 2-8-11-2; +2 +3 +4 +5	**Cr** 24; 51.996; 2-8-13-1; +2 +3 +6	**Mn** 25; 54.9380; 2-8-13-2; +2 +3 +4 +7	**Fe** 26; 55.845; 2-8-14-2; +2 +3	**Co** 27; 58.9332; 2-8-15-2; +2 +3	**Ni** 28; 58.693; 2-8-16-2; +2 +3	**Cu** 29; 63.546; 2-8-18-1; +1 +2	**Zn** 30; 65.409; 2-8-18-2; +2	**Ga** 31; 69.723; 2-8-18-3; +3	**Ge** 32; 72.64; 2-8-18-4; +2 +4	**As** 33; 74.9216; 2-8-18-5; −3 +3 +5	**Se** 34; 78.96; 2-8-18-6; −2 +4 +6	**Br** 35; 79.904; 2-8-18-7; −1 +1 +5	**Kr** 36; 83.798; 2-8-18-8; 0 +2
5	**Rb** 37; 85.4678; 2-8-18-8-1; +1	**Sr** 38; 87.62; 2-8-18-8-2; +2	**Y** 39; 88.9059; 2-8-18-9-2; +3	**Zr** 40; 91.224; 2-8-18-10-2; +4	**Nb** 41; 92.9064; 2-8-18-12-1; +3 +5	**Mo** 42; 95.94; 2-8-18-13-1; +6	**Tc** 43; (98); 2-8-18-13-2; +4 +6 +7	**Ru** 44; 101.07; 2-8-18-15-1; +3	**Rh** 45; 102.906; 2-8-18-16-1; +3	**Pd** 46; 106.42; 2-8-18-18; +2 +4	**Ag** 47; 107.868; 2-8-18-18-1; +1	**Cd** 48; 112.41; 2-8-18-18-2; +2	**In** 49; 114.818; 2-8-18-18-3; +3	**Sn** 50; 118.71; 2-8-18-18-4; +2 +4	**Sb** 51; 121.760; 2-8-18-18-5; −3 +3 +5	**Te** 52; 127.60; 2-8-18-18-6; −2 +4 +6	**I** 53; 126.904; 2-8-18-18-7; −1 +1 +5 +7	**Xe** 54; 131.29; 2-8-18-18-8; 0 +2 +4 +6
6	**Cs** 55; 132.905; 2-8-18-18-8-1; +1	**Ba** 56; 137.33; 2-8-18-18-8-2; +2	**La** 57; 138.9055; 2-8-18-18-9-2; +3	**Hf** 72; 178.49; *18-32-10-2; +4	**Ta** 73; 180.948; -18-32-11-2; +5	**W** 74; 183.84; -18-32-12-2; +6	**Re** 75; 186.207; -18-32-13-2; +4 +6 +7	**Os** 76; 190.23; -18-32-14-2; +3 +4	**Ir** 77; 192.217; -18-32-15-2; +3 +4	**Pt** 78; 195.08; -18-32-17-1; +2 +4	**Au** 79; 196.967; -18-32-18-1; +1 +3	**Hg** 80; 200.59; -18-32-18-2; +1 +2	**Tl** 81; 204.383; -18-32-18-3; +1 +3	**Pb** 82; 207.2; -18-32-18-4; +2 +4	**Bi** 83; 208.980; -18-32-18-5; +3 +5	**Po** 84; (209); -18-32-18-6; +2 +4	**At** 85; (210); -18-32-18-7	**Rn** 86; (222); -18-32-18-8; 0
7	**Fr** 87; (223); -18-32-18-8-1; +1	**Ra** 88; (226); -18-32-18-8-2; +2	**Ac** 89; (227); -18-32-18-9-2; +3	**Rf** 104; (261); +4	**Db** 105; (262)	**Sg** 106; (266)	**Bh** 107; (272)	**Hs** 108; (277)	**Mt** 109; (276)	**Ds** 110; (281)	**Rg** 111; (280)	**Cn** 112; (285)	**Uut** 113**; (284)	**Uuq** 114; (289)	**Uup** 115; (288)	**Uuh** 116; (292)	**Uus** 117; (?)	**Uuo** 118; (294)

Ce 58; 140.116; +3 +4	**Pr** 59; 140.908; +3	**Nd** 60; 144.24; +3	**Pm** 61; (145); +3	**Sm** 62; 150.36; +2 +3	**Eu** 63; 151.964; +2 +3	**Gd** 64; 157.25; +3	**Tb** 65; 158.925; +3	**Dy** 66; 162.500; +3	**Ho** 67; 164.930; +3	**Er** 68; 167.259; +3	**Tm** 69; 168.934; +3	**Yb** 70; 173.04; +2 +3	**Lu** 71; 174.9668; +3
Th 90; 232.038; +4	**Pa** 91; 231.036; +4 +5	**U** 92; 238.029; +3 +4 +5 +6	**Np** 93; (237); +3 +4 +5 +6	**Pu** 94; (244); +3 +4 +5 +6	**Am** 95; (243); +3 +4 +5 +6	**Cm** 96; (247); +3	**Bk** 97; (247); +3 +4	**Cf** 98; (251); +3	**Es** 99; (252); +3	**Fm** 100; (257); +3	**Md** 101; (258); +2 +3	**No** 102; (259); +2 +3	**Lr** 103; (262); +3

*denotes the presence of (2-8-) for elements 72 and above

**The systematic names and symbols for elements of atomic numbers 113 and above will be used until the approval of trivial names by IUPAC.

Source: *CRC Handbook of Chemistry and Physics*, 91st ed., 2010–2011, CRC Press

Table S
Properties of Selected Elements

Atomic Number	Symbol	Name	First Ionization Energy (kJ/mol)	Electro-negativity	Melting Point (K)	Boiling* Point (K)	Density** (g/cm³)	Atomic Radius (pm)
1	H	hydrogen	1312	2.2	14	20.	0.000082	32
2	He	helium	2372	—	—	4	0.000164	37
3	Li	lithium	520.	1.0	454	1615	0.534	130.
4	Be	beryllium	900.	1.6	1560.	2744	1.85	99
5	B	boron	801	2.0	2348	4273	2.34	84
6	C	carbon	1086	2.6	—	—	—	75
7	N	nitrogen	1402	3.0	63	77	0.001145	71
8	O	oxygen	1314	3.4	54	90.	0.001308	64
9	F	fluorine	1681	4.0	53	85	0.001553	60.
10	Ne	neon	2081	—	24	27	0.000825	62
11	Na	sodium	496	0.9	371	1156	0.97	160.
12	Mg	magnesium	738	1.3	923	1363	1.74	140.
13	Al	aluminum	578	1.6	933	2792	2.70	124
14	Si	silicon	787	1.9	1687	3538	2.3296	114
15	P	phosphorus (white)	1012	2.2	317	554	1.823	109
16	S	sulfur (monoclinic)	1000.	2.6	388	718	2.00	104
17	Cl	chlorine	1251	3.2	172	239	0.002898	100.
18	Ar	argon	1521	—	84	87	0.001633	101
19	K	potassium	419	0.8	337	1032	0.89	200.
20	Ca	calcium	590.	1.0	1115	1757	1.54	174
21	Sc	scandium	633	1.4	1814	3109	2.99	159
22	Ti	titanium	659	1.5	1941	3560.	4.506	148
23	V	vanadium	651	1.6	2183	3680.	6.0	144
24	Cr	chromium	653	1.7	2180.	2944	7.15	130.
25	Mn	manganese	717	1.6	1519	2334	7.3	129
26	Fe	iron	762	1.8	1811	3134	7.87	124
27	Co	cobalt	760.	1.9	1768	3200.	8.86	118
28	Ni	nickel	737	1.9	1728	3186	8.90	117
29	Cu	copper	745	1.9	1358	2835	8.96	122
30	Zn	zinc	906	1.7	693	1180.	7.134	120.
31	Ga	gallium	579	1.8	303	2477	5.91	123
32	Ge	germanium	762	2.0	1211	3106	5.3234	120.
33	As	arsenic (gray)	944	2.2	1090.	—	5.75	120.
34	Se	selenium (gray)	941	2.6	494	958	4.809	118
35	Br	bromine	1140.	3.0	266	332	3.1028	117
36	Kr	krypton	1351	—	116	120.	0.003425	116
37	Rb	rubidium	403	0.8	312	961	1.53	215
38	Sr	strontium	549	1.0	1050.	1655	2.64	190.
39	Y	yttrium	600.	1.2	1795	3618	4.47	176
40	Zr	zirconium	640.	1.3	2128	4682	6.52	164

Atomic Number	Symbol	Name	First Ionization Energy (kJ/mol)	Electro-negativity	Melting Point (K)	Boiling* Point (K)	Density** (g/cm³)	Atomic Radius (pm)
41	Nb	niobium	652	1.6	2750.	5017	8.57	156
42	Mo	molybdenum	684	2.2	2896	4912	10.2	146
43	Tc	technetium	702	2.1	2430.	4538	11	138
44	Ru	ruthenium	710.	2.2	2606	4423	12.1	136
45	Rh	rhodium	720.	2.3	2237	3968	12.4	134
46	Pd	palladium	804	2.2	1828	3236	12.0	130.
47	Ag	silver	731	1.9	1235	2435	10.5	136
48	Cd	cadmium	868	1.7	594	1040.	8.69	140.
49	In	indium	558	1.8	430.	2345	7.31	142
50	Sn	tin (white)	709	2.0	505	2875	7.287	140.
51	Sb	antimony (gray)	831	2.1	904	1860.	6.68	140.
52	Te	tellurium	869	2.1	723	1261	6.232	137
53	I	iodine	1008	2.7	387	457	4.933	136
54	Xe	xenon	1170.	2.6	161	165	0.005366	136
55	Cs	cesium	376	0.8	302	944	1.873	238
56	Ba	barium	503	0.9	1000.	2170.	3.62	206
57	La	lanthanum	538	1.1	1193	3737	6.15	194
Elements 58–71 have been omitted.								
72	Hf	hafnium	659	1.3	2506	4876	13.3	164
73	Ta	tantalum	728	1.5	3290.	5731	16.4	158
74	W	tungsten	759	1.7	3695	5828	19.3	150.
75	Re	rhenium	756	1.9	3458	5869	20.8	141
76	Os	osmium	814	2.2	3306	5285	22.587	136
77	Ir	iridium	865	2.2	2719	4701	22.562	132
78	Pt	platinum	864	2.2	2041	4098	21.5	130.
79	Au	gold	890.	2.4	1337	3129	19.3	130.
80	Hg	mercury	1007	1.9	234	630.	13.5336	132
81	Tl	thallium	589	1.8	577	1746	11.8	144
82	Pb	lead	716	1.8	600.	2022	11.3	145
83	Bi	bismuth	703	1.9	544	1837	9.79	150.
84	Po	polonium	812	2.0	527	1235	9.20	142
85	At	astatine	—	2.2	575			148
86	Rn	radon	1037	—	202	211	0.009074	146
87	Fr	francium	393	0.7	300.	—	—	242
88	Ra	radium	509	0.9	969	—	5	211
89	Ac	actinium	499	1.1	1323	3471	10.	201
Elements 90 and above have been omitted.								

*boiling point at standard pressure

**density of solids and liquids at room temperature and density of gases at 298 K and 101.3 kPa

— no data available

Source: *CRC Handbook for Chemistry and Physics*, 91st ed., 2010–2011, CRC Press

Table T
Important Formulas and Equations

Density	$d = \dfrac{m}{V}$	d = density m = mass V = volume
Mole Calculations	number of moles = $\dfrac{\text{given mass}}{\text{gram-formula mass}}$	
Percent Error	% error = $\dfrac{\text{measured value} - \text{accepted value}}{\text{accepted value}} \times 100$	
Percent Composition	% composition by mass = $\dfrac{\text{mass of part}}{\text{mass of whole}} \times 100$	
Concentration	parts per million = $\dfrac{\text{mass of solute}}{\text{mass of solution}} \times 1\,000\,000$	
	molarity = $\dfrac{\text{moles of solute}}{\text{liter of solution}}$	
Combined Gas Law	$\dfrac{P_1 V_1}{T_1} = \dfrac{P_2 V_2}{T_2}$	P = pressure V = volume T = temperature
Titration	$M_A V_A = M_B V_B$	M_A = molarity of H^+ M_B = molarity of OH^- V_A = volume of acid V_B = volume of base
Heat	$q = mC\Delta T$ $q = mH_f$ $q = mH_v$	q = heat H_f = heat of fusion m = mass H_v = heat of vaporization C = specific heat capacity ΔT = change in temperature
Temperature	K = °C + 273	K = kelvin °C = degree Celsius

432

Made in the USA
Charleston, SC
10 November 2015